Jane Barker, Exile

Jane Barker, Exile

A Literary Career
1675–1725

KATHRYN R. KING

CLARENDON PRESS · OXFORD

OXFORD
UNIVERSITY PRESS

Great Clarendon Street, Oxford OX2 6DP

Oxford University Press is a department of the University of Oxford.
It furthers the University's objective of excellence in research, scholarship,
and education by publishing worldwide in

Oxford New York

Athens Auckland Bangkok Bogotá Buenos Aires Calcutta
Cape Town Chennai Dar es Salaam Delhi Florence Hong Kong Istanbul
Karachi Kuala Lumpur Madrid Melbourne Mexico City Mumbai
Nairobi Paris São Paulo Singapore Taipei Tokyo Toronto Warsaw

with associated companies in Berlin Ibadan

Oxford is a registered trade mark of Oxford University Press
in the UK and in certain other countries

Published in the United States
by Oxford University Press Inc., New York

British Library Cataloguing in Publication Data
Data available

Library of Congress Cataloging-in-Publication Data
Data available

ISBN 0-19-818702-5

1 3 5 7 9 10 8 6 4 2

Typeset in Sabon by
Cambrian Typesetters, Frimley, Surrey

Printed in Great Britain
on acid-free paper by
T.J. International, Padstow, Cornwall

Preface and Acknowledgements

THE beginnings of this book can be traced to a graduate seminar on Swift and Pope taught twenty-five years ago by Paul
Hunter, who insisted even then that his students read around in
the 'minor' (as it was then called) fiction of the period. I came
across a Garland reprint of Barker's *A Patch-Work Screen for
the Ladies* and read, fascinated, a seemingly autobiographical
story of a single woman in the late seventeenth century who
preferred books and the life of the mind to more conventional
feminine pursuits. Who *was* this wonderfully quirky woman?
What prompted her to place before the reading public what
appeared to be her own life-story? Where did she find her narrative models? How did the author, to all appearances a genteel
Lincolnshire spinster, get mixed up late in her life with the notorious publisher Edmund Curll? But at this point in my graduate
studies—this was the mid-1970s—such questions had no ready
answers. Indeed, so far as I could tell they were nowhere being
asked, and besides I was already well on my way to becoming a
Victorianist. (The nineteenth century, it will be recalled, is
where 'early' women writers were then to be found.) So, with a
rueful glance backwards, I turned away from Jane Barker and
focused my gaze on 'early' writers of a later era.

Later, as the recovery of women writers moved steadily back in
time, I began to wonder whether any of my questions had been
answered. A little reading suggested they had not. Barker's novels
had won admirers, to be sure, but they had been little investigated, and the historical woman remained something of a
mystery. It looked as if a book needed to be written and that I
might be the one to do it. Initially I envisioned a critical analysis
along feminist lines, but before long, as a result of my participation in an NEH summer seminar on biographical research
conducted in 1992 by Paula Backscheider, my interests turned
biographical: Barker deserved, I believed, a full-fledged literary
biography. Several years of determined effort in libraries and
records offices on both sides of the Atlantic were enough to
persuade me, however, that at this late date no amount of rooting

about in the archives was likely to turn up the kind of information needed to produce a standard life-and-works, no matter
how much I might wish otherwise. Should subsequent scholars
prove me wrong, I will be the first to applaud.

If a traditional biography failed to materialize, something at
least as interesting emerged in its place. For at some point in my
researches it began to dawn that, although the information I
was unearthing told less than I had hoped about 'the life', it illu-
minated more than I would have supposed possible a long,
varied, and resonant life *as a writer*, one spanning nearly half a
century of immense literary and cultural change. At this juncture I hived off my biographical findings into an essay written
in collaboration with Jeslyn Medoff and began turning my
attention to analysis of what turned out to be a surprisingly
well-documented writing life—her literary friendships, her readers and readerships, her relations with men in the book trade,
her dialogue with inherited literary conventions. I also found
myself being drawn into parts of the culture for which my background in feminist literary history had little prepared me, until
eventually I was pursuing her activities as a writer through the
late Stuart London medical market-place, the Jacobite court at
St-Germain, the Roman Catholic community in Hanoverian
England, and the print market-place in the age of Curll, with an
eye toward discovering what Barker's odd but compelling texts
might have meant to their author and her contemporaries. The
result is *Jane Barker, Exile*, the biography of a remarkable literary career.

More people than I can hope to acknowledge here assisted in
the long process of bringing this project to completion. Thanks
are due first to Paul Hunter. Not only did he offer counsel,
encouragement, and fellowship over the course of the decade it
took me to write this book, but he also gave me the confidence
to undertake such a project in the first place. Another Emory
mentor, John Sitter, taught me what to admire in scholarly writing; I can only hope his influence is evident here. Paula
Backscheider, who introduced me to the pleasures of dust and
mildew, taught me how to do the kind of archival research on
which this study is based. Germaine Greer's astringent scepticism raised my sights, and Isobel Grundy's words and example

assured me at crucial junctures that Barker matters. To Peter Beal I owe an immeasurable debt. He lived with Jane Barker nearly as closely as I did through much of the writing of this book, and if his impatience with theory was maddening at times it forced me to submit my arguments to the discipline of fact. Doubtless a book on Barker would have been written without him, but it would have been a different and I suspect inferior piece of work.

Many people read and responded to portions of this book at various stages of its development, but I wish to thank in particular several whose comments shaped my thinking in crucial ways: Sue Lanser, Paula McDowell, Bob Markley, and Alex Pettit. Jeslyn Medoff, though often hard-pressed for time, was always happy to give an informed reading of my work. Carol Shiner Wilson was never less than generous in sharing her biographical discoveries. I should mention one other 'Barkerite': Leigh Anna Eicke has shared with me her unpublished work over the years, and I have always read it with pleasure.

Many of my colleagues at the University of Montevallo have contributed to this project, but several deserve special mention. Ellen Wright-Vance and Sidney Vance listened to my half-formed ideas about Barker, often over pizza; Sarah Palmer repeatedly took pains to make my sentences behave; Clai Rice saved me from hours of formatting difficulties. The book was so long in the making that it has been with me through three department chairs. My great thanks to Norman McMillan, Dorothy Grimes, and Glenda Weathers, who did everything in their power to find support for this project, and to Nicki Walker Masterson, who made all of our jobs easier. I have also benefited from a succession of able student assistants, of whom I must thank especially Laura Caldwell, Elizabeth Firzloff, and Lea Davis, and from a battery of interlibrary loan specialists at Carmichael Library.

I could not have written this book without financial assistance from a number of sources. A grant from the National Endowment for the Humanities enabled me to work for eight months as an NEH–Newberry Scholar at the Newberry Library in Chicago, where I profited enormously from conversations with the staff and fellow students. Short-term fellowships from the American Society of Eighteenth-Century Studies enabled me

viii PREFACE AND ACKNOWLEDGEMENTS

to work in residence at the Folger Shakespeare Library and again at the Newberry. As Osborne Fellow at the Beinecke Library of Yale University I was able to sift through unpublished Jacobite verse in the Osborne collection. For additional financial assistance I would like to thank the University of Montevallo Research and Special Projects Committee and the continuing generosity of my amazing parents, Mary and Bob King.

Christine Ferdinand, Fellow and Librarian of Magdalen College, assisted me in innumerable ways in my work on the Barker manuscript in the College library, as did that other Muse of Bibliography, Sally Speirs. To both I owe as well many pleasant memories of stays in Oxford. Edward Corp in Paris answered numerous queries about the Jacobites at St-Germain and so did Paul Monod, who also shared unpublished work. For information about Catholicism in the long eighteenth century I am grateful to Alison Shell, T. A. Burrell, and M. James Scott. For conversations about early modern medicine over some memorable meals I thank Kathryn Montgomery at the Northwestern Medical School.

For permission to reprint as part of the Epilogue revised portions of my article 'The Unaccountable Wife and Other Tales of Female Desire in Jane Barker's *A Patch-Work Screen for the Ladies*', I thank the *Eighteenth Century: Theory and Interpretation*, where it first appeared in volume 35 (1994), 155–72.

Writing books, a mentor once told me, makes you stupid, and I think I know now what he meant. To friends on the eighteenth-century conference-and-library circuit who have quickened a sometimes stupefied mind—Hans Turley, Joel Reed, Jean Marsden, Tom Lockwood, Antonia Forster, and many others—my great thanks. Special thanks to Ruth Looper, quickening agent supreme and close companion of many a year.

I met the Defoe scholar Max Novak only once, in the British Library. He will not remember our encounter, but I have never forgotten it. Told that I was working on Jane Barker he said, 'Ah, Jane Barker. She's worth getting right.' I agree, and hope I have.

Contents

List of Illustrations

(between pp. 112–113)

1. Part of Jane Barker's autograph copy of her poem 'A dialogue between Fidelia and her little nephew Martius . . .' in the Magdalen Manuscript with her thumb-print at the bottom right corner (original page size 200 x 159mm). Magdalen College Oxford, MS 343, fol. 65.

2. An Enlargement of Jane Barker's thumb-print (the original print c.30mm long). Magdalen College Oxford, MS 343, fol. 65.

3. Jane Barker's autograph preface 'to the Reader' at the beginning of the Magdalen Manuscript (original page size 220 x 159mm). Magdalen College Oxford, MS 343, fol. 1^r.

4. Jane Barker's autograph general title-page of the Magdalen Manuscript (original page size 220 x 159mm). Magdalen College Oxford, MS 343, fol. 2^r.

5. A page of the poem 'A discourse between Englands ill Genius and his companion' in the Magdalen Manuscripts, the first eleven lines in the hand of William Connock, the revisions and deletions of these lines, as well as a further ten lines of substitute text and side-note, in the hand of Jane Barker (original page size 220 x 159mm). Magdalen College Oxford, MS 343, fol. 17.

6. The first page of the poem 'Fidelia walking the Lady Abess comes to her' in the Magdalen Manuscripts, the first thirteen lines in the hand of William Connock, the next eight lines and the note in Jane Barker's hand on a slip of paper sewn in over the deleted lines (original page size 220 x 159mm). Magdalen Collge Oxford, MS 343, fol. 2^r.

7. The first page of Jane Barker's autograph letter signed, to an unnamed lady, 14 August 1730(?). The Royal Library, Windsor Castle, Stuart Papers 208/129.

8. The last page of Jane Barker's autograph letter signed, to an unnamed lady, 14 August 1730(?). The Royal Library, Windsor Castle, Stuart Papers 208/129.

1–6: *Reproduced by permission of the President and Fellows of Magdalen College, Oxford*

7–8: *Reproduced by permission of the Royal Library*

Abbreviations

BARKER TITLES

BG	*The Amours of Bosvil and Galesia* (1719)
EN	*The Entertaining Novels of Mrs. Jane Barker* (1719)
LI	*Love Intrigues; or, The History of the Amours of Bosvil and Galesia* (1713)
Lining	*The Lining of the Patch Work Screen for the Ladies* (1726)
PR	*Poetical Recreations* (1688)
PWS	*A Patch-Work Screen for the Ladies* (1723)

OTHERS

Add. MS	Additional Manuscript, British Library
BL	British Library
Bod.	Bodleian Library, Oxford
DLB	*Dictionary of Literary Biography*
DNB	*Dictionary of National Biography*
Doc. Rec.	Kathryn R. King, 'Jane Barker and her Life (1652–1732): The Documentary Record', *Eighteenth-Century Life*, 21, NS 3 (1997), 16–38, with the assistance of Jeslyn Medoff
ECL	*Eighteenth-Century Life*
ECS	*Eighteenth-Century Studies*
EMS	*English Manuscript Studies*
EWP	Carol Barash, *English Women's Poetry, 1649–1714: Politics, Community, and Linguistic Authority* (Oxford: Clarendon Press, 1996)
KR	Germaine Greer, Susan Hastings, Jeslyn Medoff, and Melinda Sansone (eds.), *Kissing the Rod: An Anthology of Seventeenth-Century Women's Verse* (New York: Farrar Straus Giroux, 1989)
LAO	Lincolnshire Archives Office
Mag. MS	Magdalen Manuscript 343, Magdalen College Oxford
N&Q	*Notes and Queries*
OED	*Oxford English Dictionary*
PB	*Post Boy*

POAS   George de Forest Lord (ed.), *Poems on Affairs of State: Augustan Satirical Verse, 1660–1714*, 7 vols. (New Haven and London: Yale UP, 1963–75)

PRO   Public Record Office, Kew

Thomas   Patrick Thomas (ed.), *The Collected Works of Katherine Philips: The Matchless Orinda*, 2 vols. (Stump Cross, Essex: Stump Cross Books, 1990)

TLS   *Times Literary Supplement*

Wilson   Carol Shiner Wilson (ed.), *The Galesia Trilogy and Selected Manuscript Poems of Jane Barker* (New York and Oxford: Oxford UP, 1997).

Note on texts: Unless otherwise indicated, all citations of the prose fictions (except for *Exilius*) are from Wilson.

Jane Barker: A Chronology

1652   Baptized, 17 May, at Blatherwick, Northamptonshire.

1662   Family takes up residence at Wilsthorp, Lincolnshire.

1675   Death of her brother Edward (b. 1650).

1681   Death of her father Thomas Barker (buried 1 Oct.) at Shingay, Cambridgeshire. He bequeaths the Wilsthorp manor house to JB and her mother.

1685   Death of Charles II, 6 Feb.; accession of James II. Living in London probably by this time; advertises her gout plaster.

1687   *Poetical Recreations* published by Benjamin Crayle (title-page dated 1688); *Scipina* said to be 'in the press' (published in 1714 as *Exilius*).

1688   Following invasion of William of Orange, James II flees to France in Dec.

1689   Moves to St-Germain, where the Jacobite court-in-exile is in residence.

1696   Has cataract operation.

1701   New Year's Day presentation of her manuscript *Poems Refering to the times* to James Francis Edward, the Prince of Wales (the 'Old Pretender', b. 10 June 1688). Death of James II, 5 Sept., at St-Germain.

1702   Death of William III, 8 Mar.; accession of Queen Anne, daughter of James II.

1704   Probable completion by this time of the three-part Magdalen Manuscript of her verse. Returns to Wilsthorp, Lincolnshire.

1713   *Amours of Bosvil and Galesia* published by Curll and Crownfield in May (under the title *Love Intrigues*).

1714   Death of Queen Anne, 1 Aug.; accession of George I, Elector of Hanover (coronation 20 Oct.). *Exilius; or, The Banish'd Roman* advertised (by 14 Aug.) and published (title-page dated 1715).

1715   Jacobite uprising in Scotland in support of James (the 'Old Pretender') in Sept. (suppressed by Apr. 1716).

1717   Obliged as a papist to register her Wilsthorp estate, 15 Oct.; involved in Chancery litigation with her niece Mary Staton.

1718   *The Christian Pilgrimage*, translated from Fénelon, published in Feb. for Lenten season. Writes letter (intercepted by Hanoverian authorities) to second duke of Ormonde, 19 Mar., regarding projected invasion of England.

1719   *The Entertaining Novels of Mrs. Jane Barker* (comprising
        Bosvil and Galesia and *Exilius*) published in July by
        Bettesworth and Curll.
1723   *A Patch-Work Screen for the Ladies* published in June by
        Curll.
1725   *The Lining of the Patch Work Screen* published in Oct. by
        Bettesworth (title-page dated 1726).
1727   Returns to France.
1730   Writes letter, 14 Aug., to Jacobite Lady, probably Mother Lucy
        Theresa Joseph, Lady Nithsdale's sister, about her breast
        'cancer' cured by the blood of James II.
1732   Dies at St-Germain (burial 29 Mar.).
1736   'Third Edition' of *The Entertaining Novels of Mrs. Jane Barker*
        published by Bettesworth, Hitch, and Curll (with apocryphal
        frontispiece portrait).

Note on Sources

Quotations from manuscript sources have been reproduced exactly as they appear in the original, including Barker's eccentric manuscript punctuation (e.g. her occasional practice of ending a line of poetry with double punctuation marks, such as ',?'). Wherever possible I have quoted the prose fictions from *The Galesia Trilogy and Selected Manuscript Poems of Jane Barker*, ed. Carol Shinen Wilson, which appeared in paperback in 1997 in Oxford's Women Writers in English series. Where other editions have been used I have indicated in a footnote the source by abbreviated title and year, e.g. *PWS* 1723. Finally, I have taken the slightly unorthodox step of designating her first published prose fiction by the title *The History of Bosvil and Galesia* on the grounds (explained within) that Barker preferred this title to the one by which it is more often known today, *Love Intrigues*.

Introduction

> I wander'd on, in hopes of better chance,
> Till cursed orange drive us all to France,
> And here we wander vagabons alone.
>
> 'A dialogue between Fidelia and her
> little nephew, Martius'

> I was greatly rejoyc'd at this my *Fall*, when I found my-self
> amongst these happy Undertakers, and hop'd to unite my-
> self in their Confraternity; but they finding some
> Manuscript *Ballads* in my Pocket, rejected me as one of
> that Race of Mortals who live on a certain barren
> Mountain 'till they are turn'd into *Camelions*; so I was
> forc'd to get away, every one hunching and pushing me,
> with Scorn and Derision.
>
> 'To the Reader', *A Patch-Work Screen for the Ladies*

BY any reckoning Jane Barker (1652–1732) was a remarkable figure. A devoted Jacobite who followed the Stuarts into exile, a learned spinster who dabbled in commercial medicine, a novelist who wrote one of very few accounts of female same-sex desire in early modern Britain, she was also one of the most important women writers to enter the literary market-place during the Augustan period. Barker published occasional verse, satires on affairs of state, a heroic romance, a translation of a French devotional manual, and the increasingly admired novels that compose the innovative, autobiographically based Galesia trilogy. Her writing life spanned a crucial half-century, from the mid-1670s to the mid-1720s. During the reign of Charles II she exchanged verse within provincial amateur circles, circulated political poetry at the Stuart court-in-exile at St-Germain at the century's turn, and emerged during the reign of George I a novelist-for-pay, an elderly and improbable instance of that new phenomenon, the female literary professional. Barker entered English literary culture from such various angles, her work touches at so many points upon the genres and media of presentation flourishing during this period of decisive transformation, her career exemplifies so richly the developments that moved literary production from aristocratically based patronage networks into the market-place, that an account of her writing life may fairly be called a study of literary culture in transition.

Barker was little known during her lifetime, however, and all but forgotten after her death. Her only volume of printed verse, *Poetical Recreations* (1688), sank quickly from sight,[1] and the one or two novels that enjoyed what scholars like to call a 'modest' success had fallen out of circulation by mid-century. She did not attract the vilification heaped upon Aphra Behn and the other highly visible 'she-wits', or the filth hurled at Elizabeth Thomas, still remembered as 'Curll's Corinna', or the sexual innuendo that clung like babes of love to Eliza Haywood's waist. And despite a (grossly misleading) reputation in some quarters for pious didacticism and the literary manner of a 'she-saint', she failed to inspire the enraptured hagiography that turned her near-contemporary the exemplary Mrs Rowe into a cultural icon. Indeed, the recorded response to Barker's work before our own century has been for the most part no response at all, a long silence broken only by the occasional derisory sniff—as when George Thorn-Drury consigned this 'close inhabitant of Obscurity' to deepest shade[2]—or the odd bemused query. The question put several times to *Notes and Queries*, 'Is anything known of her history?', elicited no useful information.[3] Why a poet and novelist we are coming to recognize as a figure of exceptional interest should have left so little impress upon her own culture is one of the puzzles to be addressed by

[1] Although a few Barker lyrics were picked up in contemporary songbooks, so far as I know the first modern anthology to include her verse is vol. vii ('The Dryden Anthology') of Edward Arber (ed.), *British Anthologies*, 10 vols. (London: Henry Frowde, 1899–1901).

[2] 'Time has not without justice left this feminine rival of Spenser, Jonson, Shakespear, Shadwell, Settle & revolting Jack Dryden, a close inhabitant of Obscurity', wrote George Thorn-Drury (1860–1931) in the 3rd vol. of his inter-leaved annotated copy of the 2nd edn. (1723) of Giles Jacob's *The Poetical Register* (Bodleian, Thorn-Drury d. 3, item 288[e]). I am grateful to Jeslyn Medoff for this reference.

[3] *N&Q*, 12th ser. 16 (Sept. 1922), 232. A query seventy years earlier (*N&Q*, 1st ser. 11 (Sept. 1852), 245), received no reply whatsoever. In 1902 the same query (*N&Q*, 9th ser. 2 (Aug. 1902), 87) prompted one respondent to report that he had 'for many years been endeavouring to find out particulars of this lady' without success (*N&Q*, 9th ser. 30 (August 1902), 171).

this book, the first full-length study of the writings and writing life of Jane Barker.[4]

Feminist criticism has already established some of the reasons Barker is worth our regard. She has been called one of the 'liveliest and most original novelists of the earlier part of the century' and praised for work that is a 'complex mixture of autobiography, fictional self-representation, and fantasy'.[5] Students of the novels have begun to explore their female rage, weird sexual fantasies, hallucinatory dreams, and homoerotic energies, while more recent criticism has drawn attention to the political commitments of the poetry.[6] A rich line of inquiry begun by Jane Spencer and extended by Kristina Straub, among others, has investigated Barker's ambivalence about her identity

---

[4] Her verse includes *Poetical Recreations* (1688), one of rather few volumes of poetry to be printed under a woman's name in the 17th cent. At the turn of the century she prepared for presentation to the young Prince of Wales (soon to be 'James III', the Old Pretender) a manuscript volume of Roman Catholic and Jacobite verse entitled 'Poems Refering to the times' (1701) of which a second copy survives as Part One of the three-part Magdalen Manuscript. The latter is a quarto volume preserving three separate collections of verse by Barker, including a 'corrected' version of the poems printed in *Poetical Recreations*. Some she revised for inclusion in the prose fictions in the Galesia trilogy, which comprises *The Amours of Bosvil and Galesia* (1713), first published under the title *Love Intrigues* and revised for inclusion in *Entertaining Novels* (1719), followed by *A Patch-Work Screen for the Ladies* (1723) and *The Lining of the Patch Work Screen for the Ladies* (1726). She also published a politically encoded romance, *Exilius* (1715)—reissued in *Entertaining Novels* (1719)—and a translation of a devotional manual by Fénelon, *The Christian Pilgrimage* (1718).

[5] Jane Spencer, 'Women Writers and the Eighteenth-Century Novel', in John Richetti (ed.), *The Cambridge Companion to the Eighteenth-Century Novel* (Cambridge: Cambridge UP, 1996), 212–35 (214); Marilyn L. Williamson, *Raising Their Voices: British Women Writers, 1650–1750* (Detroit: Wayne State UP, 1990), 103.

[6] For representations of female anger (and bodily experience), see Paula R. Backscheider, *Spectacular Politics: Theatrical Power and Mass Culture in Early Modern England* (Baltimore and London: Johns Hopkins V. P., 1993), 142–6. For dreams and the inner life, see Margaret Anne Doody, 'Deserts, Ruins and Troubled Waters: Female Dreams in Fiction and the Development of the Gothic Novel', *Genre*, 10 (1977), 529–72, esp. 532–35, and 'Jane Barker', *British Novelists, 1660–1800*, in *DLB* 39, part I (Detroit: Gale Research Co.–Bruccoli Clark, 1985), 24–30. For homoeroticism, see my 'The Unaccountable Wife and Other Tales of Female Desire in Jane Barker's *A Patch-Work Screen for the Ladies*', *The Eighteenth Century* 35 (1994), 155–72. For the political underpinnings of Barker's poetry, see Carol Barash, *English Women's Poetry, 1649–1714: Politics, Community, and Linguistic Authority* (Oxford: Clarendon P., 1996), 174–208, and Toni Bowers, 'Jacobite Difference and the Poetry of Jane Barker', *ELH* 64 (1997), 857–69.

as a woman writer.[7] That such work will go forward seems assured now that Barker's finest work is widely available, most importantly in *The Galesia Trilogy and Selected Manuscript Poems of Jane Barker* (1997) edited by Carol Shiner Wilson, which reprints three of her prose fictions and a selection of her verse in a classroom-friendly paperback edition.[8] Barker has been well served by feminist scholars and critics, and will continue to be. The chapters that follow make additional claims for Barker's significance, which I shall here briefly summarize.

First, one can scarcely exaggerate her value as a case study for the emergence of print-world literary professionalism and, more particularly, for analysis of the complex relations between manuscript and print at this transitional moment. The interplay of these two literary cultures is well documented at both early and late stages of her writing career. Barker's earliest datable verse comes from the 1670s, a time when manuscript and print flourished side by side, constituting not so much rival writing cultures as sets of overlapping and complementary literary possibilities. Over the next decades she wrote for both media, becoming one of only a handful of writers—and to my knowledge the only woman whose texts have survived in any number—to leave behind a considerable body of literary material intended for publication in both.[9] Especially valuable in this

[7] Jane Spencer, 'Creating the Woman Writer: The Autobiographical Works of Jane Barker', *Tulsa Studies in Women's Literature*, 2 (1983), 165–81, and *The Rise of the Woman Novelist: From Aphra Behn to Jane Austen* (Oxford and New York: Basil Blackwell, 1986), 62–70. Kristina Straub's revision of Spencer is brief but suggestive: see her 'Frances Burney and the Rise of the Woman Novelist', in *The Columbia History of the British Novel*, ed. John Richetti (New York: Columbia UP, 1994), 199–219, esp. 203–5. See also my 'Galesia, Jane Barker, and a Coming to Authorship', in Carol J. Singley and Susan Elizabeth Sweeney (eds.), *Anxious Power: Reading, Writing and Ambivalence in Narrative by Women*, eds. (New York: State U. of New York P., 1993), 91–104.

[8] *The Galesia Trilogy and Selected Manuscript Poems of Jane Barker* (New York and Oxford: Oxford UP, 1997), reprints *Love Intrigues, A Patch-Work Screen for the Ladies, The Lining of the Patch Work Screen*, and a selection of poems from Mag. MS. *Love Intrigues* is reprinted in Paula R. Backscheider and John J. Richetti (eds.), *Popular Fiction by Women 1660–1730: An Anthology* (Oxford: Clarendon P., 1996).

[9] For an overview of authorial attitudes toward script and print in the 17th cent., see Harold Love, 'Manuscript Versus Print in the Transmission of English Literature, 1600–1700', *BSANZ Bulletin*, 9 (1983), 95–107. For manuscript exchange and circulation in the 17th cent. more generally, see Peter Beal, *Index of English Literary Manuscripts, 1450–1700*, 4 vols. (London and New York: Bowker

regard is the Magdalen Manuscript,[10] which records Barker's participation in three different manuscript-based amateur writing communities in the latter part of the seventeenth century. Because some of this verse can be read against the cognate collection preserved in *Poetical Recreations*, we are able to track with unusual precision the passage of Barker's poetry from coterie circles to larger, more impersonal communities of readers, as will be seen in Chapter 1. Similarly, *The Amours of Bosvil and Galesia*, a prose fiction, survives in two versions, the first reflecting the more intimate possibilities of manuscript circulation and the second embodying the more distanced protocols of the market-place. We are thus able to examine the textual evolution of a work that originated in the feminine manuscript-based literary community and was only later released—or pirated into—the public literary sphere, as will be seen in Chapter 5. We have learned that too narrow a focus upon the commercial, print-oriented side of women's literary activities distorts our understanding of female literary production in the early modern period and have begun to assess women's verse in the light of recent work on female involvement in seventeenth-century manuscript culture.[11] My discovery that

and Mansell, 1980–93); Mary Hobbs, *Early Seventeenth-Century Verse Miscellany Manuscripts* (Aldershot: Scolar, 1992); Harold Love, *Scribal Publication in Seventeenth-Century England* (Oxford: Clarendon P., 1993); Arthur F. Marotti, *Manuscript, Print, and the English Renaissance Lyric* (Ithaca and London: Cornell UP, 1995); H. R. Woudhuysen, *Sir Philip Sidney and the Circulation of Manuscripts 1558–1640* (Oxford: Clarendon P., 1996); Peter Beal, *In Praise of Scribes: Manuscripts and their Makers in Seventeenth-Century England* (Oxford: Clarendon P., 1998). The ground-breaking study of women's participation in manuscript culture is Margaret J. M. Ezell, *The Patriarch's Wife: Literary Evidence and the History of the Family* (Chapel Hill and London: U. of North Carolina P., 1987). The interpenetration of print and manuscript cultures in the previous century is discussed by Margaret W. Ferguson, 'Renaissance Concepts of the "Woman Writer" ', in Helen Wilcox (ed.), *Women and Literature in Britain 1500–1700* (Cambridge: Cambridge UP, 1996), esp. 156–63. She writes: 'the existence of manuscript publication, and its use by both men and women, creates an interesting border territory on various ideological maps' (161). See also in the same collection Elizabeth H. Hageman, 'Women's Poetry in Early Modern Britain', 190–208.

[10] Mag. MS 343, Magdalen College Oxford. A selection of this verse is printed with a textual apparatus in my edition of *The Poems of Jane Barker: The Magdalen Manuscript* (Oxford: Magdalen College Occasional Paper 3, 1998).

[11] For an elegant and convincing critique of the assumptions sponsoring the feminist preoccupation with market-place writing, see Margaret J. M. Ezell, *Writing Women's Literary History* (Baltimore and London: Johns Hopkins UP, 1993).

Bosvil and Galesia, one of Barker's best-known printed volumes, was first intended for a coterie readership suggests we may need to adjust our approach to the study of prose fiction as well.

Second, Barker is an immensely important figure in the history of what might be called literary Jacobitism. The collection of political poetry she presented at the Stuart court-in-exile at St-Germain is a central Jacobite text of the 1690s and perhaps the most important Jacobite verse-history produced during the immediate post-revolutionary period. The work she published after her return to England in 1704, especially the later patchwork narratives, offers a sustained pro-Stuart response to the ongoing crisis of succession. In this context Galesia, usually read as a figure for the woman writer, is seen to stand for a bereft England repining for the lost Stuart lover. Indeed, taken together, the post-revolutionary writings constitute what is arguably the fullest, most complex imaginative representation of the dynastic fortunes of the Stuarts from the beginnings of the reign of James II in 1685 to the reign of George I (1714–27). Barker has been characterized, aptly enough, as the unofficial poet laureate of the exiled Stuart court in the 1690s.[12] We can now see, as will be argued in Chapter 4, that in the next century she would take it upon herself to speak on behalf of the troubled Catholic-Jacobite community in Hanoverian Britain, writing novels that explore the perplexed loyalties of the pro-Stuart subject in a post-Stuart kingdom.

Third, Barker figures prominently in the development of the early novel and its articulation of new modes of female subjectivity, as feminist scholarship has recognized. The Galesia fictions, generally regarded Barker's finest literary achievement, rehearse the life-story of a woman who, by degrees, slips free of the moorings of the ordinary feminine destiny to 'espouse' instead 'a Book'. In contrast to the amatory writers publishing around this time, who employed romance convention to depict in the starkest possible terms encounters between feminine powerlessness and male brutality, delivering sexual politics at

---

[12] Paul J. Korshin, Afterword [to a special issue on Jacobitism], *ELH* 64 (1997), 1091–1100 (1091).

their most excitingly lurid, Barker wrote fictions that register a quiet withdrawal from the heterosexual economy. She creates in the process a heroine almost without precedent in English fiction. Galesia, regarded by many as Barker's wry alter ego, is a sympathetically rendered 'singlewoman', to adopt Susan S. Lanser's coinage,[13] who is also a creature of the culture of print—a recognizably modern individual who knows herself in large part through silent, solitary, even furtive acts of reading and writing, a poet whose consciousness is defined as much by the private experience of texts as by her interactions as a woman within a network of familial roles and everyday social obligations. In the Galesia fictions Barker renders with minute particularity the interiorized, print-based subjectivity of an ordinary woman who finds herself propelled by her own 'uncouth' desires into a mode of existence that is anything but ordinary, and in Galesia she gives us one of the most engaging characters in the early novel.

As a case study of emergent literary professionalism, as a 'bicultural' author at home in manuscript and print, as a Jacobite writer in poetry and prose, as a pioneer of the novel of female subjectivity, and as early chronicler of an emerging, print-world individuality, Barker is an author of considerable significance. Although praised these days as 'one of the most fascinating of the early women writers recently revived by feminist literary scholarship',[14] she had until recently been assigned a rather dowdy role in literary history, being cast (if at all) as an exemplar of the new and, it need almost not be said, deeply dull strain of ladylike respectability in fiction by women. Bridget MacCarthy's relegation of Barker to the 'female school of moral didacticism' in 1946 would be reasserted with alliterative memorability by John Richetti in his more influential *Popular Fiction Before Richardson* (1969). Dubbing her novels 'pious polemics' he located her significance in the way that she, along with a handful of other high-minded early eighteenth-century women writers, brought to the scandalous early novel an insistently 'pious frame of reference' designed to render female

[13] See the Epilogue below.
[14] Sarah Prescott, 'Resolv'd to espouse a Book', *TLS* (9 Jan. 1998), 21.

8 INTRODUCTION

fiction 'impeccably respectable'.[15] Jane Spencer, in *The Rise of the Woman Novelist* (1986) and a ground-breaking earlier essay, was considerably more sympathetic, finding Barker a figure of real interest and according her a crucial (if, it now seems, problematic) role in the 'rise' of the woman novelist. None the less, her assessment of Barker's role in literary history does not move greatly beyond Richetti: she was 'one of the earliest "respectable" women novelists' who demonstrated that a woman novelist 'could be chaste, moral, and respectable'.[16] In virtually all subsequent accounts Barker is read *within* a narrative of the emerging bourgeois femininity and *against* the more flamboyant literary practices of the sex-and-scandal school of female popular fiction.[17] Again and again one encounters the assertion that the chaste (moral, pious, decorous, and above all respectable) Barker remained 'acceptable' to later generations of eighteenth-century readers, yet if any contemporaries lauded Barker's work as morally improving or paid tribute to the author as an uplifting alternative to the notoriously unedifying 'triumvirate of wit', I have not come upon their remarks. Indeed, there is little to suggest she was read at all after the second or third decade of the century and much to indicate she would have been horrified to think that one day her name would be used to stand for Rising Domestic Womanhood.

This is a woman, let it be remembered, who followed the Stuarts into exile, who lived for fifteen years at St-Germain writing in outraged support of the hereditary right of kings, and

[15] B. G. MacCarthy, *The Female Pen. Women Writers: Their Contribution to the English Novel 1621–1744* (Oxford: Blackwell for Cork UP, 1946), 251; she also, 252, pronounced the heroines 'righteous, matter-of-fact prigs'. John J. Richetti, *Popular Fiction Before Richardson: Narrative Patterns 1700–1739* (Oxford: Clarendon P., 1969), 239.

[16] Spencer, 'Creating the Woman Writer', 179. Spencer suggests but for obvious reasons declines to explore one of the problems with this assessment when in *Rise of the Woman Novelist*, 69, she notes in passing that Barker's novels seem to have been without influence.

[17] For accounts of the links between the rise of the novel and the ascendence of the ideology of bourgeois femininity, see (in addition to Spencer) Mary Poovey, *The Proper Lady and the Woman Writer: Ideology as Style in the Works of Mary Wollstonecraft, Mary Shelley and Jane Austen* (Chicago and London: U. of Chicago P., 1984); Nancy Armstrong, *Desire and Domestic Fiction: A Political History of the Novel* (New York and Oxford: Oxford UP, 1987); Janet Todd, *The Sign of Angellica: Women, Writing, and Fiction 1660–1800* (London: Virago P., 1989).

who on at least one occasion after her return to England risked imprisonment by entering into Jacobite conspiracy. Born in 1652, a mere five years after the birth of Rochester, she lived until 1732, surviving Defoe by a year. The author who alluded to Walpole in his capacity as 'The Skreen' in the title of her best known novel and who had sharp things to say about the South Sea Bubble belonged, it is astonishing to recall, to the generation that included Shadwell and Dryden. Although she watched a dynastic kingdom transform itself into the beginnings of a modern nation-state and saw its sectarian antagonisms give way to secular ambitions fuelled by commerce, international trade, and the growth of empire, she never ceased to inhabit a mental world shaped by the religio-political crises of the previous century. In the openly retrospective preface to her last novel a septuagenarian Barker characterized herself as scraping out 'an old Tune, in fashion about threescore and six years ago' (*Lining*, 179)—in 1659, that is to say, the eve of the Restoration of the Stuart monarchy. The self-portrayal points toward the paradoxical character of a literary innovator, a self-consciously modern novelist who continued to identify strongly with the values of the authoritarian, hierarchically ordered, and largely discredited Stuart world she had lost.[18] This is the figure I call *Janus* Barker, an author who looks back to traditional ways of thinking and feeling as much as she looks forward to the triumph of bourgeois domesticity, a novelist whose fictions distrust the modernity they articulate. That Barker wrote to pious and didactic purposes it would be foolish to deny; but it does not follow that she exemplifies emergent bourgeois femininity either in its manifest constraints or in its supposed 'moral authority'. The time has come to put to rest a reputation for ladylike respectability that seriously distorts the meaning of a body of work grounded in political disaffection and to begin to develop a more reliable assessment of a writing life that was not exactly 'exemplary'.

---

[18] A manuscript poem recreates in sharp detail a girlhood in which she listened enthralled to 'wond'rous storys' of civil war battles told by her family's gardener, a 'good old tippling swain', who on the anniversary of the Restoration 'skip't about the Bon-fire like a boy' (Mag. MS, fos. 65r–v). The poem, 'A dialogue between Fidelia and her little nephew, Martius, as they walk in Luxembourg', is printed in Wilson, 313–19.

In the last decade we have learned a fair amount about Barker's life. When Jane Spencer published her inaugural essay in 1983, she had to rely for biographical data upon a 1922 entry in *Notes and Queries*. The notice was five paragraphs long and the information frankly speculative—much of that wrong, as it turns out—but it was the only source in English then available.[19] Since then much has come to light. We can now reasonably surmise that at different times during her long and various life Jane Barker was an anatomy student, medical practitioner, vendor of a gout cure, political exile, head of a female household, Chancery litigant, and Jacobite agent who died at her beloved St-Germain just two months short of 80. That it is now possible to respond with something other than silence to the question, 'Is anything known of her history?' is due in no small measure to the pioneering exertions of Germaine Greer and Jeslyn Medoff, who began excavating information about Barker in the 1980s as part of the research for *Kissing the Rod: An Anthology of Seventeenth-Century Women's Verse* (1989). Since then Carol Shiner Wilson, with the assistance of Edward Corp, has carried the investigation into French archives. Their findings on the St-Germain years are reported in Wilson's introduction to *The Galesia Trilogy* along with her discoveries about Barker's family in England. The results of my own archival work are presented in a biographical essay written in collaboration with Medoff.[20] Far from being exemplary or respectable, the life that has emerged over the last decade is one best evoked by terms like exile, estrangement, and political disaffection.

To begin, the bookish Barker remained single at a time when learning and spinsterhood rendered a woman doubly suspect, circumstances long recognized and rightly emphasized in feminist accounts. But the suspect nature of her religious affiliations

[19] G. S. Gibbons, *N&Q*, 11th ser. 12 (30 Sept. 1922), 278–9, scraped together such meagre facts as were to be had from close reading of her poetry and prose fiction and, more importantly, called attention to the indispensable Mag. MS. An earlier German dissertation contains biographical information derived entirely, it appears, from Barker's writings: see Karl Stanglmaier, *Mrs. Jane Barker: Ein Beitrag zur Englischen Literaturgeschichte* (Berlin, 1906), available on microfilm from Research Publications (New Haven).

[20] Kathryn R. King, 'Jane Barker and her Life (1652–1732): The Documentary Record', *ECL* 21, NS 3 (1997), 16–38, with the assistance of Jeslyn Medoff, cited hereafter as Doc. Rec.

has received less attention. While it is generally known that she converted to Catholicism in the mid-1680s, the significance of this event is not always appreciated. In fact, conversion was the central and defining experience of Barker's life, with enormous implications for her personal existence—not least, sending her into exile in France from 1689 until 1704—and for her creative life. From the 1690s she wrote in intense if sometimes concealed identification with a community that perceived itself despised by or at best marginal to the established order. Barker came out as a papist in a world that was openly and insistently papiphobic, knowing that her religious orientation would arouse the hostility of her predominantly Protestant neighbours and possibly expose her to official harassment as well as unofficial mistrust.[21] Patricia Brückmann points out that recusant historians of the present generation are less likely than earlier ones to paint a picture of heroic suffering and persecution—seventeenth-century Roman Catholics, she notes, were for the most part 'inconvenienced rather than menaced from day to day'— but there can be no doubt that, as another historian has put it, Catholics experienced 'minor, long-term, and unremitting harassment [that] must have been both disturbing and wearing, and unquestionably the pressures to conform could be great'.[22] Those who did not yield constituted, it is often said, a community apart.[23] In affiliating herself with an outlawed community, Barker made herself subject to penal liabilities, heavy taxation

[21] See Colin Haydon, *Anti-Catholicism in Eighteenth-Century England, c.1714–80: A Political and Social Study* (Manchester and New York: Manchester UP, 1993). For the 17th cent., see John Miller, *Popery and Politics in England 1660–88* (Cambridge: Cambridge UP, 1973); Robin Clifton, 'The Popular Fear of Catholics during the English Revolution', *Past and Present* 52 (1973), 23–55; Jonathan Scott, 'England's Troubles: Exhuming the Popish Plot', in Tim Harris, Paul Seaward, and Mark Goldie (eds.), *The Politics of Religion in Restoration England* (Oxford, Basil Blackwell, 1990), 107–31.

[22] Patricia Brückmann, 'Catholicism in England', in Robert P. Maccubbin and Martha Hamilton-Phillips (eds.), *The Age of William III and Mary II: Power, Politics, and Patronage 1688–1702* (Williamsburg, Va.: The College of William and Mary, 1989), 82; Haydon, *Anti-Catholicism*, 15.

[23] The standard works on English Catholicism for this period are John Bossy, *The English Catholic Community 1570–1850* (London: Darton, Longman, and Todd, 1975) and J. C. H. Aveling, *The Handle and the Axe: The Catholic Recusants in England from Reformation to Emancipation* (London: Blond and Briggs, 1976). Geoffrey Scott extends and revises these earlier accounts in *Gothic Rage Undone: English Monks in the Age of Enlightenment* (Bath: Downside Abbey, 1992).

(from 1695 a double land tax), restrictions on her movements, surveillance, and the suspicion of the authorities.[24] Little wonder that from the ousting of the Catholic James II onwards her fictions chart an exile's sense of not-belonging, or that as late as the 1720s, when the Protestant Hanoverian succession was firmly in place, she continued to write in coded support of the dynastic claims of the Catholic House of Stuart.

Barker's Jacobite politics went well beyond a sentimental attachment to the Stuart rose, oak trees, and tartan plaids described by Paul Monod in *Jacobitism and the English People, 1688–1788* (1989) or the 'emotional Jacobitism' sometimes attributed to Pope.[25] Unlike her co-religionist Dryden and fellow Stuart apologist Behn, both of whom stayed behind to take their chances with the new regime, Barker left London for France soon after the Revolution to join the Jacobite community that settled around the Stuart court-in-exile at St-Germain-en-Laye, just outside Paris. There she lived until 1704, venting her anti-Williamite political animus in fierce verse that circulated among other Catholic members of the exile community, men and women of an unbending stamp who could be counted upon to share her uncompromising principles. After returning to England she published works of strong but often oblique Catholic-Jacobite tendency, obliged by the conditions of the market-place to develop the strategies of indirection that make the 'patchwork' fictions, *A Patch-Work Screen for the Ladies* (1723) and *The Lining of the Patch Work Screen* (1726), fascinating on so many levels. In England she continued to work for the Pretender's cause in other ways besides. We shall never know the full extent of Barker's involvement in Jacobite intrigue, but involved she unquestionably was, if only as a conduit for information: a 1718 letter intercepted by the Hanoverian authorities shows her passing along advice to the exiled Jacobite leader the duke of Ormonde regarding the

[24] See J. A. Williams, 'English Catholicism under Charles II: The Legal Position', *Recusant History*, 7 (1963), 123–43.
[25] The phrase was coined by Douglas Brooks-Davies, *Pope's* Dunciad *and the Queen of the Night: A Study in Emotional Jacobitism* (Manchester: Manchester U., 1985). For a critique of this assessment of the nature of Pope's Jacobite politics, see John Morillo, 'Seditious Anger: Achilles, James Stuart, and Jacobite Politics in Pope's *Iliad* Translation', *ECL* 19 (May 1995), 38–58.

timing for a proposed invasion of England.[26] Barker, we learn, was a hard-core Jacobite prepared to work for the overthrow, violent if necessary, of the established government. In this light her praise of nature 'dress'd' as if 'in frolick England she'd invade' in her lines on the 'Kings going to Callis this carnival 1696' acquires unexpectedly dark undercurrents. (In 1696 James left St-Germain for Calais to join an expeditionary force poised to invade England, while on the other side of the Channel a plot was afoot to assassinate William III.)[27] The authorities were right to be suspicious.

If religio-political ideological imperatives sent Barker outside the country to wait out the long duration of the 'curssed orange' years, they rendered her an exile in her own land when she returned.[28] With William of Orange dead and James's daughter Anne on the throne, Barker left France in 1704 for Wilsthorp, the Lincolnshire village where she had passed much of her early life. For the next fourteen years or so, living in the manor house and managing the farm whose leasehold she had inherited many years earlier, she struggled to make ends meet at a time when even non-Catholic small landowners collapsed under the weight of ruinous taxes. One gets the impression that she lived in the village of her girlhood virtually as an alien. Such documents as have come to light give glimpses of a woman estranged from her rural Protestant community and at odds with such family members as she could claim in England. (Her cherished Connock relations from her mother's side of the family, including at least two Jacobite military officers of some distinction, were scattered across Catholic Europe.) A niece took her to court in 1717 to recover money she claimed her aunt owed her

---

[26] The letter, which is in the BL, is discussed in Ch. 4 below.

[27] For the Assassination Plot, see Jane Garrett, *The Triumphs of Providence: The Assassination Plot, 1696* (Cambridge: Cambridge UP, 1980). There is no reason to suppose Barker knew about the plot to assassinate William.

[28] My understanding of Barker's 'exilic duration' is indebted to Michael Seidel, *Exile and the Narrative Imagination* (New Haven and London: Yale UP, 1986), especially his discussion of Crusoe's island exile, 19–43. Noting that the years of Crusoe's exile coincide with the 'alien years' of Stuart rule, he argues, 30, that *Crusoe* 'takes its place alongside traditional narratives where exilic duration is a kind of test until national history is, in a way, ready to legitimize itself. Individuals and peoples best represent themselves by metaphorically standing outside their land. See also Seidel's 'Crusoe in Exile', *PMLA* 96 (1981), 363–74.

and to gain custody of two young girls then in Barker's care, that they might be educated 'in the principles of the protestant Religion'.[29] The Jane Barker we confront in her niece's Chancery deposition is, inevitably, a pretty disagreeable character—manipulative, litigious, self-preoccupied, grasping, imperious, mean-spirited, wheedling—but beneath the exaggerations required by the occasion one may discern the grim actualities of an ageing woman of limited economic resources struggling to cope with 'necessitous Circumstances' and doing so, after the failed Jacobite uprising of 1715, in a context of mounting threats against Catholics. That by 1717 she was in perilous straits financially and involved in other lawsuits besides, as her niece claims, seems only too likely. From other documents we know she was harassed by the local authorities carrying out national orders to crack down on Catholic landowners as part of the post-1715 campaign against 'papist' enemies of the state.[30] She may have left Wilsthorp to live abroad.[31] Her relations with her neighbours may have been strained, as well. Barker was an intellectual spinster and possibly a litigious one, a practising Roman Catholic, a political malcontent who had lived outside the country for a decade and a half, residing at St-Germain, a place anathema to loyal Protestants, and if fictionalized self-representations are any indication, a woman disposed to deal haughtily with those she considered inferiors. (In one of the Chancery depositions she is said to have declared that

[29] The story of Barker's conflict with her niece, Mary Staton (formerly Henson, née Barker) can be reconstructed from documents in the PRO. I am indebted to Carol Shiner Wilson for sharing the Statons' undated answer, bound with Jane Barker's bill of complaint, 10 July 1717, in C11/237/28. (Mary's husband, John, is named co-defendant in an action initiated by Jane in 1717.) The court's order in response to Barker's bill is recorded in an entry for 23 July 1717 in Chancery Decrees and Orders, C33/327 fo. 382; the court's response to the Staton answer, dated 6 Aug. 1717, is recorded in C33/329, fo. 23. For further details of the Chancery episode, see Doc. Rec., 23–4. For women's involvement in Chancery more generally, see Amy Louise Erickson, *Women and Property in Early Modern England* (London and New York: Routledge, 1993).

[30] By a statute of 1715 Barker was required as a papist to register her estate with Kesteven Clerks of the Peace as part of a plan to put an additional special charge on two-thirds of any Catholic estate. (As a Catholic landholder she was already subject to double taxation.) See Ch. 4 below.

[31] Although the title-pages of her printed volumes continue to identify her as 'of Wilsthorpe', no evidence has surfaced to place Barker in Wilsthorp after 1717. It is possible she returned to St-Germain at around this time. See Ch. 4 below.

'sooner' than return money to her niece she would 'live a constant Prisoner to her house or leave the Kingdome': the note of high-handed obstinacy seems genuinely Barkerian.)[32] We cannot know the extent to which the heroine of the autobiographically based Galesia trilogy is a portrait of her creator, of course, but it is suggestive that Galesia grows over the course of these narratives from a brooding, self-involved, somewhat wilful girl into an elderly woman largely cut off from human society.

It is only to be expected that such a woman would be a source of irritation to her community. Or worse. In 1709 the local churchwardens brought a presentment against a woman, unnamed, residing in Barker's parish; a person 'of a scandalous Life', 'a Roman Catholick' of whom it was said, ominously, 'she is about to be removed from Wilsthorp'.[33] Our Barker? We cannot be sure. But at the very least this ambiguous reference illumines the precarious situation of a woman of heterodox tendency living estranged from a community little inclined to tolerate the unordinary.

The figure of the exile recurs in Barker's work. For all their wit and quirky humour, her prose fictions and even some of the high-spirited poetry she composed before going into exile in her middle years take as their terrain what Edward Said has called the 'perilous territory of not-belonging', the late fictions in particular charting with remarkable acuity the inner life of an odd woman largely cut off from family, community, and other traditional sources of meaning. Said's reflections on the meaning of exile in our own time may help us understand the impulses that gave rise to and shaped Barker's narratives of 'not-belonging'. Exile is an 'unhealable rift forced between a human being and a native place, between the self and its true

[32] PRO, C11/237/28.
[33] LAO, Ch. P 1709, box 4/14 (Ness Deanery). I have been unable to identify any other Catholics living in Wilsthorp at this time. The statement responds to a standard question on the visitation form: 'Is there any Person in your Parish, that lieth under a common Fame, or vehement Suspicion, of Adultery, Fornication, or other Uncleanness? Have you there any common Drunkards, Swearers, or Blasphemers of God's Name and Word? Have you any who stand excommunicate, or who countenance and keep company with such?' It was presumably the final question that qualified Barker—if it was she—for the category of a person of 'scandalous Life'.

home'.[34] Such a rupture is not to be overcome: the condition of the exile is always one of loss, deprivation, discontinuity, and acute loneliness. (It is poignant in this context to recall that Fidelia, a persona Barker invented during her first years of exile, begins her textual life in utmost isolation, shorn by her creator of all human ties: 'I mourn my parents dead', Fidelia laments, 'and mourne alone'.)[35] Exiles often use writing to 'reconstitute their broken lives in narrative form, usually by choosing to see themselves as part of a triumphant ideology or a restored people'; they compose narratives 'designed to reassemble an exile's broken history into a new whole' (Said, 'Mind of Winter', 51). The autobiographical Fidelia narrative composed at St-Germain, the story of a woman in exile and a community in diaspora, is just such an effort at reconstituting a broken life by means of fiction. The narratives written in the bleak 1720s when restoration of the Stuarts seemed a lost cause express the dilemma of the loyal subject, who must deal as best she can with her estrangement from the national life in Hanoverian Britain. In the passage from *A Patch-Work Screen for the Ladies* that serves as epigraph to this introduction, 'Jane Barker' tries to join a happy throng of people, but when she is discovered to be a poet—often in Barker a name for the Other—is rudely banished: 'I was forc'd to get away, every one hunching and pushing me, with Scorn and Derision' (53). The episode neatly encapsulates that condition of not-belonging that manifests itself, almost obsessively in the late fictions, in episodes of expulsion, banishment, and rejection, informing narrative structures that respond to an exile's longing to see a torn existence patched together into an imagined whole.

But to connect Barker's exilic themes to the circumstances of her life is probably to frame her concerns too narrowly. The preoccupation with exile that is such a marked feature of her work should be situated as well within the larger context of the constructions of national and imperial identity that emerged at this time in conjunction with what Linda Colley maintains was

[34] Edward W. Said, 'The Mind of Winter: Reflections on Life in Exile', *Harpers*, 269 (Sept. 1984), 51, 49.
[35] 'Fidelia alone lamenting her parents lately dead, and her relations gone into the west against Monmoth', Mag. MS, fo. 8.

an exclusionary, specifically Protestant brand of Britishness. In
Britons: Forging the Nation 1707–1837 Colley argues that
during the long century following the Act of Union of 1707, an
aggressive, expansionistic, and distinctly Protestant sense of
national identity, driven by imperial ambitions and fed by victories in the recurring war with Catholic France, gave meaning to
people's lives and furnished the organizing framework for the
experience of a wide range of Britons. Britons, or at least the
right kind of Britons, came to regard themselves as a privileged
people bound together by shared superiority to demonized
Others, Catholics and Jacobites chief among them. The Great
Britain codified in the Act of Union in 1707, according to
Colley, defined itself by certain exclusions, by a process of
'othering' that involved 'the unprivileging of minorities who
would not conform'. They were 'not allowed to be British so
that others could be'.[36] If Colley's thesis is accurate, then it
means that Jane Barker—Catholic, Jacobite, female, and spinster—was a member of four overlapping unprivileged minorities, groups denied citizenship in the 'newly invented nation'
and disconnected from its sources of triumphalism, self-expan-
sion, and pride (*Britons*, 55). She was the Other many times
over; and it was from an alien's perspective that she constructed
herself as an author in the years following the Revolution.

If the notion of Barker as exile helps us appreciate public
dimensions of her writings that are often overlooked, it also
offers a useful corrective to the tendency toward biographical
reductionism that weakens much Barker criticism. The keen
interest in the autobiographical foundations of the Galesia
fictions—they are, indeed, routinely quarried for 'facts' about
the life even by scholars (including myself) who concede the ill-
wisdom of doing so—has resulted in a body of criticism that, for
better or for worse, conflates author and heroine (the latter
routinely described as her stand-in, alter ego, double, or projec-
tion) and, at its most naive, reads the fictions as retellings, more
or less unmediated, of the life. (One recent writer, for example,
speaks of biographical 'silences' in the Galesia narratives as if
these fictions constitute alternative forms of the documentary

[36] Linda Colley, *Britons: Forging the Nation 1707–1837* (New Haven and
London: Yale UP, 1992), 53.

record.)[37] Even at its best, in the work of Spencer and Straub, for example, autobiographically oriented readings remain deaf to the political undertones of the novels and thus unattuned to the larger public resonances that reveal themselves once the strong bent toward self-mythologizing characteristic of much of Barker's post-revolutionary work is recognized. A single example may serve to illustrate. In an emblematic episode in *A Patch-Work Screen* the heroine, inevitably a good Anglican, confronts her not-belonging during a service at Westminster Abbey, a site meant to suggest metonymically the national religious and social order. Galesia goes to the symbolically resonant Abbey hoping to find 'Persons of my own Stamp' but, crowded and pushed there 'by the Mob', experiences herself as a grotesque outcast: the 'gathering Congregation gazing upon me as a Monster; at least I fancied so' (109). She concludes, with an exile's loneliness, 'I was here likewise alone in the midst of a great Congregation' (110). Galesia's alienation from those with whom she sought community may well reflect her creator's sense of being perpetually at odds with her world, but until we see that her sense of herself as monstrous projects as well the isolation and even paranoia of the Catholic Other within a hostile Protestant nation, we will fail to apprehend the larger, communal force of the episode. At its most politically engaged Barker's art is to turn the materials of her own life into exilic myth. It is no small part of her achievement that she was able to create out of personal experience stories for a host of Others— Catholics, Jacobites, women, spinsters—who felt themselves excluded from official constructions of national identity in post-revolutionary Britain.

Barbara Lewalski writes that the texts of early modern women are 'often too narrowly contextualized–studied chiefly in relation to other women's texts, or to modern feminist theory, or to some aspects of the period's patriarchal ideology', and I could not agree more.[38] I have come to believe that gender-driven, oppositional accounts of early modern women writers, so

37 Wilson, introd. xvi.
38 Barbara Kiefer Lewalski, *Writing Women in Jacobean England* (Cambridge and London: Harvard UP, 1993), 1.

hugely productive over the last couple of decades, have reached a point of diminishing returns and will need to be supplemented by more inclusive pictures of women's involvement in early modern culture if feminist literary history is to move forward. The present study, which attends to the religio-political origins and reverberations of Barker's work and explores links between her literary imaginings and British national life, seeks to expand the frame of reference within which we regard women's literary past and, as a corollary, to encourage a rethinking of the paradigms that have governed much literary historical work on female authorship up to the present.

In stressing Barker's political engagements I join a wave of feminist scholars intent upon recovering female political agency in the period, among them Janet Todd, Paula Backscheider, Ros Ballaster, Carol Barash, Toni Bowers, and Paula McDowell, whose work I see my own as extending but also in some ways complicating.[39] The customary alignment of Barker with the pious school of novel-writing (alongside Penelope Aubin, Elizabeth Singer Rowe, and sometimes Mary Davys) belongs to a larger polarizing strategy that divides the field of female authorship into opposing camps, the transgressive 'daughters of Behn' (noisy, scandalous, politically committed, sexually explicit) and the decorous 'daughters of Orinda' (moral, ladylike, modest, unassertive)—a good girl/bad girl split that, strangely, is still used to structure many feminist literary histories. That such a division ill-serves the larger purposes of feminist literary history has been bruited for a while now. Paula McDowell has objected to this model on the grounds that its moralized polarities flatten difference and reduce literary history to a 'spectrum of virtue and vice'. More recently Carol Barash has challenged what she does not hesitate to call the

---

[39] Some of the most interesting work on the early novel has stressed the political dimensions of women's amatory fiction. Ros Ballaster, *Seductive Forms: Women's Amatory Fiction from 1684 to 1740* (Oxford: Clarendon P., 1992), focuses on Behn, Manley, and Haywood; a more thickly textured treatment of Manley's political engagements is offered by Paula McDowell in *The Women of Grub Street: Press, Politics and Gender in the London Literary Marketplace 1678–1730* (Oxford: Clarendon P., 1998), ch. 5; for suggestive work on Haywood, see Toni O'Shaughnessy Bowers, 'Sex, Lies, and Invisibility: Amatory Fiction from the Restoration to Mid-Century', in John Richetti (ed.), *The Columbia History of the British Novel* (New York: Columbia UP, 1994), 50–72.

'false opposition' between Katherine Philips and Aphra Behn; her exposition of a web of explicitly political concerns linking a group of female poets more often considered separately or even in opposition goes a long way toward undercutting these misleading distinctions.[40] Stressing aspects of the novels that link Barker with her pro-Stuart predecessor Behn, a writer to whom she is usually contrasted, this study applies additional pressure to this dichotomous historical model as it seeks also to enrich our understanding of the political underpinnings of the early novel.

The role of religion in the writing lives of late Stuart women has barely been attended to, much less theorized.[41] In asserting the centrality of Catholicism to an understanding of Barker's career and texts, I am not thinking primarily of matters of faith, spirituality, doctrine, or devotional experience, important though these doubtless were to her; nor am I concerned, except in passing, with religious dissent as it figures resistance to sexual oppression, a matter which has received some attention in feminist accounts of seventeenth-century writing women.[42] My concern is with religion as it supplied Barker and the vast majority of her

[40] Paula McDowell, 'Consuming Women: The Life of the "Literary Lady" as Popular Culture in Eighteenth-Century England', *Genre*, 26 (1993), 219–52 (235). Barash, *EWP* 5.

[41] The reluctance of feminist literary critics and historians to take up questions of religious identity is partly explained by the candid admission of Marilyn L. Williamson, *Raising Their Voices*, 10, that 'in seventeenth-century England, religious values are social and political, but the issues are so complex that they would have required another framework besides that of gender ideology'. My own thinking on these matters profited from the workshop on Women and Catholicism in Seventeenth-Century England organized by Frances E. Dolan, Margaret W. Ferguson, and Phyllis Mack, held 22 Apr. 1995 at the U. of Maryland as part of the symposium 'Attending to Early Modern Women'.

[42] For which see work on Elizabeth Cary by Sandra K. Fischer, 'Elizabeth Cary and Tyranny, Domestic and Religious', in Margaret P. Hannay (ed.), *Silent But for the Word: Tudor Women as Patrons, Translators and Writers of Religious Works* (Kent, Oh.: Kent State UP, 1985), 225–37; Margaret W. Ferguson, 'Running on with Almost Public Voice: The Case of "E.C." ', in Florence Howe (ed.), *Tradition and the Talents of Women* (Urbana and Chicago: U. of Illinois P., 1991), 37–67; and Lewalski, *Writing Women*, ch. 7. Paul Monod, 'Jacobitism as Court Culture and Popular Culture', presented at Northeast American Society for Eighteenth-Century Studies, Sept. 1996, indicates what an analysis of Barker along these lines might look like when he observes, with an acknowledgement to Jeslyn Medoff, that Jacobitism represented to Barker 'a kind of resistance to masculine power, an opposition to the brute force of revolution, which like other Stuart publicists she equated with rape'. I am grateful to Dr. Monod for sharing this unpublished paper with me.

contemporaries with their most basic sense of identity, with that
'*context* within which people give *meanings* to their actions and
experiences, and make sense of their lives'.[43] We appear to have
little trouble acknowledging on a theoretical level that religion
constituted for Barker's age what Fredric Jameson calls the
'cultural dominant', the 'master-code in which issues are
conceived and debated'; we recognize that, in David Zaret's
words, 'religious discourse was a, if not the, predominant means
by which individuals defined and debated issues' in the emerging public sphere.[44] It is therefore all the more astonishing that
religion as a category of difference should remain so inconspic-
uous a feature in early modern cultural studies. Almost without
exception the litany of difference that is an obligatory gesture of
the cultural studies essay fails to name *the* difference central to
early modern *mentalités*. In contrast, in recent years revisionist
historians have used traditional empirical methods to reinstate
the politics of religion at the heart of English national affairs in
the period,[45] but thus far have shown little interest in the role
of religion 'below', nor have they been especially attentive to the
ways a politics of religious identity functions in relation to questions of literary expression.[46] I have tried in this study to read-
mit religion as a fundamental category of difference in the

---

[43] John Tomlinson, *Cultural Imperialism: A Critical Introduction* (London:
Pinter, 1991), 7.

[44] Fredric Jameson, 'Religion and Ideology', in Frances Barker *et al.* (eds.), *1642:
Literature and Power in the Seventeenth Century* (Colchester: U. of Essex, 1981),
317. David Zaret, 'Religion, Science, and Printing in the Public Spheres in
Seventeenth-Century England', in Craig Calhoun (ed.), *Habermas and the Public
Sphere* (Cambridge and London: MIT P., 1992), 212–35 (213). Jameson's point that
we must not confuse early modern experience of religion with our own perceptions
of religion as interiorized and privatized belief is important if we are to grasp the
public and communal meanings of religion for Barker. Religion should be understood as 'the sign of group praxis and group membership, as a badge of collective
adherence, as something like a set of pseudo-concepts whose concrete function is to
organise this or that form of communal relationship and structure' (318).

[45] Most notably J. C. D. Clark, *English Society 1688–1832: Ideology, Social
Structure and Political Practice During the Ancien Regime* (Cambridge: Cambridge
UP, 1985), ix, who sought to 're-integrate religion into an historical vision which has
been almost wholly positivist'. For a collection of essays intent upon developing this
new emphasis, see Tim Harris, Paul Seaward, and Mark Goldie (eds.), *The Politics
of Religion in Restoration England* (Oxford: Basil Blackwell, 1990).

[46] An exemplary exception is McDowell's *Women of Grub Street*, a socio-literary
study which documents the intricate connections between religion, politics, gender,
and discourse in the late Stuart period.

seventeenth and early eighteenth centuries, to restore its force as
the 'master-code' by means of which women and men of
Barker's era apprehended themselves in relation to national
history and current political struggles, and at the same time to
call attention to the multiple ways in which women constructed
their identities in the early modern period.[47]

This study departs, then, from the customary feminist
emphasis upon feminocentric traditions of lineage and influence
to concentrate instead upon a single figure in relation to multiple and sometimes overlapping circles of readership, some
female and some not. I have tried to identify the community or
communities of readers for whom Barker's surviving texts were
originally written and the traditions of reading that would have
guided these first readers' interpretations. Who, I ask, first read
a particular Barker text? What kinds of meanings would her
earliest readers find there? What codes of interpretation would
have guided their 'actualizations' of the text?[48] How, to put it
more specifically, would a fellow Jacobite read the string of
courtship disappointments that threads its way through the
Galesia trilogy? What might a sister writer-for-pay make of its
patchwork analogies? Such questions release layers of meaning
unavailable through other reading methods; they also bring into
focus elements of sociability and dialogical interplay often
slighted or ignored altogether in literary histories too ready to
consign women writers to solitude, oppositionality, and marginality. Like Terry Lovell I believe that the 'phrase "writing in
society" ' used by Raymond Williams is 'more useful for the
understanding of the history of women's writing than the

---

[47] I do not mean to suggest feminist inattention to issues of woman and religion
more generally. For an excellent study of sectarian women, see Phyllis Mack,
Visionary Women: Ecstatic Prophecy in Seventeenth-Century England (Berkeley: U.
of California P., 1992). For readings of writings by Quaker women from the mid-
17th cent., see Ezell, *Writing Women's* 132–60. For an overview of women and religion in the period, see Diane Willen, 'Women and Religion in Early Modern
England', in Sherrin Marshall (ed.), *Women in Reformation and Counter-
Reformation Europe: Public and Private Worlds* (Bloomington and Indianapolis:
Indiana UP, 1989), 140–65. Work on women and Catholicism is detailed in Ch. 3
below.

[48] Roger Chartier, 'Laborers and Voyagers: From the Text to the Reader',
Diacritics, 22 (1992), 49–61 (50), usefully distinguishes between the 'readable
space' of a text and the variations 'which govern the circumstances of their "actu-
alization" ', that is, 'readings seen as concrete practices and interpretive procedures'.

concept of "writing from the margins", whether of culture or of language itself': women writers in the eighteenth century wrote, 'if not from the center, yet from a legitimate space within emergent modern culture'.[49] Analysis of the interplay of author and readership offers, I believe, an especially promising way to map that cultural space at the same time that it suggests some of the ways feminist literary historiography might recast issues of female authorship in broader cultural and historical terms than those permitted by current oppositional models.

Such an approach also helps us understand why so many readers have sensed Barker's texts to be particularly rich inscriptions of subjectivity. From at least the 1680s the history of her writing life is the history of her shifting and often troubled identification with a succession of what might be called 'subaltern counterpublics'[50]as well as with a surprisingly wide range of reading and writing communities, including a mostly male Cambridge-based literary coterie in the 1670s and 1680s, the exile community at St-Germain in the 1690s, and the London-centred print-based literary market-place in the second and third decades of the next century. Her affiliations—real and imagined, lived and textualized—were always to some degree perplexed. As a woman who espoused the single life and identified strongly with male forms of learning, as an Anglican who converted to Catholicism, as a member of an exile community fissured along religious and national lines, as a resident in a country for nine years at war with the country of her birth, as a Jacobite papist in Protestant England, and as a genteel amateur poet turned market-place novelist under the auspices of the legendarily scurrilous Edmund Curll, Barker seems to have experienced more acutely than most what Diana Fuss calls the 'struggle to negotiate a constantly changing field of ambivalent identifications', a struggle which according to much contemporary theory constitutes subjectivity as we

[49] Terry Lovell, 'Subjective Powers? Consumption, the Reading Public, and Domestic Woman in Early Eighteenth-Century England', in Ann Bermingham and John Brewer (eds.), *The Consumption of Culture 1600–1800: Image, Object, Text* (London and New York: Routledge, 1995), 37, 38.
[50] The phrase is Nancy Fraser's in 'Rethinking the Public Sphere: A Contribution to the Critique of Actually Existing Democracy', in Craig Calhoun (ed.), *Habermas and the Public Sphere* (Cambridge and London: MIT P., 1992), 109–42 (123).

understand it today.[51] The chapters that follow consider in the light of this struggle the shifting subject-positions adopted by Barker as, in her poems and prose fictions, she repeatedly imagines herself in relation to a number of real and invented communities—academic, medical, political, religious, and literary.

Barker's perplexed response to her identity as an intellectually aspiring woman is especially acute in the early verse, written during a period of her life when she was keenly aware of the disabilities entailed by gender. Although many of these poems are intensely sociable and exhibit a surprisingly untroubled identification with men and the things of men, others brood on women's cultural peripherality, especially on their author's own exclusion from the communities of male learning with which she strongly, if in some sense impossibly, identified. The result is a group of poems of invisibility, self-absence, and exile—but a kind of exile markedly different from that expressed in the more politically engaged narratives written during and after the St-Germain years. These later narratives recur to the condition of the outsider, as has already been noted, but the author's peripherality is no longer something to be escaped or decried: it is welcomed as the ground of an identity at once personal, political, and communal—a construction of self as Jacobite exile and Catholic Other. The post-revolutionary narratives take on a strongly mythologizing cast as Barker uses the exilic themes of poverty, victimization, exclusion, persecution, and banishment to create metaphors for a community apart.

I shall be moving among these themes in the discussions that follow, which work more or less chronologically through the stages in her writing career. Chapter 1 identifies features of the manuscript verse she produced and circulated within friendship circles in the 1670s and 1680s; it attempts to reconstruct her

---

[51] Diana Fuss, *Identification Papers* (New York and London: Routledge, 1995), 34. For one very specific example, one might consider the difficulties of her position during the Nine Years War, in which the Catholic country of her residence was at war with the Protestant country of her birth. Study of Dalton's army lists suggests the likelihood that her Connock relations fought on both sides. It is probably significant that the narrator of *BG* likens the 'War between *France* and the Allies'–she declines to name England, interestingly–to a 'Civil War, Friend against Friend, Brother against Brother, Father against Son' (*BG* 7).

literary relations with a range of friends with whom she entered into poetic dialogue, the most important being the group of St John's (Cambridge) men instrumental in getting this verse into print. These robust poems of friendship, interesting in themselves, illustrate a feature that has received less attention than it deserves in treatments of women poets, still too often supposed to compose in painful isolation or to consign their feeble scribblings to the flames. Chapter 2 begins with an account of Barker's 'career' as a lay physician and then focuses on a handful of quirky poems on medicine and medical learning she wrote during the 1670s and 1680s as they project her perplexed identification with a masculine culture of learning that beckons, engages, allures, but finally eludes her. Her reconstitution of the male medical establishment in this fascinating body of verse is at once identificatory and vengeful. Chapter 3 considers the political and occasional verse she produced and circulated at St-Germain in the 1690s while she lived on the fringes of a courtly community with whom her relations were aspiring but ambiguous. I read this body of verse in the light of what Harold Love identifies as a major function of the handwritten text in the seventeenth century, namely that of joining 'groups of like-minded individuals into a community, sect or political faction, with the exchange of texts in manuscript serving to nourish a shared set of values and to enrich personal allegiances'.[52] I suggest in addition that this verse records a failed attempt to achieve patronage from members of the royal family. Chapter 4 tells the story of Barker as Jacobite novelist. It connects the plots of her major fictions to timeless Stuart myth on the one hand and their political moment on the other, and considers the spinster-heroine in relation to the Jacobite mythology of the lost lover. Chapter 5 offers an account of the complexities of Barker's passage into print, reconstructing some of the routes by which, beginning in 1713, her coterie prose fictions made their way into the market-place. It concludes with a consideration of some of her late authorial self-representations as they register and reflect upon Barker's ambivalent attitudes toward what might be called her citizenship in the modern world of print. The Epilogue takes up questions of class, sexuality, and gender

[52] Love, *Scribal Publication*, 177.

by looking closely at a single episode in Barker's fiction, the
story of an unaccountable wife, which I read as a final kind of
perplexed identification, this one involving a tension between
class- and gender-based modes of perceiving. The episode
emerges in my reading as a fragment from lesbian prehistory
which confronts readers today with perplexities of their own.

Midway through the heavily marked pages of the Magdalen
Manuscript, a book of verse Barker came to regard as a kind of
personal poetic archive, one encounters, in brown ink, a thumb
print—undoubtedly Barker's own. That the volume should
preserve the material trace of a writer who made so little
imprint on her culture is a wry irony Barker would have
enjoyed. She was a stubborn woman and highly individual, like
the pattern of whorls unique to herself that survives among
handwritten copies of her poems. But if no longer quite the
'close inhabitant of Obscurity' she once was, Barker remains in
many ways a shadowy figure. The thumb print, so teasingly
evocative, so redolent of the very idea of 'clueness', leads finally
nowhere, tells us nothing about the woman or the world in
which she lived and wrote. It stands in my mind as an allegory
of sorts for our complex relationship to the historical Jane
Barker, a woman lost to us, recoverable only by workings of the
historical imagination as its plays upon such prints and traces as
happen into our sight—Carlo Ginzburg's dispersed fragments,
'reaching us by chance, of an obscure shadowy world that can
be reconnected to our own history only by an arbitrary act'.[53]
The chapters that follow are such an arbitrary act, an imaginative reconnection with a writer of insistent singularity.

[53] Carlo Ginzburg, *The Cheese and the Worms: The Cosmos of a Sixteenth-
Century Miller*, trans. John and Anne Tedeschi (Baltimore: Johns Hopkins UP,
1980), xxvi.

PART I

c.1675–1688

Poetical Recreations

THE picture of Barker the poet that emerges from study of the fifty-odd items of verse published in *Poetical Recreations* (1688) is sharply at odds with the self-doubting, regretful, solitary, even bitter figure taking shape in recent accounts. Certainly some of the verse Barker wrote at St-Germain, the subject of an essay by Toni Bowers, can be read in support of the view that Barker experienced 'confusion and disappointment' over her sacrificial devotion to a rather austere poetic vocation.[1] But by the time Barker composed this verse she was already developing her mythology of the female poet as Virtuous Outsider, a figure associated in the St-Germain poetry of the 1690s and even more in the late prose fictions with deprivation, neglect, and banishment. The verse printed in *Poetical Recreations*, written in the 1670s and 1680s when Barker was still a young woman, tells a strikingly different story. Composed for a small but sympathetic circle (or circles) of fellow amateur poets, this is pre-eminently sociable verse. Far from recording an elegiac retreat from human company, as has been suggested, the early poetry testifies to a sustained and for the most part well-pleased companionability and shows that the writing and exchange of verse was a vital part of Barker's social existence during this period.[2] It also offers scholars today a considerable glimpse into the world of the provincial literary coterie.

The present chapter focuses on the body of verse printed as Part One of the two-part *Poetical Recreations*. These poems, which represent the earliest recorded phase of Barker's writing

---

[1] Toni Bowers, 'Jacobite Difference and the Poetry of Jane Barker', *ELH* 64 (1997), 857–69 (863).

[2] That I take a very different view of the Barker of *PR* from that advanced by Barash in *EWP* will become clear from the ensuing discussion. She posits for the collection as a whole a speaker characterized by her 'controlled—even willed—solitude' (*EWP* 201).

life, show us a coterie poet whose literary *métier* was the expression of friendship: nearly half the items are familiar epistles to friends and acquaintances.[3] One detects little of the concern for affairs of state that would mark virtually everything Barker wrote after the Revolution. Absent too is the encomiastic verse which looms so large in the output of Dryden and Behn from the 1680s and which would become a strong feature of Barker's own poetic production in the next decade when, from 1689, she began to seek patronage at the court-in-exile at St-Germain. This is not public poetry, in other words, nor is it especially political. It is occasional and familiar verse addressed to intimates. The discussion that follows teases out some of the real-life literary relationships recorded within these poems and seeks in this way to build up a picture of the network of relationships that nourished Barker's earliest efforts as a poet. I provide, that is to say, what Harold Love calls a 'centrifugal reading' of this body of verse, reading it outward as a 'trace-bearing artefact of a site or community'—of the verse-exchange circle or circles through which Barker's earliest surviving poems moved.[4] The discussion moves next to more traditional literary concerns as I situate these poems in their immediate literary contexts and in relation to classical traditions and concludes by considering some of these poems as instances of disruption and resistance, of what feminist criticism sometimes calls 'talking back'.

The Making of Poetical Recreations

We should begin by clearing up certain misconceptions. There is, first, some confusion regarding the relationship between the two parts of *Poetical Recreations*. Part One consists of more

---

[3] Unfortunately no external evidence of MS circulation of these verses before or after their printing in *PR* has survived. MS copies of *PR* poems by other contributors appear in a miscellany compiled by Oliver and Peter Le Neve, including two Crayle poems responding to poems by Barker (BL Add. MS 27,406, fos. 99r–v). None of Barker's contributions appears in current first-line indexes to manuscript verse in BL, Beinecke, Bod., Folger, Huntington, and the Brotherton Collection at Leeds. A selection of her printed poems appears in vol. 3 of Thomas Austen's Commonplace Books, begun May 1766, Harvard, MS Eng. 612, 137–205.

[4] Harold Love, *Scribal Publication in Seventeenth-Century England* (Oxford: Clarendon P., 1993), 230.

than fifty items described on the title-page as 'Occasionally Written by Mrs. Jane Barker'. Part Two, written by 'several Gentlemen of the Universities, and Others' is a verse miscellany of over three-hundred pages—three times the length of the Barker offerings—with a strongly royalist and collegiate character. Although the Part Two contributors are often identified as Barker's Cambridge friends (or even as friends of her Oxford brother, dead for more than a decade), there is little reason to link the two parts. They are in fact distinct and for the most part independent compilations, united mainly by the enterprise of the bookseller, Benjamin Crayle, a young man who had connections in university literary circles and an acquaintance with Barker. Part Two does, it is true, include a group of some eight poems to and about Barker written by Crayle himself and three to her ascribable to the Cambridge friends, but otherwise appears to have been separately assembled.[5] Second, because the title-page bears the date 1688, some commentators have mistakenly linked its publication and even its contents with the political crisis of 1688–9, but *Poetical Recreations* was on sale by December 1687, a full year before James fled to France.[6]

Barker's assertion years later that the collection had been printed without her permission need not be seriously questioned. Consider, to begin, what is missing from *Poetical Recreations*, starting with authorial front matter. The multiple layers of prefatory material interposed between reader and text proper by Margaret Cavendish—one direct address after another, her manner by turns whimsical, timorous, grandiose, and plaintive—may stand as an extreme example, but in fact

---

[5] In some cases Crayle was drawing upon his own connections. Part Two includes, for instance, poems by Hovenden Walker and Thomas Wright, writers Crayle published with some success, and B. Willie, identified as sometime master of a school in Newark-upon-Trent. Since Crayle lived in Newark until he was 16, he may have studied with Willie. This is not to discount the possibility that Part Two includes anonymous contributions by members of the Cambridge set or by other poets with unknown Barker connections. The identified poets of Part Two are in any event an obscure lot, Charles Cotton and Sir C[arr] S[croop] being the only names remembered today. Part Two also includes an unascribed epitaph on Sir Palme Fairborn by Dryden: see Hugh Macdonald (ed.), *John Dryden: A Bibliography of Early Editions and of Drydeniana* (Oxford: Clarendon P., 1939), 81.

[6] *PR* was entered in the Stationers' Register on 25 Oct. 1687, appeared in the *Term Catalogues* in Nov. 1687, and was advertised on 5 Dec. 1687 in the *London Gazette* (No. 2301).

virtually all seventeenth-century women writers who came before the public in print were demonstrably anxious to secure the reader's sympathies as quickly and as directly as possible, doing so in ways that verge at times on feminine self-parody: 'Good, Sweet, Honey, Sugar-candied READER', coaxes Aphra Behn in the Epistle to the Reader from *The Dutch Lover* (1673). Barker was not one to play at seduction, but neither was she one to let pass an opportunity to reach out to her readers: every publication in which she is known to have had a hand addresses the reader in some way. And until very late in her career she was at pains to supply her publications with a noble (or even royal) dedicatee. Since she would hardly have overlooked such matters for her volume of verse, it seems reasonable to conclude Barker played no part in preparing *Poetical Recreations* for the press, a conclusion that receives oblique confirmation from the bookseller's preface: it opens, somewhat awkwardly, '*Lest the Book might appear Naked, and unfashionable, I thought it could not be altogether unnecessary to say something by way of* Preface . . .' (sig. A3).

Scholars can be grateful that Barker later copied a selection of these poems into the Magdalen Manuscript with a note that they had been printed in 1688 'without her consent' and are 'now corrected by her own hand'.[7] The invaluable Magdalen Manuscript, a three-part collection of verse composed over many years, compiled sometime after 1701, is one of two or perhaps three literary productions whose details we can be certain Barker controlled.[8] It comes furnished with an array of prefatory materials, internal glosses, and asides that serve to negotiate in fairly complicated ways the author's relation to the readers she hoped or believed she was addressing. In addition to a very interesting dedication to the Prince of Wales (discussed below in Chapter 3), it includes two formal addresses 'To the Reader'. The first begs pardon for 'a little, idle love poem or so' and asks that the defects of the volume be overlooked as 'the

---

[7] Mag. MS, Part Three, title-page.

[8] The other is BL Add. MS 21,621, a duplicate copy of the verses composing Part One of the Mag. MS transcribed by an amanuensis under Barker's close supervision. It is described in greater detail in Ch. 3. She seems to have been closely involved as well in the publication of *EN* (1719), which includes a new dedication and a substantially revised version of *BG*.

work of a blind person'; the second, which precedes a collection
of political verse, proclaims rather truculently—this is Barker in
her High Intransigent mode—that the author need make no
'apologie to my Reader for charging whole partys with crimes in
which great numbers were not involv'd', and ends on a similar
bullish note: 'I ask no bodys pardon for what I have done'.[9]
Many of the individual poems bear marginal glosses. Some
relate a poem or particular set of lines to an event in her
personal history—in 1696 she had had her cataracts couched, at
such-and-such a time she was recovering from a dangerous
illness; some relate a detail to Jacobite interpretations of
national history, as when she notes that the skies filled with fire
on the night of the battle of Sedgemoor.[10]

Especially interesting are glosses that comment on the verses
as poetic acts. A landscape poem breaks off with an apology of
sorts—'I design'd to have made this landskip in six poems' (fo.
109), a note records; 'but the business of the world prevented
me'—and concludes with the hope that 'some better hand will
finish this designe' (fo. 109v). Manuscript verse, specialists tell
us, was inevitably collaborative, shaping itself in dialogue with
others or another, if only silently within the author's mind. The
readiness to see her work completed by an abler hand does not
indicate feminine modesty or lack of assurance, in other words,
but points to a feature of manuscript literary culture emphasized by Arthur Marotti, among others, when he observes that
manuscript verse was part of 'an ongoing social discourse', its
plastic lines inviting interaction with its readers.[11] A note to
another poem discloses that 'these athe[i]stical lines, were not

[9] The first is from the general preface (fo. 1); the second from the preface to the
'Poems Refering to the times' (fos. 5v, 6).
[10] See Jeslyn Medoff, 'Dryden, Jane Barker, and the "Fire-Works" on the Night
of the Battle of Sedgemore (1685)', N&Q, NS 35 (June 1988), 175–6.
[11] Arthur F. Marotti, Manuscript, Print, and the English Renaissance Lyric
(Ithaca and London: Cornell UP, 1995), 135. Poetic texts, he observes, were 'inher-
ently malleable, escaping authorial control to enter a social world in which recipi-
ents . . . altered what they received'. For a study of readers' dialogue with Katherine
Philips, see Elizabeth H. Hageman and Andrea Sununu, ' "More Copies of it abroad
than I could have imagin'd": Further Manuscript Texts of Katherine Philips, "the
Matchless Orinda" ', EMS 5 (1995), 127–69. For other concrete examples of readers' engagements with texts, see Peter Beal, In Praise of Scribes: Manuscripts and
their Makers in Seventeenth-Century England (Oxford: Clarendon P., 1998), 25–6,
96–100, 124.

given to the Prince'—the 12-year-old Prince of Wales was dedicatee of Part One of the Magdalen Manuscript—'but being in
the original, they are here incerted' (fo. 36).[12] A note elsewhere
heads off the accusations of plagiarism that inevitably dogged
women poets at this time with a disclaimer: had she known 'the
poem calld naboths vinyard'—*Naboth's Vineyard* by John
Caryll, also an exile at St-Germain—she 'would not have put
her sicle in an others harvest' (fo. 21v).[13] In the manuscript
volume Barker is repeatedly seen reaching out to her readers in
various ways, a circumstance strengthening the conclusion that
she did not prepare *Poetical Recreations* for the press and thus
cautioning against uncritical use of the printed volume in
accounts of women's print-world involvements and self-repre-
sentational strategies. Maureen E. Mulvihill, for example,
counts Barker among the growing number of 'professional'
Restoration women writers who 'boldly published their
surnames' when it is almost certainly the boldness of the bookseller's commercial instincts we have to thank for the appearance of the author's name on the title-page.[14]

How, then, did this body of verse find its way into print? The
initiative may have come from her Cambridge friends, a group
of St John's College men with whom she evidently exchanged
poetry for many years. They furnished commendatory verses
and the Virgilian epigraph, as we learn from the long title of one

[12] The lines deemed unsuitable for the Prince accuse providence of almost malig-
nant mismanagement: 'Thus Providence cheats foolls, and fooll the wise | Lulling us
into stupid letergies, | Till worthless fools the worthiest men dispise' (Mag. MS, fo.
36). In the presentation version, this harsh reflection is softened into a question: 'If
Heav'n be just, and good, O tell me then, | Why are the just made preys to wicked
men?' (BL Add. MS 21,621, fo. 52v). The lines are from 'Fidelia walking the Lady
Abess comes to her'.

[13] The poem is 'Fidelia and her friend the third dialogue'. *Naboth's Vineyard*, by
John Caryll, titular Lord Caryll (1625-1711), appeared in a folio edition in 1679:
see E. F. Mengel (ed.), *POAS*, ii. 82. For female responses to the inevitable charges
of plagiarism, see *KR* 306.

[14] Maureen E. Mulvihill, 'A Feminist Link in the Old Boys' Network: The
Cosseting of Katherine Philips', in Mary Anne Schofield and Cecilia Macheski
(eds.), *Curtain Calls: British and American Women and the Theater, 1660–1820*
(Athens: Ohio UP, 1991), 71–104 (74). Also problematic is the assumption of
authorial intent and control that underpins Barash's reading of *PR* as an ordered
narrative in *EWP* 181–95. It is odd, given Barash's interest in the notion of collec-
tion-as-narrative, that she does not use Part Three of the Magdalen MS, where the
arrangement *is* demonstrably authorial.

of her manuscript poems, 'To my friends who prais'd my Poems, and at the begining of the little printed book placed this motto. —— pucherimma virgo Incedit, magnâ juvenum stiplante catervâ (Virg.[)]' (fo. 57).[15] We can only guess at their motives, if indeed it was the Cambridge friends who instigated publication, but Barker's poem 'To my friends' supplies materials with which to speculate on how she felt about seeing her work pass into print. On the surface the poem glows with gratitude to the 'band of gallant youths' whose encouragement and praise inspired her to write poetry:

> I doubt not to come safe to glories port,
> Since I have such a troop for my escort,
> This band of gallant youths, bear me along,
> Who teach me how to sing, then praise my song,
> Such wreaths and branches, they've bestow'd on me,
> I look like Daphne turn'd into a tree,
> Whilst these young sons of Phoebus dance around
> And sing the praise of her themselves have crown'd.
> (fo. 57; printed in Wilson, 307–8)

The affection for the friends praised as the 'gayest, sweetest, gentlest, youths on earth' (l. 15) seems unforced, yet the image of self as Daphne/the laurel tree enthronged by a band of perhaps overly eager sons of Apollo is equivocal in its implications: it may hint at ambiguities of which Barker herself was not wholly aware. The submerged allusion to the Ovidian story of Apollo's near-rape of Daphne and her transformation into a tree may, that is to say, point toward feelings of coercion, exposure, and shame not unlike those detected by Kristina Straub in Anne Killigrew's roughly contemporaneous 'Upon the saying that my Verses', where the poet-speaker's 'fantasy of a love-relationship'

---

[15] The commendatory verses include Philaster's 'To Madam Jane Barker, On Her Incomparable POEMS' and Exilius's 'To the Ingenious AUTHOUR, Mrs. JANE BARKER, ON HER POEMS'. Philaster is identified elsewhere in the volume as J[ohn] N[ewton], a fellow of St John's; Exilius as 'a Gentleman of St John's College'. Fidelius, author of 'To the Incomparable GALÆCIA, On the Publication of Her POEMS', may also be a member of the Cambridge set but is not identified as such. The line is from Aeneid 1. 496. The friends have substituted virgo for Dido to fashion a playful tribute: Barker becomes, loosely translated, the loveliest of virgins, attended by a throng of young men. The commendatory verse is discussed by Barash, EWP 178–80, who also reproduces the title-page. There is no basis for her claim, 178 n. 57, that it was Barker who reworked Virgil for the title-page.

with Apollo is 'charged with dangerous and sinister possibilities'.[16] Does Barker intend to associate these Cantabrigian 'sons of Phoebus' with the sexual menace of their Ovidian predecessor and in this way to express the feelings of exposure generated by what was arguably a forced entry into print? Or do we see here a poet not in full control of the implications of her allusions? (The question of technical control remains an open one with Barker, I think.) Or, as seems to me more likely, does a metaphorical subtext suggestive of rape and male sexual menace evince the existence of perplexed feelings—of confused resentment, even of violation—that under the circumstances Barker might have been reluctant to confront much less articulate?

The other known player in the making of *Poetical Recreations* is Benjamin Crayle, a bookseller still in his twenties, new to the trade and ambitious to carve out a niche. Over the previous decade the literary market-place had seen a small but visible surge in printed poetry by women. Volumes by 'Ephelia', Aphra Behn, and Anne Killigrew had recently appeared, prompting Lady Masham late in 1685 to call women's verse 'much the Fasion of late'.[17] As an enterprising young bookseller-publisher with an eye to a developing market, Crayle may have believed that a woman's name on the title-page would attract readers. In December 1687 he placed in the *London Gazette* an advertisement for *Poetical Recreations* that featured Barker's name—the single instance I have found of Crayle's promoting one of his titles in a newspaper—which may suggest he believed his own appeal to the 'fasion' for verse by women might meet with commercial success.

Crayle could easily have had on hand copy sufficient to assemble Part One. He and Barker had been friends since 1684 or thereabouts, at least as he tells the story, and although Barker does not refer explicitly to Crayle in any of her writings, the fact

[16] Kristina Straub, 'Indecent Liberties with a Poet: Audience and the Metaphor of Rape in Killigrew's "Upon the saying that my Verses" and Pope's *Arbuthnot*', *Tulsa Studies in Women's Literature*, 6 (1987), 27–45 (31). For examples of the handling of the story of Daphne and Apollo in poems by Behn and 'Philo-Philippa' as well as Killigrew, see Dorothy Mermin, 'Women Becoming Poets: Katherine Philips, Aphra Behn, Anne Finch', *ELH* 57 (1990), 335–55; see 349–51.
[17] Letter from Lady Masham to John Locke, 14 Dec. 1685, in E. S. De Beer (ed.), *The Correspondence of John Locke*, 8 vols. (Oxford: Clarendon P., 1976), ii. 762.

that she appears to have been living in lodgings in Newgate Street just a few blocks away from his shop in St Paul's lends credence to his claim that he had known her for three years.[18] They certainly exchanged verse. At least eight poems by Crayle to or about Barker are printed in Part Two of *Poetical Recreations* (172–99) in a group of twelve poems identified in the table of contents as 'done by the Publisher'. They tell (among other things) the story of his love for 'Cosmelia', his name for Barker in her literary incarnation as his beloved. (Other Crayle poems address her as 'Galecia' or 'Galæcia', variants of the coterie name she used with the Cambridge circle, and 'Mrs. Jane Barker'.) A couple of Crayle's efforts respond to poems by Barker printed in Part One.[19] Barker's part in the exchange is less certain, but it is possible that Crayle, eight years her junior, is the 'Young Lover' addressed in several lyrics discussed below. That they were actually lovers seems unlikely. Crayle, a bachelor in his mid-twenties, a younger son of a well-to-do Newark family, possessed gentlemanly literary aspirations: he may have been indulging in conventional poetical gallantries with a woman who shared his taste for literary play. Alternatively, as an aspiring print entrepreneur he may have contrived to give the impression of a romantic involvement with Cosmelia/Barker in order to lend piquancy to what, in spite of a handful of recent titles, was still a relatively unusual thing: a printed collection of verse by a woman. Indeed, he may have concocted an amatory tale in verse in order to recast the culturally ambiguous or uncertain relationship between male bookseller and female poet along comfortably familiar romance lines.[20] In any event, by 1687 the bookseller, assisted by one or

---

[18] For her Newgate residence see Doc. Rec. 21–2, and n. 52. The claim of a three-year acquaintance comes in Crayle's 'On his Secret Passion for Cosmelia', published in Part Two of *PR*, which would seem to date the beginnings of their friendship to 1684.

[19] For example, he responded to Barker's 'A Virgin Life' with 'A *Batchelor's Life*, in pursuit of Mrs. BARKER's Verses in Praise of a *Single Life*', the latter of which begins, 'Since, O ye Pow'rs, it is by your decree, | For *Women* I've so great *indiff'rencie*' (*PR* 2. 197). Barker had written, 'Since, O ye Pow'rs, ye have bestow'd on me | So great a kindness for Virginity' (*PR* 1. 12). Unless otherwise indicated, subsequent references to *PR* are to Part One and will be indicated parenthetically in the text.

[20] For examples from earlier in the century (and before) of the way manuscript lyrics were given fictionalized romantic frames in print, see Marotti, *Manuscript*,

more of the Cambridge circle, was able to assemble for publication a considerable body of verse by Jane Barker.

'I often read your Lines, and oft admire'

David Vieth famously observed of Rochester's *Poems* (1680) that the volume, which is 'not in essence a printed collection at all', is 'valuable to literary scholars mainly insofar as it preserves features of its manuscript source'.[21] With the huge qualification that the interest of Part One of *Poetical Recreations* is not reducible to its textual properties, something similar might be said of this volume as well, for it preserves and makes available for study the coterie usages of the (now lost) manuscript source(s). Because Barker later 'corrected' many of these printed poems for inclusion in Part Three of the Magdalen Manuscript, we can identify quite precisely the kinds of changes she felt were required to bring coterie forms into accord with the decorums suitable for the wider readership imagined for the more 'public' manuscript volume. We are thus confronted with the intriguing paradox that a printed source represents the more 'private' usages and a manuscript source the more 'public' ones.

In the Magdalen Manuscript, for example, personal references are removed or obscured. A 'Mr. G.P.' identified at the end of the printed text by his Christian name '*George*' (*PR* 96) is addressed in the more circumspect manuscript simply as 'dear'. In the same poem a reference to '*Shin-gay*' (*PR* 95), a Cambridgeshire hamlet where Barker evidently spent time, has been replaced by 'Willsthorp', for reasons that remain unclear.[22] The printed collection also includes some twenty poems she declined to copy into the Magdalen Manuscript; taken together

---

219–22. For a poem illustrative of some of the ambiguities of the male book-seller/female poet relationship, see Crayle's 'To my Ingenious Friend, Mrs. JANE BARKER, on my Publishing her Romance of SCIPINA' (*PR* 2. 194). Additional details about Crayle can be found in my 'Jane Barker, *Poetical Recreations*, and the Sociable Text', *ELH* 61 (1994), 551–70: see 558 and 568–9 nn. 22, 23, and 24.

[21] David M. Vieth, *Attribution in Restoration Poetry: A Study of Rochester's Poems of 1680* (New Haven and London: Yale UP, 1963), 4.

[22] Shingay is a biographical puzzle. Barker's father, Thomas, died there in 1681 and was buried in the chapel; yet his business in this Cambridgeshire village remains unknown. See Doc. Rec. 20.

they indicate categories of verse Barker considered unfit for wider circulation. They are mainly of two sorts. The first includes conventional and easily forgotten songs of the kind that fill verse miscellanies and songbooks of the period, lyrics that begin 'As Am'rous *Corydon* was laid' (*PR* 83) and 'The *Heart* you left, when you took mine' (*PR* 81). Perhaps Barker did not think highly enough of them to sanction them for inclusion in the Magdalen Manuscript, possibly because they seemed trifling, undignified, or jejune.[23] The second takes us into more fertile territory, biographically speaking, for these are strongly personal poems touching on matters of death, grief, and sickness. They include three poems on the death of her brother, Edward, a poem '*To my Dear Cousin Mrs. M.T. after the Death of her Husband and Son*', and '*On my Mother and my Lady* W ——, *who both lay sick at the same time under the Hands of Dr. Paman*'.[24] She did not, it is clear, deem poems occasioned by family sorrows suitable for exchange outside intimate coterie circles.

A valuable feature of these verses for students of women's literary practices is that, read centrifugally as trace-bearing artefacts of poetic communities, to use Harold Love's language, many of them yield information about the exchange circles through which they passed. Those hoping for information

---

[23] In view of Barker's failure to leave much of an impress on her culture, it is interesting to discover that the two songs named above, and a third, a drinking song which begins 'Troy had a breed of brave stout men', are the only poems from *PR* known to have been reprinted in her lifetime (they were also set to music) and are so very *un*Barkerian as to raise the possibility they were written by someone else. She does not include them in the Magdalen MS or the prose fictions. James Fitzmaurice has suggested, plausibly, that 'A Bachanalian Song', as the drinking song is called in *PR*, may have been an attempt to mimic undergraduate tavern humour. See James Fitzmaurice, 'Jane Barker and the Tree of Knowledge at Cambridge University', *Renaissance Forum*, 3 (1998), para. 14. For reprintings of the three songs (in songbooks of 1690, 1714, and 1720), see Cyrus Lawrence Day and Eleanore Boswell Murrie, *English Song-Books 1651–1702: A Bibliography with a First-Line Index of Songs* (London: Bibliographical Society at the UP, Oxford, 1940 (for 1937)), Nos. 197, 1317, and 3479.

[24] The drowning simile developed in the opening lines of the Paman poem may find an echo in Lady Chudleigh's 'To the Learn'd and Ingenious Dr. *Musgrave* of *Exeter*', ll. 23–9, printed in *Poems on Several Occasions* (1703) and reprinted in Margaret J. M. Ezell (ed.), *The Poems and Prose of Mary, Lady Chudleigh* (New York and Oxford: Oxford UP, 1993), 121. For more on Dr Henry Paman (1626–95), see Ch. 2 below.

about female friendships and networks of mutual support will be disappointed, however. Nearly all the literary friends discoverable are male. They include the Cambridge students, one of whom, John Newton ('Philaster'), of Uffington, Lincolnshire, lived in her neighbourhood; at least one lawyer; and some assorted country gentlemen—men, that is to say, of the professional and perhaps lower gentry classes. Only one poem addressed to a woman appears in the entire collection, lines of consolation '*To my Dear Cousin Mrs. M.T. after the Death of her Husband and Son*', although a second poem memorializes a female friendship in striking ways.[25]

The virtual absence of female addressees is startling given Barker's reputation as poet of female friendships and is at odds with what we have learned about the female orientation of women's manuscript networks in the seventeenth century.[26] Perhaps in this way too Barker was eccentric. Or perhaps the male-directedness of this verse is a function of the circumstances of their publication: copied, compiled, complimented, printed and sold by men, they may reasonably be presumed to reflect male interests. Since there is no compelling reason to believe that *Poetical Recreations* represents all or even the greater part of Barker's poetic output from the 1670s and 1680s—for all we know she exchanged yet as many poems with women friends far removed from academic networks or the attentions of London booksellers—we simply have no way of knowing the full extent of Barker's corpus in 1687, much less what a collection of verses compiled and arranged by Barker herself might have looked like, although Part Three of the Magdalen Manuscript may give some indication. But even allowing for male bias in selection, it must be said that the surviving verse strongly challenges descriptions of Barker as poet of female communities current in standard reference works and critical accounts.[27] The persistence of

---

[25] 'On the DEATH of my Dear Friend and Play-fellow, Mrs E.D. having Dream'd the night before I heard thereof, that I had lost a Pearl' is discussed below.

[26] For women's literary networks, see Margaret Ezell, *The Patriarch's Wife: Literary Evidence and the History of the Family* (Chapel Hill and London: U. of North Carolina P., 1987), ch. 3; and Marotti, *Manuscript*, 48–61. The Perdita Project, at Trent University of Nottingham, is in the process of establishing a database to facilitate study of these networks.

[27] The headnote to the Barker selections in Moira Ferguson, *First Feminists: British Women Writers 1578–1799* (Bloomington: Indiana UP; Old Westbury, NY:

this feminocentric construct in the face of a raft of counter-evidence illustrates strikingly the phenomenon Germaine Greer calls 'the Sappho problem', that is, the scholarly tendency to recreate early modern women poets in the image of present desires: 'All estimations of the nature of Sappho's achievement', she reminds us, 'have more to do with the politics of contem-porary poetry than anything that was actually going on 2,600 years ago'.[28] Gender politics today favours literary sororeality; *ergo* Barker's *Poetical Recreations* is found to project an ideal of female community, never mind that the actual network of corre-spondents and literary friends recorded in its twenty-odd famil-iar verse epistles is overwhelmingly male. Greer is certainly right to say that we often hail women writers as 'kindred spirits with-out knowing whether they were or not', and we would do well to listen when she urges that 'Scholarly ethics require that we try a great deal harder to get at the truth about them' (xvii).

Although largely silent on the matter of female friendships, the early verse abounds in materials relating to Barker's rela-tions with a surprisingly wide range of male literary friends. Consider, to begin, some of the men to whom she wrote verse. They include her '*Reverend Friend Mr. H.*'—the local rector, George Hawen, whom she thanks for presenting her with two books, *The Reasonableness of Christianity* and *The History of King Charles the First*; '*Sir F.W.*'—a young man, evidently, to whom she presented a copy of Cowley's juvenilia and whose early poetical efforts she encouraged;[29] '*Mr. G.P.*', her 'Adopted Brother', whom she seeks to dissuade from marriage; a hapless '*Young Lover*' whose amorous overtures she mocks; a '*Cousin Mr. E.F.*' whose excellent painting she praises; '*Dr. R.S.*', an indifferent lover whose indifference leaves her unmoved; her '*Unkle Colonel C*' (Connock) whose return to the Netherlands was celebrated by his adoring troops; the Cambridge friends

The Feminist P., 1985), 172, tells us, for example, that her poems 'attach emphatic significance to female friendship'. See also Maureen Bell, George Parfitt, and Simon Shepherd, *A Biographical Dictionary of English Women Writers 1580–1720* (Boston: G. K. Hall, 1990), 17. Barash, *EWP* 181, finds in *PR* 'an ideal of female community which she models on Katherine Philips's Society of Friendship'. The latter, incidentally, was actually composed of both women and men.

[28] Germaine Greer, *Slip-Shod Sibyls: Recognition, Rejection and the Woman Poet* (London: Viking, 1995), xvi.

[29] He is possibly the son of the 'Lady W.' of the Paman poem.

with whom she exchanged verses in the 1680s; a Mr Hill who
wrote verses to the Duchess of York when she visited
Cambridge; an 'Honoured Friend, Mr. *E.S—t*'; 'Mr. C.B.' whose
singing was incomparable; her 'Unkind STREPHON', that object
of sexual obsession well known to readers of her fictions as the
slippery lover Bosvil; and finally her 'unkind Friend, *Little Tom
King*', identified elsewhere as 'Mr. *S.L.*' and possibly the original of Strephon/Bosvil.[30]

What does this impressive range of poetic addressees and
correspondents have to tell us? First, we get a strong sense of the
intense *sociability* of Barker's verse-writing practice. While these
poems are concerned with personal occasions, none could be
described as pious, inward-looking, or domestically circum-
scribed; they shape themselves, rather, within an interactive social
space and exhibit traits of what might be called textual gregari-
ousness—intellectual playfulness, shared allusiveness, an ongoing
textual give-and-take. Literary sociability enabled Barker to enter
mental worlds otherwise inaccessible to her, to construct a zone
of contact with learned communities that was crucial to her self-
image as an educated woman engaged, however marginally, in the
nation's intellectual life. Not surprisingly, she cultivated relationships with men associated with the universities, ranging from her
brother Edward (a student at Oxford, not, as is sometimes said,
Cambridge), to the unidentified Mr Hill (whose 'whole ascent',
she puns, 'shall learned *Cambridge* grace'),[31] to the men of St
John's. It may be no exaggeration to say that verse exchange

---

[30] Internal evidence suggests that Strephon/Bosvil, Little Tom King, and Mr S.L.
may be the same person. The *PR* poem 'To my unkind Friend, *Little Tom King*' (65)
reappears, shortened and revised, in Mag. MS as 'On Strephon's pretending business
to be the cause of his long absence', suggesting the shared identity of Strephon and
'Little Tom King'. That the latter and 'Mr. S.L.' are the same person is indicated by
the *PR* poem 'To my Friend Mr. *S.L.* on his Receiving the Name of *Little Tom King*',
entitled in Mag. MS 'To my friend mr —— on my calling him Little tom King' (fo.
106). If one person, his identity remains unknown. On the chance others may wish
to try to hunt him down, I offer the following clues, taken from *BG*: he practised law
and may have been a friend of her brother Edward (d. 1675), was related to the
Barkers, and came from a town or village some twenty miles north of Wilsthorp.

[31] 'To Mr. HILL, *on his Verses to the Dutchess of* YORK, *when she was at*
Cambridge'. The next couplet continues the pun: 'for now the World shall know |
That *Woods* and *Hills* of wit in *Cambridge* grow' (*PR* 5). A marginal gloss in Mag.
MS identifies 'Wood' as having 'made a speech in prose' (fo. 88v) on the same occasion. Hill may be Richard Hill, who was made a fellow of St John's in 1679, and
was later appointed Ambassador to the Hague. See the entry on Hill in the *DNB*.

with men was tantamount to intellectual survival for Barker, even if in actual practice it left some sour aftertastes, as will be seen.

We also learn of the range of stances Barker was capable of assuming, her manner and tones varying according to the nature of her relationship with her poetic correspondent. With Mr E.S., for example, she appears deferential, gracious, and intellectually engaged, as if composing her best self for a valued and slightly superior friend. Mr E.S. may in fact have been one of her first poetic mentors, for she likens him to a father who, having encouraged an infant's first 'babbling Rhimes', must be prepared to endure a parent's fate, 'the plague of Cradle-noise'.[32] In a second epistle to Mr E.S. she wittily compliments her 'Honoured Friend' on his bringing back to life her dead muse:

> Oft has my *Muse* and I fall'n out,
> And I as oft have banish'd her my Breast;
> But such, alas, still was her interest,
> And still to bring her purposes about:
> So great her cunning in insinuation,
> That she soon gain'd her wish'd-for restoration:
> But when I found this wou'd not do,
> A Violent Death I put her to.
> But see, my Friend, how your All-pow'rfull Pen
> (O Miracle!) has rais'd her from the Dead again.
> ('A Second EPISTLE. *To my Honoured Friend*
> *Mr. E.S.*', PR 70)

Readers acquainted with the novels of the Galesia trilogy will recognize in this passage a light-hearted treatment of a familiar tug-of-war between creativity and silence. Carol Barash has called attention to the 'unresolved tension between the claims of poetry, politics, and romance' that informs this passage and Barker's work more generally, and points out that ambivalence about writing is here cleverly worked out in royalist metaphors of exile, regicide, and restoration: the poet-speaker who would silence her muse is likened to a rebel who seeks first to banish the monarch-muse and then, in Cromwellian fashion, put her to a 'Violent Death' (*EWP* 175). But it should be noticed that

---

[32] 'To my Honoured Friend, Mr. *E. S—t*'., PR 42.

Barker's poet-self quickly springs back to life in order to pay tribute to the restorative powers of the friend whose 'All-pow'r-full Pen' has 'rais'd her from the Dead again'. The topos of the resurrected muse is conventional in seventeenth-century poetry of praise—John Oldham, for example, likened the attentions of a friend to 'a pow'rful Cordial' that infuses new life into a 'speechless gasping Muse'[33]—but in her witty usage Barker unexpectedly combines royalist metaphor, national history, biblical allusion, and ironic self-portrayal in such a way as to create an unusual compliment to an older man whom she was clearly determined to honour with her full intelligence. If the poem's political figures express the inevitable ambivalence of the writing woman, her 'tortured relationship with her muse', as Barash puts it, the economic images introduced in the second stanza proclaim the speaker's sense of the richly productive rela-tionship between friendship and poetry: her muse 'thrive[s]' upon the 'Stock' of Mr. E.S.'s encouragement and the poet seeks with these complimentary lines to 'pay the Int'rest of Acknowledgment'. When Barker reordered the *Poetical Recreations* poems for Part Three of the Magdalen Manuscript she concluded with a group of six poems about poetry, placing last this poem of affirmation of the writing self, poetic mentor-ship, and literary friendship.[34]

With the poet she identifies only as her 'Young Lover', a gallant (Crayle?) whose evidently vapid poetic accolades she more than once has occasion to mock-repulse, she adopts a tone of good-humoured contempt.[35] It is a manner she may have learned from Katherine Philips. Philips, admired by feminist readers for her ability to create in verse a ' "counter-universe"

---

[33] John Oldham, '*A Letter from the Country to a Friend in Town, giving an Account of the Author's Inclinations to* Poetry', ll. 7–8, in Harold F. Brooks (ed.), *The Poems of John Oldham* (Oxford: Clarendon P., 1987), 149. For examples of Cowley's and Dryden's use of the topos, see the commentary on these lines on 430.

[34] Re-entitled 'To my friend mr —— on his perswading me to poetry' in Mag. MS (fo. 131). The Barker portion of PR ends with the pessimistic '*Resolved never to Versifie more*', which may reflect an order imposed by Crayle. Barker did not include the latter poem in Mag. MS.

[35] PWS associates these poems with the Cambridge friends, but her manner in them is unlike that in any of the poems known to be addressed to the students, which tend to be classically based.

of female friendship',[36] is known nowadays more for elegant lyricism than for regulated scorn. But it is possible she was appreciated by the women who followed her for an edgy, acerbic quality we do not always hear today. Barker's indebtedness to Philips as a source of poetic identity is by now a commonplace of feminist literary history, but her technical debt remains little investigated. Indeed, because it has been somewhat vaguely assumed that it was the *idea* of Orinda—the much-celebrated poetic icon—more than the example of her verse and literary manner that loomed so large for women of Barker's generation, our understanding of the full range of Philips's influence remains rudimentary. It is useful, then, to discover that Barker used Philips's *'An Answer to another perswading a Lady to Marriage'* as a formal model for her own 'To My Young Lover. A Song'. Philips's dissuasion to marriage begins:

> Forbear bold Youth, all's Heaven here,
> And what you do aver,
> To others Courtship may appear,
> 'Tis Sacriledge to her.[37]

Barker's 'Song', which uses the same stanza form and a similar rhyme scheme, opens with an unmistakable verbal echo:

> To praise sweet Youth, do thou forbear,
> Where there is no desert;
> For, alas, *Encomiums* here,
> Are Jewels thrown i'th' dirt.   (PR 64)

Philips goes on, caustically, to chastize the 'bold Youth' for presuming to think a woman worshipped as a 'publick Deity' might condescend to dwindle into his 'petty Houshold God' (Thomas, i. 227). Barker exhibits some of the Orindan scorn in her address to her own Young Lover, but the persona she creates is playful, more inclined to tease than scold the young man for his sexual naivety. Another poem in this group, 'To My Young Lover On His Vow', sets out to quash the expressions of adoration streaming from the Young Lover's pen. The speaker—who,

[36] Paula R. Backscheider, *Spectacular Politics: Theatrical Power and Mass Culture in Early Modern England* (Baltimore and London: Johns Hopkins UP, 1993), 75.
[37] Thomas, i. 227.

unusually for Barker, occupies the position of the idealized Petrarchan mistress—adopts an attitude of mocking scepticism toward a young poetaster who 'know'st not what it is' to love:

> Sweet *Youth*, thou know'st not what it is
> To be Love's *Votary*;
> Where thou must for the smallest bliss,
> Kneel, beg, and sigh, and cry.
> *Probationer* thou should'st be first,
> That thereby thou may'st try,
> Whether thou can'st endure the worst
> Of Love's *austerity*.   (PR 62–3)

Barker adopts a tongue-in-cheek version of Orinda's dissuasive manner in a verse letter to Mr G.P. upon the *'nigh approach of his Nuptials'* (PR 11).[38] ('Then let not Marriage thee in danger draw', she mock-cautions, 'Unless thou'rt bit with Love's Tarantula': the final phrase neatly sums up her characteristically jaundiced view of love's frenzies.) The epistle rewrites from a male point of view the anti-marriage position advanced by the female speaker of Philips's 'A marry^d state', a conventional but spirited poem against marriage that begins, 'A marry^d state affords but little ease: | The best of husbands are so hard to please' (Thomas, i. 254).[39] Where Philips limns conjugality's discontents from the point of view of the beleaguered wife, who must contend with 'Blustering husbands', 'pangs of child birth', 'children's crys', and 'worldly crosses', Barker melts down these elements into a warning to a man: his days will be filled with 'Crosses, crying Children, scolding Dame'.[40]

---

[38] Barker and her set drew upon the practices of the *précieuses* and Orindan traditions of love advocacy—one member of the circle writing verse on behalf of the love interest of another. For examples see 'To my Friend EXILLUS, *on his persuading me to Marry Old* Damon' (PR 1. 14) and, from the second part of *PR*, Benjamin Crayle's 'The Young Lover's Advocate: Being an Answer to a Copy of Verses. *Written by* Galæcia *to her* Young Lover *on his* Vow' (2. 192). See Thomas, i. 351, for the practice within Orinda's circle.

[39] It may have been written to warn a friend off marriage. Thomas, i. 397, describes the poem, probably addressed to Anne Barlow, as 'an early example of Orinda's practice of attempting to make or mar matches amongst her friends'.

[40] She develops the anti-marriage position from her own perspective in 'To *my* Friend EXILLUS, *on his persuading me to Marry Old* Damon': she taxes husbands with habitual jealousy ('Not only He-friends innocent as thou, | But he'll mistrust She-friends and Heav'n too') and figures herself in marriage as a once 'brave Horse' forced to 'tug a nasty Dray' (PR 15).

Sounding the note of cynicism characteristic of much fashion-able verse of the time, she likens marital existence to dwelling in the midst of tolling bells or among a herd of sheep:

> Yet prithee don't its joys too much esteem,
> It will not prove what distance makes it seem:
> Bells are good musick, if they're not too nigh,
> But sure 'ts base living in a Belfery.
> To see Lambs skip o're Hills is pretty sport
> But who wou'd justle with them in their Court?   (PR 11)

and arrives, finally, at something very like the position of casual contempt for marriage found in libertine Restoration verse: 'Ah, pity thy good humour should be spoil'd, | The glory of thy wit and friendship soil'd' (PR 11). This she follows with the urbane lines of witty dissuasion that struck Robert Southey with suffi-cient force more than a hundred years later that he entered them into his commonplace book, along with some reflections:

> From Married Man wit's Current never flows,
> But grave and dull, as standing Pond, he grows;
> Whilst th' other like a gentle stream do's play,
> With this World's pebbles, which obstruct his way.   (PR 12)

'A very pretty expression', Southey writes of the image of masculine wit as a gentle stream flowing easily over the pebbles placed in its way, 'villainously applied'.[41]

One other poem to George P. has survived. 'To My Adopted BROTHER, Mr. G.P. On my frequent Writing to Him', another of her complimentary verses to a brother poet, is a romp in iambic tetrameters, a 'sort of borlesk' (as she calls it in the Magdalen Manuscript), the high spirits and impromptu rhymes of which recall Behn's 'A Letter to Mr. *Creech* at *Oxford*, Written in the last great Frost'.[42] Beginning on a note of amused self-depreca-tion Barker mocks her compulsion to versify: poetic epistles to

[41] John Wood Warter (ed.), *Southey's Common-Place Book*, 4th ser., 4 vols. (London: Longman, Brown, Green, and Longmans, 1851), iv. 296. The lines on the curative powers of the 'cephalic cowslip', 'diuretic woodbine', 'splenetic columbine', and 'scorbutic rose' in '*The Prospect of a* LANDSKIP' also gave him pause: they were as 'scurvy epithets as were ever applied by fair lady to fine flowers' (iv. 296). Southey's copy of *PR* is at the Victoria and Albert Museum, Dyce 788.
[42] First printed in *Miscellany, Being A Collection of Poems By several Hands. Together with Reflections on Morality, or Seneca Unmasqued* (London: J. Hindmarsh, 1685), 73–7.

the man she calls her adopted brother fall out of the trees like
goose feathers:

> Dear Brother, You will think that now,
> *Epistles* grow on every Bow,
> O'th' multitude of *Shin-gay* Trees,
> And so drop off like *Soland* Geese.

She then rings changes on the feathery wit conceit. Her poems,
their matter as airy and insubstantial as goose feathers, are pies
filled with down instead of the solid meat of wit and sense:

> In this the *Analogie* holds forth,
> They are produc'd of airy froth;
> .   .   .   .   .   .
> For when you find they want the heat
> Of *Wit* and *Sence* to make them meat;
> And that the inside's only down,
> Soft as the *scope* they grew upon:
> You'll curse the *Winds* officious wings,
> Because to you no good it brings.   (*PR* 95)

She mock-protests that he must leave off praising her poems
lest, spurred on by his kind words, she set out to 'plague both
genteel Fops and Rabble' with more of her 'Nonsence, Rhime
and Babble' (*PR* 96). The 'borlesk' furnishes an illustration of
Margaret Doody's claim that women poets of the Augustan
period were especially at home in tetrameter couplets, a form in
which they could 'exhibit wit without being thought too arro-
gant';[43] and though it has nothing to match the impudence of
Behn's rhymes ('a Poet' | 'no wit'; 'truth to tell' | 'Doggerell'),
reveals a Barker with a surprising gift for poetical clowning and
an obvious delight in creating herself as a figure of fun.

The final relationship to be considered is the most complex
and, on the surviving evidence, perhaps the most important in
her early literary life. In *A Patch-Work Screen for the Ladies*
(1723), written some four decades later, Barker devotes considerable space to Galesia's literary friendship with a group of
Cambridge students. Since this account is surely based upon the
real-life friendships glimpsed in *Poetical Recreations*, it seems

---

[43] Margaret Anne Doody, *The Daring Muse: Augustan Poetry Reconsidered*
(Cambridge: Cambridge UP, 1985), 242.

worth summarizing here. The acquaintance was initiated by a young man Galesia identifies only as 'a Kinsman a Student at the University'—possibly John Newton of nearby Uffington, whose mother was a Barker[44]—who brought with him to her home in the country his college friends, whose 'youthful and witty Conversation' she came to value (*PWS* 92). They 'came now and then, a little to relax their College Discipline, and unbend the Streightness of their Study; bringing with them little Books, now Pamphlets, and Songs' and 'convers'd with me by Writing; sometimes Verse, sometimes Prose, which ingaged my Replies in the same manner' (*PWS* 93). Some of the most interesting poems in *Poetical Recreations* are addressed to the Cambridge set: '*An Invitation to my Friends at* Cambridge', '*To my Friend* EXILLUS, *on his persuading me to Marry Old* Damon', '*To my Friends* against POETRY', and '*Resolved never to Versifie more*'.[45] That this friendship was a source of pain as well as pleasure is the suggestion of a bittersweet moment in *Patch-Work Screen* in which the friends gather at a drinking place at Cambridge to sing a ballad composed by Galesia, doing so with such noisy abandon that a proctor, suspecting a woman in their midst, tries to break up the merriment. But of course no woman is present: '*finding no Female amongst us, [he] drank the innocent Author's Health, and departed*' (*PWS* 100). In the male academic setting the female poet is at once celebrated and excluded.

If this episode underscores themes of female absence and invisibility, the manuscript poem 'To my friends', discussed earlier, develops themes of reciprocity and mutuality. The female speaker permits herself not only to bask in the glory of the admiration of her learned young friends but also, more unusually, to cast herself as their literary 'copartner':

---

[44] Newton, 'Philaster' of the verse, is further identified in *PR* as 'J.N., *Fellow of St.* John's *Colledge*, Cambridge'. He was admitted as a sizar 10 June 1678, received a BA in 1682, an MA in 1685; was a Fellow from 1685 to 1700 and then rector of King's Cliff, Northamptonshire, until his death in 1714. I am grateful to Alison M. Pearn for sharing with me the St John's College Biographical Record Sheet on Newton. Uffington, where Newton's family lived, was only a few miles from Wilsthorp.

[45] The latter prompted Newton (as 'Philaster') to write a poem in response (*PR* 2. 33–4). For another poem written to Barker by Newton, see my 'Jane Barker, Mary Leapor and a Chain of Very Odd Contingencies', *English Language Notes*, 33 (1996), 14–27.

> Ye learned youths, most learned of your time,
> Of all your Reverend mothers sons the prime,
> Ye gayest, sweetest, gentlest, youths on earth
> Tell me what constellation rul'd my birth,?
> That I'm become copartner of your bays,
> And what's more glorious, subject of your praise.
>   (Mag. MS, fo. 57v, printed in Wilson, 308)

The playful insistence on the youthfulness of these friends some decade or so her juniors, even reminding them of their ties to their 'Reverend mothers', would appear to be part of an ongoing joke between Barker and the Cambridge set, as James Fitzmaurice has observed.[46] It may also represent an assertion of a kind of hierarchy of age by which Barker was able to claim for herself some small part of the superiority routinely ceded men as intellectual beings and in this way frame, however awkwardly, a cross-gender friendship more egalitarian in its possibilities than most women permitted themselves to imagine.

If the epistles to her Cambridge friends project the witty sociability of near-equals, the fact that Barker seeks to work within—as well as against—what we regard today as masculine discourse suggests a degree of cultural ambitiousness on her part. In 'To My Friends against POETRY' she writes as a Restoration wit, a man about town, using the commonplace figure of the whorish muse, for instance, to depict the debased state of modern poetry: the muses are 'all grown *Prostitutes*' (*PR* 95 (misn.)) and the desire for literary fame is an '*itch*' as 'hard to cure as Dice or Whore' (*PR* 96).[47] This same modishly satiric (and by our lights masculinist) poem-against-poetry opens, confidently, with an echo of Ovid: 'Dear Friends, if you'll be rul'd by me, | Beware o'th' Charms of *Poetry*'.[48] Another of

---

[46] Fitzmaurice, 'Jane Barker', notices that Newton made a similar joke in 'To Mrs. JANE BARKER, on her most Delightfull and Excellent *Romance* of SCIPINA, now in the Press' when he praised the prose romance, mischievously, as one that might safely be read by young men without giving their '*Lady Mothers*' reason to fear for the 'debauch't *innocence*' of their sons (*PR* 2. 32).

[47] For a poem which recycles many of the same commonplaces, see Nahum Tate's 'On the Present Corrupted State of Poetry', *Poems Written on Several Occasions*, 2nd edn. 'enlarged' (London: B. Tooke, 1684), 16.

[48] A 1685 paraphrase of one of Ovid's elegies, identified as 'Elegy the 7th , Book the 3d , *Miscellany Poems and Translations by Oxford Hands* (London: Anthony Stephens, 1685), 150, includes the lines, 'Young men if you are wise be rul'd by me,

the Cambridge poems, 'Resolved never to Versifie more', employs a swaggering man-about-town idiom. No more can one produce verse in London than one can expect the whores of 'Bridewell, or of Stews' (PR 108) to be moved except by a good whipping, the male-ventriloquizing speaker complains.

The self-division produced by identification with male intellectual life is revealed with poignant clarity in the most interesting poem of this group, 'An Invitation to my Friends at Cambridge', an idiosyncratic reworking of the poem of invitation to the countryside. Barker rewrites the *beatus vir* topos that is a feature of this poetic kind in such a way as to transform the expected affirmation of happy virtuous retirement into a tonally complicated protest against the speaker's exclusion from a communal intellectual life.[49] The epistle begins conventionally with praise of the country as the site of simplicity, wholesomeness, and innocence. Midway through, however, neo-stoic commonplace gives way to ironies that call into question the untroubled vision of a rural 'Paradise'. Drawing upon an ironized symbolism of the Fall, Barker suggests that even in the ideal simplicity of the countryside women are denied the full measure of happiness reserved for the *beatus vir*. For in women's 'cold Clime'—according to humoral theory women were the cooler and moister sex—the Tree of Knowledge cannot grow:

> the Tree of Knowledge won't grow here:
> Though in its culture I have spent some time,
> Yet it disdains to grow in our cold Clime,
> Where it can neither Fruit nor Leaves produce
> Good for its owner, or the publick use.   (PR 3)

| Learn not our fruitless Arts of Poetry'. A. D. Melville, *Ovid: The Love Poems* (Oxford and New York: Oxford UP, 1990), 70, translates the lines, from *Amores* 3. 8, thus: 'Learn, if you're wise, not what we know, we idlers, | But battle-lines and wild alarms of war' (ll. 25–6). It is unclear whether Barker is invoking Ovid or expressing a poetic commonplace such as is found, for example, in John Oldham's 'A Satyr . . . Dissuading the Author from the Study of Poetry': 'Take heed betimes, repent, and learn of me | To shun the dang'rous Rocks of Poetry': see Brooks, *Poems of John Oldham*, 239.

[49] For 17th-cent. uses of the topos of the *beatus vir*, see vol. 1 of Maren-Sofie Røstvig, *The Happy Man: Studies in the Metamorphoses of a Classical Ideal*, 2nd. edn. (Oslo: Norwegian Universities P., 1962). In this monumental study Barker is overlooked, although Katherine Philips receives close treatment.

Barker thus reworks the expulsion from Eden into a bitter little feminist parable about female exclusion from sites of learning,[50] here depicted with almost comical literalness as Cambridge, which emerges as a kind of cap-and-gown, for-men-only Garden of Intellectual Delights. The fruits of *this* garden are reserved for male consumption:

> Altho' our Eyes
> Do serve our longing-Souls to tantalize,
> Whilst kinder fate[51] for you do's constitute
> Luxurious Banquets of this dainty Fruit.
> Whose *Tree* most fresh and flourishing do's grow,
> E'er since it was transplanted amongst you.
>
> (PR 3–4)

That her exclusion may have cultural origins, as the word 'transplanted' would seem to suggest, only adds to the sense of frustration and perhaps unformulated resentment that hovers around the lines of praise with which the epistle ends. The friends become the tree which she is denied, *their* virtues its fruits 'bright and fair', and *her* complaint modulates into a gracious if perhaps inwardly costly tribute to *their* learning. Barker manages to convey affection for her young friends while expressing exasperation that male privilege renders them oblivious to the rewards of the 'kinder fate' she cannot enjoy. When Barker included 'An Invitation' in *Patch-Work Screen* she has Galesia describe the poem as 'plain and innocent' (95). Plain and innocent? Not exactly. This is a poem that twits as it invites.

If the *Poetical Recreations* verse is any indication, poetry by women in this period exhibits a greater range of tones, moods, manners, and voices than existing feminist paradigms, with their heavy stress upon gender difference and patriarchal silencing, prepare us to recognize. In the epistles to the mentor-figure,

---

[50] Anne Finch would do something similar in the ending of 'Poem, Occasion'd by the Sight of the 4th Epistle Lib. Epist: I. of Horace', which, as Hilda L. Smith, *Reason's Disciples: Seventeenth-Century English Feminists* (Urbana: U. of Illinois P., 1982), 162, has observed, 'would condemn the male monopoly of knowledge and the subordination of women to their pleasure, ostensibly because a woman had first eaten of the tree of knowledge'.

[51] For 'kinder fate' Mag. MS and *PWS* substitute the more hardened 'god and nature', suggesting perhaps a more pessimistic view of gender relations later in her life.

Mr. E.S., we see gestures of deference, to be sure, but in other epistles we find evidence of witty and classically based exchanges with men on quasi-equal terms, and elsewhere we find lyrics of playful superiority in which an older and more worldly woman exercises her wit at the expense of a Young Lover. We encounter the sly subversion feminist criticism has taught us to expect, but also expressions of quite straightforward disgruntlement—one epistle reproaching an unkind male friend with being too busy to pay attention to her, another warning against squalling children and scolding wife. We find feminist complaint, but also outbreaks of poetical rambunctiousness such as the 'borlesk' to George P. Such findings suggest that students of women's writing would do well to develop protocols of reading responsive to dialogical and sociable as well as subversive and contestatory elements of poetry by women.

Finally, admirers of the historical Barker will find that some of these poems preserve personal details or circumstances that carry considerable biographical interest. Especially poignant is the elegiac 'On the DEATH of my Dear Friend and Play-fellow, Mrs E.D. having Dream'd the night before I heard thereof, that I had lost a Pearl', the only real representation of a female friendship in the printed collection and the closest thing to a direct reminiscence of childhood to be found in her work.[52] The poem begins with a celebration of the beauty and preciousness of friendship in the lyrical Orindan mode:

> I Dream'd I lost a Pearl, and so it prov'd;
> I lost a Friend much above Pearls belov'd:
> A Pearl perhaps adorns some outward part,
> But Friendship decks each corner of the heart:
> Friendship's a *Gem*, whose Lustre do's out-shine
> All that's below the heav'nly *Crystaline*.   (PR 18)

This is lovely, in an uncharacteristically idealizing way. In the

---

[52] The verse epistle 'To my Dear Cousin Mrs. M.T. after the Death of her Husband and Son' (PR 59) is too sententious ('dry your Eyes, but chear your brow'; 'Rouse up your Soul') to shed much light on the relationship. For a brief discussion of 'To my Dear Cousin' in the context of female-authored 17th-cent. elegies, see Kate Lilley, 'True State Within: Women's Elegy 1640–1700', in Isobel Grundy and Susan Wiseman (eds.), Women, Writing, History 1640–1740 (Athens: U. of Georgia P., 1992), 72–92 (78–9).

section that follows lyricism gives way to memories of the days when she and her friend rambled the fields around Wilsthorp in childish play. They would feast on 'Pocket-Apples, Plumbs, and such delights',[53] make flower garlands, play at games with pebbles, and finally, when tired, stretch out lazily on 'Beds of Vi'lets' under cool shade (*PR* 19). It is a pleasing picture, a rare moment of lovingly recalled female comradeship, and stands in marked contrast to the sometimes bleak chronicles of girlhood offered in *Bosvil and Galesia* and *Patch-Work Screen*, where Galesia seems something of a loner, a solitary woman living in the remembered past at some remove from other people; almost, it would seem, an outcast by nature.

'Those Goblings which so many have betray'd'

So far this account has emphasized verse and verse-writing practices that are strongly oriented toward men and male literary values. It is a curious fact, however, that a number of the poems in *Poetical Recreations* resist or even refuse the heterosexual relation. Some of the most interesting confront the sexual mystifications—the 'Goblings which so many have betray'd'—that draw women into disastrous marriages and disabling sexual relations and expose as delusive many of those same conceptions of romantic love that feminist theory in our century has identified with the ideology of compulsory heterosexuality. Indeed some of these poems seem almost to respond in advance to Adrienne Rich's call to examine critically 'heterosexuality as a political institution which disempowers women'.[54] Barker receives no mention in Hilda L. Smith's study of English feminism in the second half of the seventeenth century, which seems fair enough. Barker brooded long and often on gender injustices (especially as they affected her own intellectual life), but she stopped short of full-fledged feminist analysis. In this she stands in contrast to Mary Astell, Elizabeth Elstob, the anonymous author of *An Essay in Defence of the Female Sex*, and other writers who as a

---

53 This detail is omitted from the Magdalen version.
54 Adrienne Rich, 'Compulsory Heterosexuality and Lesbian Existence', in *Blood, Bread, and Poetry: Selected Prose 1979–1985* (New York and London: Norton, 1986), 23–75 (23).

group 'did not simply criticize women's position in society, but saw social change as necessary to restoring women's rightful opportunities'.[55] Barker was unable to reject received views of the 'natural', divinely sanctioned subordination of women but neither could she accept her own secondary status, and so she engaged in a kind of compensatory exceptionalism:[56]she would never sign herself a 'lover of her Sex', as Mary Astell did in *A Serious Proposal to the Ladies* (1694). And, oddly perhaps, she produced none of the celebrations of female homoerotic desire that turn up with some regularity in verse by women in the second half of the seventeenth century, among them Katherine Philips, Aphra Behn, Lady Mary Chudleigh, and Elizabeth Singer.[57] None the less, some of Barker's most interesting verses challenge the sexual status quo in quite remarkable ways. These poems are the subject of the remainder of this chapter.

'To Ovid's HEROINES *in his Epistles*' protests against the sexualized view of Woman advanced in *Ovid's Epistles* (1680), the hugely successful Dryden–Tonson collaboration that went through four editions by 1688.[58] A collection of monologues spoken (mostly) by abandoned women, *Ovid's Epistles* is

[55] Smith, *Reason's Disciples*, 5.

[56] As for example in her assessment of female learning: 'But let the World confine or enlarge Learning as they please, I care not; I do not regret the Time I bestow'd in its Company, it having been my good Friend . . ., tho' I am not so generous, by Way of Return, to pass my Word for its good Behaviour in our Sex, always, and in all Persons' (*BG* 37).

[57] For an overview of feminist friendship poetry in the late Stuart period, see Smith, *Reason's Disciples*, ch. 5. The best treatment of Philips in her sapphic aspect is Harriet Andreadis, 'The Sapphic Platonics of Katherine Philips, 1632–1664', *Signs: Journal of Women in Culture and Society*, 15 (1989), 34–60; for a critique, see Arlene Stiebel, 'Subversive Sexuality: Masking the Erotic in Poems by Katherine Philips and Aphra Behn', in Claude J. Summers and Ted-Larry Pebworth (eds.), *Renaissance Discourses of Desire* (Columbia and London: U. of Missouri P., 1993), 223–36. For Behn, see Carol Barash, 'The Political Possibilities of Desire: Teaching the Erotic Poems of Behn', in Christopher Fox (ed.), *Teaching Eighteenth-Century Poetry* (New York: AMS P., 1990), 159–76. For Elizabeth Singer Rowe's homoerotic friendship verse, see Marilyn L. Williamson, *Raising Their Voices: British Women Writers, 1650–1750* (Detroit: Wayne State UP, 1990), 111–12.

[58] *Ovid's Epistles, Translated by Several Hands* (London: Tonson, 1680). One of the hands was that of the unlearned Aphra Behn, the excellence of whose translation, according to Dryden, gave classically trained male translators 'occasion to be asham'd' (preface, sig. a4). The Barker poem receives brief mention by John Kerrigan, 'Introd.', *Motives of Woe: Shakespeare and 'Female Complaint': A Critical Anthology* (Oxford: Clarendon P., 1991), 75, in the context of a valuable discussion of 17th-cent. female complaint.

unremitting in its fascination with the spectacle of feminine grief, suffering, rage, and despair. (Sappho's epistle, for example, a long suicide note filled with heterosexual burnings and expirings, begins, 'While *Phaon* to the flaming Ætna flies, | Consum'd with no less Fires poor *Sapho* dies. | I burn, I burn, like kindled Fields of Corn, | When by the driving Winds the flames are born'.)[59] Dryden may have been nervous about the volume's reception, for he was at some pains to counter the reputation for heated eroticism that made the *Epistles* (or as they are also known, the *Heroides*) suspect reading matter for the ladies. Ovid had 'taken a most becoming care' not to offend against feminine modesty; his 'amorous Expressions go no further than virtue may allow, and therefore may be read, as he intended them, by Matrons without a blush' (preface, sig. A7v). Barker was not impressed. She fired back with a poem that bypasses Dryden to speak directly to the female speakers of the *Epistles*, the 'Bright *Shees*' betrayed twice over by these amatory complaints, urging them to 'put on the Armour' of their 'scorn' and 'fix' their sexual feelings 'with Frost':

> Bright *Shees*, what Glories had your Names acquir'd,
> Had you consum'd those whom your Beauties fir'd,
> Had laugh'd to see them burn, and so retir'd:
>
> Then they cou'd ne'er have glory'd in their shames,
> Either to *Roman*, or to *English* Dames,
> Had you but warm'd, not melted in their flames.
>
> You'd not been wrack'd then on despair's rough coast,
> Nor yet by storms of Perjuries been toss'd,
> Had you but fix'd your flowing Love with Frost.
>
> Had you put on the Armour of your scorn,
> (That *Gem* which do's our Beauties most adorn)
> What hardy *Hero* durst have been forsworn.
>
> But since they found such *lenity* in you,
> Their crime so Epidemical do's grow,
> That all have, or do, or would be doing so.
>
> (*PR* 28–9)

---

[59] Sir Carr Scroop, 'Sapho to Phaon', *Ovid's Epistles*, 1. Barker would have been particularly annoyed by the display of feminine self-disregard found in the passage in which Sappho describes herself wandering the streets with dishevelled hair and torn clothes, forgetting 'Vertue, Fame, and all but thee' (4).

Barker would probably have agreed wholeheartedly with Germaine Greer's characterization of the amatory complaint as a 'sadistic mode which enacts the despoliation of deflowered women'.[60] Her counter-complaint expresses contempt for a genre that debases women and for readers who derive voyeuristic pleasure from exhibitions of feminine abjection; it also excoriates male sexual freedom, now grown 'Epidemical'. Her disgust with the licence granted men to express an often predatory sexuality was shared by plenty of other women, among them the amatory novelists, but where Behn, Manley, and Haywood chronicled in their fictions the extremities of victimization with what I suspect Barker would have regarded unseemly relish, Barker wanted nothing to do with female victimization. Like her contemporaries Mary Astell and Mary Lady Chudleigh (and a host of nineteenth- and twentieth-century feminists besides) she chose rather to emphasize the enabling possibilities of female self-sovereignty. Her aim was to encourage dignity and self-control: she counselled women to wear the 'Armour' of their 'scorn'.[61]

The removal from the heterosexual relation recommended to Ovid's heroines is accomplished with Barkerian quirkiness in 'On the Apothecary's Filing my Bills amongst the Doctors', a wonderfully self-laudatory celebration of the speaker's triumphs as a 'fam'd Physician'. (Barker's medical practice will be taken up in detail in the next chapter.) Midway through comes a digression that supplies the familiar story of abjection-in-abandonment with an ending never envisioned by Ovid or his male successors. Rejection at the hands of the 'False Strephon', which should produce languors, hair-tearing, or self-immolation, turns out to be the first step in a journey toward dignified selfhood *and* a medical practice. The speaker could now 'almost bless' her jilting lover, for had he 'been true' she would have 'liv'd in sottish ease' and studied only 'how to love and please'. She was

---

[60] Germaine Greer, 'How to Invent a Poet', TLS (25 June 1993), 7–8 (7).

[61] The early 18th-cent. novelist Mary Davys made a similar point in the preface to the two-volume The Works of Mrs. Davys (London: H. Woodfall, 1725), where she argued that the impetus for regulation of the sexual passions would have to come from women: 'if the reformation would once again begin from our sex, the men would follow it in spite of their hearts, for it is we have given up our empire, betrayed by rebels among ourselves'. The reference to rebels within may be a glance at the amatory novelists.

a fool, she now knows, 'to sigh, weep, almost dye, | Little fore-
thinking of this present joy' (*PR* 32–3). Ovidian complaint is
thus dispatched in a single unenchanted line—'Fool that I was
to sigh, weep, almost dye'—and the reader is shunted from the
well-charted territory of feminine abjection to contemplate a
'present joy' grounded in a condition of female intellectual and
emotional self-sufficiency such as male poets seldom showed
themselves disposed to imagine. Barker was not the first woman
poet moved to rewrite Ovid nor the last to intimate that female
joys need not revolve around a phallic axis.[62] But I know of no
other poet who delivers the abandoned woman from the 'sottish
ease' of romantic love and its self-erasing studies in amatory
pleasure to the more bracing satisfactions of physick.

As a poet Barker leaned always toward the astringent.
Nowhere in the early verse does one find that indulgence in
sensuous luxuriousness so richly present in the pastorals of
Aphra Behn, for example. Indeed, one is hard-pressed to
discover anywhere in the corpus, early or late, material that
might be called erotic, despite the fact that she wrote during a
time when female authors, poets and later novelists, were developing a speciality in the 'soft', 'warm', and 'melting'. *Poetical
Recreations* does include a scattering of amatory lyrics,
however. Although many are undistinguished, others are
remarkable for the way they wryly rework the symbols and
imagery of male amatory traditions. Among the most interesting is a handful of anti-*carpe diem* poems which, like the two
anti-Ovidian poems just examined, ironize inherited poetic
conventions in such a way as to subvert received poetic fictions
of 'Woman', especially those that collapse female worth into
(perishable) beauty and (transient) sexual attractiveness in the
eyes of men.

The *carpe diem* rendering of women as rapidly fading objects
of male desire, their beauty inseparable from the pathos of its
extinction, provoked a variety of responses from Barker's
female contemporaries. In a clever about-face Lady Chudleigh
turns the whole *carpe diem* tradition against any man weak-
minded enough to become prey to a woman's physical charms.

---

[62] For 17th-cent. rewritings of Ovidian complaint, including verse by Killigrew,
Behn, and Barker, see Kerrigan, *Motives of Woe*, 67–83.

A 1703 'Song' reminds an all-too susceptible shepherd that beauty is 'worthless, fading, flying' and asks, coolly, 'Who would for Trifles think of dying?' Another 'Song' by Chudleigh chides Narcissus for being enslaved to his own physical beauty: 'What will you do' when that 'lovely beauteous Face' to 'old Age give[s] place?'[63] Narcissus, interestingly, is made to suffer the *carpe diem* woman's fate: he is transformed into a flower. Anne Finch in 'The Petition for an Absolute Retreat', an adaptation of the time-is-flying convention that advances a refreshingly reciprocal understanding of sexual pleasure, depicts the amatory couple—husband and wife in her revisioning—as discovering their mutual enjoyments within, rather than outside or against, temporality: they 'Spent the swiftly flying Time, | Spent their own and Nature's Prime, | In Love'.[64]

As a mountain of feminist criticism has demonstrated, poets who write amatory verse from a specifically female point of view inevitably disrupt a whole train of established poetic conventions that inscribe women as passive objects of desire. Barker's poems are disruptive in a way peculiar to herself. She creates female speakers who identify themselves with the image of perishing beauty promulgated by the *carpe diem* tradition so as to fashion themselves as objects of non-desire, rejected objects. She seems especially intrigued by the possibilities for ironic self-representation achievable by means of controlled distortions of the metaphors of the tradition, especially the central one of the fading flower. Any metaphor consists of two parts: the vehicle, that which carries or embodies the meaning, and the tenor, that which is meant. In the standard *carpe diem* metaphor of the fading flower, the vehicle not only embodies the idea of the loss of feminine beauty but also evokes the supposed poignance of that loss in ways that, as often as not, partake of the elegantly sadistic. ('Then die', Waller apostrophizes the lovely rose, that she may 'read in thee' the 'common fate of all things rare'.) Barker's method is to detach the vehicle, the flower, from its cluster of associations with feminine beauty and to insist instead upon its spoiled, ragged, overblown, and discarded aspects. Her

---

[63] Ezell, *Poems*, 73, 116.
[64] Myra Reynolds (ed.), *The Poems of Anne Countess of Winchilsea* (Chicago: U. of Chicago P., 1903), 72.

speaker identifies herself, that is to say, with the flower in its dying and unlovely aspect, never with the flower in its delicate if perishing beauty. She is a withered tulip or rose:

> For I no more deserve Applause,
> Now Youth and Beauty's fled;
> Than a *Tulip*, or a *Rose*,
> When its fair Leaves are shed.
> ('To My Young Lover. A
> Song', *PR* 64)

Her face is past its bloom:

> Incautious *Youth*, why do'st thou so mis-place
> Thy fine *Encomiums* on an o'er-blown Face.
> ('To my Young Lover', *PR* 61)

The young lover's compliments to his aged beloved are no less out of season than April flowers placed upon a pear bough in autumn (St Michael's pear ripens around Michaelmas, that is, in late September):

> Then chuse some budding *Beauty*, which in time
> May crown thy Wishes in thy blooming prime:
> For nought can make a more preposterous show,
> Than *April* Flowers stuck on St. *Michael*'s Bow.
> ('To My Young Lover', *PR* 61)

The pain of sexual rejection hovering around these images of self-as-faded-flower emerges full-blown as it were in 'A song', a two-stanza manuscript poem from the Magdalen Manuscript. The speaker's comparison of the unpenetrated vagina of the aging 'Galaecia' to an overblown rose puts to unsettling use conventional associations between rosebuds and virginity, sexual initiation and defloration.

> When poor Galæcia aged grew,
> young strephon in his prime,
> The nosgay which to her was due,
> Poor nymph she gave to him,
> Which coldly he receiv'd and sed,
> Alas I her bemoan,
> This nosgay's like her maiden-head
> The roses are o'er blown.
> (Mag. MS, fo. 84; printed in
> Wilson, 330)

The remarkably dismal rendering of female sexual rejection achieved by this inversion of a stock Cavalier compliment is unlike anything I have encountered in women's verse of the period, though the lines may bear comparison with those in Rochester's 'The Imperfect Enjoyment' where the speaker's prematurely spent penis lies 'Shrunk up, and Sapless, like a wither'd *Flow'r*'.[65] Inevitably 'A song' invites biographical speculation, but one need not read these lines confessionally to recognize that one of Barker's major strengths is her ability to bend inherited poetic conventions to what can be rather disturbing purposes.

In 'A Virgin Life' she uses conventions derived from popular contemporary forms and classical retirement verse to unmask the fictions that bind women to men and marriage and to re-imagine in positive terms female existence outside matrimony. This is one of Barker's best known poems and undoubtedly one of the finest. Sometimes described as a homage to Katherine Philips, whose 'The Virgin' has been proposed (wrongly I think) as its model, these lines in praise of the single life have more recently been read as an expression of the author's Catholicism. George Parfitt, for example, observes that 'without naming the Blessed Virgin' Barker 'has access to the Catholic position'; the poem's emphasis is 'distinctly Catholic in its concern for virginity'. Paul Monod makes the suggestive point that her praise of virginity challenges the 'Protestant acceptance of marriage as necessary to social order'.[66] So far as I can tell, however, the *Poetical Recreations* verse shows little if any trace of the author's Catholicism. I suspect that these poems, 'A Virgin Life' included, were written prior to her conversion. (For poems written from a Catholic position one should consult the markedly different 'Fidelia' poems in Part One of the Magdalen

---

[65] Keith Walker (ed.), *The Poems of John Wilmot Earl of Rochester* (Oxford: Basil Blackwell, 1984), 31, l. 45. Behn picks up and modifies the image in 'The Disappointment', l. 114, in Janet Todd (ed.), *The Works of Aphra Behn*, i: *Poetry* (London: William Pickering, 1992), 68, when she refers obliquely to the post-ejaculatory penis as being 'Cold as Flow'rs bath'd in the Morning-Dew'.

[66] George Parfitt, *English Poetry of the Seventeenth Century*, 2nd edn. (London and New York: Longman, 1992), 236, 237; Paul Monod, 'Jacobitism as Court Culture and Popular Culture', paper delivered at Northeast American Society for Eighteenth-Century Studies, Sept. 1996. See also Williamson, *Raising Their Voices*, 105.

Manuscript, treated in Chapter 3.) In any event, 'A Virgin Life' is perhaps best approached, like 'An Invitation to my Friends at Cambridge', as an appropriation of the classical topos of the happy retired life.

Poems in praise of the single life, examples of which can be found in the work of Mary Astell, Lady Chudleigh, Sarah Fyge, Elizabeth Singer, and Catherine Trotter and many others,[67] were extremely popular in the 1680s and 1690s. Like many such poems Barker's 'A Virgin Life' begins with the speaker's petition to the higher powers that she not be overpowered by the force of men's 'almost Omnipotent Amours':

> Since, O ye Pow'rs, ye have bestow'd on me
> So great a Kindness for Virginity,
> Suffer me not to fall into the Pow'rs
> Of Mens almost Omnipotent Amours.   (PR 12)

Petitions of this sort were common in poetry by women in the 1680s.[68] Mrs Taylor begins a song against passion by calling upon 'Ye Virgin Pow'rs' to defend her heart against the 'sawcy Love, or nicer Art' that 'beguile' most of 'our Sex'; a wavering nymph in a song probably adapted by Aphra Behn beseeches Pan that she never 'fall in love' and thus 'Resign' her 'happy Liberty'; Alinda in one of Killigrew's pastoral dialogues pleads with 'ye Favouring Gods' to 'defend' her 'flocks from Wolves' and her 'Heart from Love'.[69] Also conventional is the negative portrayal of marriage which follows, when Barker sardonically compares marriage to a 'Lyon's Den' into which naive young women, like so many 'harmless Kids' being 'purs'd by Men', flee for refuge.

Yet, unusually for poems of this sort, Barker is less concerned

---

[67] For the anti-marriage stance as sophisticated female literary convention, see Ezell, Patriarch's Wife, 106–8. Her attribution to Barker of 'The Preference of a Single Life before Marriage' is inaccurate; the poem, which appears in Part Two of PR, is by an anonymous male contributor.

[68] The petitionary formula was also used by men. John Norris's 'Sitting in an Arbour', published in 1684, begins, 'Thus ye good powers, thus let me ever be | Secure, retir'd, from love and business free': qtd. in Røstvig, The Happy Man, 273, who observes that these lines 'may owe something to Horace's ode III, 16'.

[69] Elizabeth Taylor, 'Song, Made by Mrs. Taylor', in KR 296; Aphra Behn, 'Song in the same Play [The Wavering Nymph or Mad Amyntas], by the Wavering Nymph', in Todd, Works, i. 64; Anne Killigrew, 'Pastoral Dialogue', in Poems by Mrs Anne Killigrew (London: Samuel Lowndes, 1686), 58.

with advancing a critique of marriage than with establishing the single life as a genuine alternative to the conjugal one—no easy task in a world in which, as one historian puts it, 'to live outside marriage and the family was almost inconceivable'.[70] This difference in emphasis can be seen by comparison with two well-known praise-of-single-life poems from the time, 'The Emulation' by Sarah Fyge and 'To the Ladies' by Lady Chudleigh. Both are critical of the institution of marriage, seen to disadvantage women and serve male interests, and both depict marriage as a 'fatal slavery' for women, entailing loss of liberty, happiness, and even selfhood. ('Then comes the last, the fatal slavery, | The Husband with insulting Tyranny | Can have ill Manners justified by Law; | For Men all join to keep the Wife in awe', as Fyge puts it.) Women readers are urged to 'shun, oh! Shun that wretched state'.[71] But where Fyge, Chudleigh, and others invoke the freedoms and pleasures of the single life so as to throw into starker relief the self-extinction demanded of wives, Barker takes seriously the single life on its own terms. She seems, indeed, little interested in marriage generally: seldom is she moved to denounce the insulting tyrannies of husbands or anatomize the miseries of their victim-spouses.[72] Her central concern is to redefine the single life—understood as virtuous retirement from the distractions of the matrimonial order—as the basis for a distinctively female version of the *beatus vir* ideal of the happy, well-ordered existence.

First, though, she had to recuperate the negative image of the old maid, as the never-married woman was coming to be called, by insisting upon the foolishness of certain 'mad conceptions' which historians tell us were gaining cultural force at precisely this time as part of an emerging and very nasty anti-old maid

[70] Olwen Hufton, *The Prospect Before Her: A History of Women in Western Europe*, i: *1500–1800* (New York: Alfred A. Knopf, 1996), 63.

[71] 'The Emulation', in Sarah Fyge [Egerton], *Poems on Several Occasions, Together with a Pastoral* (London: J. Nutt, [1706]), 108. Chudleigh, 'To the Ladies', in Ezell, *Poems*, 84. (Marriage, Chudleigh writes, 83–4, is that 'fatal Knot' that 'nothing, nothing can divide'; once married woman is 'govern'd by a Nod' and 'fear[s] her Husband as her God: | Him still must serve, him still obey, | And nothing act, and nothing say, | But what her haughty Lord thinks fit, | Who with the Pow'r, has all the Wit'.)

[72] An exception is 'To my Friend EXILLUS, *on his persauding me to Marry Old Damon*', which comments ironically on the tendency of husbandly 'kindness' to 'improve' to jealousy (*PR* 14).

discourse.[73] The woman who declines to marry is *not* 'foul
deformity' in the 'ugliest dress'; her existence is *not* 'all
wretchedness'.

> Ah lovely State how strange it is to see,
> What mad conceptions some have made of thee,
> As though thy Being was all wretchedness,
> Or foul deformity i'th' ugliest dress;
> Whereas thy Beauty's pure, Celestial,
> Thy thoughts Divine, thy Words Angelical.
>
> (*PR* 12–13)

Having thus constructed an image of the single life as lovely,
beautiful, celestial, divine, and angelical to counter the 'mad
conceptions' that needlessly malign and humiliate unmarried
women, Barker is ready to redefine the social existence of the
single woman in radically new ethical terms: she is properly
understood as a member in her own right of the larger community and stands at the centre of her own network of social, religious, and political obligations.

> Her Neighb'ring Poor she do's adopt her Heirs,
> And less she cares for her own good then theirs;
> And by Obedience testifies she can
> Be's good a Subject as the stoutest Man.
> She to her Church such filial duty pays,
> That one would think she'd liv'd i'th' pristine days.
> Her Closet, where she do's much time bestow,
> Is both her Library and Chappel too,
> Where she enjoys society alone,
> I'th Great Three-One—
> She drives her whole Lives business to these Ends,
> To serve her God, enjoy her Books and Friends.
>
> (*PR* 13)

She adopts for her 'Heirs' the 'Neighb'ring Poor', pays 'filial
duty' to the Church, and shows by her 'Obedience' that she is
as 'good a Subject as the stoutest Man'. Virtues which when
defined in feminine terms carry narrowly parochial meanings—
obedience and filial duty for example—are thus resituated
within a larger ethical framework in which they acquire more

---

[73] This anti-old maid discourse is discussed in greater detail in the Epilogue
below.

comprehensive civic and religious meanings. Prised from its associations with feminine submissiveness, 'obedience' comes to signify a broadly civic virtue; severed from the patriarchal family and its association with modes of daughterly obligation, 'filial duty' implies a relationship with God and the Church. The single woman's contribution to the social order extends well beyond biological reproduction and the patriarchal household: she serves the neighbouring poor, the *polis*, and God. Earlier in the century Margaret Cavendish argued differently: 'we Women', she wrote in *Sociable Letters*, 'are not made Citizens of the Commonwealth, we hold no Offices, nor bear we any Authority therein'; 'if we be not Citizens in the Commonwealth, I know no reason we should be Subjects to the Commonwealth'.[74] In 'A Virgin Life' Barker imagines what Cavendish found so unimaginable, a meaningful existence for a woman apart from her subjected position within the family, and she frames this existence in terms of a reconceived understanding of the ideal female life, the *beata femina*, that unfolds independently of marriage, the family, and her culture's reproductive imperatives.

Marilyn Williamson is certainly right, then, when she observes that for Barker 'the celibate life of single blessedness was a realistic alternative for women', but she may not go far enough.[75] The radical nature of Barker's aim is more easily grasped when 'A Virgin Life' is read alongside Katherine Philips's 'The Virgin', a poem sometimes cited as its precursor. Philips's demure speaker enumerates the 'things that make a Virgin please'—middling beauty, kindness, genuine innocence, pleasing conversation, moderate liveliness, and so on, in the manner of Martial's epigram 10. 47, on which it is based.[76] Although it is hard to imagine Barker rejecting altogether anything written by her beloved Orinda, one can be sure she

[74] Margaret Cavendish, *CCXI. Sociable Letters, Written by the Thrice Noble, Illustrious, and Excellent Princess, the Lady Marchioness of Newcastle* (London: William Wilson, 1664), 27.

[75] Williamson, *Raising Their Voices*, 105.

[76] Thomas, i. 207. Martial's Epigram 10. 47, which envisions the happy life as moderation in all things, begins, 'Since dearest Friend, 'tis your desire to see | A true Receipt of Happiness from Me; | These are the chief Ingredients . . .'. Philips seems to have been echoing Jonson's translation, which begins, 'The Things that make the happier life, are these.' Both quotes are in Røstvig, 40, 61.

would have been unimpressed by this list of pleasing attributes. They would have struck her as superficial at best and on at least one point, the notion that it is the virgin's part to please, down-right wrong-headed. Whether or not Barker was rewriting a precursor poem, she clearly sought to remove virginity from the firmament of self-effacing feminine virtues in which Philips and others were inclined to place it and associate it instead with refusal of a matrimonial order that ill-serves women's interests. In Barker's poem, as in her work more generally, virginity is an image for an ethically ordered existence lived under one's own control, a new kind of *beata femina* ideal. The ideal thus proposed offers, it seems to me, a challenge to the heteropatri-archy at least as bold as the expressions of sexual freedom for which more overtly transgressive women writers are nowadays sometimes lauded.

It seems odd that what might fairly be called a poetry of hetero-sexual refusal should have originated in a matrix of cross-gender sociability. We have seen that the verse printed in *Poetical Recreations* was written mostly to men, and analysis of individual poems shows that they imitate, sometimes ironi-cally but oftentimes not, male literary codes. Barker clearly regarded verse-exchange friendships with learned men as opportunities to extend her zone of contact with elite mascu-line culture, and in some of these poems she identifies closely with male subject-positions. But she writes from positions of female resistance, as well, and in 'A Virgin Life' in particular identifies with a kind of female selfhood that enacts itself outside relationships with men and the heterosexual economy—in what we might term, following Theresa de Lauretis, a feminist 'elsewhere', an imagined space in the margins of the dominant matrimonial order.[77] The rather puzzling silence of these poems on the question of female friendships, female community, or same-sex desire—puzzling in the light of the image of Barker that has emerged over the last

[77] The feminist 'elsewhere' is to be found in 'spaces in the margins of hegemonic discourses, social spaces carved in the interstices of institutions and in the chinks and cracks of the power-knowledge apparati': see Theresa de Lauretis, *Technologies of Gender: Essays on Theory, Film, and Fiction* (Bloomington and Indianapolis: Indiana UP, 1987), 25.

decade, to be sure, but puzzling in view of Barker's own ideological leanings as well—may possibly be explained by the
circumstances of their production and circulation. For these are
first and foremost *sociable* utterances, currency of exchange
with men whose friendship she regards as vitally important, if
at times rather troubling. The next chapter takes up a small
group of poems from *Poetical Recreations* in which her identifications with men are at their most perplexed.

2

Physick, Verse, and Female Subjectivity

THE handful of poems on medical themes discussed in this chapter exemplify with sometimes painful clarity the contradictions of Barker's position as a learned woman who identified with, but was excluded from, men's communities of learning. That these poems exhibit considerable intellectual confusion might almost go without saying. Female identification with a male point of view, as Adrienne Rich has observed, results in 'synapses in thought, denials of feeling, wishful thinking, a profound sexual and intellectual confusion' in which 'many women engage . . . and from which no woman is permanently and utterly free'—features of what Rich calls 'doublethink'.[1] In the last chapter we saw Barker using sociable verse to gain admission to a kind of Cambridge of the mind. Here we shall see her using poetic fantasy to claim belonging with the medical establishment, a mode of investment in male interests that would prove even less possible to sustain.

Until recently orthodox feminist analysis has tended to regard 'doublethink' as first and foremost a symptom of patriarchal distortion, akin to co-optation and silencing, and to treat 'male-identified' writing as spurious, impure, or merely imitative—and in any case lamentable—with the result that we lack critical tools for thinking about what used to be called, not without opprobrium, 'immasculated' female subjectivities.[2] The

---

[1] Adrienne Rich, 'Compulsory Heterosexuality and Lesbian Existence', in *Blood, Bread, and Poetry: Selected Prose 1979–1985* (New York and London: Norton, 1986), 23–75 (48).

[2] The term is Judith Fetterly's in *The Resisting Reader: A Feminist Approach to American Fiction* (Bloomington: Indiana UP, 1978). She defines 'immasculation' as the process whereby 'women are taught to think as men, to identify with a male point of view, and to accept as normal and legitimate a male system of values, one of whose central principles is misogyny' (xx).

psychoanalytic model of subjectivity developed by Diana Fuss in *Identification Papers* may offer a more fruitful approach to early modern women's writings. Subjectivity, as she proposes we understand it, is not tied to one kind of identification or another, is neither male- nor female-directed, but is rather constituted by an array of ambivalent identifications. These travel a 'double circuit, allowing for the possibility of multiple and contradictory identifications coexisting in the subject at the same time'. When Barker's medical poems are read in the light of what Fuss elegantly calls the 'struggle to negotiate a constantly changing field of ambivalent identifications',[3] they turn out to be unusually rich sites for study of female subjectivity constructed in tension with prevailing gender codes. That the struggle to construct an identity embracing both learning and femaleness—categories seventeenth-century gender ideology rendered disjunct—should occur within a field charged with self-doubt is hardly surprising. It is more to be wondered that Barker was able in the best of these poems to show so clearly the effort required to 'negotiate a constantly changing field of ambivalent identifications' and in this way reveal something of what it meant to be a woman of mind in a world in which female intellectual attainment was rendered ridiculous, grotesque, or invisible.

Dr Barker's Famous Gout Plaster

Although these poems fascinate today as expressions of female subjectivity, Barker seems to have been motivated to write them by a desire to get on the record personal accomplishments liable to remain outside history. As Galesia says of the most self-laudatory of these poems, 'so *I celebrated my own Praise*, according to the Proverb, *for want of good Neighbours to do it for me*' (*PWS* 119). Assuming that the medical poems have a basis in biographical fact, as I am persuaded they do, they tell us that Barker possessed not only skill in 'physick', an area of medicine not yet closed off to women but also, somewhat unexpectedly,

[3] Diana Fuss, *Identification Papers* (New York and London: Routledge, 1995), 34. Subsequent references will be indicated parenthetically in the text.

a more than passing acquaintance with academic medicine. In
the early verse and later prose fictions she would devote considerable attention to her involvement in medicine, relating
engagements with 'physick' that on occasion took her deep into
male-only intellectual territories. Passages in *The Amours of
Bosvil and Galesia* (1713) and *A Patch-Work Screen for the
Ladies* (1723) suggest that under the tutelage of her brother, a
medical student as she represents him, she received an unusually
erudite medical education; they further suggest that for a time
in the 1680s she practised medicine in London and, as we
discover from the seemingly autobiographical account offered
in '*On the* Apothecary's *Filing my Bills amongst the* Doctors',
went so far as to prescribe medications. The latter was a highly
unorthodox—and risky—proceeding which could have landed
her before the authorities. (By statute, the right to prescribe
through an apothecary was reserved to male academic practitioners licensed by the College of Physicians; anyone prescribing
illicitly could in theory by prosecuted by the College, though in
practice few actually were by this time.)[4] 'Anatomy', an ambitious voyage in verse through the seventeenth-century anatomical body, bears witness to Barker's extensive knowledge of the
academic medicine of her day.[5] These self-representations,
which appear to be unknown to medical historians and remain
little studied by literary critics, are an important source for
investigation of lay and female involvement in medicine in the
Restoration generally. More to our purposes here, they constitute our chief source of information about Barker's activities as
a healer and furnish a crucial context for study of Barker's
ambivalent identification with forms of male learning.

Recent accounts of Barker's life confine themselves to vague
references to her activities as a 'healer' or 'medical practitioner'
or else they make claims for which there is no evidence, that she
supported herself by means of a medical practice, for example.
It seems worth while to begin, then, by clarifying what can be
known about her real-life medical activities, starting with the

---

[4] For the legal battle over the right to prescribe at this time, see Harold J. Cook,
'The Rose Case Reconsidered: Physicians, Apothecaries, and the Law in Augustan
England', *Journal of the History of Medicine*, 45 (1990), 527–55.
[5] Both poems survive in three versions, *PR*, Mag. MS, and *PWS*.

fact that, with minor exceptions, virtually everything 'known' derives from fictionalized self-representations (or from what, to be more accurate, we *take* to be self-representations) and must therefore be used with caution. Some corroborating evidence is furnished by commendatory verses from the 1680s that praise her skill in physick—in her one sees '*Medicine* at once improv'd, and Poetrie', in 'her sight no bold *Disease* durst stand'[6]— though we must allow for the possibility that such praise represents male gallantry exercising itself in flattery of a woman's chosen image of self at least as much as evidence for any real-life skill or actual medical practice. Regarding the latter there exists, it must be said, no 'official' documentation. She acquired no university degree, of course, but neither (so far as I have been able to discover) did she seek to be licensed by the authorities, as a number of women did at this time—various kinds of evidence, including the records of city companies and ecclesiastical licensing authorities, show that quite ordinary women practised medicine for a living within 'official', that is, licensed, channels[7]—although given that at this time the major part of health care was delivered outside official structures of documentation, this negative evidence proves nothing.

One need not automatically discount Barker as a source, however, especially since everything she relates is consistent with what is known about female involvement in early modern medicine.[8] That medicine played an important role in the educa-

---

[6] 'Fidelius', 'To the Incomparable Galæcia, On the Publication of her Poems' (*PR*, sig. a2v); Benjamin Crayle, 'To Clarinda, On his Deserting her, and loving *Cosmelia*' (*PR* 2. 186).

[7] Specialities known to have licensed female practitioners include midwifery, surgery, phlebotomy (blood-letting), and bone-setting. For names see the typescript at the Wellcome Institute (MS 5354). For the admission of women to the company of barber-surgeons, see Sidney Young, *Annals of the Barber Surgeons* (London: Blades, East and Blades, 1890), 260; for the story of the 'surgeoness', see A. L. Wyman, 'The Surgeoness: The Female Practitioner of Surgery 1400–1800', *Medical History*, 28 (1984), 22–41.

[8] Women's involvement in early modern medicine has attracted much attention in recent decades. Studies I have found helpful include Margaret Pelling and Charles Webster, 'Medical Practitioners', in Charles Webster (ed.), *Health, Medicine and Mortality in the Sixteenth Century* (Cambridge: Cambridge UP, 1979), 165–235; Margaret Pelling, 'Medical Practice in Early Modern England: Trade or Profession?', in Wilfrid Prest (ed.), *The Professions in Early Modern England* (London: Croom Helm, 1987), 90–128; Lucinda Beier, *Sufferers and Healers: The Experience of Illness in Seventeenth-Century England* (London and New York:

tion of women in the period has long been recognized. Josephine Gardiner reports that there is 'scarcely a description of the upbringing of girls at this time which omits all reference to the "study of Physick" ',[9] and I am reminded by Peter Beal that manuscript cookery books of the period almost invariably include medical receipts as well: a recipe for gingerbread, for instance, might share the page with one for gout plaster. Women of the aristocratic and gentry classes were expected to attend to the health needs of the family, the household, and often the poor in the surrounding neighbourhood, which would have included preparing herbal remedies and other medicines, dressing wounds, performing minor surgery, even in some cases bone-setting.[10] Indeed, skill in medicine was expected from female members of the upper ranges of the servant class as well. A manual quoted by Alice Clark states that well-placed house-keepers were expected to 'have a competent knowledge in Physick and Chyrurgery, that they may be able to help their maimed, sick and indigent Neighbours'.[11] All of which is to say that as a well-bred country gentlewoman Barker would have acquired in due course the skills and knowledge to practise medicine had she wished.

With the proviso that what follows can be at best roughly suggestive, I shall outline what might reasonably be inferred about Barker's medical practice by reading relevant passages in the fictions against what is known about health care at this time. If one assumes that the account of Galesia's London

Routledge and Kegan Paul, 1987); Doreen Nagy, *Popular Medicine in Seventeenth-Century England* (Bowling Green, Oh.: Bowling Green State Univ. Popular P., 1988). Still indispensable is Alice Clark, *Working Life of Women in the Seventeenth Century* (1919; repr. London and New York: Routledge, 1992), ch. 6.

  [9] Dorothy Gardiner, *English Girlhood at School: A Study of Women's Education through Twelve Centuries* (Oxford: Oxford UP and London: Humphrey Mildord, 1929), 262. For the place of medicine in a girl's education in the 17th cent., see 262-4.

  [10] A classic example would be Lady Halkett (1622-99): 'In the summer season she vyed with the Bee or Ant in gathering Herbs, Flowers, Worms, Snails, &c, for the Still or Limbeck for the Mortar or Boyling Pan; and was ordinarily then in a Dress fitted for her Still-House, making preparations of extracted Waters, Spirits, Ointments, Conserves, Salves, Powders, which she ministred every Wednesday to a multitude of Poor infirm Persons, besides what she dayly sent abroad to persons of all Ranks who consulted her in their Maladies': from *Life of Lady Halkett* (1701), qtd. in Gardiner, *English Girlhood*, 263-4.

  [11] Clark, *Working Life*, 255.

practice offered in *Patch-Work Screen* is based on her author's
own experience, then Barker would have been what her
contemporaries termed a physician, the rough equivalent of
what nowadays we call an internist. Physicians diagnosed
internal disorders, gave advice, and prescribed medications.
(Galesia was sought in her lodgings for 'Advice in divers sorts
of Maladies'; she wrote *'Bills* in *Latin,* with the same manner
of *Cyphers* and *Directions* as Doctors do' (*PWS* 116).) They
were distinguished from surgeons, who attended to external
disorders—wounds, sores, tumours, and venereal disease.
Although the latter was a recognized female speciality, Galesia
pointedly declines to treat venereal complaints. (A patient thus
infected she recommends to a physician of her acquaintance,
more accustomed to the 'immodest Harangues necessary on
such Occasions' (*PWS* 113).) During the Restoration period
the category physician was by modern standards almost unbe-
lievably elastic and heterogeneous, embracing men and
women, official and unofficial practitioners, commercial oper-
ators and university-trained professionals, all drawn from
across a wide social range. A physician was often but not
always licensed. Not all physicians were, or professed to be,
doctors: a doctor, strictly speaking, had been granted a university degree, an MD,[12] but in practice some doctors were self-
declared. Many received training from a family
member—sometimes a mother but more often a father or
older brother. (Galesia received training from an older brother,
a medical student at Oxford, Paris, and Leiden, who helped
her learn Latin, botany, herbal medicine, anatomy, and physiology. She also read contemporary scientific medicine and by
her account made such progress 'as to understand *Harvey*'s
Circulation of the Blood, and *Lower*'s Motion of the Heart'
(*PWS* 82).)
    Did Barker earn a living through medicine as is sometimes
stated? It is impossible to say. We do know she was at pains to
construct Galesia as one who heals without regard for recognition, professional prestige, or financial reward—as, in short, a

[12] The latter required about fourteen years of university study, seven to complete
the arts course and another seven devoted to medicine. See Pelling and Webster,
'Medical Practitioners', 189, for a profile of the learned physician.

genteel amateur.[13] (Galesia professes to treat the sick in London
for the 'Pleasure I took in thus doing good' (*PWS* 116); she
earlier resolved to learn the use of simples—herbal medicine—
purely for the 'Good of my Country-Neighbours' (*BG* 15).) In
this regard, as in few others, Galesia treads a well-worn exemplary path. The shining ideal of the female healer who selflessly
practises medicine for the good of others and, no less important,
does so without encroaching upon male prerogatives—the
Good Woman of conduct books and sermons—was endlessly
extolled in the seventeenth century. One Good Woman was
praised for having ministered to 'divers poor folks, that were
otherwise destitute of help'; another for being 'compassionate in
Heart and charitably helpful with Phisick Cloathes
Nourishment or Counsels to any in misery'; another for 'having
bene above 40 yeares a willing nurse, midwife, surgeon, and in
part physitian to all both rich and poore; without expecting
reward'.[14] The 'charitableness' of the Good Woman's medicine
often brought about remarkable cures, for 'God gives a *peculiar
Blessing* to the Practice of those Women' whose only design is
in 'the doing Good'.[15] One funeral sermon praises her for caring
for the poor when a doctor is not available or, tellingly, afford-
able; for declining to prescribe where she 'may have the Advice
of the Learned'; and for curbing any desire to indulge in independent thought.[16] The Good Woman—deferential, self-effacing, and unpaid—is scrupulous not to compete with men
economically or to intrude if ever so slightly upon their
appointed sphere of learning and authority.

In view of this portrayal of Galesia as genteel amateur, it is

---

[13] At the lower reaches of the socioeconomic scale many women sought to make
a living through paid health care, mainly as nurses, midwives, and 'cunning women',
where the earnings were meager and the work often foul and dangerous. When
women did try to compete economically with men they often found themselves
attacked and suppressed, which explains why so much female medical work was
concentrated among the poor. Barker is at some pains to distinguish Galesia from
lower orders of female practitioners such as nurses, one of whom is depicted in *PWS*
as occupying a 'mean servile Station' (119).

[14] Quoted by Wyman, 'Surgeoness', 32, 31, 32. The last two are memorial
inscriptions.

[15] Timothy Rogers, *The Character of a Good Woman, Both in a Single and
Marry'd State* (London: John Harris, 1697), 43. The sermon was occasioned by the
death of Elizabeth Dunton, John Dunton's first wife.

[16] Rogers, *Character*, 43.

fascinating to find a piece of external evidence which suggests her creator may have dabbled in market-place medicine, that Barker may indeed have been something of a 'quack'.[17] The evidence comes in the form of a 1685 advertisement for '*Dr. Barkers* Famous *Gout Plaister*', the plaster said to be on sale at Benjamin Crayle's bookshop at the Lamb in Fleet Street for five shillings a roll. (It will relieve the pain in 'Twelve Hours time, with the Paroxysm of the Distemper, and in time may effect a perfect Cure'.)[18] Had the Famous Gout Plaster been vended elsewhere there would be little reason to suspect the hand of our author: commercial remedies were often sold by booksellers, and the name Barker was far from uncommon.[19] But the shop being Crayle's gives pause. Barker and her first publisher could have been acquainted by this time, for she may have been living in Newgate Street, just a short distance from Crayle's shop in Fleet Street near St Paul's Churchyard.[20] Three years later he would print in *Poetical Recreations* a poem whose speaker brags of her conquest over the 'sturdy *Gout*'; and according to a note added much later when that same poem was included in *Patch-Work Screen*, the author had possessed a 'particular Arcanum for the Gout'.[21] Given Barker's close association with Crayle, her claim on two widely separated occasions to special expertise in cure of the gout, and the fact that in the 1680s little distinction was made between the domestic remedies routinely

[17] See Harold J. Cook, *The Decline of the Old Medical Regime in Stuart London* (Ithaca and London: Cornell UP, 1986), ch. 1, for an overview of the medical market-place of London in the 17th-cent.; for commercial medicine more particularly, see Roy Porter, *Health for Sale: Quackery in England 1660–1850* (Manchester and New York: Manchester UP, 1989).

[18] The advertisement appears at the end of a list of Crayle titles on the final leaf in the anonymous *Delightful and Ingenious Novels: Being Choice and Excellent Stories of Amours, Tragical and Comical* (1685), available on microfilm in Early English Books, 1641–1700, reel 64: 3.

[19] For the link between booksellers and commercial medicines in the late 17th cent., see John Alden, 'Pills and Publishing: Some Notes on the English Book Trade, 1660–1715', *Library*, 5th ser. 7 (1952), 21–37. In 1679 the bookseller Benjamin Harris, who also carried an assortment of medicines, advertised in his newspaper, *Domestick Intelligence*, his own remedy for 'the Griping of the Guts'. See also R. B. Walker, 'Advertising in London Newspapers, 1650–1750', *Business History*, 15 (1973), 112–30, esp. 115.

[20] See Doc. Rec. n. 52.

[21] *A Patch-Work Screen for the Ladies* (London: Curll and Payne, 1723), 57. Wilson misprints as 'acanura'.

prepared by country gentlewoman and the proprietary medicines more and more produced for public sale,[22] one surmises that in the mid-1680s Jane Barker probably did sell, for five shillings a roll, a commercial remedy for the gout.[23] Whether she also attended the ill for pay there is simply no way of knowing. However, one of her most intriguing poems, 'On the Apothecary's *Filing my Bills amongst the* Doctors', gives reason to believe that at roughly this same time she wrote prescriptions in medical Latin convincing enough to fool the London apothecaries.

'*Just so* I celebrated my own Praise'

It might be said of patriarchy, as Diana Fuss has of colonialism, that as a system of domination and subordination it works 'in part by policing the boundaries of cultural intelligibility, legislating and regulating which identities attain full cultural signification and which do not' (*Identification*, 143). Barker's failure as a learned woman to achieve cultural intelligibility accounts in no small part for the bitter-sweet taste that remains after one has savoured the self-praise of 'On the Apothecaries', an exuberant piece of female braggadocio all the more glorious when read against the code of goodwomanly self-effacement sketched earlier. The female speaker not only boasts of finding

---

[22] The continuities between domestic, commercial, and professional modes of health care at this time are discussed by Mary E. Fissell, *Patients, Power, and the Poor in Eighteenth-Century Bristol* (Cambridge: Cambridge UP, 1991), ch. 3, esp. 37–48. Domestic gout remedies were common. Of the twenty or so manuscript receipt books at the Wellcome Institute consulted for this study, nearly every one has at least one gout remedy. Some are quite complicated, and perhaps impractical in London, but others could be easily and cheaply prepared: a gout plaster might require no more than soap, egg yolk, sack lees, and wheat bran.

[23] Printed notices surviving from the last decades of the 17th cent. indicate that many women offered health products for sale in the market-place. A number of bills and notices produced by practitioners identifying themselves as women are available for study at the British Library, Wellcome Institute, and in the John Johnson Collection at the Bodleian. By my rough estimate an identifiably female practitioner is found in about 10 per cent of the ads in these collections. Patricia Crawford, 'Printed Advertisements for Women Medical Practitioners in London, 1670–1710', *Society for the Social History of Medicine: Bulletin*, 35 (1984), 66–70, working with a somewhat smaller base of advertisements, counted a total of 66 ads from 1660 to 1710 which mention a female practitioner (66).

a cure for gout but also reflects with considerable complacency that 'since the Learn'd exalt' her 'Fame' it is 'no Arrogance' (*PR* 34) on her part to do the same. Yet on rereading, her self-satisfaction comes to seem increasingly thin and even self-mocking as the reader notices how, in subtle ways, the poem exposes the way (unauthorized) knowledge, knowledge without cultural legitimation, renders a woman invisible. 'On the Apothecaries' depicts what might be called, adapting Fuss, the vanishing point of cultural intelligibility in patriarchy.

The poem opens disarmingly with a gesture suggestive of the submission due to male authority. 'I Hope I shan't be blam'd', the speaker murmurs with proper deference, but immediately she lifts downcast eyes and proclaims herself 'proud' to be enrolled among the university-trained doctors who make up the 'Learned Croud'. For ten more lines she relishes the pleasures of her identity as a 'fam'd *Physician*'. It is an identity depicted, significantly, in terms of two male precedents, prelapsarian Adam and post-conversion Saul:

> I Hope I shan't be blam'd if I am proud,
> That I'm admitted 'mongst this Learned Croud;
> To be proud of a Fortune so sublime,
> Methinks is rather Duty, than a Crime:
> Were not my Thoughts exalted in this state,
> I should not make thereof due estimate:
> And sure one cause of *Adam*'s fall was this,
> He knew not the just worth of *Paradise*;
> But with this honour I'm so satisfy'd,
> The *Antients* were not more when *Deify'd*:
> For this transcends all common happiness,
> And is a Glory that exceeds excess.
> This 'tis, makes me a fam'd *Physician* grow,
> As *Saul* 'mongst *Prophets* turn'd a *Prophet* too.   (*PR* 31)

The strategy of male identification adopted here serves at once to elevate and lend cultural authority to her achievements and to bypass the problematic suggestions of feminine mental deficiency inevitably associated with Eve and her intellectually fallen daughters. However, when she begins to brag about the triumph of her '*Female* hands' over the gout, which 'all *Male* power withstands', she turns from biblical male models to heroic ancient women, inserting herself in a female genealogy that aligns her medical victory with the military triumphs of the Old Testament heroines Deborah and Judith and the conquests of the mythological Assyrian queen Semiramis.

> The sturdy *Gout*, which all *Male* power withstands,
> Is overcome by my soft *Female* hands:
> Not *Deb'ra, Judith,* or *Semiramis*
> Could boast of Conquests half so great as this;
> More than they slew, I save in this Disease.
>
> (*PR* 31)

She presents herself, as Carol Barash has noted, as a *femme forte*, the strong martial woman (*EWP* 190), but the identification is equivocal, for in the process of associating herself with a tradition of female heroism she also distinguishes herself from its exponents: 'More than they slew, I save in this Disease'. A *femme forte* she may be, but she is also, paradoxically, a conqueror who saves, a 'soft' female who overcomes a 'sturdy' disease.

We are thus invited to contemplate the much greater paradox that prompted her to sing her own praises in the first place. Her self-proclaimed place as a 'fam'd *Physician*' is hers only so long as her successful textual impersonation of 'real' doctors continues undetected, only so long as her actual identity as an unlicensed female practitioner remains unknown. She must operate by stealth and is, impossibly, 'fam'd' only so long as she is invisible. She all but admits the untenability of her position when, toward the end of the poem, she proposes to her muse that together they should 'praise and please our selves in doing so' (*PR* 34). The hint that the 'Glory that exceeds excess' she imagines for herself is just that, fantastical wishful thinking, would be made explicit decades later when in *Patch-Work Screen* Barker followed the poem with commentary that brings to the fore the elements of 'doublethink' implicit within the poem proper. 'Thus, Madam', observes the narrator, an older and more self-aware version of the young Galesia who composed the poem, 'as People before a Looking-glass, please themselves with their own Shapes and Features, though, perhaps, such as please no-body else; just so *I celebrated my own Praise*, according to the Proverb, *for want of good Neighbours to do it for me*' (*PWS* 119). We gaze at Galesia gazing at herself in a verse looking-glass of her own creating, reminded by this bit of regressus that outside the verse/glass Galesia-the-famed-physician has no intelligible being. The triumphs she celebrates, the power of her soft female hands, are fictive 'solutions' to the contradictions of her position—not unlike what one must finally call her preposterous victory over gout, a disease acknowledged at the time to be chronic, agonizingly painful, and stubbornly resistant to medical alleviation. The poem undoes its own claims to power and in the process exposes with great originality what it is to be a learned woman in a social order that renders such oddities invisible.[24]

If 'Apothecaries' situates itself at the vanishing point of cultural intelligibility, the next poem to be discussed addresses itself to men located at one of the very centres of cultural signification. '*An Invitation to my Friends at* Cambridge' is not, strictly speaking, a medical poem, but it registers very clearly the ambivalent attitude toward male learning that shapes the poems in this group and surfaces here and there in moments of confused resentment, of 'doublethink'. Elaine Hobby is certainly right to say that Barker's 'major preoccupation' as a writer is 'women's exclusion from the male world, and from male education', but such a formulation may underplay the extent to which Barker struggles to align herself with male interests and values, especially those associated with learning and the intellectual life.[25] Carol Barash seeks a more nuanced understanding when she observes that the 'speaker's desire for men is entwined with her desire for knowledge', but it is hard to know exactly what 'desire for men' might mean here (*EWP* 182). Perhaps it is more helpful to turn again to language provided by Fuss: the poem charts a 'struggle to negotiate a constantly changing field of ambivalent identifications' (*Identification*, 34). We might say, by way of refining Barash's observation, that the speaker oscillates between an unconcealed envy of male intellectual privilege, verging at times on bitterness, as Williamson

---

[24] Or monstrous. In *BG* Galesia compares the learned woman to a bloated toad: 'Men will not allow it [learning] to be our Sphere, so consequently we can never be suppos'd to move in it gracefully; but like the Toad in the Fable, that affected to swell itself as big as the Ox, and to burst in the Enterprize' (*BG* 37).
[25] Elaine Hobby, *Virtue of Necessity: English Women's Writing 1649–1688* (Ann Arbor: U. of Michigan P., 1989), 161.

has suggested,[26] and a fantasized and unstable identification with an imagined community of learned men. The point can be illustrated by considering some of the ambiguities of the Tree of Knowledge as Barker develops this symbol in the final section of the poem.

Barker plays upon conventional associations of the Tree with transgressive desire and divine punishment, linking prohibitions against female learning with Eve's desire for forbidden knowledge. Speaking at first for womankind the speaker concedes that 'in our Maker's Laws we've made a breach' and that as punishment women are forbidden to 'touch' the fruits that once we 'gather'd' (*PR* 3). The Fall is thus conceived (for women) as a descent into intellectual deprivation and hunger. Hereafter learning will be reserved for men, whose 'kinder fate' is to eat freely at 'Luxurious Banquets of this dainty Fruit' (*PR* 4). Women are left with their unsatisfied and unsatisfiable desires: 'our Eyes | Do serve our longing-Souls to tantalize' (*PR* 3). But as a signifier of transgressive female desire the symbolic Tree generates ambiguities most critics decline to pursue. Jean Martinolich points out, for example, that Barker 'inverts the idea of the Tree of Knowledge as a prohibitive object, a thing to be avoided, and glorifies it as something to be pursued',[27] and Hobby similarly underscores the association of the Tree with the desire of women to 'leave the "Garden" of their confinement' (*Virtue*,162). But both readings sidestep the inconvenient fact that in every version of the poem the Tree is linked not only with desire ('our longing-Souls') but also with female intellectual incapacity. The speaker laments:

> But that the *Tree* of *Knowledge* won't grow here:
> Though in its *culture* I have spent some time,
> Yet it disdains to grow in our cold *Clime*,
> Where it can neither Fruit nor Leaves produce
> Good for its owner, or the publick use.   (*PR* 3)

[26] Marilyn L. Williamson, *Raising Their Voices: British Women Writers, 1650–1750* (Detroit: Wayne State UP, 1990), 104.

[27] Martinolich makes this point in 'Self-Effacement in Patriarchal Education: An Analysis of Milton's Eve and the Narrative Voice in Jane Barker's "A Farewell to Poetry, With a Long Digression on Anatomy" and "An Invitation to my Learned Friends at Cambridge" ', an unpublished paper which furnished the starting place for my own thinking about the medical poems. This chapter has benefited from her perceptive criticisms.

When Barker copied the poem into the Magdalen Manuscript she placed in the margin next to the last line a note, 'learning being usless in women' (fo. 87), and in 1723 she glossed 'our cold *Clime*' as 'A Female Capacity' (*PWS* 95). What are we to make of the deprecatory, even perhaps misogynistic tendency of this paratextual material? Does Barker mean for it to provoke resistance, to invoke a whole unjust cultural inheritance that functions to bind women to an intellectually fallen condition? Or is she articulating without apparent irony or subversive intent the terms of an oppressive gender ideology that women must simply learn to live with?

The remainder of the poem only heightens the ambiguity—or is it doublethink? For at this point a crucial realignment occurs. As if unable or unwilling to sustain the self-extinguishing implications of an identification with female intellectual incapacity, the speaker switches to an identification with her male friends signalled by a pronominal shift from first to second person. The concluding lines focus upon the friends, happily settled at Cambridge, where the male Tree 'most fresh and flourishing do's grow'. Curiously, she now introduces a cluster of arboreal metaphors whose effect is to assimilate the flourishing intellectual attributes of the friends—their wit, philosophy, judgement, fancy, virtues—to the Tree of Learning, from which they are in the end virtually indistinguishable:

> And you in *Wit* grow as its branches high,
> Deep as its *Root* too in *Philosophy*;
> Large as its spreading *Arms* your Reasons grow,
> Close as its *Umbrage* do's your *Judgments* show;
> Fresh as its *Leaves* your sprouting *fancies* are,
> Your *Vertues* as its *Fruits* are bright and fair.   (PR 4)

That these arborescent friends substitute for the lost and unattainable female Tree suggests desire for a full intellectual life too painful to be sustained. The substitutive conclusion would seem to correspond to the interior mechanism Freud had in mind when he observed that the most obvious reaction to the loss of a love-object is 'to identify oneself with it, to replace it from within, as it were, by identification'.[28] For Barker this meant

---

[28] Sigmund Freud, *An Outline of Psycho-Analysis*, qtd. in Fuss, *Identification*, 1.

replacing the lost (since the Fall) possibility of learning with male friends whose intellectual flourishing takes the place of her own thwarted desires.

In these two poems, exclusion from spheres of male medical authority ('Apothecaries') and from institutions of male learning ('An Invitation') is associated with themes of power, invisibility, guilty desire, and self-estrangement, which are themselves linked to the contradictions of gender. When Barker reads the medical establishment through her preoccupation with distinctions of class, however, the effect is quite different. In '*On my Mother and my Lady W——, who both lay sick at the same time under the Hands of Dr.* Paman' (*PR* 42), the speaker identifies unequivocally with elite male medicine, represented by the well-known London physician Dr Henry Paman,[29] against 'Base *Quakery*', showing herself in this context to be a staunch upholder of social and professional hierarchies. 'Ah happy *Paman*', she writes, 'let no *Quack* intrude where thou do'st come, | To crop thy *Fame*, or haste thy *Patients* doom' (*PR* 43). Whatever her resentments over her *own* exclusions as a woman, Barker was no critic of elite medicine in itself; it would probably be a mistake to identify her with a radical critique of learned medicine such as that associated with her contemporary Thomas Sydenham, for example.[30] But no sooner does gender enter the picture than her thinking slides into ambivalence, uncertainty, and weirdly shifting identifications. A striking case in point is her elegy on her brother, depicted (as he is elsewhere in her verse and prose fiction) as an accomplished medical student who died tragically young.[31]

In its mixed messages and uncertain bearing 'On the Death of my Brother' is perhaps the strangest of Barker's medical poems.

[29] According to the *DNB*, Paman (1626–95), a fellow of the College of Physicians from 1687, resided at Lambeth Palace 1677–89, removing when he declined to take the oaths to William III.

[30] For the support of elite men and women for learned medicine as part of the necessary hierarchical order, see Robert L. Martensen, ' "Habit of Reason": Anatomy and Anglicanism in Restoration England', *Bulletin of the History of Medicine*, 66 (Winter 1992), 511–35, esp. 522–3. The duchess of Newcastle vigorously supported elite medicine: to do otherwise would be to support 'Hereticks' (523).

[31] Edward Barker, an Oxford student who had recently completed an MA, almost certainly died in 1675, when Jane was around 23. See Doc. Rec. 19.

It begins conventionally enough: the speaker, occupying the familiar subject-position of the grieving sister, apostrophizes sorrow in the mildly erotic language characteristic of many elegies in terms that might be said to verge on the incestuous, as if to express the immensity of her loss: she invites sorrow to 'embrace' her 'yielding heart', calling her grief 'the faithfull'st Lover I have left' (PR 47). Next—and again in accordance with convention—she praises her brother's medical attainments (his 'growing Art made Death afraid'), depicts in heroic terms his losing battle with death in the form of 'a Feavour' (PR 48), and laments her own terrible loss (PR 49). But when she attempts to 'display' to 'all the World' his 'Matchless worth' (PR 49) the speaker begins to falter, declaring herself unequal to the task of eulogizing her brother. Such moments are not exactly unknown in the elegy, of course, but Barker responds with a strategy all her own: she repeats the words spoken at her brother's funeral by the old doctors whose pronouncements supply the lament with its bizarrely inadequate consolation. 'I cannot blame you for lamenting so', one of the doctors is made to say,

> 'Since better friend no friend did e'er forego;
> 'A publick Sorrow for this loss is due,
> 'The Nation surely, Madam, mourns with you.   (PR 50)

That the female mourner resents her displacement from the discourse of public grief is the suggestion of a disgruntled aside that calls attention to her own erasure: the assembled physicians, she earlier remarks, 'seem'd to grudge me in their grief a part' (PR 50).

What is one to make of an elegy in which the grieving subject relinquishes her own elegiac voice? Kate Lilley argues that it is not a relinquishment at all. Reading 'On the Death of my Brother' in the light of the seventeenth-century familial elegy by women, she finds Barker driven by a dual need to legitimize a woman's private grief and to rescue her sorrow from male appropriations: the poem 'calls for and dramatizes a public and professional mourning' while privileging the grief of a sister over that of the old doctors. In such a reading the concluding lines represent not a silencing or a surrender of poetic authority but rather a rhetorical resolution of her fear of male usurpation. Their speech constitutes 'a public, professional endorsement of her own familial priority as the authentic origin of mourning'.[32] This interpretation is both plausible and appealing, and yet there are surely equally plausible ways of reading these lines. Older strains of feminist criticism could readily see in them a deference to masculine authority that betrays gendered anxieties of author- ship; a more recent kind of criticism might, by a small adjustment of the critical lens, discover that what looks like feminine deference conceals a bold power claim—'The Nation surely, Madam, mourns with you'—and then argue that Barker deliberately appro- priates a masculine voice so as to lend proper public gravitas to her private, feminine grief. But I remain struck by the note of aggriev- ement within the grief, by the noise of an only partly concealed resentment directed toward members of a medical 'old boys' network who 'grudge me in their grief a part'. However one decides to read Barker's intentions, the ending of 'On the Death of my Brother' would seem to give muted expression to the confused anger that results when the female subject confronts male medical authority and finds herself vanishing into cultural unintelligibility.

The most complex rendering of female subjectivity to be considered here is found in the final poem in the medical group, 'Anatomy', an ambitious attempt to turn a body of academic anatomical knowledge into verse. This poem, Barker's most sustained examination of the double circuit travelled by the learned woman's ambivalent identifications, throws light on late seventeenth-century understandings of the body's interior, on lay understandings of recent medical discoveries, and on the way an educated woman in the post-Harvey era sought to assimilate the findings of the new physiology to older Galenic models. 'Anatomy' is important on so many levels that it deserves a section of its own.

'A long degression on anatomy'

In *A Patch-Work Screen for the Ladies* Galesia offers an account of the circumstances which occasioned the writing of

---

[32] Kate Lilley, 'True State Within: Women's Elegy 1640–1700', in Isobel Grundy and Susan Wiseman (eds.), *Women, Writing, History 1640–1740* (Athens: U. of Georgia P., 1992), 72–92 (83).

'Anatomy'.[33] She professes herself unable to explain why she undertook so odd a venture, '*Physick* being as little reducible' to verse 'as *Law*' (*PWS* 85)—the allusion is to Ovid's rendering into verse of law—but is able to trace the beginnings of the project to the period in her life when she was nearly undone by the unexpected death of her brother.[34] Devastated, she sought relief in study of his medical textbooks, returning obsessively to pages which bore markings in his hand and lingering in tears over his notes. 'I read those Books he had most studied', she recalls, 'where I often found his Hand-writing, by way of Remarks, which always caus'd a new Flux of Tears' (*PWS* 84). When at last she began to emerge from her depression she decided to render into verse portions of the books 'on which I had seen my Brother most intent': 'I at last resolv'd to begin with a Body of *Anatomy*, and between whiles, to reduce it into Verse' (*PWS* 85), almost as if such an undertaking would enable her to sustain contact with her brother. This is a poignant anecdote, subtle in its understanding of the logic of grief, and has about it a feeling of truth that leads one to believe Barker was working from her own experience. It is, therefore, fascinating to discover that in writing 'Anatomy' Barker was almost certainly drawing upon a textbook that Edward Barker might well have studied.

The book is Caspar Bartholin's *Anatomicae institutiones corporis humani*, a dissecting manual used by university students across Europe. The 'institutions', first published in 1611, is said to have been 'the best standard anatomical text then available'.[35] From 1633 it was specially printed for use by Oxford students,[36] and in 1641 was issued by Caspar's son Thomas (1616–80) in a revised form designed to take account of such recent findings as Harvey's circulation of the blood. The

[33] My discussion uses the text revised for *PWS*.

[34] For some cultural dimensions of the poem's preoccupation with mortality and loss, see Jonathan Sawday, *The Body Emblazoned: Dissection and the Human Body in Renaissance Culture* (London and New York: Routledge, 1995). He briefly discusses the poem on 268.

[35] Robert G. Frank, Jr., *Harvey and the Oxford Physiologists: Scientific Ideas and Social Interaction* (Berkeley: U. of California P., 1980), 26.

[36] K. F. Russell, *British Anatomy 1525–1800: A Bibliography of Works published in Britain, America and on the Continent*, 2nd edn. (Winchester: St Paul's Bibliographies, 1987), xxiii. ˋ

updated manual, which corrected many Galenic errors in the light of seventeenth-century physiological discoveries, was to prove foundational for several generations of revisionist 'moderns' whose experiments and observations would move Western medicine further and further from its Galenic roots, a paradigm shift which forms an important part of the background of the poem. Since Barker knew some Latin, she may have studied an untranslated version of Bartholin,[37] or she may have consulted the Culpeper and Cole translation which came out in the 1660s.[38] My own study of this translation shows that in writing her 'long degression on anatomy' Barker followed fairly closely the content and arrangement of the updated *Anatomy*, but introduced some significant departures.

The poem, which follows the female poet-speaker on a journey through the anatomical body, takes as its starting point the anatomical lore set forth by Bartholin—either Caspar (1585–1629), his son Thomas (1616–80), or some combination of the two as represented by the revised manual first printed in 1641—who figures as the speaker's first mentor-guide.

> Now BARTHOLINE, the first of all this Row,[39]
> Does to me *Nature's Architecture* show;
> How the *Foundation*, first, of *Earth* is laid;
> Then, how the *Pillars* of *Strong-Bones* are made.
>
> (*PWS* 86)

For both the macrostructure of the anatomical body and the progression through its chief parts Barker followed Bartholin: her three bodily 'courts' correspond to what he called the three bellies—the lowest belly, 'commonly called Abdomen or the

---

[37] In Mag. MS Barker supplied Latin glosses for her anatomy poem along with the information that she 'learnt latin by reading the latin poets' (fo. 127). The *Anatomicae institutiones corporis humani* (1611) was reprinted five times. Thomas's revised version, *Anatomia, ex Caspari Bartholini parentis Institutionibus*, acknowledging the work of Harvey, produced with the help of Jan de Wales, was first printed in Leiden in 1641; 2nd and 3rd editions came out in 1645 and 1651.

[38] *Bartholinus Anatomy; Made from the Precepts of his Father*, trans. Nicholas Culpeper and Abdiah Cole (London: John Streator, 1668). Russell's *Bibliography* records a 1662 edition.

[39] Row of classical medical tomes, that is. The earliest extant version of the poem begins by naming classical medical writers—Aristotle, Hippocrates, Gallen, Socrates, and (the legendary) Aesculapius—whom she hails as her 'new Acquaintance' (*PR* 99). It is hard to know why Socrates is included in this list.

Paunch', which contains the liver and 'Natural parts'; the middle belly or chest, which contains the heart and 'vital parts'; and the uppermost belly or head, which contains the brain and 'Animal parts'.⁴⁰ Barker's interior journey begins in the abdomen (the 'first court'), moves on to the chest (the 'second court'), and then to the brain (the 'third court')—although in a crucial addendum that amounts to a rewriting of both Bartholin and his Galenic models, Barker has her poet-speaker return to the heart as if to a newly discovered site of corporeal vitality. The language, in the early parts especially, echoes Bartholin as well. Four of his early chapters, for example—'Of the Skin', 'Of Fat' ('De Pinguedine'), 'Of Membranes' (the *membrana carnosa*), and 'Of the Muscles in General'—she compresses into four swift lines: 'The *Walls* consist of *Carneous-Parts* within, | The Out-side *pinguid*, overlay'd with *Skin*; | The *Fret-work*, *Muscles*, *Arteries* and *Veins*, | With their Implexures' (*PWS* 86).

Twenty-five lines into the poem a crucial shift occurs. The poet-speaker, up to this point a dutiful student of 'Bartholine', now acquires a new pair of mentor-conductors, William Harvey (1578–1657) and Thomas Willis (1621–75), who will themselves be joined at the poem's close by Richard Lower (1631–91). Exponents of the new physiology, these three leading medical theorists from Barker's own country and century at once exemplify and represent the displacement of the Galenic 'ancients' by the scientific 'moderns'. When in 1628 Harvey announced the circulation of the blood, generally acknowledged to be 'the single most important discovery in the history of the physiological sciences', he inaugurated a period of intensive medical investigation, much of it centred at Oxford, from the late 1640s to the middle of the 1670s—when Barker may have

---

⁴⁰ *Bartholinus Anatomy*, sig. D2v. The sequence corresponds to that used during actual anatomical demonstrations, which began in the abdominal cavity so as to reduce the risk of putrefaction. In 1624 Richard Tomlin specified as part of the terms of the Tomlins Readership in Anatomy at Oxford that dissections were to proceed in the following manner: 'One day, or at most two, after death four hours had to be spent in demonstrating the organs that decayed first—'the partes commonly called Naturall videlicet Liver Spleene Stomacke Guttes &c.' The 'Vitall' organs—'Hart Lunges &c.'—were demonstrated the following day, and on the next day 'the Animall partes and faculties videlicet the Brayne &c',: H. M. Sinclair and A. H. T. Robb-Smith, *A Short History of Anatomical Teaching in Oxford* (Oxford: Oxford UP, 1950), 11–12.

begun the poem—during which time 'English anatomists and chemists completely refashioned our knowledge of the function of the human body'.[41] The appearance at the site of anatomical instruction of these three medical researchers signals a shift from an ancient anatomical orientation (body as structure) to a modern physiological one (body as function).

Their appearance also marks a decisive transformation in the speaker-student's relation to male pedagogical authority. With Bartholin she is a passive recipient of instruction, her proper role being to receive what her conductor imparts: he 'Does to me *Nature*'s *Architecture* show'. When Harvey and Willis take over, the student-mentor relationship loosens and ancient hierarchies begin to relax, as the ambiguous word *bid* ('WILLIS and HARVEY bid me follow them') may suggest. (*Bid* may imply either a command or an invitation.) The language becomes more expansive, metaphorical, even a bit whimsical. The stomach, Bartholin's '*Ventriculus*'—a 'little Belly' (18)— becomes Barker's '*Kitchen* call'd *Ventriculus*'; beneath it, approached through the pylorus, is what Bartholin called 'the guts' and Barker 'the *Dining-Room*' where, charmingly, 'the *Lacteans* take their sweet Repast' (in Bartholin the lactæans, or venæ lacteæ, are somewhat inelegantly said to 'suck Chyle' out of the gut (24)). The shading of the old active/passive mentor/student relation into something more reciprocal is also reflected in the shift in pronouns from *they* and *me* ('*They* brought *me* to the first & largest Court') to first-person plural:

> We view'd the Kitchen called Ventriculus;
> Then pass'd *we* through the Space call'd Pylorus;
> .   .   .   .
> This & much more *we* saw; from thence *we* went
> Into the next Court by a small Ascent.
> (*PWS* 87, 88; emph. mine)

And then, remarkably, the *we* is replaced by an *I*, as the astonished speaker gazes at the heart, which seems an endlessly self-renewing fountain, marvellous and unaccountable. Her own wonderment in the face of this 'strange Prodigy', this

---

[41] Frank, *Harvey*, xii.

'*Fountain* like a *Furnace*',[42] becomes momentarily the subject of the poem:

> Bless me! said I; what Rarities are here!
> A *Fountain* like a *Furnace* did appear,
> Still boiling o'er, and running out so fast,
> That one wou'd think its Eflux, cou'd not last:
> Yet it sustain'd no Loss, as I cou'd see,
> Which made me think it a strange Prodigy.

Harvey is now made to address her directly.

> Come on, says HARVEY, don't stand gazing here;
> But follow me, and I thy Doubts will clear.
>
> (*PWS* 88)

She is encouraged to extrapolate knowledge from her direct experience of the functioning body, as Harvey invites her to discover, as he did through his own experiments—through, that is, the evidence of her eyes and her own reasoning upon what she sees—the truth of the circulation of the blood.

As the speaker and her mentors now begin their 'Journey with the *Blood*', the metaphorical framework shifts to accommodate new physiological understandings of the body. The architectural metaphors of the Bartholin section—the three 'courts', the 'foundation' of earth, 'pillars' of bone, and decorative 'fretwork' of entwined arteries and veins—yield to images of motion, energy, fluidity, and labyrinthine indeterminacy. The traditional anatomical body-as-structure—stable, permanent, intricate, fixed, knowable—is transformed into a mysterious territory through which veins and arteries, sinuous streams, wind as if through a maze:

> Then we began our Journey with the *Blood*,
> Trac'd the Meanders of its Purple Flood.
> Thus we thro' many Labyrinths did pass,
> In such, I am sure, old *Dædalus* ne'er was.
> Sometimes i'th' Out-Works, sometimes the *First-Court*,
> Sometimes i'th' *Third* these winding Streams would sport—
>
> (*PWS* 89)

---

[42] The image of the boiling fountain-furnace goes back to the ancient medical writings, where the heart was understood to be the body's furnace or internal oven, that is, its main source of heat; Bartholin's *Anatomy* depicted the heart as a '*Fountain of Heat*' (100).

and the speaker, now an explorer of the interior, is thus invited
to trace the 'Meanders of its Purple Flood', an image found in
other poems in praise of Harvey.[43] Eventually the blood-trav-
ellers return to the place where they began, and it now falls to
the student-speaker to draw the lesson. The shift from *we* to *I* is
again worth noting:

> And after some small Traverses about,
> Came to the Place where *we* before set out:
> Then *I* perceiv'd, how HARVEY all made good,
> By th' Circles of the Circulating Blood,
> As Fountains have their Water from the Sea,
> To which again they do themselves convey.
>
> (*PWS* 90; emph. mine)

In her evolving relation to both her guide-mentors and the
anatomical body, the speaker thus replicates transformations in
the individual's relation to various forms of authority, both
ancient and modern. She begins in passive deference to
Bartholin, figured within the poem less as a human being than
as a textbook, but before long submission to the authority of
the written text gives way to something more akin to an intellectual partnership with actual human beings nearer at hand,
Harvey and Willis; they are joined at the close by Richard
Lower, who is made to address the speaker as 'dear *Cousin*'.[44]
In the process we are invited to watch the speaker pursuing her
own desires for knowledge, figured in her rapt gaze at the
strange prodigy of the boiling fountain. A good inductive
Baconian, she is eager to break away from habits of mind
grounded in submission to written authority and embrace

[43] John Collop's 'On Doctor Harvey' from *Poesis Rediviva* (1656) celebrates
Harvey as an extraordinary explorer sailing interior seas: 'Thou set'st up sail,
swim'st through the purple flood, | Which blush'd before, 'cause never understood.
| Thou circlest through our *Microcosm*, and we | Learn more then th' world, our
selvs, new worlds by thee': Conrad Hilberry, *The Poems of John Collop* (Madison:
U. of Wisconsin P., 1962), 102. Cowley's 'Ode. *Upon* Dr. *Harvey*', in A. R. Waller
(ed.), *The English Writings of Abraham Cowley*, 2 vols. (Cambridge: Cambridge UP,
1905–6), i. 416, has Harvey pursue 'long-hunted' nature into the very bloodstream:
'She leap't at last into the winding streams of blood; | Of mans *Meander* all the
Purple reaches made, | Till at the heart she stay'd . . .'. For a discussion of the
Cowley poem, see Sawday, *Body Emblazoned*, 239–41.

[44] Lower, from Tremeer, Cornwall, was related to Barker on her mother's
(Connock) side. See Doc. Rec. 31 n. 17.

discoveries stemming from observation and experimental investigation—rather like her mentor Willis, who declared that he would credit only 'Nature and ocular demonstrations'.[45] 'Then I', the speaker says, the metrical stress falling squarely on the perceiving *I*, 'perceiv'd, how HARVEY all made good'. In this area, at least, Barker adopts a progressive stance: as regards scientific discovery she is squarely on the side of the moderns.

'Anatomy' is then a complex journey through medical history as well as interior space, a progress from ancient to modern models of the body in which the speaker, depicting herself as a student of learned medicine in the post-Harveyan era, explores her own relation to both inherited systems of Galenic authority and the new epistemological modes associated with the Oxford physiologists of the preceding decades. Yet certain inconsistencies within this general pattern suggest that Barker may not have entirely understood the implications of her material or, as I prefer to think, that she deliberately misrepresented her sources. I should like briefly to consider the most glaring of these inconsistencies, her curiously out-of-date treatment of the liver. Since few of my readers will be familiar with the shift of conceptual models at issue here, I shall briefly review seventeenth-century thinking on the subject.

Liver-function constituted something of a crux in mid-seventeenth-century medical thought. According to traditional Galenic doctrine, the liver was the body's main blood-making ('sanguificating') organ. Bartholin was quite unequivocal on this point: the 'Action of the Liver is Sanguification' (35); the liver is 'the Organ of Blood-making, and the beginning of the Veins' (32). What this means is that blood was thought to originate in the liver and flow outward through the veins. As Phineas Fletcher puts it in *Purple Island*, the veins 'rising from the liver' are 'appointed to contein, concoct and distribute the bloud'; 'from the liver rise all the springs of bloud, which runnes in the veins'.[46] (Blood was known to be transported by the

---

[45] Willis, preface to *Anatomy of the Brain and Nerves*; qtd. in Martensen, 'Habit of Reason', 514.

[46] Qtd. in Marjorie Hope Nicolson, *The Breaking of the Circle: Studies in the Effect of the 'New Science' Upon Seventeenth-Century Poetry*, rev. edn. (New York: Columbia UP, 1960), 137–8. She notes, 138, that the passages from *Purple Island*, published five years after the publication of Harvey's discoveries, show no awareness of the doctrine of circulation.

arteries as well, but they were thought to constitute a separate system designed to deliver to the brain a more highly charged blood from the left side of the heart.) Harvey's discovery that blood circulates through the veins and arteries, its movement driven by the action of the heart, rendered obsolete the Galenic view of the liver and veins, forcing theorists to locate blood production elsewhere. Richard Lower, for example, in *Tractatus de Corde*, a book mentioned in *Patch-Work Screen*, removed blood production to the heart.[47] Although the conservative view of the 'sanguificating' liver persisted in some medical texts into the 1670s—the obstetrical writer Jane Sharp, for example, described the liver as a 'fountain of *blood*'[48]—by 1676 Charles Goodall could declare in his account of the Royal College of Physicians that removal of 'sanguification' from the liver was one of those discoveries that had 'obtain'd the universal consent of all the ingenious of our Faculty'.[49] Barker's description of the liver as 'Sanguificating the whole mass of *Chyle*' and then 'pour[ing] it forth to mix with other *Blood*' (*PWS* 88) represents, in other words, an understanding her medically learned contemporaries would have found out of date.

Perhaps Barker was hedging her bets, as the editors of *Kissing the Rod* suggest, like Milton—unsure whether the Ptolemaic or Copernican system of the planets was true—or perhaps she was simply unable to assimilate fully the implications of the medical texts she read. But the latter conclusion sits oddly with other things we know. Harvey's views on circulation had long since been accepted within the medical and larger learned community, and as early as the 1650s ideas of blood circulation had begun to enter poetic discourse.[50] One of the first to invoke Harveyan ideas was Margaret Cavendish, whose '*The* Motion *of the*

---

[47] See R. T. Gunther, *Early Science in Oxford*, ix: De Corde *by Richard Lower, London 1669*, trans. K. J. Franklin (Oxford: for the Subscribers, 1932), 94–5. This account leaves out the liver altogether.

[48] Audrey Eccles, *Obstetrics and Gynaecology in Tudor and Stuart England* (London and Canberra: Croom Helm, 1982), 21. She reports that obstetrical handbooks did not incorporate Harvey until the late 1670s.

[49] Charles Goodall, *The Colledge of Physicians Vindicated, And the true State of Physick in this Nation Faithfully Represented* (London: Walter Kettilby, 1676), 46. He credits Glisson with this discovery. Goodall's son Charles contributed verses to the second part of *Poetical Recreations* under the name 'Mr. C.G. of Æton-Colledge'; he may be the author of the commendatory verse signed by 'C.G.'

[50] See Nicolson, *Breaking of the Circle*, ch. 4, esp. 130–41.

Blood' was printed in *Poems and Fancies* (1653) the same year that Harvey's *de Motu* first appeared in an English translation. (Her poem begins: '*Some* by *Industry* of *Learning* found, | That all the *Blood* like to the *Sea* runs round: | From two great *Arteries* the *Blood* it runs | Through all the *Veines*, to the same backe comes'.)[51] Traditional notions of the 'sanguificating' liver had been discredited by, among others, Harvey and Lower, men with whom Barker explicitly aligns herself in this poem. In *Patch-Work Screen* she underscores that alignment by identifying them as the medical writers Galesia studied and most admired: 'I made such Progress in *Anatomy*, as to understand *Harvey's* Circulation of the Blood, and *Lower's* Motion of the Heart' (82).[52] Moreover, there is no gainsaying Barker's impressive command of the materials in Bartholin's *Anatomicae institutiones* and, what is even more important here, her incorporation of post-Harveyan elements into the Bartholinian framework of 'Anatomy'.[53] She showed herself quite capable, in other words, of making sense of the findings of contemporary medical science when it suited her purposes.

We should at least consider then that her 'misreading' of liver function was a calculated effect. This possibility assumes a more subtle and artistically deliberative Barker than most critics

---

[51] Margaret Cavendish, *Poems, and Fancies: Written by the Right Honourable, the Lady Margaret Countesse of Newcastle* (London: J. Martin and J. Allestrye, 1653), 42. Habitually impatient with fact and sensory observation, the famously arachnid Cavendish quickly begins to spin a speculative web, discovering in the circulation of the blood an analogy for understanding the weather as a circulatory process—with sunbeams, each a '*blazing Ship*', carrying heat ('*warme Nourishment*') to earth and returning to the sun with moisture. In a marginal gloss Cavendish explains the process of rain-production in terms of human physiology: '*When the* Sun *draws up more* Moisture *then it can digest, it turns to Raine, or Wind*' (43).

[52] 'My Time and Thoughts were taken up in *Harvey, Willis*, and such-like Authors, which my Brother help'd me to understand and relish', she says on the next page, adding, ruefully, studies such as these 'serv'd to make me unfit Company for every body' (*PWS* 83).

[53] She follows Bartholin in her reference to the 'modern' lacteals (discovered in the 17th cent.) but goes beyond him in including a reference to bile. The latter may be a nod toward Francis Glisson, whose account of sanguification, according to Charles Goodall, *The Royal College of Physicians of London Founded and Established by Law* (London: for Walter Kettilby, 1684), sig. Ss4v, represented bile as formed by 'continual concoction of the bloud'. Barker may have had something like this in mind when she depicted the liver as 'severing the *Crural Parts* from *Bile*' (*PWS* 88).

would now grant, but arguably what looks at first like waffling on her part may represent a strategy for dramatizing the struggle to accommodate new scientific findings to older conceptual models belonging to the classical Galenic tradition.[54] Thus understood the poem's inconsistencies could be said to figure the confused, shifting, and contradictory play of scientific understandings during a time of paradigm shift. That Barker was capable of such subtle intent finds some support in her most intriguing revision. In the earliest version of the poem the mentor-role played by Thomas Willis, a pioneer of modern understandings of the nervous system, was assigned to the Leiden professor 'Walæus', or Jan de Wale (1604–49), an advocate of the new ideas about circulation and one of Harvey's earliest defenders. Their names were often linked. Bartholin, for example, credits '*Harvey* and *Walæus*' together with discovery of the circulation of the blood.[55] Given Barker's preoccupation in 'Anatomy' with new understandings of blood and circulation, Walæus would seem a natural choice for mentor.

Why, then, starting with the Magdalen Manuscript, would she replace Walæus with Thomas Willis (1621–75), a researcher-physician best known for his work on the brain and nerves?[56] Biographical circumstances may offer some explanation. Willis died in 1675, the same year Edward Barker did, and he had been connected with Christ Church, where Edward received his MA, also in 1675.[57] His collected works were first

---

54 I owe this reading to a suggestion from Harold Cook.

55 Introduction, *Bartholinus*, sig. D. Walæus assisted Thomas Bartholin in the production of the revised manual, in which he makes frequent appearances as an authority; the volume concludes with two letters from him on the motion of the chyle and the blood.

56 Thomas Willis (1621–75), England's leading scientific physician at the time of his death, Sedleian Professor of Natural Philosophy at Oxford from 1660, and one of the founders of the Royal Society, published in 1664 the fullest account to date of the nervous system. Barker appears to echo him in her description of the brain as 'the *fertile Womb*, | From whence the *Spirits-Animal* do come: | Which are mysteriously ingender'd here, | Of Spirits, from *arterial Blood* and Air' (*PWS* 89). For an assessment of Willis's intellectual influence in the 1670s, see Martensen, 'Habit of Reason'. The failure of Barash, *EWP* 193, to recognize 'womb' as referring to the brain leads her to misrepresent the passage as a 'controversy over links between the female reproductive body and the nature of creativity'.

57 Richard Lower (1631–91) was also associated with Oxford for fifteen years beginning in 1649, when he was elected to a studentship at Christ Church. He was Willis's student, assistant, and collaborator, deriving from him an interest in the circulatory system. They remained associated until Willis's death in 1675.

translated in the 1680s; Barker might be expected to seek them out, for intellectual reasons as well as for their associations with her brother. Willis was, moreover, the sort of person that, politically and ideologically, Barker would have admired: a learned man who fought for the King during the wars and suffered for his loyalty. In this he was a good match with Harvey, who had been physician to Charles I until 1647 and, after 1642, took refuge in royalist Oxford.

Yet one is tempted to speculate that the turn to Willis may be connected to Barker's perception of herself as a learned woman as well. Medical historians point out that Willis's emphasis on the primacy of the brain and nerves, a 'departure from the contemporary English preoccupation with the blood', introduced into scientific thought a 'neurocentric' model for understanding of the economy of the human organism.[58] The Willisian brain-centred model may have had special implications for women, traditionally thought to be driven to irrationality and emotional excess by the all-powerful, centrally controlling, and hysteria-prone womb. To install the sexless brain at the centre of the hitherto womb-propelled female body was to put in place a physiological paradigm that allowed for the possibility of less reductive models for comprehending female nature. Calling attention to the importance of this shift, Anthony Fletcher seems at first to be overstating the case when he suggests that the neurocentric model may have served to promote the phenomenon he calls the 'new morally responsible woman', but in light of Barker's substitution of Willis for Wallæus, it is fascinating to consider that such a shift may indeed have offered women a chance to 'make some kind of stab, puny as it might be beside that of men, at adopting rationality in their personal relationships', an opportunity to contemplate less hystericized, more cerebral modes of female being.[59] The removal of the blood-and-heart man for the new brain-and-nerves man in the revised version of Barker's anatomy poem may represent an approving nod toward a paradigm which implied a whole new range of possibilities for odd

[58] Martensen, "Habit of Reason', 515.
[59] Anthony Fletcher, 'The Decline and Fall of the Lusty Woman' [rev. of Olwen Hufton's *The Prospect Before Her*], *TLS* (15 Dec. 1995), 8.

women—including one who undertook to write a 'long degression on anatomy'.

'Desire of Knowledge, cost us very dear'

For this erudite 'degression' is, inevitably, a meditation on the problems of identity confronting the woman of learning compelled always to regard herself through the lens of cultural definitions of intellectually deficient femininity. Thus far I have not mentioned the ten-line passage early in the poem in which, unsettlingly, the student-speaker expatiates in her own voice on women's intellectual inferiority. It is not at first clear that the student has taken over the discourse from her mentor-conductor; indeed, it comes as something of a shock to discover from the reference to '*our Sex*' midway through the passage that the hitherto mute female student is now speaking, arguing from the Fall (' 'cause *our Sex* precipitated first') for the inevitability of female intellectual deprivation ('*Ignorance*, e'er since, became our Share').

> For 'twas the *Eye*, that first discern'd the *Food*,
> As *pleasing to itself*, for eating *good*,
> Then was persuaded, that it wou'd refine
> The *half-wise Soul*, and make it all Divine.
> But O how dearly *Wisdom's* bought with Sin,
> Which shuts out *Grace*; lets *Death & Darkness* in.
> And 'cause *our Sex* precipitated first,
> To Pains, and Ignorance *we* since are curs'd.
> Desire of *Knowledge*, cost *us* very dear;
> For *Ignorance*, e'er since, became our Share.
>
> (*PWS* 87)

It is easy enough to read this passage as a complex piece of feminist resistance, a sly ventriloquizing of discourses of feminine subservience which serves to mock and undermine the ideology of male intellectual supremacy that underpins the surrounding poem.[60] But I am struck by the way other elements of the poem

[60] Support for such a reading might be found in Joseph Wittreich's finding in *Feminist Milton* (Ithaca and London: Cornell UP, 1987), 54, that in the debates of the 1680s over received notions of male supremacy 'Milton's Eve is enabling for women, a figure through whom they can advance and whom they can use to benefit their own polemical positions'.

resist this interpretation. In a provocative analysis Jean Martinolich argues that this lesson in anatomy puts on display what the seventeenth century would have regarded as the proper relationship between the female learner and male figures of authority. That is to say, Barker places her student before Bartholin in a position of passivity all too familiar to seventeenth-century women accustomed to an education on the lines set down by Vives and the conduct-book writers that followed him: Bartholin speaks, she listens. She is then passed on to other male mentors, encouraged to see through their eyes and submit to their views. When the student-speaker slips free of male control long enough to gaze in wonder at the workings of the heart, Harvey, mindful perhaps of the dangerous susceptibilities of the female eye, admonishes her not to 'stand gazing here'. Even when she pauses to moralize in the most orthodox terms on the dire consequences for women of the Fall, her discourse goes unattended—'But as I was inlarging on this Theme, | WILLIS and HARVEY bid me follow them'—and when intellectual controversy breaks out around her, it is Harvey who 'by Fact and Reason' settles the dispute. Barker's regulated female subject, Martinolich concludes, is subordinated from beginning to end to male discourse and male authority.[61]

If this analysis is reliable, and I must say I find it compelling, then the seemingly misogynistic endorsement of the story of Eve's punishment inserted by Barker in her learned digression on anatomy may stand as an ambiguous parable about the self-doubts, the 'doublethink' that afflicts an intellectual woman in a cultural order that renders her at once, paradoxically, invisible and monstrous. Although Barker tried to write her way into visibility, to enter by way of verse into real and imagined learned communities, she ended up producing, in the medical poems in particular, a body of work that speaks on its lower frequencies about the guilt, confusion, and self-distrust experienced by women at a time when female refusals of ignorance inspired deep suspicion, not least in learned women themselves.

[61] Martinolich, 'Self-Effacement'.

PART II

1685–1701

3

Catholicism, 'our holy King', and St-Germain

JANE BARKER left behind two considerable bodies of verse. The first, the coterie verse preserved in *Poetical Recreations* (1688), shows a young woman engaged in sociable verse exchange with a network of male friends as a way of sustaining her self-image as a woman of intellectual and literary attainment. The second, occasional and political verse written for the most part during Barker's fifteen years of exile (1689–1704) at the Stuart court at St-Germain-en-Laye to circulate within the exile community, is the subject of the present chapter. Bitter, righteous, fiercely pro-Stuart, the St-Germain poems offer a picture of a devoted Jacobite of middle years, a Catholic convert and political exile, who sought recognition at the Stuart court-in-exile and, what is more extraordinary, felt herself obliged and authorized to compose a substantial verse-history intended to expose the 'madness and mallice' of the times.

The St-Germain verse is compiled in the first two parts of the three-part Magdalen Manuscript.[1] Part One, a collection of twenty political poems 'Refering to the times' said to be 'Occasionaly writ according to the different circumstance of time and place' (fo. 7), was completed by late 1700. Internal evidence suggests most of the poems were begun earlier, probably between 1685 and 1691 or so. Part Two consists of twenty-seven complimentary and occasional verses written for the most part at St-Germain, many as part of a campaign for notice at the court-in-exile.[2] (The third part, the selection of 'corrected'

---

[1] Magdalen MS 343, Magdalen College Oxford. A selection, with textual apparatus, can be found in my *The Poems of Jane Barker: The Magdalen Manuscript* (Oxford: Magdalen College Occasional Paper 3, 1998). Sixteen poems from the second part are reprinted in Wilson.

[2] The title-page of Part Two indicates the 'greatest part' of these verses 'were

versions of the *Poetical Recreations* verse discussed in Chapter
1, will not concern us here.) Taken together, *Poetical
Recreations* and the Magdalen Manuscript constitute important
and barely explored sources for the study of women's poetic
practices in the late seventeenth century. They also exhibit two
phases in the literary career of a woman who began as a
genteel—if eccentric—provincial amateur and evolved, after the
trauma of 1688–9, into a political poet and later a Jacobite
novelist whose aim, explicit or (as became increasingly the case)
covert, was to vindicate Jacobite truth from the aspersions of its
many enemies.

   The discussion begins with an incident from the last years of
Barker's life involving cancer, a holy king, and an 'od' present,
turns attention to the verse-chronicle she assembled in 1700 to
proclaim the imminent triumph of Stuart history, and then
sketches two additional contexts for the St-Germain verse—her
conversion to Catholicism and ambiguous relation to the Stuart
court—before taking up the question of literary authority. I
analyse Barker's authority as a poet in relation to Jacobite politics, especially what has been called the politics of paranoia
among the exiled Stuart followers.[3] My overarching argument
is that from the 1690s Barker wrote to supply the exiles of her
generation with a mythology of banished righteousness.
Depicting herself and her fellow exiles as driven by 'cursed
orange' to 'wander vagabons alone',[4] she creates fictions of
persecution, banishment, suffering, and heroic fidelity designed
to sustain a people in diaspora and turn the bleakness of exile
into an affirmation of Jacobite ideals.[5] In Fidelia, a persona
created for the St-Germain poems and found nowhere else in the
surviving works, she creates an exemplary figure, a Catholic

writ since the author was in France' (fo. 39), which would appear to date this group
to no later than 1704, when Barker returned to England. The latest poem datable
with any certainty is an elegy on the death of James II, who died 5 Sept. 1701.

   [3] Edward Gregg, 'The Politics of Paranoia', in Eveline Cruickshanks and Jeremy
Black (eds.), *The Jacobite Challenge* (Edinburgh: John Donald, 1988), 42–56.

   [4] 'A dialogue between Fidelia and her little nephew, Martius', fo. 66v.

   [5] My discussion of Barker's use of exemplary suffering in her Jacobite texts is
indebted to Valerie Rumbold's analysis of Mary Caesar's attempt to assimilate loss
and disappointment to her belief in the ultimate triumph of Jacobitism: see 'The
Jacobite vision of Mary Caesar', in Isobel Grundy and Susan Wiseman (eds.),
Women, Writing, History 1640–1740 (Athens: U. of Georgia P., 1992), 178–98.

convert and Stuart loyalist able to remain staunch even when the cost is deprivation and poverty.[6] In the seemingly autobiographical St-Germain verse Barker composes stories of sacrificial devotion congenial to the outlook of other uncompromising Jacobite exiles, fashioning myths that express in equal measure the virtuous ideals and shared paranoia of the tribe.

An 'od' present

In 1730, two years before her death just short of 80, Barker sent to an unnamed recipient what many will agree is an 'od' present: a tumour expelled years earlier from her breast. She sent the tumour, or what remained of it, to a lady, probably Mother Lucy Theresa Joseph, prioress of Augustinians in Bruges, whom Barker may have known many years earlier when, as Lady Lucy Herbert, she lodged at the palace of St-Germain.[7] The letter accompanying this strange offering rehearses the progress of the cancer, as Barker thought it,[8] from origins to cure: it is a remarkable piece of clinical observation, clear, exact, and vivid, if by our lights somewhat grotesque.[9] The tumour first appeared 'in form of a grain of oatmeal' when

[6] Toni Bowers argues differently in 'Jacobite Difference and the Poetry of Jane Barker', *ELH* 64 (1997), 857–69, where she heavily stresses what she sees as Barker's doubts about the Jacobite project. Needless to say I do not agree that Barker is a 'deeply equivocal' Jacobite (868).

[7] According to Henrietta Tayler, *Lady Nithsdale and her Family* (London: Lindsay Drummond, [1939],12, Lady Lucy Herbert, daughter of the duke of Powis, lived at St-Germain until Feb. 1693, when she entered the convent at Bruges; she was there professed June 1693, aged 24.

[8] 'I knew it to be a cancer, and therfore looked upon it as a deaths head, and so resolved to let it work its will, or rathe[r] the will of god, only addressd, my prayrs, to our holy King, touching it with his blood which I had on a little rag.' It was probably a cyst.

[9] The account is one of an extremely small number of texts from before our own century in which a woman comments upon her breast disease, the most famous being Frances Burney's harrowing account of her mastectomy in 1811. For discussions of this account, see Julia Epstein, 'Writing the Unspeakable: Fanny Burney's Mastectomy and the Fictive Body', *Representations*, 16 (Fall 1986), 131–66, and *The Iron Pen: Frances Burney and the Politics of Women's Writing* (Madison: U. of Wisconsin P., 1989), ch. 2; and John Wiltshire, 'Fanny Burney's Face, Madame D'Arblay's Veil', in Marie Mulvey Roberts and Roy Porter (eds.), *Literature and Medicine during the Eighteenth Century* (London and New York: Routledge, 1993), 245–65.

it caused 'great iching and between whiles, pricking and shooting' and then emerged 'from under its little mole-hill' until, by degrees, 'its whole vile body' worked free of her breast and hung 'by a little string like a white thred'. Of this extrusion, we learn, there were 'divers witnesses', some of whom urged her to clip the little string. She steadily refused, and rightly so, for in time the dangling cancer was found to have dropped away among the bed clothes, 'no soar or any manner of corruptio[n] appearing' in the now restored breast: 'the part parfectly well'.[10]

Doubtless it was unusual to dispatch, unsolicited, bits of expelled body tissue. So much the apologetic opening concedes: 'I begg pardon for this liberty I take in making yr La[dyshi]p so od a present'. But in terms of Barker's own mental world the odd present makes good sense. The meaning of the transaction is to be sought, first, in 'pre-medical' understandings of bodily experience. The flesh, according to such understandings, was to be regarded as a medium for transmission of messages from God and bodily events as signifiers of the divine will. Sickness and bodily affliction possessed, that is to say, social and public dimensions that would recede from view as disease came to be medicalized, to be reconceived as a set of largely private, interiorized physiological processes interpretable only by designated medical personnel and indeed, often invisible to the lay eye. But for Barker and her contemporaries the body was still an arena in which God on occasion chose to make his judgement visible: an abnormal tissue mass could be a powerfully implicative

[10] The letter is in the Royal Archives, Windsor Castle (SP 208/129), incorrectly dated 1738. It is reprinted in Tayler, *Lady Nithsdale*, 239–40, misdated 1739, attributed to an otherwise unidentified 'I. Barker.' Tayler identifies the recipient, whom Barker addressed as 'Madam' and 'your Ladyship', as Mother Lucy Theresa Joseph, whose sister, Lady Nithsdale, is named in the letter. The letter is difficult to date. The superscribed date appears to read 'Aug 14:73°', which may mean [17]13, the '7' possibly being a 1. However, internal references to a 'little neece'—if one of the Henson girls, she would have been improbably young to be one of the 'divers witnesses'—and the external evidence of the resumption of the canonization movement around 1730 persuade me that the correct interpretation is [1]730. For Barker's Henson nieces, see Doc. Rec. 23–4. Edward Corp, one of the leading historians of the St-Germain court, questions my dating. He points out that by 1730 Father Sabran, to whom Barker suggested the evidence might be directed, had left Saint-Omer, and was an elderly man living in retirement, aged 78. Would she, he asks, really have considered sending him evidence at that stage? He is inclined to date the letter to 1713, when Sabran was rector of the Jesuit College at Saint-Omer.

signifier. Charles II, for example, was tormented by a tumour in his right hand after he signed away the lives of the Popish Plot martyrs. His Catholic wife knew what the tumour meant: 'Nor did the Queen omit to signify to his Majesty that this seemed to be a judgment of God upon him for having with that hand signed the death warrant'.[11] In a world in which God expressed displeasure through bodily events, the line between public and private history, between the body politic and the body corporeal, was practically non-existent and a tumour, say, might carry religio-political resonances we must now work to recover.

To such resonances Barker was instinctively attuned. The expulsion of her tumour, we learn elsewhere in the letter, was achieved through the intercession of 'our holy King' (James II) whose blood, soaked up in 'a little rag' and applied to the diseased flesh, worked a miraculous cure.[12] Barker was not the only woman cured through the agency of James's blood. Within months of his death in September 1701, men, but more often women, began reporting cures. By 1702 'the world', in the words of a contemporary, was 'taking alarm at miracles said to be wrought at King James' Tomb'.[13] Many involved bits of cloth that had touched the dead king or had been dipped in his blood at the embalming. An Ursuline nun claimed to be cured by a piece of cloth that had been dipped in his blood.[14] A Dominican sister was cured of a 'horrid fluxion on her face by applying a little of ye King's Blood'; one woman, a 'most sad helpless creature', was restored to health by donning 'a smock y^t had touched ye Kings Coffin'.[15] The tradition of healing

[11] Henry Foley, *Records of the English Province of the Society of Jesus*, 7 vols. (London: Burns and Oates, 1879), v. 94.
[12] The royal blood cured her 'little neeces' swollen eye as well: 'I kneelld doun and touched it [the eye] with the Kings blood in form of a cross, saying The Kings blood touch, God heal, the Eye retir'd into its place, the nose and face became well and and [*sic*] never had any return since, much nor little . . .'.
[13] Bennet Weldon, *A Chronicle of the English Benedictine Monks from the Renewing of their Congregation in the Days of Queen Mary, to the Death of King James II* [London: J. Hodaes, 1882], 249.
[14] Geoffrey Scott, ' "Sacredness of Majesty": The English Benedictines and the Cult of King James II', *Royal Stuart Papers*, 23 (Huntingdon: The Royal Stuart Society, 1984), 4. For other sources, see Falconer Madan (ed.), *Stuart Papers Relating Chiefly to Queen Mary of Modena and the Exiled Court of King James II*, 2 vols. (London: J. B. Nichols and Sons, 1889), ii. 514–35.
[15] BL Add. MS 10,118, fos. 436r, 436v.

through the agency of a handkerchief or piece of cloth goes back at least to the New Testament,[16] but to Catholics at the time of James's death the combined elements of blood, rags, and miraculous healing would have recalled the thaumaturgic relics associated with the Popish Plot martyrs in 1679. Accounts of the executed martyrs abound with stories of the miracle-producing powers of handkerchiefs soaked in blood from their quartered bodies: God gave these 'sacred relics, which had been gathered up by the pious Catholics, the power of healing diseases'. One such cure involved the wife of a gardener, afflicted for five years with an 'obstinate' disease. As usual in these cases, the medical men had given up, but when she sought divine aid through the intercession of the Popish Plot martyrs she 'received it without delay': 'Having swallowed the liquid in which a handkerchief with some of their blood on it had been dipped, she was instantly restored to health. Many others, both Catholics and Protestants, had been cured of fevers by the same means.'[17] Elizabeth Cellier, the Roman Catholic midwife and political activist three times pilloried for her involvement in plotting during the Exclusion Crisis, is reported to have acquired a handkerchief dipped in the blood of Richard Langhorne, the Catholic attorney who acted on behalf of the Jesuit martyrs, executed in 1679.[18] Like Barker, it is interesting to discover, Cellier followed the royal family into exile at St-Germain.[19]

The odd present has a specific occasion as well. Around roughly 1730 a campaign to canonize James II that had begun nearly three decades earlier and then sputtered into inactivity was resumed in earnest. The campaign had a distinctly Jacobite political agenda. From James I onward the monarch's divinely sanctioned right to rule was linked in Stuart propaganda with the miracle-producing powers of the royal body, especially the power to heal by touch (most commonly scrofula, the king's

---

[16] Acts 19: 11-12: 'And God wrought special miracles by the hands of Paul: So that from his body were brought unto the sick handkerchiefs or aprons, and the diseases departed from them, and the evil spirits went out of them.'

[17] Foley, *Records*, v. 85.

[18] Thomas Dangerfield, *The Case of Tho. Dangerfield: with Some Remarkable Passages that happened at the Tryals of Elizabeth Cellier the Popish Midwife, and the Earl of Castlemain* (London: for the Author, 1680), 10.

[19] Edward Corp has found references to Cellier in the unpublished Stuart papers, confirming speculation that she had moved to St-Germain after the Revolution.

evil) thought to descend from Edward the Confessor to the *rightful* kings of England. After 1689 the royal touch served in Jacobite propaganda to distinguish rightful king from usurper, James from William: the latter famously disdained to touch for the king's evil, deriding the practice as papist superstition. 'For the Jacobites', as one historian explains it, 'this was the one gift which could not be snatched from a *de jure* king; it was the witness of continuous divine sanction to his rule, a birthright which ensured a certain reverence was given to the exiled Stuarts even in their darkest hours.'[20] Since miracles of healing attested to the legitimacy no less than the sanctity of the Stuart line, it is easy to say why Jacobites would work to publicize the healing powers of James's blood and look upon his canoniza- tion as a means to advance Jacobite political claims. The years immediately following James's death saw the first serious attempt at canonization, resulting in the recording of at least forty authenticated miraculous cures, mostly from 1701 and 1702, the majority of which involved women.[21]

Nothing came of it at the time, but around 1730 the move- ment began to stir, at which point Barker enters the story. Her letter was obviously intended as evidence for deliberations at Rome: the careful description of the progress of the disease, the reference to 'divers witnesses', the writer's solemn assurance of

---

[20] Scott, ' "Sacredness of Majesty" ', 5. For a summary account of the Stuart kings and the royal touch, see Paul Kléber Monod, *Jacobitism and the English People, 1688–1788* (Cambridge: Cambridge UP, 1989), 127–32. For Charles II specifically, see Harold M. Weber, *Paper Bullets: Print and Kingship under Charles II* (Lexington: U. of Kentucky P., 1996), 50–87. The standard treatment is Marc Bloch, *The Royal Touch: Sacred Monarchy and Scrofula in England and France*, trans. J. E. Anderson (London: Routledge and Kegan Paul, 1973), who demon- strates that James administered the royal touch liberally. From 1686 the touching ritual became more and more Catholic, James using Catholic clergy, invoking the Virgin and saints, and making the sign of the cross (219).

[21] Scott, 'Sacredness of Majesty'. It is unclear whether women were more likely to experience a miraculous cure, come forward with their stories, or have their stories entered into the official records. There is a study to be done of women's role in promoting the cult of James's holiness. The Visitation nuns at Chaillot, for exam- ple, not only sent out a *Lettre circulaire* publishing the news of his miraculous cures but also distributed secondary relics, 'pieces of cloth' that had 'touched the king's coffin, or been placed under his heart in their chapel, or had once belonged to him' ('Sacredness of Majesty', 4). Presumably the nuns intended to prepare the ground for a fresh crop of miraculous cures as against the official record-keeping left to men, suggesting a gendered division of religious labour worth further investigation.

'the truth of this attestation', indeed, the inclusion of the material evidence of the cancer (or cyst) as corroboration make her immediate purpose sufficiently clear. It is poignant to consider this aged and unrepentant Jacobite, living now in apartments just two blocks from the old palace at St-Germain-en-Laye, once home to the royal family and court, taking up the pen once again on behalf of the Stuarts. Nearly three decades had passed since James's death, more than four since she had followed him to France. Barker must have been painfully aware when she parted with the long-expelled tumour that she was one of the dwindling number of the faithful who could bear personal witness to the saintliness of the man she continued to call 'our holy King'.

'Poems Refering to the times'

The merging of political activism and Jacobite faith exemplified by this letter of attestation finds expression in nearly everything Barker wrote from the 1690s onwards, starting with the remarkable 'A Collection of Poems Refering to the times' (1701).[22] This ambitious multilayered collection, compiled for presentation to the Prince of Wales (the 12-year-old James Francis Stuart, destined to become the Old Pretender), is a sequence of twenty poems on religio-political themes that chronicle affairs of state from 1685, when James took the throne, to 1691 or so, when his military efforts to reclaim it met with defeat in Ireland. Running throughout are satiric glimpses of an England gone mad, a country given over in James's absence to 'Rebells, Hereticks, Debauchees and knaves'.[23] It is

---

[22] The collection survives in two similar manuscript versions: Part One of Mag. MS and BL Add. MS 21,621, the latter a calf-bound quarto volume generally assumed to be the copy presented to the Prince of Wales. Certain physical imperfections suggest that the BL volume may not have been the actual presentation copy, however. Peter Beal, manuscript expert at Sotheby's, thinks it possible it was a prototype, a copy retained for private use, or one intended for wider circulation in the St-Germain community. Evidence for the latter possibility is found in the language of a preface 'To the Reader' (discussed later in this chapter) which suggests the volume was intended to be read outside court circles. I am grateful to Dr Beal for his counsel on this matter.

[23] 'Englands ill Genius and his companion after the Battell of the Boyn' (fo. 33v).

a sign of her epic aspirations that Barker uses two great military events to frame the narrative, the Battle of Sedgemoor (1685)[24] and the surrender of Limerick (1691), with many of the intervening poems continuing the military and political emphasis. These poems attempt to make sense of the disasters befalling England since James's accession, providing Jacobite perspectives on such events as the outbreak of anti-Catholic violence in London after the king's forced flight, the failure of the Jacobite siege at Londonderry, the defeat at the Battle of the Boyne, the collapse of the Irish resistance and ensuing scattering of James's supporters. At the exact centre is James's flight to France, which is fitting given the chronicle's preoccupation with exile and the Jacobite diaspora.

An expression of the Jacobite historical imagination, the 'Poems Refering to the times' is also a personal history. Interwoven among the poems of national import are others rehearsing the seemingly private spiritual history of Fidelia—the Catholic persona invented for the St-Germain verse—poems which tell the story of Fidelia's conversion and subsequent attempts to consolidate a somewhat troubled new identity as a Roman Catholic among the other exiles in France. A narrative of national and personal crisis, the sequence mingles public and private themes, comic and tragic modes, actual and invented characters to form a self-conscious generic mix, combining elements from political satire, spiritual autobiography, conversion narrative, military chronicle, and religious apologia. In this regard 'Poems Refering to the times' has affinities with the royalist tragicomedies from earlier in the century discussed by Lois Potter, expressing from a late-century, female, and Jacobite point of view the confused nature of recent events.[25] They recall as well seventeenth-century prophetic writings by women, which likewise refuse to separate out political and religious,

---

[24] It is characteristic of the multi-perspectival methods employed in this collection that Barker should include four poems about the Battle of Sedgemoor, two spoken by Fidelia, one by England's Good Genius, and one by Lucifer and his fiends. They are 'Fidelia alone lamenting her parents lately dead, and her relations gone into the west against Monmoth' (fo. 8), 'On the Victory at Sedgemore' (fo. 9v), 'England's good Genius [on the victory]' (fo. 10), and 'On Sedge-more victory by Lucifer and his Fiends' (fo. 10v).

[25] See Lois Potter, *Secret Rites and Secret Writing: Royalist Literature, 1641–1660* (Cambridge: Cambridge UP, 1989), ch. 3, esp. 80–5.

national and personal themes. As Paula McDowell has observed, 'issues of spirituality were not private, personal matters' in such writings, but were rather 'public matters of urgent national importance, inseparable from problems of institutions and power'.[26]

Take by way of illustration 'Fidelia alone lamenting her parents lately dead, and her relations gone into the west against Monmoth' (fo. 8), the first poem in the sequence. It seems at first glance intensely private. An anguished Fidelia is 'alone', the title tells us, 'lamenting her parents lately dead', and in the opening lines she is seen to face even more terrible anxieties, for such kin as remain to her are then fighting, and perhaps dying, at Sedgemoor. In contemplating their fate on the battlefield she is compelled to contemplate her own radical isolation:

> I mourn my parents dead, and mourne alone,
> For all my other friends, to th' wars are gone;
> Were they but here, they'd help me bear a share,
> But I their presence want, their danger fear.   (fo. 8)

In the cognate scene in *Patch-Work Screen* Galesia broods on the horror of Sedgemoor at her mother's bedside;[27] Fidelia, however, is constructed as utterly alone. Shorn of parents, kin and community, she returns obsessively to images of death and destruction of those dearest to her:

> Alas! methinks I hear the bullets fly;
> I see a cousin wounded, brother dy;
> I hear my aged Uncles dying groans,
> And see by's side, his grandson's shattered bones—

At a time when personal identity was thoroughly bound up in the sense of an ongoing family destiny, this anxious vision of orphanhood raised to a terrifying level, envisioned as the loss of

---

[26] Paula McDowell, *The Women of Grub Street: Press, Politics, and Gender in the London Literary Marketplace 1678–1730* (Oxford: Clarendon P., 1998), 177.

[27] The cognate scene in *PWS* (159–60) recapitulates the basic situation of the Fidelia poem and recycles almost unaltered six lines of the ironically commendatory 'prayer' for Monmouth muttered by an old female neighbour and overheard by Galesia/Fidelia. In *PWS* the 'prayer', entitled 'A *Hymn*. Sung in a *Psalm* Tune', is sung by 'an Old Gentlewoman' who lodged next door. In Mag. MS she is identified as 'an old m[enda]cious presb[yrte]rian' and excoriated by Fidelia as a blasphemous 'curss'd woman' (fo. 9). To the six lines from 'Fidelia alone' Barker added in *PWS* a final triplet, replacing a much harsher one calling for James's fall.

all kin, may be the ultimate expression of personal isolation. (Galesia, in *Patch-Work Screen*, faces the loss of her mother only.)[28] But as the lines that follow indicate, personal loss is inseparable from national upheaval, for Fidelia's almost empathic imaginings of the battered bodies of her kinsmen give way to a vision of 'Barbarians' on the English shore:

> Nay I not only see, and hear, but feel
> In my poor tender heart, th' obdurate steel.
> Whilst all the fields with bodyes coverd o'er,
> And all the riv'lets running with fresh gore,
> As if Barbarians had been on our shoar.   (fo. 8)

Personal and national crisis merge, and we are able to glimpse in this moment something of the reciprocal relation between public macrohistory and private microhistory that organizes the sequence as a whole. We can discern, in other words, the workings of a process of analogical conversion which according to Michael McKeon informs much early novelistic narrative. The early modern imagination, he points out, often sought to understand 'large, public macrohistories' by way of 'smaller, more accessible, private microhistories of individual and familial life', a process which he terms the 'analogical conversion of the macronarrative of recent history to the microplots of private lives' or what we might call, more simply, the conversion of history into story. The Fidelia story bears just such an analogical relation to public events. By means of this private history of a woman positioned on the edge of great events, a micronarrative of personal loss and exile, Barker tries to comprehend the nearly incomprehensible, the events of recent national history, foremost among them the expulsion of James II from his kingdom. The effect is to collapse what McKeon aptly calls the

---

[28] The death of Galesia's mother is linked also to the death of Charles II (*PWS* 152–3). We do not know whether Barker's mother was alive in 1685, but given the entangling of national and personal themes in her work, it is not unlikely Barker would invent a dead, or dying, mother for the novelistic occasion. Delarivier Manley, sharing her era's indifference to matters of factual accuracy, linked the death of her royalist father, Sir Roger Manley, with the Revolution of 1688–9: her 'truly loyal' father retired to the country after William took over the throne, dying soon after 'in apprehension of what would befall his unhappy country'. In fact her father had died in 1687. See Fidelis Morgan, *A Woman of No Character: An Autobiography of Mrs Manley* (London and Boston: Faber and Faber, 1986), 36–8.

'chaste, modern antithesis of "history" and "story" ' into the 'rich indeterminancy' more characteristic of the seventeenth century.[29] It is also to point toward the novelistic strategies Barker would develop more fully in the next century: in the Galesia fictions she would use the life-story of an ordinary if singular women to render intelligible the confusions of early Georgian existence.

'Methinks a Virgin should a virgin hear'

It is typical of Barker that personal and national turmoil should be embroiled with religious crisis as well: later in 'Fidelia alone' the speaker, driven to the end of her interior resources, will reach out to the Virgin. Identification with Catholicism, an outlawed religion, was the defining fact of Barker's existence from her mid-thirties onward. But for information about her conversion we have little more than the account provided by Fidelia in the 'Poems Refering to the times', which moves from doubts about the Church of England, through conversion under the guidance of 'Benit's sons' (the Benedictines),[30] to her perplexed position as an object of distrust among her new co-religionists. Since it is generally assumed that Fidelia speaks for Barker in her identity as a convert, the charge of opportunism with which she is taxed in one of the dialogues—'You chang'd your faith, to be in the court mode, | For fassion sake you

[29] Michael McKeon, *The Origins of the English Novel 1600–1740* (Baltimore: Johns Hopkins UP, 1987), 215, 229, 270.

[30] Benedictine connections are suggested by at least three Magdalen poems: 'Fidelia arguing with her self on the difficulty of finding the true Religion' (fo. 11v); 'Fidelia having seen the Convent at St James' (fo. 13v), lines in praise of the royal chapel served during the reign of James II by sixteen Benedictine monks; and 'To Madam Fitz James, on the day of her profession, at Pontoise, she taking the name of St Ignace' (fo. 45), which places her at the Benedictine convent at Pontoise, not far from St-Germain, in Apr. 1690 when Arabella Fitzjames, daughter of James II and Arabella Churchill, made her profession. The Benedictines were closely associated with the Stuart court: see David Lunn, *The English Benedictines, 1540–1688: From Reformation to Revolution* (London: Burns and Oates and New York: Barnes and Noble, 1980), 121–45; James Flint, 'James II and the English Benedictines', *American Benedictine Review*, 39 (1988), 113–32; Geoffrey Scott, *Gothic Rage Undone: English Monks in the Age of Enlightenment* (Bath: Downside Abbey, 1992).

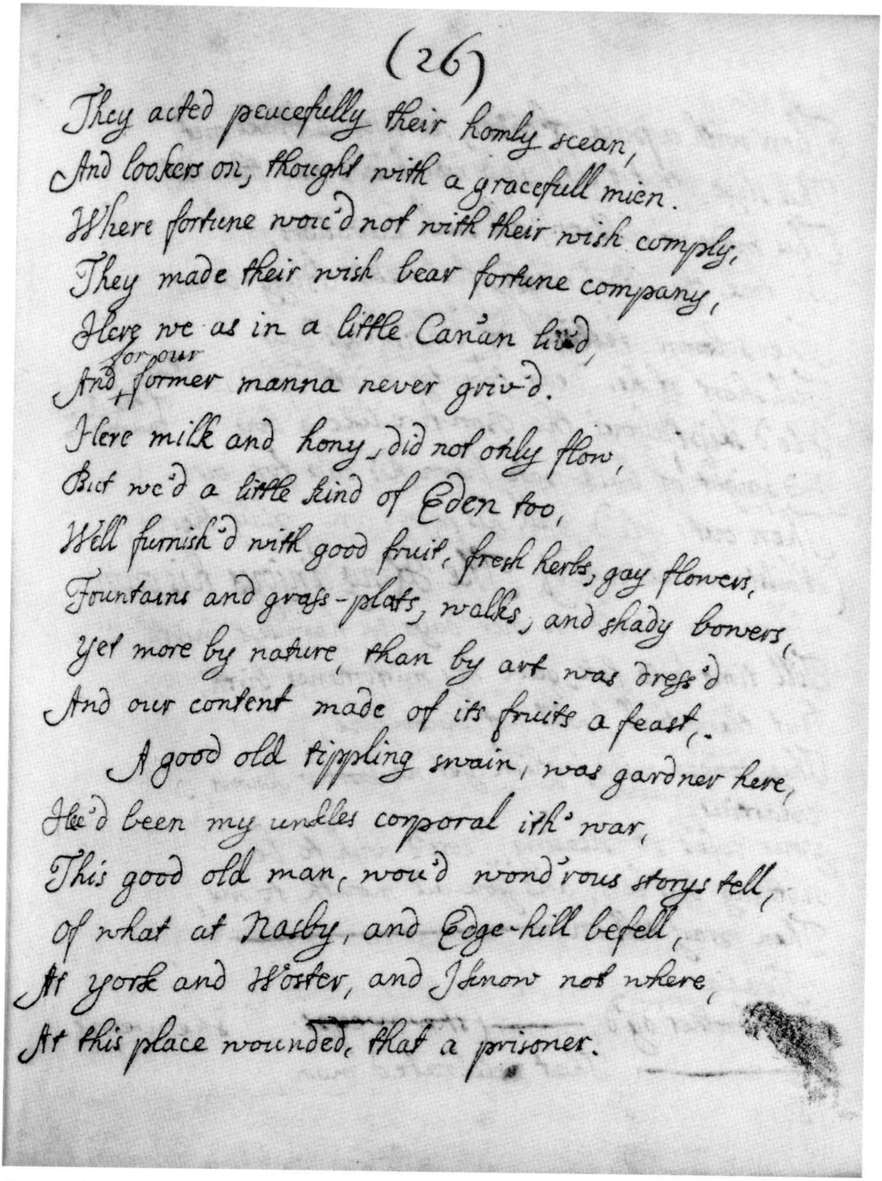

(26)

They acted peacefully their homly scean,
And lookers on, thought with a gracefull mien.
Where fortune wou'd not with their wish comply,
They made their wish bear fortune company,
Here we as in a little Canan liv'd,
And former manna never griv'd.
for our
Here milk and hony, did not only flow,
But we'd a little kind of Eden too,
Well furnish'd with good fruit, fresh herbs, gay flowers,
Fountains and grass-plats, walks, and shady bowers,
Yet more by nature, than by art was dress'd
And our content made of its fruits a feast.
    A good old tippling swain, was gardner here,
He'd been my uncles corporal ith' war,
This good old man, wou'd wond'rous storys tell,
Of what at Nasby, and Edge-hill befell,
At york and Worster, and I know not where,
At this place wounded, that a prisoner.

FIG 1. Part of Jane Barker's autograph copy of her poem 'A dialogue between
Fidelia and her little nephew Martius . . .' in the Magdalen Manuscript with her
thumb-print at the bottom right corner (original page size 220 x 159mm).
Magdalen College Oxford, MS 343, fol. 65. *Reproduced by Permission of the
President and Fellows of Magdalen College, Oxford*

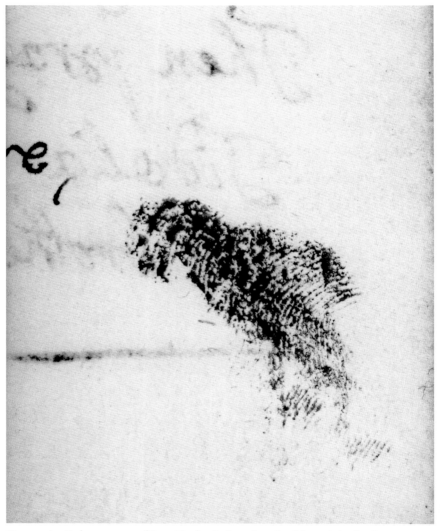

FIG 2. An Enlargement of Jane Barker's thumb-print (the original print *c*.30mm long). Magdalen College Oxford, MS 343, fol. 65. *Reproduced by Permission of the President and Fellows of Magdalen College, Oxford*

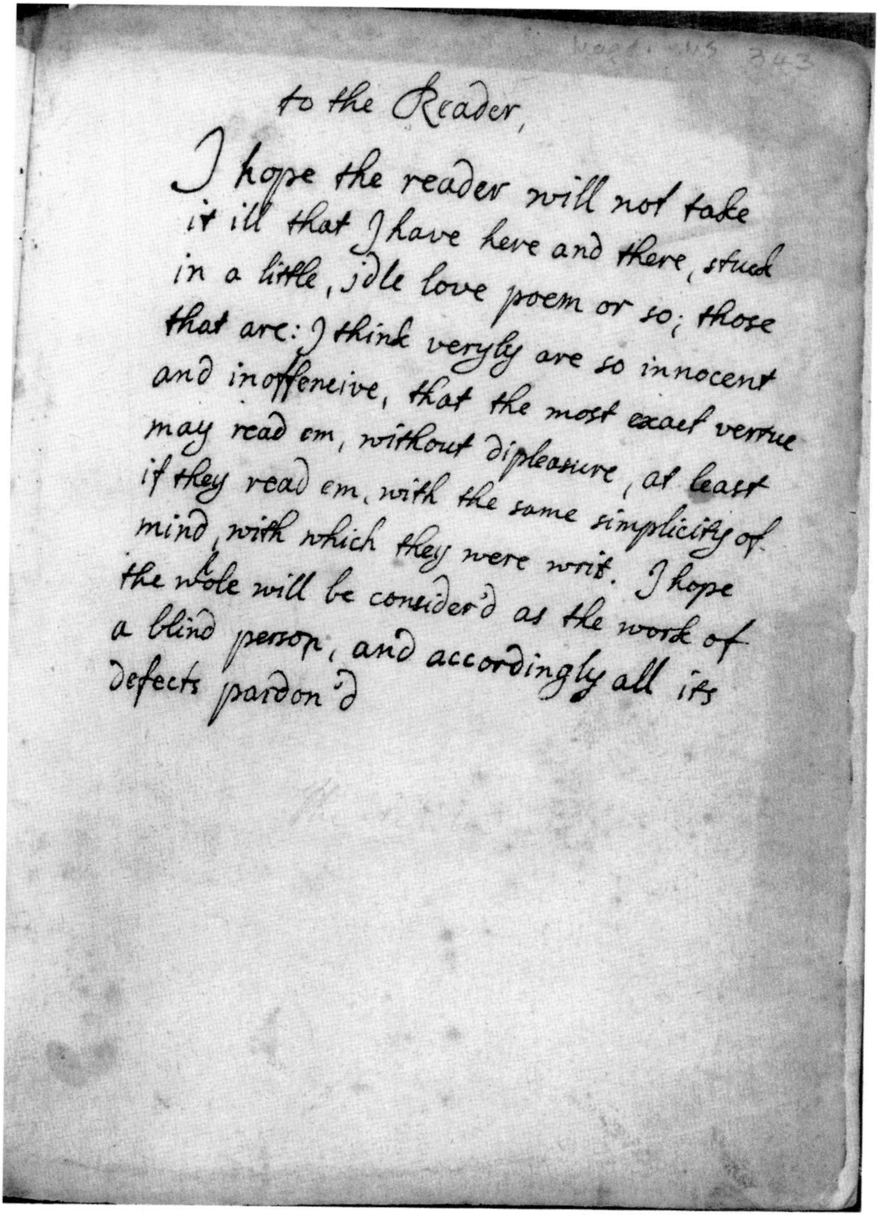

to the Reader,

I hope the reader will not take
it ill that I have here and there, stuck
in a little, idle love poem or so; those
that are: I think veryly are so innocent
and inoffensive, that the most exact vertue
may read em, without displeasure, at least
if they read em, with the same simplicity of
mind, with which they were writ. I hope
the whole will be consider'd as the work of
a blind person, and accordingly all its
defects pardon'd

Fig 3. Jane Barker's autograph preface 'to the Reader' at the beginning of the
Magdalen Manuscript (original page size 220 x 159mm). Magdalen College
Oxford, MS 343, fol. 1ʳ. *Reproduced by Permission of the President and Fellows
of Magdalen College, Oxford*

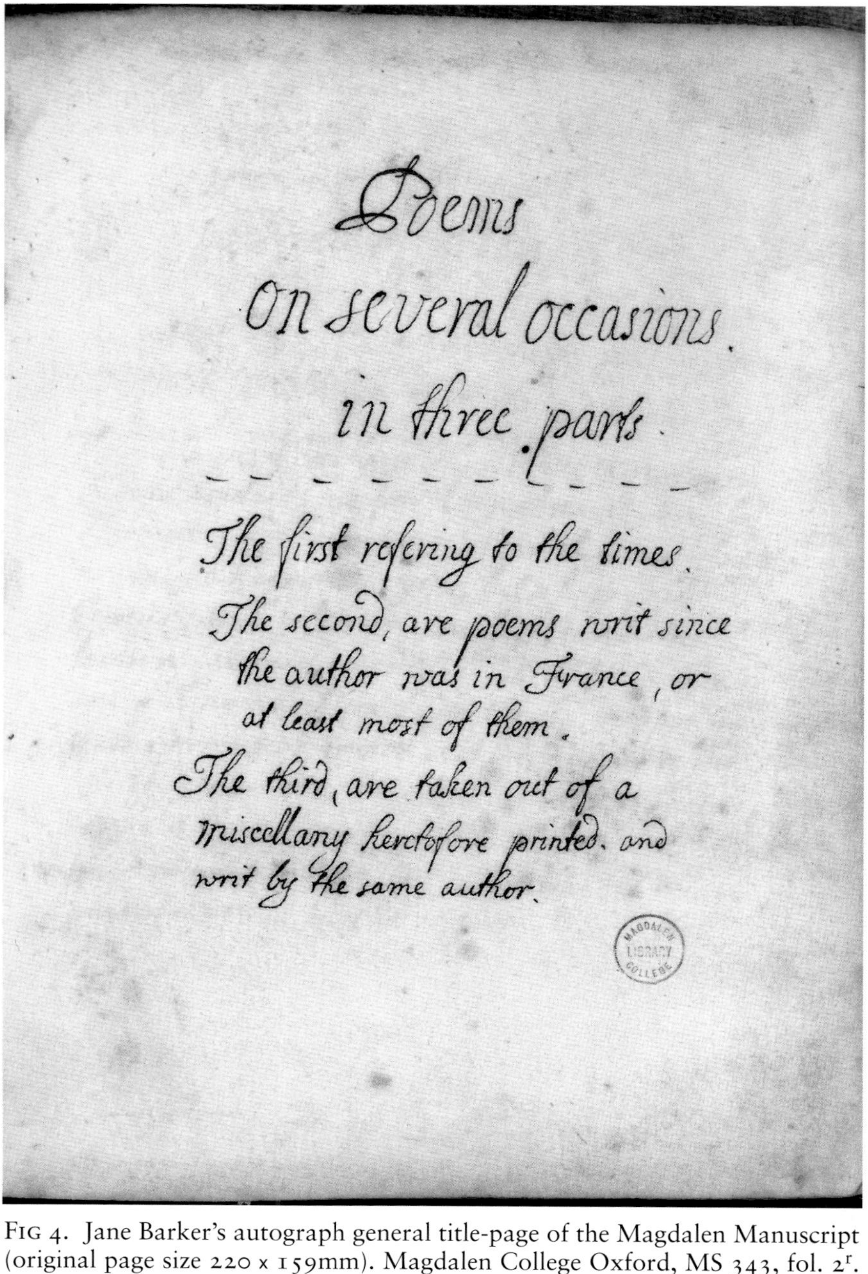

Poems

on several occasions.

in three parts.

— — — — — — — — —

The first refering to the times.

The second, are poems writ since the author was in France, or at least most of them.

The third, are taken out of a miscellany heretofore printed. and writ by the same author.

FIG 4. Jane Barker's autograph general title-page of the Magdalen Manuscript (original page size 220 x 159mm). Magdalen College Oxford, MS 343, fol. 2^r. *Reproduced by Permission of the President and Fellows of Magdalen College, Oxford*

New pieces still of property they broach,
Which on the Crowns prerogative encroach,
And people with disloyalty debauch.

~~Nei did their ~~Thei~~ God blessings so dispense~~
~~On people without gratitude or sence~~
    strange
~~Such a pack our Hell could never shew~~
~~As is this non resisting canting crew.~~
~~Genius~~ ~~But prithee stop thy peevish clamor here,~~
~~Here spend thy time to make their character.~~
~~We know in every thing they are our fools,~~
    In
~~Their Bodys, Fortunes, reputation, souls~~

neer did their God, his blessings so dispence
on people without gratitude or sence.
Their Parliments are Rebells, clergie knaves   *+the*
Their states-men bubles, and the people slaves,   *meani*
    clerg
genius   They well deserve the chain of slavery
Who take such pains to cast of liberty.
But let that pass we'll not complain since wee
By their overthrow, set up our monarchy,
We know in every thing, they are Hells fools
In bodys, fortunes, reputations souls.

FIG 5. A page of the poem 'A discourse between Englands ill Genius and his companion' in the Magdalen Manuscripts, the first eleven lines in the hand of William Connock, the revisions and deletions of these lines, as well as a further ten lines of substitute text and side-note, in the hand of Jane Barker (original page size 220 x 159mm). Magdalen College Oxford, MS 343, fol. 17. *Reproduced by Permission of the President and Fellows of Magdalen College, Oxford*

Fidelia walking
the Lady Abess comes to her.

Abess. The news is come, that Irland is quite lost,
Their army is arivd upon our coast,
I'th' list oth dead, no frind of yours I find,
In sparing them, Heav'n has I hope been kind.

Fidelia That is some comfort, but the publick loss,
Is still a bitter cup, a heavy cross.
What have we done, good God what have we done?
That on our heads this punishment is thrown,
Our King's a saint, and we are martyrs all,
And in our cause, Heav'ns cause too seems to fall,
It makes one ready to think all a cheat,
And that Religion's but a trick of state,
Since Providence, does not its cause defend,

How can we on this Providence depend,
When Providence wants will or power to grant
Our want of merit must supply that want
Thus Providence cheats fooll's, and fooll the wise
dulling us into stupid letergies,
Till worthless fools the worthiest men dispise.

Abess, Accuse not heav'n, Heav'n's always just and good,
Although its ways be n't alway understood,

note these athestical lines, were not given to the
Prince, but being in the original, they are
here inserted.

FIG 6. The first page of the poem 'Fidelia walking the Lady Abess comes to
her' in the Magdalen Manuscripts, the first thirteen lines in the hand of William
Connock, the next eight lines and the note in Jane Barker's hand on a slip of paper
sewn in over the deleted lines (original page size 220 x 159mm). Magdalen
College Oxford, MS 343, fol. 2ʳ. *Reproduced by Permission of the President and
Fellows of Magdalen College, Oxford*

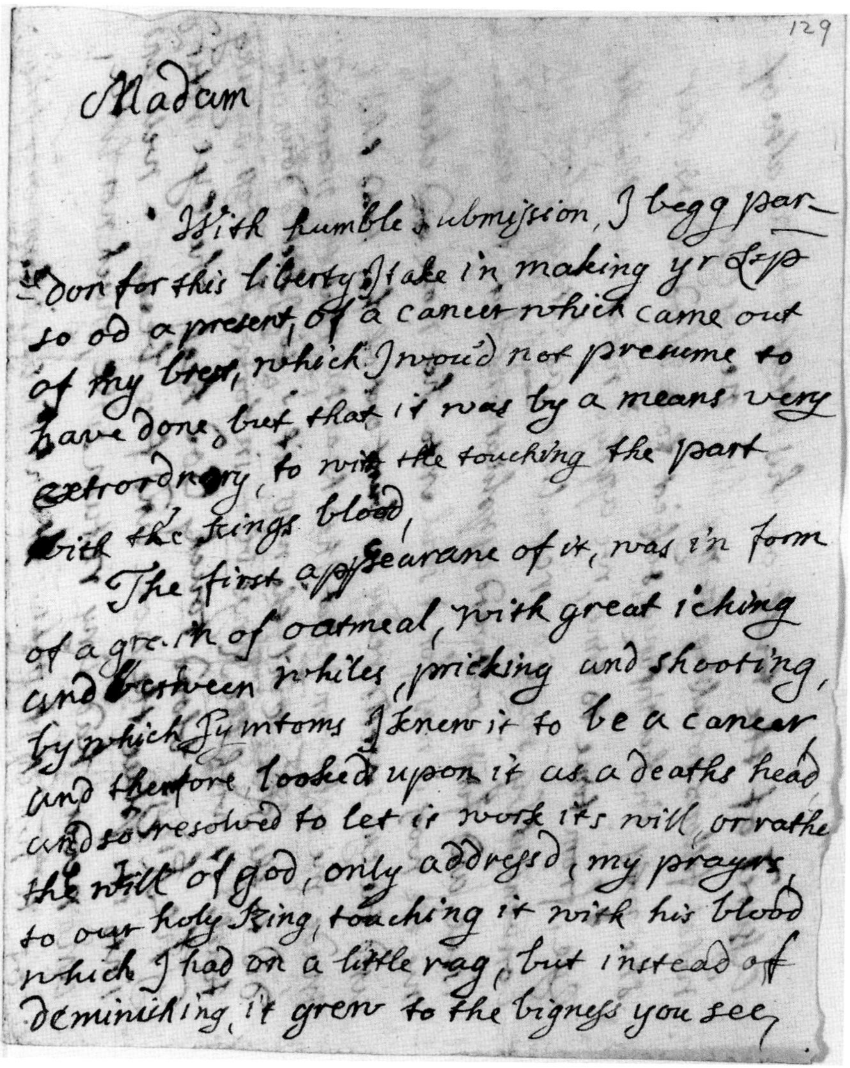

129

Madam

   With humble submission, I begg pardon for this liberty j take in making yr L:sp
so od a present of a cancer which came out
of my brest, which j wou'd not presume to
have done, but that it was by a means very
extrordnary, to wit the touching the part
with the kings blood,
   The first appearane of it, was in form
of a grem of oatmeal, with great iching
and between whiles, pricking and shooting,
by which symtoms j knew it to be a cancer
and therfore looked upon it as a deaths head
and so resolved to let it work its will, or rathe
the will of god, only addressd my prayrs,
to our holy King, touching it with his blood
which j had on a little rag, but insteed of
deminishing, it grew to the bigness you see,

FIG 7. The first page of Jane Barker's autograph letter signed, to an unnamed
lady, 14 August 1730(?). The Royal Library, Windsor Castle, Stuart Papers
208/129. *Reproduced by permission of the Royal Library*

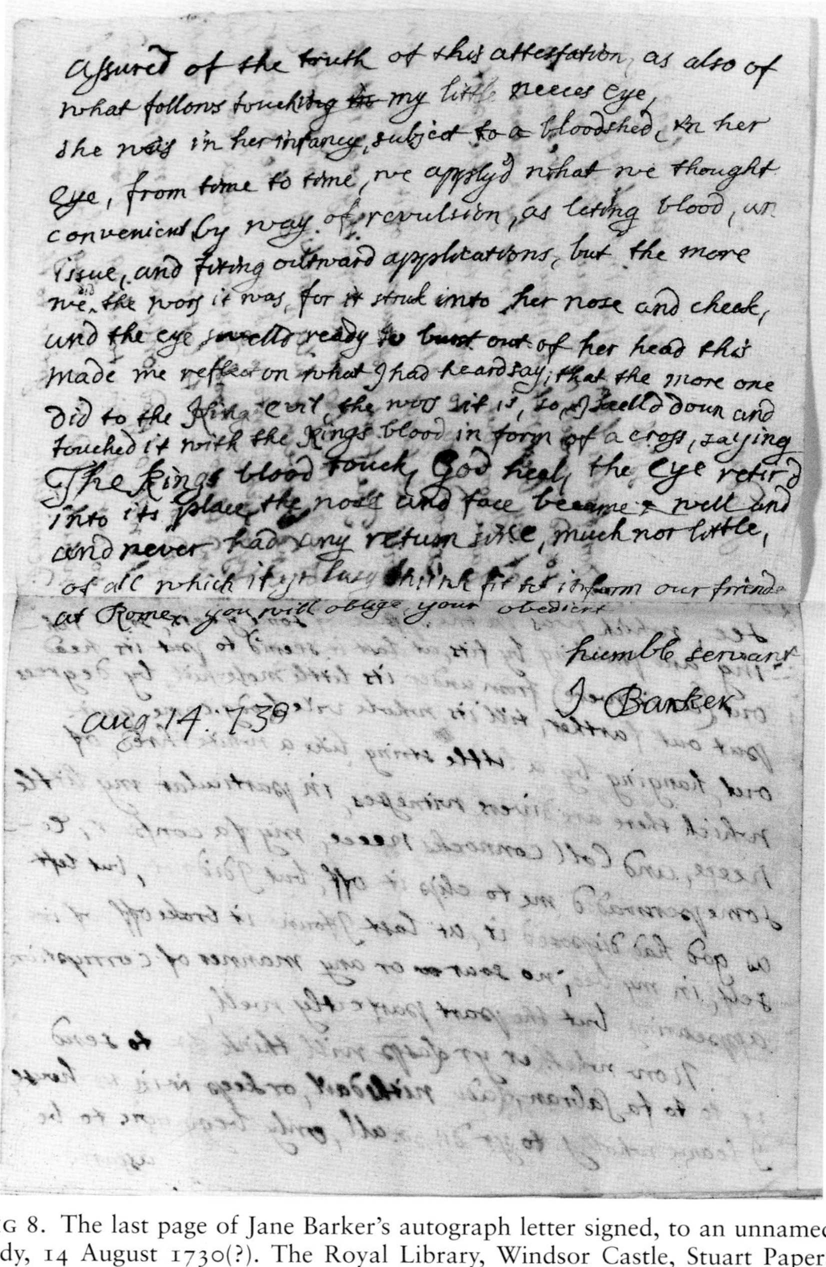

assured of the truth of this attestation, as also of
what follows touching my little neeces eye,
she was in her infancy subject to a bloodshed in her
eye, from time to time, we apply'd what we thought
convenient by way of revulsion, as leting blood, an
issue, and fixing outward applications, but the more
we, the worse it was, for it struck into her nose and cheak,
and the eye swelld ready to burst out of her head this
made me reflect on what I had heard say; that the more one
did to the King evil the worse it is, to, kneeld down and
touched it with the Kings blood in form of a cross, saying
The Kings blood touch, God heal, the eye retird
into its place, the nose and face became well and
and never had any return since, much nor little,
of all which if you... think fit to inform our friends
at Roane you will oblige your obedient

humble servant
J. Barker

aug: 14: 730

FIG 8. The last page of Jane Barker's autograph letter signed, to an unnamed
lady, 14 August 1730(?). The Royal Library, Windsor Castle, Stuart Papers
208/129. *Reproduced by permission of the Royal Library*

change and eat your God'—has been thought to indicate that Barker was received into the Church during James II's reign.[31] In truth we do not know. Accusations of opportunism were rife at the time, most famously in the case of Dryden, and it is possible Barker was invoking a commonplace so as to make Fidelia speak for broader Catholic experience. 'I have made my Fidelia speak the common dialect of Catholicks' (fo. 6), she writes in the preface, and we are warned to remain alert to the potentially collective dimension of Fidelia's utterances.

On the other hand, the biographical record gives no reason to suppose Barker did *not* convert sometime between 1685 and 1688. We know she was baptized into the Church of England, for an early poem addressed to the rector of Wilsthorp parish church asserts that she 'gain'd the knowledge of all saving truth' (fo. 96) under his tutelage, suggesting instruction in the Anglican faith, while the parish register shows that her father, Thomas, served as a church officer—all of which points toward a solidly Church of England background.[32] Her mother, Anne, was a Connock, however, and on her side of the family one does find evidence of Catholicism.[33] Although Anne Barker's name

[31] 'Second Dialogue', fo. 19v.

[32] Her baptism, 17 May 1652, is recorded in the Blatherwick Parish Register, 1621–89, Northamptonshire Record Office, 34 P/1. The poem is 'To my Reverend friend mr H—— on his presenting me the Reasonableness of christianity: and the History of king Charles th[e] 1st' (fo. 96), printed in *PR* 8–10. The 'mr H——' of the title is George Hawen, rector of the Greatford cum Wilsthorpe parish from 1643 to his death in 1691. I am grateful to Elizabeth Wood, LAO Archivist, for these dates. Thomas Barker was signatory to the parish register for 1672 along with 'Geo. Hawen': LAO, Gretford-cum-Wilsthorp parish registers, 4/422.

[33] It seems significant that while Anne's branch of the Connock family has proved impossible to trace in parish (i.e. Church of England) records, members do turn up in military records in contexts strongly suggestive of Catholicism. A Major William Connock (d. 1704)—probably the brother of Timon and oldest son of Jane's cousin William (d. 1738)—quit Dutch service in March 1688 along with other Catholic officers in order to serve James; he joined one of three mostly Roman Catholic infantry regiments in the pay of Louis XIV. See Charles Dalton (ed.), *English Army Lists and Commission Registers 1661–1714*, 6 vols. (London: Eyre and Spottiswoode, 1892–1904), ii. 155 and ii. 230. It is suggestive that other military Connocks appear to have served outside England, where they would not be subject to the Test Act. According to John Childs, *The Army, James II, and the Glorious Revolution* (Manchester: Manchester UP, 1980), 18–19, 'Roman catholic officers who fought for Charles II did so in Tangier, France, Portugal, the Anglo-Dutch Brigade, and in the colonies where they were far removed from the prying eyes of parliament and the provisions of the two Test Acts'.

appears in none of the Lincolnshire recusancy lists, she may have been a 'church-Papist' (outwardly or occasionally conforming) or an undeclared recusant, practising the faith of her branch of the family within the relative safety of the home. She would not have been the first Englishwoman to recreate domestically the religious observances officially outlawed in public all the while her husband conformed to the Church of England.[34] Jane would have been raised in both faiths or at least in sympathy with Catholicism—a situation not uncommon at a time when penal laws and recusancy fines, to say nothing of anti-papist prejudice, constrained Catholics to conceal or disguise their religious affiliations, making it 'difficult at the best of times to define what is meant by a Catholic in seventeenth-century England', as Alison Shell has observed.[35] Jane may have been an Anglican convert or a closeted Catholic who chose to come out during James's Catholicizing reign. In any event, for the remainder of her life there is not the slightest doubt of her religious persuasion.

Although the seven Fidelia poems can be described accurately enough as spiritual autobiography, only superficially are they poems of spiritual anguish. The pre-conversion poems do gesture toward a crisis of conscience, to be sure, but the gestures are formulaic and the outcome is never really in question. Indeed Fidelia declares herself 'asham'd' of being a Protestant midway through the first poem, and any doubts as to where she is heading are quickly dispelled when in the same poem Fidelia reaches out, unwittingly—so the poem's rhetoric would have us believe—in prayer to the Virgin, promising that if James's forces win at Sedgemoor and her kin are returned to her, she will

34 Single women and widows could be fined for recusancy, but married women with conforming husbands created problems for the authorities, who, according to Merry E. Wiesner, *Women and Gender in Early Modern Europe* (Cambridge: Cambridge UP, 1993), 202, were seldom willing 'to back measures which would allow a wife to be legally responsible as an individual for her religious choices and put her husband's property at risk'. This gave English women, who arranged private masses in the home and sometimes sheltered priests, an important religious role not enjoyed by women on the Continent, resulting in an Anglo-Catholicism that was domestic rather than parish-oriented.

35 Alison Shell, 'Popish Plots: *The Feign'd Curtizans* in Context', in Janet Todd (ed.), *Aphra Behn Studies* (Cambridge: Cambridge UP, 1996), 30–49 (30). She distinguishes between church-Papists, recusants, and crypto-Catholics, including in the latter category Aphra Behn.

search 'with all the power I can' for the 'surest way to thy bles'd son God man'.[36] Four poems later we watch Fidelia struggle against her attraction to a despised religion, 'a Church by persecutions torn' (fo. 12v), but in a moment of grace and passive acceptance of the true faith, all resistance to 'the true Religion' dissolves:

> Now now I feell th' effect of Heav'nly love,
> That nothing e'er my constancy can move.
> Sure pleasant are the repasts of the just,
> Since in this tast I find so great a gust.
> Hence then all worldly joys I might pursue,
> With Benit's sons, I will go bid adue,
> In pennance my baptismal vows renew.[37]

The Fidelia poems are not, then, enactments of doubt and confusion in the manner of spiritual autobiographies, though they sometimes echo the conventions of the genre ('Thus I by doubts, and hopes, and fears am toss'd, | And in the labyrinth of disputes are lost' (fo. 12v.)), nor are they struggles at affirming a relationship with God in the manner of Donne or Herbert. Still less are they exercises in piety in the manner of countless minor devotional poets. More surprisingly, perhaps, they contain little of the contemplative mystical spirituality that we might expect from a follower of the famously quietist Fénelon.[38] They are perhaps best regarded as poems of religious identity—attempts by a recent convert not only to affirm the

---

[36] 'Fidelia alone lamenting her parents lately dead, and her relations gone into the west against Monmoth' (fo. 8v).

[37] 'Fidelia arguing with her self on the difficulty of finding the true Religion' (fo. 13). The poem is reprinted in KR, where the editors interpret these lines to mean that Barker/Fidelia has 'decided to go into what Catholics nowadays call retreat under the spiritual direction of the Benedictines. She would be expected to make a general confession ("pennance") and renew her baptismal vows' (360). Barker's rendering of the conversion experience might fruitfully be compared with that of the Benedictine monk Maurus Corker, best known for converting Dryden during the reign of James II (among a reputed thousand others during the 1670s and 1680s). According to Scott, Gothic Rage, 114, Corker 'saw his conversion as the result of a passive acceptance of the light of faith rather than as the fruit of intellectual argument'; he hoped his account in A Rational Account given by a Young Gentleman . . . of the Motives and Reason why he became a Roman-Catholic (c.1700) 'might stimulate readers into following the same path'.

[38] Her translation of devotional meditations by Fénelon is discussed below in Ch. 4.

saving value of a new faith but also to grapple with the difficulties of an identity that renders her an outsider in newly
perplexed ways. Fidelia, 'a poor forlorn', embraces persecution
and provokes the 'general scorn' of her former 'friends' when
she forsakes the Church of England;[39] but as a convert she
meets with scorn in a new guise. Such, at any rate, is the implication of a passage given to England's Good Genius in which
converts are said to 'suffer to excess' because they are suspect to
all parties. Between the Church of England, wrathful and
vindictive, and the Catholic community, coolly suspicious, their
'generous souls' are 'ground', for 'neither [party] thinks a
converts concience sound':

> They run as 'twer the gantlet twixt the blows,
> Of jealous tepid friends, and peevish foes
> Affronted by the party, which they leave,
> The other does with coldness them receive,
> Betwixt these two their generous souls are ground,
> And neither thinks a converts concience sound:
> Leaving that side, which wrath and vengance blinds,
> On t'other side he no protection finds,
> But like a ship o'erset betwixt two winds.
> ('Englands good Genius and Philanthrophel his
> companion', fols. 35r–v)

Only within the shelter of a convent does Fidelia experience the
sense of connectedness she had longed for from the first; and in
the French Lady Abbess who offers her comfort in the final
poems she finds a replacement for the various mothers, familial,
national, and religious—the Church of England is earlier
described as 'my first mother' (fo. 12v) and a 'tender mother,
friend, and governes' (fo. 17v)[40]— she has lost or has had to
forsake.

To some degree, then, the conversion narrative nested in the
'Poems Refering to the times' enacts a version of that 'quest
for a specifically female community' that Isobel Grundy has
identified as central to the tradition of early historical writing

---

[39] 'Fidelia arguing with her self on the difficulty of finding the true Religion' (fo.
12v).
[40] 'Fidelia arguing with her self on the difficulty of finding the true Religion' and
'Fidelia and her friend on her becoming a Catholic first dialogue'.

by English nuns.[41] With works in this tradition it shares a preoccupation with the destiny of the female outsider and a narrative drive to merge the arc of the individual life with that of a religious community. But where the nuns studied by Grundy eventually find a secure, sustaining place within an enclosed female world, Fidelia remains partly estranged from all communities, an outsider even after her conversion to the true faith. The most crucial struggle in the sequence is to be found, in fact, not in 'Fidelia arguing with her self on the difficulty of finding the true Religion', in which, as we have seen, the spiritual crisis is rather easily resolved, but rather in the protracted temptation enacted in 'Fidelia and her friend', a dialogue in which her political loyalties are severely tested. Her 'friend', an Anglican of accommodating temper, tries to convince Fidelia to arrive at a private peace with the new regime, to compromise her principles for the sake of expedience. His arguments begin on a private and personal note— why should she 'such hardships undergo'? (fo. 26)—but quickly modulate into a public register more insidious in its appeal. The high-minded Fidelia is able to brush aside a bribe from the new government with ease; more seductive is the promise of political agency, of effectual intervention in the current dynastic and constitutional crisis. She may 'be phisician to the state', he urges, and its 'convulsions cure, at least abate' (fo. 26)—a temptation that, given Barker's self-image as a lay physician, we can surmise was meant to carry considerable potency. When she fails to budge, he offers fame and glory greater than any the 'Romans their heroick matrons gave' if she would only consent to speak out (publish?) against the Stuarts:[42]

[41] Isobel Grundy, 'Women's History? Writings by English Nuns', in Isobel Grundy and Susan Wiseman (eds.), *Women, Writing, History 1640–1740* (Athens: U. of Georgia P., 1992), 126–38 (127).

[42] Aphra Behn's rather different (poetic) response to a similar (real-life) occasion, her temptation by Bishop Gilbert Burnet in the spring of 1689, can be seen in *A Pindaric Poem to the Reverend Doctor Burnet, On The Honour He Did Me of Enquiring After Me and My Muse*. For a discussion of the poem in its political contexts, see McDowell, *Women of Grub Street*, 1–4, and Virginia Crompton, ' "For when the act is done and finish't cleane, | what should the poet doe, but shift the scene?": Propaganda, Professionalism and Aphra Behn', in Janet Todd (ed.), *Aphra Behn Studies* (Cambridge: Cambridge UP, 1996), 130–53, esp. 141–4.

> Your countrys good, and your own safty too
> Your honour profit, all ask this of you.
> For which Ill answer you'l more glorys have,
> Than Romans their heroick matrons gave.
> You'd be our Saviouress, our Heroine
> If you'd but speak the truth o'th' Prince and Queen.
>
> (fo. 26v)

This too failing, he reminds her that her own party of unbending Stuart adherents is small and weak, their 'feeble voices, can but feebly blame'. Simple prudence, to say nothing of glory, argues for her casting her lot with the men and women of compromise whose 'loud huzzas, shall exalt y^r fame'. Finally, he urges her to 'Speak, speak the truth, and fix the tottering state' (fo. 26v) but even this final grandiose temptation she is able to withstand; she will 'quit this land till better times ensue' (fo. 27). The story of Jesus's temptation in the wilderness that supplies the religious background of these lines invests the steadfastness of the aptly named Fidelia with a spiritual dimension that extends well beyond one woman's determination to refuse political expediency. Her triumph over the twin temptations of religious apostasy and ideological compromise combined with her willingness to embrace the uncertain prospects of exile abroad makes her an ideal exemplar of the Jacobite faith.[43]

'The Muses fleece lys dry'

Barker's personal circumstances at St-Germain may never be known, but close reading of the verse in the first two parts of the Magdalen Manuscript enables informed speculation about her place in the exile community at St-Germain-en-Laye and its literary culture.[44] A manuscript poem addressed to the Prince of

[43] The poem which follows, 'Fidelia in France meets one of Portsmoth officers', presents a series of physical ordeals from a male point of view: a soldier remains true to James in spite of being 'prisond, menac'd, tortur'd' by 'that monster Orange' (fo. 27v). He escapes and, despite frostbite so bad it rots his limbs, makes his way back to his true master.

[44] For an overview of the literary culture at St-Germain, see Eveline Cruickshanks and Edward Corp, 'Introd.', in Eveline Cruickshanks and Edward Corp (eds.), The Stuart Court in Exile and the Jacobites (London and Rio Grande: Hambledon P., 1995), xvii–xix. For the role of verse-writing in Jacobite gentry culture in England,

Wales on his first birthday locates her among the exiled Jacobites by June 1689, suggesting Barker left for St-Germain not many months after James II set up court there.[45] This would make her one of as many as 40,000 men and women from the British Isles who sought refuge in France in the aftermath of the Revolution and of a much smaller number who took up residence at St-Germain, where early in 1689 the Stuarts established a court-in-exile in the old royal palace lent them by Louis XIV. The court numbered some thousand people (husbands, wives, and children included), mostly English and Scots, and mostly Roman Catholic. Since accommodations at the palace were limited, many took lodgings in the surrounding community along with other exiles not directly connected with the court.[46] Barker's residence in the 1690s is not known, but several decades later she took up lodgings in the Chancellerie, a royal building not far from the palace that had been divided since 1689 into apartments for the Jacobites and others.[47]

To gauge Barker's standing at court or in the exile community we must rely upon such information as can be teased out of the poems in the Magdalen Manuscript, since she is mentioned in no surviving memoirs, correspondence, or royal household lists.[48] There is nothing to suggest a position at court or connec-

see ch. 9 of Monod, *Jacobitism*, esp. 286–8. For John Caryll (1625–1711), who wrote verse, and David Nairne (1655–1740), who collaborated with Caryll on English translations of the Psalms and other parts of the Bible, see Edward Gregg, 'New Light on the Authorship of the *Life of James II*', *English Historical Review*, 108 (1993), 947–65 (952). For Richard Maitland, earl of Lauderdale, who translated Virgil, see Margaret Boddy, 'The Manuscripts and Printed Editions of the Translation of Virgil Made by Richard Maitland, Fourth Earl of Lauderdale, and the Connexion with Dryden', *N&Q*, NS 12 (1965), 144–50.

[45] The poem is somewhat strangely entitled 'To His Royal Highness the Prince of Wales, on His birth day 1689: or 99', the pair of dates suggesting the possibility that it was revised, or perhaps simply recirculated, in 1699. References to the fighting in Ireland date the composition of the poem to 1689. London was a dangerous place for Catholics at the time, and her relations with her brother, a Protestant with whom she may have been living in Newgate Street, may have been strained.

[46] For life in St-Germain, see the papers in Cruickshanks and Corp (eds.), *Stuart Court*, esp. Nathalie Genet-Rouffiac, 'Jacobites in Paris and Saint-Germain-en-Laye', 15–38.

[47] The Chancellerie is given as her residence in her death notice. See Wilson, xxvi.

[48] The only archival trace of her presence in St-Germain, a reference in the parochial register from 1691, suggests links with the community's legal classes. On 29 Jan. 1691 Barker stood godmother to Christine Winiffe, born to Dorothy (née Ford) and George Winiffe, a London lawyer. See C. E. Lart (ed.), *The Parochial*

tions with any of the well-known courtiers, diplomats, or political figures who chose to follow the king into exile—men like the dramatist and poet George Etherege, for example, who set off from his diplomatic post in Ratisbon as soon as he heard of James's arrival in Paris, 'being resolv'd to live and dy in serving him faithfully'.[49] Barker was a Connock, however, and some of her younger relations would achieve distinction in the next century. In 1702 a James Connock was sworn in as Gentleman of the Privy Chamber. Timon—the 'little Martius' of the Magdalen verse and son of Jane's cousin, Colonel William Connock—was knighted in 1707; his wife, daughter to one of James II's Secretaries of State, had been maid of honour to Queen Mary of Modena. William Connock, the 'dear cosen' of Barker's verse, would be knighted in 1732 by James III in recognition of the services of his son Timon, an aide-de-camp to Philip V of Spain; William's interment in 1738 in the church at St-Germain indicates some social stature.[50] What any of this says about Barker's situation in the 1690s is uncertain: she may have been 'known at court' in the 1690s, as her editor asserts (Wilson, xxviii), but it would be difficult to prove.

We can be certain that she did her best to get known there, however. The occasional verse assembled in Part Two includes a number of complimentary poems addressed to highly placed

Registers of St.Germain-en-Laye: Jacobite Extracts of Births Marriages and Deaths, 2 vols. (London: St Catherine P., 1910–12), i. 137. Her co-sponsor and co-signatory, Robert Brent, was an attorney of importance in the pre-Revolutionary Catholic world, head of the commission of 'regulators' that in 1687–8 attempted to pack Parliament in a pro-Catholic direction. I am grateful to Paul Hopkins for information about Brent. The claim made by James Winn, Janet Todd, and others that she served as a maid of honour to Mary of Modena is without basis: there is no record of her having a position in the royal household.

[49] Frederick Bracher (ed.), *Letters of Sir George Etherege* (Berkeley: U. of California P., 1974), 266. On 3 Jan. Etherege had written: 'The Zeal I have to serve his Majesty makes me very uneasy in a place where I cannot shew it as I wou'd do, wherefore I think of coming to England. . . . My allegiance and my gratitude tell me it is base to be unactive when my King and my Masters Crown and person are in danger' (264–5).

[50] *Calendar of the Stuart Papers*, 7 vols. (London: HMSO, 1902), i. 176, 211; Marquis of Ruvigny and Raineval, *The Jacobite Peerage* (Edinburgh: T. C. and E. C. Jack, 1904), 37. For more on the Connocks at St-Germain, see Wilson, xxvi–xxvii.

members of the exile community, including five members of the royal family.[51] Twice, in 1689 and 1699, she honoured the birthday of the Prince of Wales with a poem and, once at least, with a present—a 'Calvary set in a vinyard'. In 1694, for the birthday of the king, she composed lines spoken by a suitably abject Penelope-as-England who, smitten with remorse, yearns for the return of her Ulysses-as-James. (Penelope's renewed love for her absent husband expresses what Edward Gregg calls 'an absolute article of political faith on the part of the exiles': those who remained in the British Isles 'only awaited an opportunity to display their true political colours'.)[52] In a 1696 poem to Mary of Modena she apologizes that ill health—Barker was recovering from an eye operation—prevented her from being on hand to see the king off to Calais ('It was not want of zeal, but want of sight', she assures the queen, 'That I did neither come, nor speak nor write').[53] She congratulated James's natural daughter, Arabella FitzJames, upon the latter's taking of vows at the Benedictine convent at nearby Pontoise in a ceremony Barker appears to have witnessed; it includes some curiously sectarian lines of praise ('If English Protestants your beautys saw, | They'd add new fury, to their furious law').[54] She complimented the royal princess Louise Maria, younger sister of the Prince of Wales, born 28 June 1692,[55] and lesser figures as well: an Augustinian nun, identified only as 'Dame ——', known for her 'curious gum-work' (fo. 46); someone she calls 'my dear Clarinthia'; a painter, one Mr Mosier; the Cambridge friends. Part Two also includes two elegies, one on the death of John

[51] Behn's attempt to secure Stuart patronage is discussed by Deborah C. Payne, ' "And poets shall by patron-princes live": Aphra Behn and Patronage', in Mary Anne Schofield and Cecilia Macheski (eds.), *Curtain Calls: British and American Women and the Theater, 1660–1820* (Athens, Oh.: Ohio UP, 1991), 105–19. For Manley, see Ros Ballaster, *Seductive Forms: Women's Amatory Fiction from 1684 to 1740* (Oxford: Clarendon P., 1992), 117–19.

[52] Gregg, 'Politics of Paranoia', 43. The poem, 'On The kings birth-day, writ at st Germains. 1694:', concludes: 'Then come my Lord return believe | your honour I ll mentain, | If you can but this once forgive | I'll never sin again' (fo. 42).

[53] 'To Her Majesty the Queen, on the Kings going to Callis this carnival 1696:' (fo. 43).

[54] 'To Madam Fitz James, on the day of her profession, at Pontoise, she taking the name of St Ignace' (fo. 45v).

[55] For whom see Susan Cole, 'Princess Over the Water: A Memoir of Louise Marie Stuart (1692–1712)', *Royal Stuart Papers*, 18 (Royal Stuart Society, 1981).

Cecil, fifth earl of Exeter from 1700,[56] another on the death of King James II from 1701.[57]

But Barker's great bid for recognition and patronage came in 1700 when, assisted by her cousin William Connock, she prepared a New Year's gift for the Prince of Wales: a presentation volume of the Jacobite verse-history 'A Collection of Poems Refering to the times; since the Kings accession to the Crown' (BL Add. MS 21,621).[58] The volume, comprising nearly ninety quarto pages of loyal verse, testifies to its author's belief that her 'ideas about matters of state mattered enough' to transmit in poetic form to the Prince of Wales and his supporters, according to Jeslyn Medoff, and she is surely right.[59] Every page is instinct with the conviction that national history filtered through the eyes of an ordinary woman possesses value. But missing from Medoff's sympathetic account is recognition that the gift was also, to put it baldly, a genteel species of begging: 'what must become of me an insect scribler', Barker asks her royal dedicatee, 'except enliven'd by the rays of your Royal

[56] The Cecils, the leading family in the Stamford area, owned the Wilsthorp, Lincolnshire property leased by Barker's family from 1662. *BG* (1713) and *EN* (1719) were dedicated to the earl's daughter-in-law, the countess of Exeter.

[57] That Barker's verse circulated at St-Germain seems certain but proof is thin. A copy of her elegy on the death of James II appears unattributed in BL Add. MS 10,118, fols. 410r–411r, a compilation of materials for a history of James completed by 1706, included so that 'nothing may perish coming to my hand yᵗ sounds forth yᵉ praises of this Royall Victime of yᵉ True Faith' (fo. 410r). Ascribed in the BL catalogue to Joseph Johnston, Prior of the English Benedictines of St Edmund in Paris, the volume was actually produced by Ralph Benet Weldon (1674–1713), a monk at St Edmund's. A second instance of copying exists but circumstances suggest the original was encountered far from St-Germain, probably in the neighbourhood of Stamford–Wilsthorp–Burghley House in the south-western corner of Lincolnshire. A version of her 1700 elegy on the death of the earl of Exeter was copied by Charles Caesar of Great Gransden, Huntingdonshire, into a commonplace book (BL Add. MS 43,410, fo. 160r) and ascribed without comment to 'J. Barker'. The commonplace book is dated 1705, at which time Caesar was living in Stamford, only a few miles from Wilsthorp, where Barker had been living since 1704, and from Burghley House, seat of the Cecil family. Caesar probably encountered the elegy locally.

[58] MS presentation volumes by women were relatively uncommon in the 17th cent.: see Margaret J. M. Ezell, *The Patriarch's Wife: Literary Evidence and the History of the Family* (Chapel Hill and London: U. of North Carolina P., 1987), 66–8. She might have included Mary Astell, who in 1689 presented a volume of her verse to archbishop Sancroft (Bod., MS Rawl. poet. 154, fos. 50–97).

[59] Jeslyn Medoff, ' "A temerity allmost to madness": Jane Barker as Jacobite Poet/Historian', paper presented at Northeast American Society for Eighteenth-Century Studies, Sept. 1996.

Highnes's protection, which at your feet I begg with profound respect and humility'.[60]

For her copyist she turned to her cousin William Connock, whose involvement in the project may suggest the volume was intended to promote the interests of the Connock family at court.[61] William's hand, although unprofessional, was neat, firm, and distinct.[62] Hers, clear but quirky, was at this time rather sloppy, given to blots and ink spills. Having long suffered from failing eyesight, which she attributed to cataracts, Barker, aged 43, elected in 1696 to have her eyes couched, a procedure which involved inserting a needle into the eye in order to move the clouded lens out of the line of vision. The operation must have been dreadful to contemplate. Assuming the sufferer was not left fully blind (from sepsis or injury), she or he would thereafter have difficulty seeing and would need to use a powerful magnifying glass to read or write at all. Couching had left her, by her own description, 'a blind person', able to write but only with difficulty, as the messy pages of her portions of the Magdalen Manuscript poignantly attest.[63] To produce copy suitable for presentation at court she would need the assistance of an amanuensis. William, a soldier who had seen active service in the Nine Years War wars between England and France, possessed an acceptable hand and, in the present lull in hostilities, the necessary time. The Treaty of Ryswick (1697), which

[60] For patron–client relationships within the context of scribal publication, see Harold Love, *Scribal Publication in Seventeenth-Century England* (Oxford: Clarendon P., 1993), 58–65 and 178–9.

[61] If so, then Barker was acting in accord with aristocratic codes that throughout the 17th cent. encouraged female participation in politics in support of family interests. See Lois G. Schwoerer, 'Women and the Glorious Revolution', *Albion*, 18 (1986), 195–218, esp. 210–11.

[62] The identity of the hand can be established by comparison with that found in three letters by Connock from 1726 to 1727 in the BL (Add. MS 21,896, fos.1r–v, 3–4v, 11–12v).

[63] The Magdalen MS refers in several places to vision problems. The dedication from late 1700 opens with a reference to 'blindness and misfortunes' (fo. 3); a preface from the same time attributes 'slips of the pen, and defects in the English' to 'long absence and blindness' (fo. 6); an undated preface 'to the Reader' (probably no later than 1704) asks that the volume be 'consider'd as the work of a blind person' (fo. 1). A marginal note to a 1696 poem in Part Two ('To Her Majesty the Queen, on the Kings going to Callis this carnival 1696:'), fo. 43, indicates that her eyes were then 'bound doun' in consequence of an operation: 'her catharact was then couched'.

marked the start of an interval of peace that would last until the outbreak of the War of Spanish Succession in 1702, left him at leisure to help his cousin with what must have been a time-consuming scribal project.

William is an intriguing instance of a little-studied phenomenon, the male amanuensis to a woman writer, and as such takes a place alongside, from roughly this same period, the husbands of Anne Finch and Margaret Cavendish. Literary history has shown itself full of admiration for Milton's daughters, Wordsworth's sister, and Hardy's second wife, to name only a few of the scores of women whose secretarial services on behalf of celebrated male authors traditional scholars were pleased to extol and feminists more recently to deplore, but has exhibited scant interest in the menfolk who have performed similar services on behalf of women. One wishes more could be learned about William Connock.[64] As 'dear cosen Coll—' he is praised in one of the Magdalen poems for his heroic actions at the siege at Limerick, where 'the bold Rebells'' fell by 'Connock's battery, rais'd within the wall'.[65] From his burial notice we know that after the Irish campaigns he served in the wars on the continent in Toby Bourke's regiment, resided at the Chancellerie (where he was joined by Jane late in her life, if not earlier), and died in 1738, aged 89, surviving by six years 'Cosin Barker'.[66] One of our rather few glimpses of the histor-

[64] According to Ruvigny and Raineval, *Jacobite Peerage*, 37, William, created baronet in 1732 by 'James III', was the grandson of George Connock, born 1575, of the family of Connock of Treworgy, Cornwall.

[65] 'To My dear cosen Coll—at his return out of Irland into france' (fo. 47). The 'cousin wounded' (fo. 8) at Sedgemoor in 'Fidelia alone' may refer to William; his name does not, however, turn up in Dalton's *Lists*, although a Major William Connock (d. 1704), who was Captain of Col. Roger McElligot's [Irish] Regiment of Foot, does. He may be the son of cousin William and older brother of Timon, a possibility supported by a line in 'To My dear cosen' indicating that her cousin the Colonel had a son fighting in Ireland. The Part Three poem 'To my unkle Colonel C— after his return into the Low countrys' (fo. 100) would suggest the possibility of a third military Connock, possibly the father of cousin William. According to Childs, *Army*, 119–20, the Anglo-Dutch Brigade, having fought in the Confederate army between 1674 and 1678, returned to the Netherlands in 1678. This may be the occasion of the 'return into the Low countrys' poem.

[66] For Bourke, see Micheline Kerney Walsh, 'Toby Bourke, Ambassador of James III at the Court of Philip V, 1705–13', in Eveline Cruickshanks and Edward Corp (eds.), *The Stuart Court in Exile and the Jacobites* (London and Rio Grande: Hambledon P., 1995), 143–53.

ical Barker comes in letters by William to his son Timon, one (14 January 1726) reporting that he received word that 'Cos. Barker' was 'very ill & had receivd the Blessed Sacrament', another (26 May 1727) indicating she was on her way to France: 'I expect every day a lettre from Cosin Barker of her beeing arived at Diep'.[67] He was obviously a respected figure at St-Germain and known to James III in Rome, though perhaps not well. A letter of 7 December 1738 relating the burial of 'old Coll. Connock' notes, 'I believe H[is] M[ajesty] may remember him, he was an Officer that had served with distinction in ye first war after ye Revolution'.[68]

New Year's Day was a traditional occasion for tendering royal compliments, and this particular New Years Day—1 January 1701—would have seemed an unusually propitious time to seek favour at the Jacobite court. Never had the likelihood that James Francis Edward, the Prince of Wales, would succeed to the English throne seemed greater. Hopes at St-Germain had been at a fever pitch since mid-August, when news of the death of William, duke of Gloucester, Anne's last surviving heir, raised expectations that the Prince of Wales, Anne's half-brother, would be named next-in-line. 'I need not tell you how pleased they are, and confident of being soon in *England*', reported the English ambassador in a dispatch of 18 August. Six days earlier he had reported that they 'were never in such great hopes at *St. Germains* as they are now'. Throughout the autumn and early winter the message remained much the same: 'For of late the *St. Germains* People are so high, that they think it is now our time to court them' (9 October); '[they] are grown to so great a height as is not to be imagined' (11 October); '[they] think their Game so very sure' (11 December). Then in early November Philip of Anjou (the grandson of Louis XIV) was named successor to the Spanish Crown, concentrating yet more power in the House of Bourbon, still the House of Stuart's best hope. 'I do assure you there is great Joy at *St. Germains*', the ambassador wrote; 'the

[67] BL Add. MS 21,896, fos. 1, 11v.
[68] Letter from Dicconson to Edgar, Royal Archives, Stuart Papers, 211/110. The parish register recording his burial describes him as 'chevalier baronnet d'Angleterre, colonel réformé d'infanterie, à la suite du régiment de Bourke'. I am grateful to Edward Corp for sharing this information with me.

late King [i.e. James II] goes this day to wait on the Duke of Anjou'.[69]

The presentation copy of the 'Poems Refering to the times' was obviously prepared in this mood of Jacobite exhilaration. The dedication begins on a sanguine note: 'The daydawn of happiness which begins to break in Europe conducts me ... to wish your Highness not only a happy new year, but a happy new Century'. The verses themselves are rather bleak, the author warns—they chronicle the decline of James's fortunes from their apex in 1685, when he crushed Monmouth's rebellion, to the loss in 1691 of Ireland—but this revisitation of the 'madness and mallice which concluded the old [century]' may 'give as it were a gust to coming Felicity'. To provide the sequence the felicitous close that the recent upturn in events seemed to warrant she supplied a new ending, a poem with the gloating title 'Hell's Regret, for the peace & unity like to ensue the Duke of Anjou's accession to the Crown of Spain', obviously composed in the last month or so to take advantage of developments in Spain.[70] It stands as a kind of exultant coda, a declaration of the triumph of Stuart history, to a group of poems otherwise focused on the bitter afflictions visited upon England in the absence of its rightful Stuart rulers and was doubtless designed to share in, and perhaps capitalize on, the ebullient mood at court. That ebullience would collapse soon enough, along with the promise of 'peace & unity' that occasioned such regret in hell. By May 1701 English forces were assembling in Holland; the next month the Act of Settlement establishing a Protestant succession would squelch all remaining hopes that the Catholic Prince of Wales would succeed peacefully to the throne.

[69] Christian Cole, *Historical and Political Memoirs* (London: J. Millan, 1735), 195, 188, 217, 219, 260, 245. The mood did not last. The ambassador, the duke of Manchester, posted at the court at Versailles, reports on 5 Mar. 1701 that the 'only Hopes they have now left at *St. Germains* are, that they are to be restored by a *French* Power in a short time, and the Intrigues carried on in *Scotland* are too apparent to be doubted on' (323). See also vol. ii of Duke of Manchester, *Court and Society from Elizabeth to Anne*, 2 vols. (London: Hurst and Blackett, 1864).

[70] 'Hell's Regret' could have been begun no earlier than 8 Nov. when, according to Cole, news of the King of Spain's death arrived at Paris. The poem is tipped in the BL volume, fos. 54r–55v, obviously a late insertion, indicating it was composed after the volume had been sent off for binding.

It is not known what notice was taken of Jane Barker's New Year's gift to the prince,[71] but a Part Two poem raises suspicion that her grand bid for royal protection came to naught.[72] 'Reflections on mr Cowleys words, The Muses fleece lys dry'[73] takes its title from a line in an ode by Abraham Cowley, 'The Complaint', in which the poet, one of Barker's literary heroes and himself an exile at an earlier Stuart court, reflects self-pityingly upon his neglect at the hands of Charles II after the Restoration. (Cowley failed to receive the preferment he had had every reason to expect in return for his services to the exiled royal family during the Interregnum.) The poet goes unrewarded ('the Muses fleece was dry'), he complains, while Charles freely bestows his bounty ('The fruitful seed of Heaven') upon others:

> And upon all the quickned ground,
> The fruitful seed of Heaven did brooding lye,
> And nothing but the Muses Fleece was dry.[74]

A well-publicized instance of grousing over royal neglect and ingratitude, 'The Complaint' was notorious in Cowley's and

---

[71] The volume now in the British Library, which may or may not have been the actual presentation copy (see n. 22 above), eventually came into the possession of Anne-Charlotte de Crussol de Florensac, duchesse d'Aiguillon, for it bears a book plate with her arms engraved sometime after her marriage in 1718 to Armand-Louis du Plessis-Richelieu (1683–1750). A pencilled note in the volume mistakenly identifies the arms as belonging to her husband, the duc d'Aiguillon. I have been informed by Edward Corp that the duchesse lived at the Château du Val at Rueil, midway between Paris and St-Germain, which means she resided near the Jacobites from 1718 onwards. She may have received the manuscript directly from Jane Barker herself or it may have been transmitted through courtly circles.

[72] Other women had known similar disappointment. Elizabeth Cellier, Catholic convert and midwife, sought and secured King James's approval of her plan for a college of midwives and a Royal Hospital in 1687 but received no financial support: see Anne Barbeau Gardiner, 'Elizabeth Cellier in 1688 on Envious Doctors and Heroic Midwives Ancient and Modern', *ECL* 14 (Feb. 1990), 24–34. Aphra Behn's struggles with both Stuart brothers are described by Janet Todd in *The Secret Life of Aphra Behn* (London: Andre Deutsch, 1996). James II did not become Behn's special patron, as she had hoped; indeed during his brief reign 'he had hardly patronised anyone significant' among the English poets, concentrating instead on his various Catholicizing projects (395).

[73] Mag. MS, fo. 81; printed in Wilson, 329–30.

[74] A. R. Waller (ed.), *The English Writings of Abraham Cowley*, 2 vols. (Cambridge, Cambridge UP, 1905–6), i. 437. Cf. the story of Gideon and the fleece, Judges 6: 36–40.

Barker's time;[75] it is impossible not to hear in Barker's bitter little poem an application to herself of Cowley's well-known resentments.[76]

The prediction of an unseasonable withering of 'buding Loyalty' with which Barker's poem begins seems a barbed reference to the poor record of recent Stuart monarchs in regard to patronage of deserving poets. ' 'Tis that unluckey sentance'— that is, Cowley's charge that the Muse's fleece lies untouched by royal favour—which has turned erstwhile loyal poets against monarchs:

> 'Tis that unluckey sentance which has lost
> More hearts than wou'd have conquer'd Ceasors host
> It is to buding Loyalty a frost.

But if the advice-to-kings stance adopted at the beginning of the poem is meant to hint darkly at the folly of treating a poet badly, Barker quickly retreats from this quasi-threatening posture to suggest that neglect is part of a poet's fate:

> And what's yet worse, it ever must remain,
> unkindness to a poet's dy'd in grain.

But then she cannot resist further dark intimations:

> If poets neither drink nor porrige have,
> They will not cough, but they'll talk in their grave,
> Tis ominous to treat a poet ill,
> As tis our merry chimny guests to kill.

She ends by invoking the examples of Cowley and Butler ('Hudibras'),[77] two poets whose names stood as virtual

---

[75] He is mildly ridiculed in one Session of the Poets for 'print[ing] his pitiful Melancholy': see Jean Loiseau, Abraham Cowley's Reputation in England (Paris: Henri Didier, 1931), 11. In the next century Samuel Johnson wrote, 'he published his pretensions and his discontent in an ode called The Complaint, in which he styles himself the melancholy Cowley. This met with the usual fortune of complaints, and seems to have excited more contempt than pity': George Birkbeck Hill (ed.), Lives of the English Poets by Samuel Johnson, 3 vols. (New York: Octagon Books, 1967), i. 14–15.

[76] Behn also draws upon 'The Complaint' in her post-revolutionary poem to Gilbert Burnet, 'A Pindaric Poem to the Reverend Doctor Burnet, On The Honour He Did Me of Enquiring After Me and My Muse: see Todd, Secret Life, 427, and 509 n. 8.

[77] She might have mentioned Dryden as well, who never managed to collect from

bywords for her generation for writers abandoned to poverty and neglect:[78]

> The world admir'd, this mighty Cowleys wit
> But more admir'd, he had not bread to eat,
> Not only his, but Hudibras's name,
> Serves to immortalize mans crying shame,
> In true necessity his days he pass'd,
> And by the parish, was inter'd at last.
>
> (fos. 81r–v)

Barker implicitly enrolls herself, that is to say, in the company of deserving but impoverished poets passed over for royal favour. It is surely significant that she placed these sulky lines at the end of a group of poems that show her assuming a variety of patronage-seeking postures—including, as we have seen, direct addresses to members of the royal family. It is notable too that nowhere in Part Two of the Magdalen Manuscript does she include the lines of praise or thanks, the tributes to royal bounty and munificence, one would expect of a royal client well treated.[79] We find instead a sour little poem exhibiting considerable resentment that the 'Muses fleece lys dry'.

'An insect scribler'

But the materials in the Magdalen Manuscript tell also of a rather more successful effort at literary self-authorization. A major concern in feminist literary history has been the exploration of

---

Charles II all the pay owed him: see Michael Foss, *The Age of Patronage: The Arts in England 1660–1750* (Ithaca: Cornell UP, 1971), 48, 62; in 1685 he was owed 1,245 pounds. For a record of official payments, see James Winn, *John Dryden and his World* (New Haven and London: Yale UP, 1987), 525–31. According to Paul J. Korshin, 'Types of Eighteenth-Century Literary Patronage', *ECS* 7 (1974), 453–73, royal support for writers in the Restoration was 'not common' (457).

[78] As early as 1683, in a letter to Laurence Hyde, earl of Rochester, Dryden linked the two as examples of poverty and neglect: '''Tis enough for one Age to have neglected Mr Cowley, and sterv'd Mr. Buttler': qtd. in Rachel Trickett, *The Honest Muse: A Study in Augustan Verse* (Oxford: Clarendon P., 1967), 65. As Trickett observes, 66, Dryden and John Oldham 'had begun to suggest the idea of a pantheon of unfortunate great writers from Spenser to Cowley and Butler who had been neglected by their age'.

[79] The one poem of gratitude, interestingly, is addressed to the Cambridge students who saw her earlier poems into print in *PR*.

gender as a source or constituent of female literary authority, the assumption being that a woman's identity as a writer is closely aligned with her identity as a woman and, further, that at this particular juncture her marginality could be turned to social, moral, and political advantage. As Ros Ballaster puts it in an important study, women writers at this time (she names Behn and Manley), succeeded in constructing the female writer 'as a political agent, precisely by virtue of her position at the margins of the political order'.[80] I would not deny the huge role gender plays in women's strategies of literary self-authorization, far from it, but my work on the St-Germain verse suggests that too intent a focus on gender excludes from consideration elements at least as important as those it makes visible. When in the preface to the 'Poems Refering to the times' Barker declares herself 'not in a station to know what springs mov'd this mad machin of Rebellion' (fo. 6), she is undoubtedly speaking 'as a woman', as Carol Barash has observed,[81] but she speaks as much more besides—as an ideological hard-liner, a Roman Catholic convert, a Jacobite non-compounder. To place gender at the centre of the story of women as political agents is, ironically, to miss out on much of their politics.

Insistence on the centrality of gender leads to problems of the sort that crop up in the discussion of the Magdalen Manuscript offered by Barash. She is right, I think, to characterize Barker's poetic stance in the political poems as that of prophetic outsider; however, her effort to find in them an extended effort on Barker's part to construct herself as a virginal Catholic poet in relation to an imagined female community and to install Mary of Modena as the 'authoritative centre' of what Barash wants us to believe is a body of feminocentric political verse creates at least two problems. First, it requires that she seriously misrepresent the general tendency of the Magdalen verse. Such concern as is exhibited for female literary affiliations is, in fact, fleeting at best, and, more damagingly for her argument, Mary of Modena is very little apparent. Indeed, it is somewhat surprising, given the marked courtly orientation of this body of verse, to find that the queen figures with real significance in only

---

[80] Ballaster, *Seductive Forms*, 3.
[81] Carol Barash, *EWP* 198.

two of the forty-eight long poems under consideration—for a total of no more than thirty lines. Barash's claim that it is the 'alien and marginalized female monarch, rather than the would-be (or reigning) king, who attracts the poet's attention and focuses her desire for legitimate authority' is simply not tenable.[82] Second, and more directly relevant to my purposes here, preoccupation with themes of female community obscures the extent to which these verses are implicated in a very different kind of identity politics. Barker, it seems to me, writes less 'as a woman' in the Magdalen verse than as a divine-right monarchist and Roman Catholic of a particularly uncompromising sort. First and foremost she constructs herself as an ideological purist among the exiles at St-Germain, and her regnant aim is to stand firm against the concessionary views of the so-called 'compounders', the mainly Anglican supporters of James who sought restoration on strictly limited terms.[83] For Barker literary self-authorization was bound up in Jacobite politics, which at the contentious court of St-Germain was often a politics of paranoia in which members of many factions felt themselves to belong to a persecuted, deep-suffering minority. Such a climate was productive of verse of a particularly self-righteous stamp.

To some extent the self-righteousness of the verse Barker circulated at St-Germain is characteristic of Jacobite verse more generally, for the 'Jacobite Muse', as Paul Monod observes, 'was clothed in doggerel, and her music was crude'.[84] Certainly these poems lack subtlety, grace, or any of the other elements traditional criticism honours with the phrase 'literary value'. Except for a few quietly reflective moments, mainly in the Fidelia poems, they bristle with fury, moral indignation, and implacable

---

[82] Barash, *EWP* 175. Her support of the claim, 204, seriously distorts the evidence: the 'long poem in praise of Mary of Modena' is in fact no more than a fourteen-line passage embedded in a long assault on Protestant England. Praise of Mary occurs in only two poems, one in Part One and the other in Part Two; by far the greater part of Barker's panegyric takes James II as its subject.

[83] For a summary overview of the differences between the 'compounders' and the 'non-compounders', see John Miller, *James II: A Study in Kingship* (1978; London: Methuen, 1991), 236–7.

[84] Monod, *Jacobitism*, 45. His chapter on Jacobite verse, 45–69, provides a good overview. See also Murray G. H. Pittock, *Poetry and Jacobite Politics in Eighteenth-Century Britain and Ireland* (Cambridge: Cambridge UP, 1994).

certitude. Fidelia can be memorably unsoftspoken, and is capable of wonderful abusiveness. William of Orange is 'currsed', a 'monster'.[85] The Anglican Church is a syphilitic Jezebel 'with ulcers coverd o'er' and 'insects . . . in every festerd sore' (fo. 22). The English people are 'worse than Judas' (fo. 23). The Anglican preachers who abandoned James are Sphinxes who bring forth death to whole cities (fo. 30v). An old Presbyterian woman with gall enough to offer up a prayer for Monmouth is a 'croaking toad, and scriech-owl . . . fit to teach the Devils to harangue' (fo. 9); her countrymen are 'gull'd, with folly and deceit' (fo. 28v). So assured is Fidelia of the truth of her convictions that she does not hesitate to rain curses upon her enemies— '[I] wish all cursses Hell cou'd e'er invent, | May light on those, who caus'd [James's] banishment' (fo. 23)[86]—or, in the manner of an Old Testament prophet, to pronounce judgement upon her wayward contemporaries: when generations to come look back upon these mad times, England will be thought hell and the English devils—or 'monsters, bearing tusks and claws, | To tear their neighbors as they do their laws' (fo. 30).[87]

Lines such as these provide striking evidence of the 'older, more subversive traditions' of politically engaged writing by women, traditions which Paula McDowell has convincingly argued were gradually erased from the cultural memory over the course of the eighteenth century, to be replaced in the nineteenth by a sanitized, bloodless, and intensively marketed construct of the apolitical literary lady.[88] We hear in Barker much the same note of resounding certitude voiced in the early verse of Elizabeth Singer ('Philomela', later the famously pious Mrs Rowe) when, in the same decade but from the other end of the political spectrum, she called upon God to punish William's enemies at the Battle of the Boyne: 'So now, great God, wrapt in

[85] Barker's other imagined speakers can be even more abusive. The Portsmouth soldier calls William a 'monster', 'tyrant', 'anti Pope', 'Dutch Hodge=pot of all wickedness', and, in a couplet deleted from the presentation copy, 'A tyrant and a hipocrite compleat, | Adore the Devil if he'd but make him great' ('Fidelia in France meets one of Portsmoth officers', fos. 27v–28v).
[86] 'Fidelia weeping for the Kings departure at the Revolution'. For 'weeping' BL has 'lamenting' (fo. 34).
[87] 'Fidelia in a Convent garden the Abess comes to her'.
[88] Paula McDowell, 'Consuming Women: The Life of the "Literary Lady" as Popular Culture in Eighteenth-Century England', *Genre*, 26 (1993), 219–52.

avenging *Thunder*, | Meet thine and *William's Foes*, and tread them *groveling* under'.[89] We are reminded how anachronistic it is to expect the verse of early modern women to yield the qualities of mild benignancy that the sentimental notions of femininity of a later age have encouraged us to attach to the idea of 'the woman poet'.

Barker's poems also participate in what Monod has described as the basic Jacobite cosmology.[90] History is thought to consist of a recurring struggle between lawful, divinely appointed monarchy and the forces of evil—today William, yesterday Cromwell, and before him 'that gyant Henry' (Henry VIII), to whose closing of the monasteries, a crime of enormous proportions, Barker traces many of the current national troubles. James is a saint, his enemies satanic. Rebellion is the work of the devil, and the events of recent history—the Test Act, the Exclusion Bill, the Battle of the Boyne—are authored by Lucifer, who, as prototype of all rebels, is a recurring figure in Barker's political verse (as he is in Jacobite verse in general). Hell, a 'place prepar'd for all that e'er rebell' (fo. 10), is the setting for several monologues spoken by Lucifer and England's Ill Genius, the great champions of William, 'our dearest Orange' (fo. 37).[91] Some poems depict a 'jubelee in Hell' (fo. 24) following a Protestant victory of one sort or another; others employ the topos of hell-in-an-uproar beloved of late seventeenth-century political satirists.[92] For Barker, as for other political satirists,

---

[89] 'A Pindaric *Poem* on Habakkuk', *Poems on Several Occasions. Written by Philomela* (London: John Dunton, 1696), 21. History of the transmission of Singer's verse provides a little known instance of the depoliticization of women's writings. In the 1690s, when she began to publish verse, her political engagements received praise: a 1696 commendatory verse lauds her championing of William ('No Pen *but* yours can match *the* Heroes Sword') and urges that she continue giving political lessons ('*Let harden'd Traitors know what 'tis to' abuse* | *The Patience of a* King *and of a* Muse', sig. A8). In the preface to a 1737 2nd edition, xvii, Curll explains why some of the 1696 political poems were omitted and others put in their place: Rowe's friends were 'desirous' of omitting some 'as favouring of *Party-Reflection* and the *Heat of Youth*, since *cooled* by stricter *Judgment*'.

[90] Monod, *Jacobitism*, esp. 45–62.

[91] Five of the twenty 'Poems Refering to the times' are set in hell.

[92] See 'A discours between England's ill Genius and his Companion on the jubelee in Hell' in which the English are shown to have allied themselves, unwittingly, with the devil's party ('They ran, and bawld, and huzza'd up hells' cause, | And fancyd 'twas, for liberty and laws' (fo. 24v)). For slightly later Jacobite satire making use of the hell-in-an-uproar topos, see 'The Devil and Burnet', which begins 'The Devils

hell offers opportunities for ironic inversions, as when Protestant fear of Catholicism is put into the mouths of Lucifer and his fellow 'direfull' fiends, who debate methods to 'stop this mighty growth of Popery' (fos. 15r, 15v).[93] Their councils in hell parody those in William's England, while England, so far as Fidelia is concerned, *is* hell.

The exuberant excesses of these poems belong to a world in which the battle to proclaim religious truth performed itself in highly theatricalized public spectacles, in annual pope-and-the-devil processions, for example, or the executions and public dismemberments of the Popish Plot martyrs. (In 'Fidelia weeping for the Kings departure at the Revolution' a mock procession behind a crucified cat figures importantly; for the cheering 'Rabble' in this representation of London anti-Catholic hysteria late in 1688 Fidelia has only contempt: 'Great is the folly of a headless crew, | Who still o'er-shoot themselves in all they do' (fo. 23v).)[94] In both public spectacle and privately circulated verse the drama of religious truth played itself out in heightened and polarized ways; absolute evil disputing absolute good in rituals of diabolism and purity. The squalling cats in the pope effigy, the blood dripping from the daggers of the attendants in the pope processions, the pope cast into the fire by the devil, the disembowelled priests hung at Tyburn: all are of a piece with Barker's heavily ironic jubilees in hell and invented dialogues in convent gardens, part of an invented world in which the contest over religious and political truth expressed itself in the starkest possible antitheses between evil and good.

Readers who come to the 'Poems Refering to the times' familiar only with the ironies of the later Galesia narratives may be startled by the strident absolutism of this verse. They should keep in mind that at this time political writers seldom sought (or

were bawling when Burnet descending | Transported them so that they left off contending; | Old Beelzebub ran the good Bishop to meet . . .' (Bod. MS Rawl. poet. 155, p. 100; other versions in Bod. MS Eng. misc. c. 116, fo. 7; Bod. MS Eng. poet. e. 87, p. 98). See also Monod, *Jacobitism*, 49–62.

[93] 'A discourse between England's Ill Genius and his companion'. At a council called by Lucifer the fiends discuss what they regard as hell's most urgent concern: 'The world's allmost by Popery o'errun' (fo. 15).

[94] For the riots of November and December, see Tim Harris, 'London Crowds and the Revolution of 1688', in Eveline Cruickshanks (ed.), *By Force or By Default? The Revolution of 1688–1689* (Edinburgh: John Donald, 1989), 44–64.

were rewarded for) moral complexity or subtle ironized truths. Indeed, Dryden is one of the very authors who regularly achieved in his political verse the kind of complexity we like to think inheres in works of 'real' literature. But he did not leave England: he lived out the 1690s 'a commercially-minded Jacobite who continued to produce stage works and lucrative translations in London, but never visited St. Germain'.[95] If the qualities that make the Galesia fictions so appealing to modern readers are largely absent in Barker's privately circulated manuscript verse, this is in part because Barker was writing not for an open and diverse print-based community, such as Dryden's in London, but rather for a small band of co-religionists whom she could rely upon to share her furious indignation. The political poems are tribal utterances meant to circulate through a confined 'scribal reading circle', to use Harold Love's terminology, and like any such circle the militantly Catholic community at St-Germain was characterized by 'coherence and inward-turned autonomy'.[96] Its readers required neither irony nor subtlety. Love's observation on the satiric lampoon, with which Barker's political verse has affinities, is helpful: its decorum 'was one of outspokenness in all things, a fact that helps explain why so productive a genre produced so few lasting masterpieces'. When irony appears in 'scriptorial satire', it usually does so 'in the form of heavy sarcasm'.[97] As will be seen in the next chapter, when she began to publish in the market-place of print Barker would be forced to develop more oblique strategies, but in the St-Germain verse her literary authority was firmly grounded in her straightforward enunciation of Jacobite truth.

Indeed, in places her very language can be seen as performative of Jacobite truth. This is strikingly the case in the dedication to the Prince of Wales, which may usefully be regarded as a kind of 'arena' in which a carefully crafted language of obeisance expresses metaphorically Jacobite ideals of loyalty and obeisance.[98] Take the 'insect scribler' reference mentioned

[95] Paul Monod, 'Jacobitism as Court Culture and Popular Culture', paper presented at Northeast American Society for Eighteenth-Century Studies, Sept. 1996.

[96] Love, Scribal, 184.   [97] Love, Scribal, 308.

[98] I am drawing here on Payne's analysis of the dedication as 'one of the "arenas" in which patronage is transformed into a powerful cultural metaphor': see her 'Behn and Patronage', 114.

earlier. It is easy to see why such a self-representation, read alongside the author's later deprecatory concession that her fingers were meant rather to 'wield the needle and distaf', might suggest the concealment of literary ambition behind the protective cover of a self-effacing femininity.[99] But to foreground gender in this way is to read as feminine modesty what is more crucially an expression of a Jacobite (and, more generally, a conservative seventeenth-century) world-view based upon divinely sanctioned social distinctions. For in Barker's usage humility tropes such as these are bound up in notions of divine-right monarchy and the properly submissive political subject. The notion of the sacredness of monarchy is underscored by the biblically resonant language—taken from Exodus, fittingly—which Barker adopts to praise the 'piller of fire' (fo. 4v) which has brought her, one of the chosen people, 'to the most desirable presence of your Royal Highness, the haven of happiness, the asylum of vertue, and the reward of Loyalty' (fo. 4v). As the appropriately worshipful subject she is vastly below and distant from him: an 'insect scribler'; one who 'with awfull respect' can but 'admire at distance, those glories in which you are incircul'd' (fo. 5). Even an insect, however, is free to remind a monarch of his obligations: 'Now if it far'd thus with this great man [Dryden], what must become of me an insect scribler, except enliven'd by the rays of your Royal Highnes's protection' (fo. 4). The attitude of extreme humility performed by the language serves then as a kind of metaphor to project at once an attitude of mind and an ideal relationship between sovereign and subject and, by extension, to invoke a whole world of divinely ordered distinctions of hierarchy and rank. Viewed in this light the dedication is a remarkably assured statement of authorial purpose: far from inscribing gendered anxieties of authorship or excusing herself in what have been called tropes of undoing, Barker affirms Jacobite ideals of divine-right monarchy and performs the unswerving fealty of truly loyal subjects—such as herself.

One sign of Barker's confidence is her alignment of the 'Poems Refering to the times' with comparable works by the two foremost male poets of the time, Abraham Cowley and

[99] Barash, *EWP*, 198.

John Dryden. (Katherine Philips, who will figure prominently in Barker's later novelistic self-authorizations, makes no appearance in the St-Germain verse, perhaps because Orinda's largely lyrical poetic oeuvre offered no precedent for the kind of epic scope Barker sought in her Jacobite verse-chronicle. It is only when she enters the market-place as a novelist, writing as a woman for women readers, that Barker will emphasize her place in a female line of poetic descent epitomized by Orinda.) She begins by comparing herself with the Cowley of *The Civil War*, the long poem he abandoned when a string of parliamentary victories deprived the verse-history of its hoped-for royalist conclusion. Her assumption of the role of loyalist historian is, she concedes, 'somwhat audacious for so feeble a capacity' (fo. 3), adding with calculated modesty, 'if the learned Mr Cowley found so great a difficulty in writing the transactions of his time [*his history of the civil wars*] that he suppressd them after written, the enterprise in me must needs seem a temerity allmost to madness' (fos. 3r–v).[100] In this way she establishes herself a successor of the 'mighty Cowley', as she calls him elsewhere, the royalist man of letters still regarded by many of her contemporaries as the greatest English poet of the age. She next constructs herself in relation to a more recent precursor, 'that learned and great wit' Dryden, a declared Catholic like herself, naming *The Hind and the Panther* as a model for her own apologia for her conversion to Catholicism. Like him, she is destined to suffer in the cause of religious truth. (It is probably to Dryden that she pays homage later in the dedication when she refers to loyal writers, who, though remaining behind in England, 'have not bowd the knee to Baal': their 'learned pens' might 'have performd this work more anply [amply] and gracefully' (fo. 4).) Adopting a manner that combines deference and audacity, she thus inserts herself in a prestigious and deeply serious tradition of royalist poetic intervention in religio-political crisis. In this

---

[100] In the preface to his *Poems* (1656) Cowley explained, 'I have cast away all such pieces as I wrote during the time of the late troubles, with any relation to the differences that caused them; as among others, *three Books of the Civil War it self*, reaching as far as the first *Battel* of *Newbury*, where the succeeding *misfortunes* of the *party* stopt the *work*': Waller, *Abraham Cowley*, i. 9. A part was published in 1679 as *A Poem on the Late Civil War*, the only printing in the 17th cent. Her reference to her 'temerity' may echo Cowley's description in the 1656 preface of the Pindaric form as '*bold, even to Temeritie*' (Waller, i. 11).

context the 'insect scribler' image acquires additional resonance, for it can be seen to belong not only to the decorum of royal address but also to a tradition of authorial 'modesty formulas', which, as Curtius has demonstrated, can be traced back to the Old Testament and classical rhetoric. (He includes in his discussion of topoi of self-deprecation a medieval poet who called himself 'a louse'.)[101] Modesty topoi enabled Barker not only to position herself in a suitably obeisant relation to the monarch but also to join the company of serious, classically based authors for whom authorial self-deprecation was one of the oldest cards in the deck of self-authorizing tricks.

If we turn now to the preface 'To the reader' that follows the dedication, we see that in addressing a more general readership she sets aside the extremes of deference adopted for an address to royalty and assumes instead a righteous, Old Testament manner, stressing the rough, angry, but above all truthful nature of her representation of the madness and frenzy of the recent past. In addressing a non-royal readership she grounds her authority in her commitment to harsh truth. She disavows special knowledge or access to privileged information ('I was not in a station to know what springs mov'd this mad machin of Rebellion'); instead she testifies to truths that all can recognize, her authority grounded in shared experience: 'I have onely told what all the world saw and heard'. Even the roughness of the verse is made a condition of its truthfulness. She will 'leave elegancy to the great and learned writers': her verses are not well-wrought pieces of literary artifice, but simple truth. If her words seem plain and rude ('too lively'), then the objects of her attack should look to their own crimes: 'If any herein see the portrature of their actions, make an ill figure, let them blame the original, not the hand for drawing the copys too lively'. This aggressively unapologetic preface is framed by statements that underscore her disregard for conventions of polite modesty, deference, or even gentleness. 'I suppose I need not make an apologie', it begins, and ends on exactly the same note: 'I ask no bodys pardon for what I have done, touching the subject'. This remarkable preface is worth quoting in full:

---

[101] Ernst Robert Curtius, *European Literature and the Latin Middle Ages*, trans. Willard R. Trask (1953; Princeton: Princeton UP, 1990), 83–5.

I suppose I need not make an apologie to my Reader for charging whole partys with crimes in which great numbers were not involv'd, for since matter of fact demonstrates that the major part were; the minor must forgive this non exemption, till their proper merit distinguish their persons, or attone for their party.

It is hard to writ an affair of this kind for tis certain, many will be offended, scarce any pleasd; consequently the author condemn'd on all hands, but an honest writer who takes Justice for rewarde, and Vertue for a Crown, cares not who weres the wreaths of popular applause. Every soldjer is not a general, yet every one that does his duty in his station is commendable: and if in this I have done mine honestly; I leave elegancy to the great and learned writers; I was not in a station to know what springs mov'd this mad machin of Rebellion, I have onely told what all the world saw and heard: I have made my Fidelia speak the common dialect of Catholicks, and her friend that of the Church of England: If any herein see the portrature of their actions, make an ill figure, let them blame the original, not the hand for drawing the copys too lively. I ask no bodys pardon for what I have done, touching the subject, the slips of the pen, and defects in the English caus'd by long absence and blindness every generous reader will pardon gratis. and there in lay an obligation on | their humble servant (fos. 5v–6).

'Malice or faction sure beguiles your sight'

There is little in the present debates over culture and history that would have surprised Barker. As an exiled adherent of a much calumniated king, a 'fugitive' as one of the poems puts it, and as a Roman Catholic in an aggressively Protestant country, she knew first-hand that representations of past and contemporary political affairs were anything but objective or 'value-free'. Moreover, she came to political writing at a time when the press was seen to be able to 'promulgate new, subversive fictions with an irresistible force and rapidity'.[102] Everything Barker wrote in the decades following the Revolution registers an acute (and often appalled) sense that what goes by the name of truth within the political nation is to an overwhelming extent a product of those who controlled the press. Well into the 1720s she continued to brood

---

[102] Love, *Scribal*, 171. For a provocative study of the relation between print culture and political intervention in the late 17th cent., see Weber, *Paper Bullets*.

over the power of fiction and fiction-makers to manufacture whole new orders of reality within the expanding culture of print. In the more hectic certitudes of the St-Germain verse, written in the immediate context of a propaganda war the print-savvy Williamites had little trouble winning,[103] she returns again and again to contemplate the gap between Protestant propaganda—'forgerys they strove the world to cheat' (fo. 32)—and Jacobite truth, by turns frustrated over and infuriated by the power of Protestant fictions to define her reality. The likes of a William of Orange can 'flatter, threaten, faun, swear, ly for gain'[104] and see his print-driven lies choke out the truth.

> Nothing he [James] said, or did, was judg'd aright,
> But white was still made black, and black made white.
> ('Fidelia in a Convent garden the Abess comes to
> her', fo. 31)

She is at once shocked and outraged by the way 'lys, aspersions, calmnys' (fo. 32) could turn even James's supporters against him.[105] Fittingly, Lucifer's hell is imagined as a kind of ministry for anti-Catholic propaganda, and Lucifer's agent, England's 'ill Genius', is essentially a master of disinformation, sent into England after the defeat of Protestantism at Sedgemoor to subvert by lies:

> Go tempt the people, and new sins devise,
> Puzzell their brains, with jealousies and lyes
> Of slavery and arbitrary power,
> Of leagues with France, and thousand follys more,
> In all things make the government to blame,
> At the last cast, sometimes one wins the game.[106]

The English people are unthinking, easily duped; once 'stout'

---

[103] For William's shrewd management of popular opinion, see Lois G. Schwoerer, 'Propaganda in the Revolution of 1688–89', *American Historical Review*, 82 (1977), 843–74; and David Hayton, 'The Propaganda War', in W. A. Maguire (ed.), *Kings in Conflict: The Revolutionary War in Ireland and its Aftermath 1689–1750* (Belfast: Blackstaff P., 1990), 106–21. James, as Hayton reports, 'seemed often content to rely on his authority as the divinely anointed king' (113).

[104] 'Fidelia in France meets one of the Portsmoth officers', BL Add. MS 21,621, fo. 41. Cancelled in Mag. MS.

[105] 'Fidelia in a Convent garden the Abess comes to her' (fos. 29v–32v) is the most sustained treatment of this theme.

[106] 'A discourse between Englands ill Genius and his companion' (fo. 15).

they are now 'debauch'd' by Protestant heresy, wholly at the mercy of satanic lies (fo. 10v).[107] They are easily deluded by such fabrications as the Popish Plot—described by the exasperated Fidelia as a 'fantome wond'rously begot, | By wond'rous mallice, on a wond'rous Sot'[108]—and, more wondrous still, by the egregious fiction of the 'warming-pan' birth.[109]

Barker never ceased fulminating against the 'warming-pan' fiction, which symbolized to her the power of print to propagate and render inevitable the most astonishing lies. In *Exilius*, published in 1714 but written earlier, in part perhaps at St-Germain, she invents for her fictional Mauritania an incident reminiscent of the warming-pan fiction which heaps scorn upon the deluders and a weak-minded populace so easily deluded:

This Conceit was so push'd on by those Princes, whose Interest it was that the King should have no Son, that the greater Part of *Mauritania* either believ'd, or pretended to believe this real Prince to be an Impostor; by which one sees, how easy it is to impose upon a Populace, who are generally ready to receive any Notion, though never so ridiculous, if it does but diminish the Power of their Superiors (*Exilius*, ii. 56).

She returned to the theme again in her last published work, *The Lining of the Patch Work Screen* (1726), in the tale, from an unnamed printed volume, relating the 'many false Stories invented against the Queen and the Prince' (206). This allusion to the warming-pan fiction from nearly four decades earlier concludes, slyly, with the crypto-Jacobite narrator getting the last word: 'Thus the little [printed] Story ended, without telling what Misery befel the King and Kingdom, by the *Moors*, who overran the Country for many Years after' (210).

---

[107] 'England's Good Genius' (fo. 10v).

[108] 'Fidelia and her friend on her becoming a Catholick first dialogue' (fo. 19). In a brief but suggestive discussion of Titus Oates's *A true narrative of the horrid plot and conspiracy of the Popish party against the life of His Sacred Majesty* (1679), Love, *Scribal*, 171–2, observes that 'Oates's incredibly circumstantial accounts of imaginary papist intrigues bombarded its readers with a whole new construction of reality, richly metonymic and virtually unfalsifiable. . . . Indeed, the study of literary realism in English might more profitably commence with the *Narrative* and its imitations than with *Robinson Crusoe*, which surely learned many techniques from it.'

[109] In the 'Second Dialogue' Fidelia defends Mary of Modena against the 'malice [that] makes her not be understood' (fo. 20v). For her defence of James and an attack on Whig and Protestant misrepresentations of the birth of the Prince of Wales, see 'Fidelia in a Convent garden the Abess comes to her' (fos. 29v–32v).

Revisionist work by recent Jacobite historians emphasizes the ideological differences dividing what was once thought to be a highly unified exile community at St-Germain. St-Germain, in the picture that has been emerging, was fissured along religious, national, and factional lines: Catholics and Protestants; English, Irish, and Scots; and various political groups at court all jockeyed for place in a community riven by conflict. Although bound in theory by 'their common desire to restore the House of Stuart to the British throne', in practice, as Edward Gregg and others have argued, the Jacobites were less a 'unified, single-minded movement' than a nonce collection of 'shifting coalitions and alliances in the manner of most modern political parties'.[110] Rivalries could be sharp and bitter. It is clear Barker aligned herself with the 'non-compounders', the most intransigent of the Jacobites at St-Germain. These were Catholic hardliners who rejected the compromise sought by the mainly Anglican 'compounders' who proposed restoration on strictly limited terms and called for assurances that measures for the advancement of Catholics in England such as those pursued by James during his brief reign would not be repeated. To Barker and her kind compounding with the Anglican establishment was anathema. Having exchanged security and position in the British Isles for the bleak uncertainties of exile, the non-compounders formed a 'a solid bloc of reactionaries', as one historian puts it.[111] The thought of moderating their insistence on the restoration of anything less than a *divine-right* monarch or other than a *Catholic* Stuart—for plans were afoot to convert the Prince of Wales to Protestantism—was totally unacceptable.[112] Were James to compromise in the manner proposed by the compounders, he would 'weaken his moral position and that of his supporters; moreover, as most of the exiles had suffered some loss through their fidelity, would not compromise

---

[110] Gregg, 'Politics of Paranoia', 42, 43.

[111] George Hilton Jones, *Charles Middleton: The Life and Times of a Restoration Politician* (Chicago and London: U. of Chicago P., 1967), 255.

[112] Manchester, 11 Dec. 1700, reports fears among the Jacobites that the Prince will be carried away to England, with his consent, to convert to the Church of England; among the hard-line Catholic party 'the changing of his Religion will never be suffered, and they have lately declared that they would rather see him dead': see Cole, *Historical*, 260.

mean sacrifice of the loyal to the factious and rebellious?'[113] Their ideal was unswerving fidelity. It was an ideal that Fidelia in her Old Testament-prophetic manner was intended to project, one that drew strength from its opposition to real and imagined enemies.

We can begin to understand, then, why in the prefatory materials Barker would represent herself as an embattled truth-teller ringed about by enemies. ('It is hard to writ an affair of this kind for tis certain, many will be offended, scarce any pleasd; consequently the author condemn'd on all hands'.) On the face of it this expectation of wholesale hostility seems odd and even fanciful since Barker is obviously writing for her own kind, for other Stuart zealots. Why then depict herself as having gained by her truth-telling 'much Hatred and many enemys' (dedication, fo. 3v) and as certain to be 'condemn'd on all hands' (preface, fo. 5v)? Were she really writing for hostile readers she would have been obliged to fashion a more open and accommodating persona—along the lines, perhaps, of the judiciously fair-minded one fashioned by Dryden for his preface to *The Hind and the Panther*; but her polarizing strategy, her aggressive refusal to exempt anyone from her attack exactly reverses the conciliatory strategy adopted by Dryden when he affirmed he would satirize only the 'refractory and disobedient on either side'.[114] Barker sought in fact to repudiate the middle ground Dryden attempted to open. She had no interest at this point in engaging what we have learned from Habermas to call the contestatory public sphere of letters. The poetry she produced and circulated at St-Germain belongs rather to an older world of scribal transmission in which the exchange of manuscript verse served to consolidate communal bonds, to 'nourish and articulate a corporate ideology'.[115] Her purposes were indeed almost tribal: she wrote to excoriate communally recognized enemies and stiffen the resolve of a band of intransigents, her imprecations verging on a form of social ritual. It is a kind of writing to which she would never return.

[113] Jones, *Charles Middleton*, 255.
[114] Earl Miner (ed.), *The Works of John Dryden*, iii: *Poems 1685–1692* (Berkeley and Los Angeles: U. of California P., 1969), 119.
[115] Love, *Scribal*, 181.

PART III

1713–1725

4

A Jacobite Novelist

THE next two chapters explore features of the prose fictions Barker published in the literary market-place between 1713 and 1725. The emphasis of the present chapter upon their religio-political aspects departs sharply from existing approaches, which tend to concentrate upon gender-and-genres themes in relation to feminist paradigms of female authorship or to pursue the meanings of Barker's autobiographical self-inscriptions. I would not gainsay the value of such approaches or challenge the view of Barker they imply. Barker is in fact a supremely self-regarding writer, mindful of her gendered singularity and fascinated with the many ways to tell her own story; and it seems undeniable, if hard to prove, that her heroine, Galesia—poet, healer, virgin, *femme savante*, and odd woman—is in many ways a self-portrait. However, when the complex self-fashionings of the prose fictions, the Galesia trilogy in particular,[1] are read in relation to their own political moment, these narratives emerge as complex elegiac responses to the declining fortunes of the exiled Stuarts and their followers in England.[2]

---

[1] The Galesia trilogy, as it is coming to be known, comprises *The Amours of Bosvil and Galesia*, first published as *Love Intrigues* (1713), *A Patch-Work Screen for the Ladies* (1723), and *The Lining of the Patch Work Screen* (1725; the title-page has 1726).

[2] Recent years have seen an explosion of work on Jacobitism and literature. For non-canonical Jacobite verse, see Paul Monod, *Jacobitism and the English People, 1688–1788* (Cambridge: Cambridge UP, 1989), ch. 2, and Murray G. H. Pittock, *Poetry and Jacobite Politics in Eighteenth-Century Britain and Ireland* (Cambridge: Cambridge UP, 1994). For Jacobitism in the mainstream tradition, see Howard Erskine-Hill, *Poetry of Opposition and Revolution: Dryden to Wordsworth* (Oxford: Clarendon P., 1996). For Dryden, see Alan Roper, *Dryden's Poetic Kingdoms* (New York: Barnes and Noble, 1965), 165–84; William J. Cameron, 'John Dryden's Jacobitism', in Harold Love (ed.), *Restoration Literature: Critical Approaches* (London: Methuen, 1972), 277–308. For Pope, see Douglas Brooks-Davies, *Pope's Dunciad and the Queen of the Night: A Study in Emotional Jacobitism* (Manchester: Manchester UP, 1985); Howard Erskine-Hill, 'Pope: The Political Poet in his Time', *ECS* 15 (1981–2), 123–48; John M. Aden, *Pope's Once*

That Barker's career as a market-place novelist overlaps closely with the reign of the first of the Hanoverians, George I (1714–27) is no coincidence. These were years of intense Jacobite, or anti-Hanoverian, activity—the two were never easily distinguishable—protests, plots, conspiracies, alarms, riots, abortive and actual invasions, including in 1715–16 a full-fledged uprising, the Fifteen, one of the most serious of several attempts in the first half of the century to overthrow the Hanoverian government. With its ongoing unrest over the question of the succession, the period from 1714 to 1723 was the 'most widespread and the most dangerous' of the 'three great waves' of Jacobite agitation that threatened the English government between 1689 and 1754.[3] (It was during the first of these waves, 1689–96, that Barker composed much of the St-Germain verse discussed in the previous chapter.) The failure of the Fifteen, as will be seen, had disastrous consequences for the English Catholic community: from this point on Jacobite political activism would be largely a Protestant phenomenon. Barker remained stalwart, however. A former inhabitant of St-Germain, kin to ex-officers in James's army and at least one officer presently in the service of Philip V of Spain, a person whose name was known to the exiled duke of Ormonde, she evidently had connections with the Jacobite underground. A 1718 letter to Ormonde demonstrates she was implicated in Jacobite plotting at high levels, and it is possible she lent covert assistance to the Pretender in ways no longer discoverable. She continued to write with a Jacobite purpose, but starting in 1714 she began publishing in the literary market-place and would require strategies of indirection to advance her Catholic-Jacobite programme.

Critics have shown little interest in the political dimensions of the novels and until recently have failed to recognize their

and Future Kings (Knoxville: U. of Tennessee P., 1978); John Morillo, 'Seditious Anger: Achilles, James Stuart, and Jacobite Politics in Pope's Iliad Translation', ECL 19 (1995), 38–58. For Swift, see Ian Higgins, Swift's Politics: A Study in Disaffection (Cambridge: Cambridge UP, 1994). For Anne Finch, see Charles H. Hinnant, 'Anne Finch and Jacobitism: Approaching the Wellesley College Manuscript', Journal of Family History, 21 (1996), 496–502. For an overview of novels of the 1740s having Jacobite themes, see Jerry C. Beasley, Novels of the 1740s (Athens: U. of Georgia P., 1982), 13–15. Although most were anti-Stuart, they 'capitalized on the aura of romance' surrounding the 'Forty-Five' (14).

3 Monod, Jacobitism, 11. The third wave was from 1745 to 1754.

deep immersion in a Jacobite world-view,[4] while studies of the links between women, politics, and the novel such as those provided by Ros Ballaster, Catherine Gallagher, and Paula McDowell omit Barker from consideration. Yet Barker was, arguably, England's leading producer of Jacobite fiction. The discussion that follows focuses upon her career as a Jacobite novelist, beginning with *Exilius* in 1714, published just weeks after the death of Queen Anne, and ending in 1725 with *The Lining of the Patch Work Screen*, a work that wrestles with the implications for English Jacobites of the failure of the Jacobite cause. (Her first published prose fiction, *The Amours of Bosvil and Galesia* (1713), better known as *Love Intrigues*, presents a special case and will be treated in the next chapter.) Barker was no propagandist; she did not attempt political interventions in the manner of Tory party-writer Delarivier Manley. Although she shared her predecessor's anti-Whig animus as well as her appreciation of the political possibilities of market-place fiction, Barker wrote quiet, realistic stories far removed in tone and intent from the lurid sex-and-scandal allegories that brought Manley infamy but also contributed, it has been thought, to the fall of the Whig ministry in 1710.[5] None the less, the plots and central situation of the Galesia stories, even the heroine's identity as a spinster, would have carried strong political resonances for contemporary readers attuned to Jacobite interpretative codes. Read through these codes and against the backdrop of the ongoing crisis over the succession—a sustained conflict that constitutes, it seems to me, a crucial context for everything Barker published between 1714 and 1725—her prose fictions present themselves as highly allusive political meditations designed to express the hopes and anxieties of politically disaffected readers, Catholics and Jacobites especially, in ways we are only now beginning to recognize.

[4] Jerry Beasley, 'Politics and Moral Idealism: The Achievement of Some Early Women Novelists', in Mary Anne Schofield and Cecilia Macheski (eds.), *Fetter'd or Free? British Women Novelists, 1670–1815* (Athens and London: Ohio UP, 1986), 216–36 (226), for example, describes *Exilius* as a 'didactic romance' with neither 'hidden partisan interest' nor reflections on 'contemporary political history'. See also William H. McBurney, 'Edmund Curll, Mrs. Jane Barker, and the English Novel', *Philological Quarterly*, 37 (1958), 385–99, esp. 390.

[5] Gwendolyn B. Needham, 'Mary de la Riviére Manley, Tory Defender', *Huntington Library Quarterly*, 12 (1948–9), 253–88 (263).

Exilius; or, The Banish'd Roman

Although the title-page reads 1715, *Exilius; or, The Banish'd Roman*, an old-fashioned heroic romance, appeared in August 1714 during the interval between the death of Queen Anne, the last of the Stuarts, and the arrival of George I from Hanover.[6] (The post-dating is typical of its publisher, Edmund Curll, who found it expedient to prolong thus a work's claim to currency.)[7] The weeks and months following Anne's death saw a flood of pro-Stuart writing as fears about the Hanoverian succession and the change of ministry gave rise to pro-Jacobite riots and demonstrations. Throughout the kingdom, according to historian Kathleen Wilson, political anxieties found expression in a Tory-Jacobitism that would provide the 'dominant idiom of protest in the extra-parliamentary nation between 1715 and 1722'.[8] In its own way *Exilius* frames a fittingly pro-Stuart response to the succession crisis of 1714. Turning on a bewildering array of returns from exile, its plot organized around crises of obligation and authority displaced onto a variety of father–child relationships, *Exilius* develops the themes of loyalty, constancy, and obligation beloved of Stuart supporters in the seventeenth century and their Jacobite successors in the next. In the manner of the French heroic romance of the previous century, Madeleine de Scudéry's *Clélie* (1654–61) for example, she used Roman history to comment on present affairs of state;[9] as with the royalist dramas of the 1680s to which it is

---

[6] Although the political reference of the title has been recognized, no one has attempted a political reading. The only sustained discussion of *Exilius* to date is Eleanor Wikborg, 'The Expression of the Forbidden in Romance Form: Genre as Possibility in Jane Barker's *Exilius*', *Genre*, 22 (1989), 3–19, which examines its rendering of female sexuality within the framework of romance.

[7] *The Monthly Catalogue* No. 4 for Aug. 1714 lists as published that month 'Mrs. Barker's New Entertaining Romance, call'd Exilius: Or, the banish'd Roman' (25). *Exilius* was advertised 14 and 21 Aug. in the *Post Man* (No. 11050), and 14 Aug. in *Post Boy* (No. 3006), where it is said to be published 19 Aug. Queen Anne died 1 Aug.

[8] Kathleen Wilson, *The Sense of the People: Politics, Culture and Imperialism in England, 1715–1785* (Cambridge: Cambridge UP, 1995), 102. For ideological conflict in the post-succession years, see ch. 2.

[9] Annabel Patterson, *Censorship and Interpretation: The Conditions of Writing and Reading in Early Modern England* (Madison: U. of Wisconsin P., 1984), 186, reports that de Scudéry may have used Tarquin in *Clélie* to represent Cromwell.

related, the extravagantly heroic plot inscribes codes of loyalty and obligation shown to be inviolable even under the most egregious conditions, including attempted rape and incest.[10] By reaffirming these old-fashioned royalist virtues and celebrating a determination to remain faithful at all costs, Barker offers in *Exilius* a fiction designed, it would seem, to strengthen Jacobite resolve to resist the House of Hanover and bring home the true king.

Readers are right to feel there is something retro about *Exilius*, however. Parts had in fact been written much earlier, as far back perhaps as the early 1680s in response to the Exclusion Crisis.[11] Commendatory verses printed in *Poetical Recreations* reveal that an earlier version of *Exilius*, then entitled *Scipina*, was 'in the Press' in 1687—why it failed to appear is unknown—and that the romance had been read in manuscript by members of the Cambridge circle, two of whom wrote under names shared by characters in the romance ('Exilius' and 'Fidelius'), suggesting its coterie origins.[12] It seems reasonable to speculate, then, that the episode in which the princess Galecia runs her lover through with a sword was written with a view toward amusing the Cambridge friends, who would have been all too familiar with Barker's obsession with Strephon/Bosvil (called Boccus in *Exilius*), the unreliable suitor whose perfidy

[10] See Susan Staves, *Players' Scepters: Fictions of Authority in the Restoration* (Lincoln and London: U. of Nebraska P., 1979), and J. Douglas Canfield, 'Royalism's Last Dramatic Stand: English Political Tragedy, 1679–89', *Studies in Philology*, 82 (1985), 234–63.

[11] Barker appears to have worked on the romance over a period of many years. Parts completed by 1687, when it was called *Scipina*, probably included the Egyptian episode (i. 103–14), which echoes crises from the 1680s, including the Exclusion Crisis (1678–83) and Monmouth's rebellion (1685). The history of the Queen of Egypt (i. 118–33), a monarch with secret Jewish—i.e. Roman Catholic—inclinations, may date from the 1680s as well. Vol. ii contains material suggestive of Barker's post-revolution preoccupations: the nature of cultural misrepresentations (ii. 41), the warming-pan calumnies (ii. 55–6), prophecies about the triumphs of the house of Scipio (ii. 60–1), bitter reflections on the cheats and impostures practised by priests (ii. 89–90). Some of this material may have been written at St-Germain, or later.

[12] The verses, printed in the second part of *PR*, are 'To Mrs. JANE BARKER, on her most Delightfull and Excellent *Romance* of SCIPINA, now in the Press' (2. 29), by J[ohn] N[ewton]; 'To the Incomparable AUTHOR, Mrs. JANE BARKER, On her Excellent ROMANCE of SCIPINA', by an unidentified '*Gentleman of* St. John's *College*, Cambridge' (2. 35), and 'To my Ingenious Friend, Mrs. JANE BARKER, on my Publishing her Romance of SCIPINA' (2. 194), by Benjamin Crayle.

was evidently the subject of verse exchanged within this circle. A further example of coded, in-group humour may be found in John Newton's tongue-in-cheek observation that 'Young *Country Squires*' may read *Scipina* 'without *offence*, | Nor *Lady Mothers* fear their debauch't *Innocence*' (*PR* 2. 32), a mischievous gender reversal that suggests he and Barker may have been enjoying a private joke.

We do not know whether Barker had a hand either in initiating or in stopping publication of *Scipina* or why publication was delayed nearly three decades. One of the first hints the romance had resurfaced under a new title comes on 14 August 1714 in the *Post Boy* (No. 3006): 'Next Thursday will be publish'd, in a neat Pocket-Vol. EXILIUS; or, *The Banish'd Roman*: A new Romance, in Two Parts'. Curll may have rushed the book through the press to take advantage of the political moment. (On 5 August, just days after Anne died, he published a pamphlet on her death: he 'must have been first in the field', his biographer comments.)[13] In any event *Exilius* came out at last in the context of widespread apprehensions about the Hanoverian succession. Fitted out with a topical, politically allusive title, this high-minded story of constant love and banished Romans, a piece of coterie fiction dating back to the Restoration and begun in response to a different Stuart crisis, emerged a deeply (if in a sense inadvertently) Jacobite work. It seems right Barker should assume the role of market-place writer at the precise moment of the passing of the Stuart era.

She did not consider herself a market-place author, however, not yet anyway. She seemed rather to imagine herself as writing in the tradition of aristocratic sixteenth- and seventeenth-century royalist romance,[14] if a dedication dated 10 June 1715 is any indication.[15] She casts herself in the role of a latter-day

---

[13] Ralph Straus, *The Unspeakable Curll: Being Some Account of Edmund Curll Bookseller* (London: Chapman and Hall, 1927), 229. The pamphlet was entitled *The State of the Nation*.

[14] For which tradition see Lois Potter, *Secret Rites and Secret Writing: Royalist Literature, 1641–1660* (Cambridge: Cambridge UP, 1989), esp. ch. 3, and Patterson, *Censorship*, esp. ch. 4.

[15] The dedication to the countess of Exeter, first printed in *EN* (1719), was undated until 1736 when it appeared in the 'third edition' of *EN* (no 'second edition' has been found). It is reprinted in Wilson, 2–4, as the dedication to what the editor calls *Love Intrigues*.

Sir Philip Sidney, 'whose steps with awful Distance, I now take Leave to trace', and calls attention to the affinities between her own 'Roman Heroes' and 'his Arcadians'.[16] Perhaps she saw Exilius as providing the present generation of Stuart loyalists with what, according to Annabel Patterson, Sidney's Arcadia gave royalists in the seventeenth century: pro-Stuart commentary in the guise of romance, 'a key to class solidarity, a language in which to express and assess their own recent history'.[17]

Exilius is in many ways an angry work, filled with a Jacobite's contempt for the credulity of the lower orders, ready to fall for the absurdity of the fiction of the warming-pan birth, and fury at the fear-mongering tactics of those with an illegitimate hold on power,[18] but it remains Barker's most sanguine fiction. The multiple weddings with which it closes exhibit the triumph of 'unfashionable Constancy', as the dedication puts it, and proclaim faith in the power of loyalty, honour, moral integrity, and steadfast love—sacred ideals in the Jacobite constellation of virtues—to triumph over adverse circumstance. Such faith would fade in the novels to come. A Patch-Work Screen for the Ladies and The Lining of the Patch Work Screen, written after the spectacular failure of the Fifteen and the collapse of other lesser Jacobite restoration attempts, deliberately reject the affirmations of marriage in order to explore the uncertain circumstances of the woman never-married, a spinster and an exile who never quite makes it home. If Exilius uses romance, exalted love, and a heroic idiom to project Jacobite faith, the more pessimistic patchwork novels for which she is better known turn away from love, marriage, and the heroic possibilities of the past to confront instead the gritty, here-and-now experience of loss,

---

[16] Dedication, EN (1736), sig. A2.

[17] Patterson, Censorship, 25. We can hear a particularly pointed appeal to Jacobite sentiment in the dedication to the countess of Exeter: 'It is in your Power, Madam, to dissipate all those Clouds of Tribulation which encircled these my Roman Lovers, from the Time of their Separation at Rome, 'till their Return to their Father's House in the Country' (Wilson, 3).

[18] The episode of the Mauritanians, who believe dead a prince standing among them, offers a sardonic gloss on the warming-pan fiction (Exilius, ii. 55–6). For other treatments of this fiction between 1688 and 1745, see Rachel J. Weil, 'The Politics of Legitimacy: Women and the Warming-pan Scandal', in Lois G. Schwoerer (ed.), The Revolution of 1688–1689: Changing Perspectives (Cambridge: Cambridge UP, 1992), 65–82.

disappointment, loneliness, and compromised loyalty in early
Georgian Britain.

The Christian Pilgrimage

Her next publication was not a fiction at all, however, but a
translation of Lenten meditations by the French prelate and
man of letters François de Salignac Fénelon (1651–1715), the
archbishop of Cambrai. The octavo volume, advertised in the
Post Boy on 18 February 1718 (No. 4456) as 'This Day'
published, came out under the auspices of Curll and Charles
Rivington as *The Christian Pilgrimage*,[19] dedicated to the
countess of Nottingham. She was a High Anglican reputed to
have Catholic sympathies; her husband had recently been
dismissed from office for his opposition to the government in
the aftermath of the Fifteen.[20] The Catholic devotional manual
was obviously intended for a Protestant audience: Barker
sought to make Fénelon 'speak *English*, in the Dialect of the
Church of *England*' ('Dedication', ii–iii).[21]

Given Fénelon's strong market value at this time Curll's part

[19] A similar ad, *PB*, No. 4459 (25 Feb.), quotes from Barker's preface: she undertook the translation so that the 'Protestant Reader might not be depriv'd of the most
Useful and Profitable Book of Devotion in the World'.

[20] According to *POAS*, v. 206, the countess was reputed to be devoted 'to the
forms and ceremonies thought to be "papist" by less rigid Anglicans'. She was Anne
Hatton, second wife of Daniel Finch, second earl of Nottingham, dismissed from
office in 1716 when he tried to dissuade the king from executing the Scottish lords;
they made their home at Burley-on-the-Hill, near Oakham, Rutland, not twenty
miles from Wilsthorp. The dedication may reflect political sympathy with a local
powerful family that suffered for its opposition, Barker's Catholicizing programme,
or (probably) both.

[21] It is the only Curll publication to be listed in a bibliography of 18th-cent.
Catholic publications running to nearly 3,000 items: see F. Blom, J. Blom, F.
Korsten, G. Scott, *English Catholic Books 1701–1800: A Bibliography* (Aldershot,
Hampshire: Scolar P., 1996), item 1039. The volume has an engraved frontispiece
of the Crucifixion by Michael van der Gucht. Catholic historian and bibliographer
Geoffrey Scott reports that such engravings were becoming quite rare in English
Catholic books by this time, bibliographic evidence that the translation was proba-
bly destined for a Protestant readership. Barker never published under Catholic
auspices or engaged in open Catholic apologetics or controversy. For the latter, see
Robert Blackey, 'A War of Words: The Significance of the Propaganda Conflict
Between English Catholics and Protestants, 1715–1745', *Catholic Historical
Review*, 58 (1973), 534–55.

in the venture is not difficult to understand. The decade witnessed a veritable outpouring of Fénelon titles from mainstream (that is, non-Catholic) presses. The previous year, 1717, Curll had brought out a highly successful new translation by John Ozell of Fénelon's *Telemachus* (1699), said to have established 'the cult for the Archbishop of Cambrai'.[22] By 1720 it had gone into a third edition. Though little read today *Telemachus*—part didactic romance, part political theory, part mirror-for-princes treatise, and part *cause scandale* for what was universally thought to be its attack on the absolutism of Louis XIV—was extraordinarily influential in its time, the 'most notorious, then the most renowned book of the early eighteenth century'.[23] Barker sought to draw upon its prestige when on the title-page she described *Exilius* as 'Written After the Manner of TELEMACHUS, For the Instruction of Some Young LADIES of Quality', although in fact the two books are not much alike.

If Curll's involvement in the publication of *The Christian Pilgrimage* requires little explanation, Barker's motives are more complicated and are, as usual, bound up in her Catholic-Jacobite agenda. To understand why she might want to translate a French Roman Catholic devotional manual at this particular juncture, and publish it through the auspices of a Protestant publisher,[24] we need to recall the crisis in which hard-line Jacobite members of the English Catholic community found themselves early in 1716 when government forces managed successfully to quash the Jacobite rebellion. Catholics had been heavily involved in the Fifteen and faced severe reprisals from a government determined to crush all future Catholic opposition. Prominent members of the Catholic aristocracy and gentry were imprisoned and in some cases executed—the hapless young earl

---

[22] James Herbert Davis, Jr., *Fénelon* (Boston: G. K. Hall-Twayne, 1979), 108.

[23] A. T. Gable, 'The Prince and the Mirror, Louis XIV, Fénelon, Royal Narcissism and the Legacy of Machiavelli', *Seventeenth-Century French Studies*, 15 (1993), 243–68 (244). For a summary of the impact and influence of *Télémaque* generally, see Davis, *Fénelon*, 107–10.

[24] She might, for example, have published with an established Catholic bookseller such as Thomas Meighan, who the year before had published for a Catholic readership a Fénelon devotional manual, *Pious Reflections for Every Day of the Month* (1717). This and *Christian Pilgrimage* are the only Fénelon titles from the decade listed in Blom, *English Catholic Books*, out of only five for the entire century.

of Derwentwater lost his head—and many priests were forced
into hiding. Catholic landowners of all ranks and regions were
threatened with additional charges on estates already subject to
double land taxes; some faced forfeitures. As a known papist
Barker was herself obliged by a 1715 statute to register her
estate in Wilsthorp; documents preserved in the Lincolnshire
Archives Office show that she submitted a deposition on 15
October 1717, just before the government's deadline.[25] The
English Catholic community was deeply shaken by these events.
Indeed, as Colin Haydon has observed, 'for contemporary
Catholics the aftermath of the uprising had the potential to
develop into one of the greatest crises for their church since
Elizabethan times'.[26] Leading members of the gentry and nobil-
ity renounced their faith in order to hold onto their property;
those who did not looked for ways to assure the authorities of
their political loyalty. To the consternation of many Catholic
Jacobites a group of churchmen, led by Bishop John Talbot
Stonor and Dr Thomas Strickland, went so far as to draft for
the community's use an oath that would enable Catholics
anxious to protect their estates to swear allegiance to George
I.[27] In short, government measures designed to sap Catholic
opposition to the established order largely succeeded.
Historians Geoffrey Holmes and Daniel Szechi report that from
1716 Catholic support of Jacobite plots was 'minimal': the
'dwindling Catholic élite was no longer prepared to risk what it
had left by rebelling' while the larger Catholic community 'was
forced into quietism to protect itself'.[28] Hereafter the impetus

[25] For the 1715 statute and registration, see Edgar E. Estcourt and John Orlebar
Payne, *The English Catholic Nonjurors of 1715: Being a Summary of the Register
of their Estates* (London: Burns and Oates, [1885]). The LAO holds two documents
relating to Barker's registration of her estate: 'Schedules and Letters of Attorney,
1717' and 'Kesteven Quarter Sessions. Papists' Estates. Rolls. 1717'; both bear her
signature. The same information is recorded in documents in the PRO: FEC 1/1200
(Abstracts of Papists Estates) and FEC 1/1201 (Returns).
[26] Colin Haydon, *Anti-Catholicism in Eighteenth-Century England, c.1714–80:
A Political and Social Study* (Manchester and New York: Manchester UP, 1993),
104. My account of the post-15 reprisals and their effects on the Catholic community draws from Haydon, 103–16.
[27] For the movement to recognize the legitimacy of George I, see Haydon, *Anti-
Catholicism*, 104–5, and Geoffrey Scott, *Gothic Rage Undone: English Monks in
the Age of Enlightenment* (Bath: Downside Abbey, 1992), 56–7.
[28] Geoffrey Holmes and Daniel Szechi, *The Age of Oligarchy: Pre-industrial
Britain, 1722–1783* (London and New York: Longman, 1993), 90.

for Jacobite conspiracy would come principally from Protestants, as evidenced by the Atterbury plot exposed in 1722, named after one of the central conspirators, the Anglican bishop Francis Atterbury: it was a plan for a foreign invasion hatched at the very highest levels of the Church of England. Catholics who retained their commitment to Jacobite activism were compelled to adopt strategies of accommodation to pursue their political ends. *The Christian Pilgrimage*, which seeks to reframe Anglican understandings of Catholicism in such a way as to secure greater toleration for the Catholic community, represents one such strategy. Barker makes Fénelon speak 'in the Dialect of the Church of *England*' so that the volume might be 'universally beneficial', to which end she expunges a few Catholic bits, some Hail Marys for example, in order '*to prevent any sudden Disgust the Protestant Reader might take at the Sight of it*'.[29] Barker's translation is an instance of 'protestantization', that is to say, a kind of sanitizing process whereby 'Catholic publications, especially works of devotion' were deliberately 'purged of all-too Catholic elements, and provided with an introduction warning the Protestant reader'.[30] But Barker's purposes went beyond making Catholic materials palatable to non-Catholic readers and beyond extending the common ground between Catholics and Anglicans, important though these were to her greater aim, which was, to soften resistance to the notion of a Catholic monarch on the English throne.

For such a project Fénelon was ideal. Why? To begin with, he was a revered figure not only in English Jacobite circles, where his role as counsellor to the Pretender would have been well

---

[29] 'Dedication', iii; 'The Translator to the Reader', sig. Bv.

[30] Blom, *English Catholic Books*, xxiv. In 1715, for example, Whitelocke Bulstrode composed a preface for some essays written by his Catholic father, Sir Richard Bulstrode, during the latter's exile at St-Germain, intended to ' "soften" the Catholic nature of the work'. The collection is entitled *Miscellaneous Essays. With the Life and Conversion of St. Mary Magdalen* (London: Jonas Browne, 1715). The Anglican non-juror George Hickes attempted something similar in the previous decade in his translation of *Instructions for the Education of a Daughter, By the Author of Telemachus* (London: Jonah Bowyer, 1707). His dedication to the duchess of Ormonde stresses the absence of everything mainstream English readers might find suspect in Catholicism: one finds no 'Superstition' or 'Indiscreet Zeal', no recourse to images, saints, angels, relics, beads, or prayers for the dead.

known, but in broader circles as well—for reasons wrapped up, ironically, in British xenophobia and anti-French prejudice. At the turn of the century Louis XIV, infuriated by certain passages in *Télémaque*, had banished Fénelon from Versailles to the remote frontier diocese of Cambrai: ill-treatment at the hands of the French king counted for much among Barker's contemporaries. For another thing, Fénelon's particular brand of Catholicism, quietist and mystical, appealed to Anglicans of a highly spiritual turn of mind. The compilers of *English Catholic Books* include his devotional writings (along with those of Thomas à Kempis) in a select category of 'spiritual classics' destined to remain 'popular across the denominational divide throughout the century'.[31] But even more importantly, perhaps, Fénelon—famously mild, gentle, urbane, tolerant, universalist, even in a sense anti-French—offered an effective counterbalance to English stereotypes of 'superstitious' and 'tyrannical' papists, an answer of sorts to the anti-Catholic propaganda churned out by government writers nothing loath to whip up support for George I and the Whig ministry around long-standing fears of Catholic atrocities.[32] In such a papiphobic climate the benign example of Fénelon and his devotional writing would offer reassurance to an English public all too inclined to assume Catholics capable of the worst kind of militancy and superstition and in this way, perhaps, diminish antipathy toward the notion of a Catholic Stuart on the English throne.

Barker's use of a conciliatory, ostensibly universalizing stance that at once masks and advances her Jacobite purposes associates her with such well-known Stuart adherents as Thomas Southcott (1670–1748) and his friend Andrew Michael Ramsay (1686–1743), the former a Benedictine monk with close links to the Stuart court-in-exile, the latter the Scots Catholic convert who edited Fénelon and published the first biography. Although there is no evidence that Barker knew Southcott or Ramsay, it is clear they all appreciated Fénelon's tactical importance to the restoration cause. In 1723 Andrew ('Chevalier') Ramsay published a deeply sympathetic *Life of Fénelon* in the hope,

---

[31] Blom, *English Catholic Books*, xiii.
[32] For anti-Catholicism in the early Georgian period, see Haydon, *Anti-Catholicism*, esp. chs. 3 and 4.

according to Geoffrey Scott, that non-Catholic readers 'would be impressed' by Fénelon's willingness to suffer 'for his principles' and to 'distinguish essential elements of Catholicism from its trappings'.[33] (As Ramsay put it, somewhat disingenuously, in the *Life*, 'Pure Love and humble Faith are the whole of the Catholick Religion'.)[34] Southcott vigorously promoted Ramsay's *Life*, Scott argues, because he was persuaded that Fénelon's teachings on 'disinterested love' would draw Anglicans of a particularly spiritual turn of mind closer to Catholicism.[35] From 1723, in other words, Fénelon would be a key element in the British Catholic-Jacobite programme. At a time when many of the Pretender's Protestant supporters urged him to renounce his religion, Catholic Jacobites such as Southcott and Ramsay chose for obvious reasons to devise strategies for cultivating greater popular acceptance of his Catholicism, a tolerance which would in turn remove from the minds of many Britons what amounted to the chief obstacle to a Stuart Restoration, the Pretender's repugnant religion. Historians would do well to consider that five years earlier Barker had embarked upon much the same project.

The Patchwork Narratives

Five years would pass before Barker brought out a new work, possibly because she had once more gone to live abroad.[36] About these years nothing is known beyond the fact that, in 1718, only a month after the publication of *Christian*

---

[33] Scott, *Gothic Rage*, 129.

[34] [Andrew Ramsay], *The Life of François de Salignac De la Motte Fénelon, Archbishop and Duke of Cambray* (London: Paul Vaillant and James Woodman, 1723), 241. For an account of the *Life* (which, however, underplays its Jacobite implications) see G. D. Henderson, *Chevalier Ramsay* (London: Thomas Nelson and Sons, 1952), ch. 7.

[35] Scott, *Gothic Rage*, 128. See also 114–15.

[36] She may have resided in St-Germain and Rome for part of these years. A letter from her nephew Timon Connock to John Hay, dated 20 Feb. 1720, Royal Archives, Stuart Papers 46/14, expresses mortification that his 'poor Ant'—unfortunately she goes unnamed—had 'taken the desperate resolution' of leaving St-Germain to starve in Rome (where the Pretender now made his court). Since Timon had at least one other aunt living at St-Germain, it is impossible to know whether the letter concerns Jane. I am grateful to Edward Corp for sharing this letter.

Pilgrimage, Barker wrote a letter to the exiled Ormonde passing on information regarding a proposed invasion scheme. (We know about this letter only because it was intercepted and duly copied into a letterbook by the bemused authorities: 'On ignore qui est Barker'.)[37] *A Patch-Work Screen for the Ladies* was published in June 1723,[38] the same month Bishop Atterbury went into exile and just one month after the hanging of the Jacobite conspirator Christopher Layer. The sequel, *The Lining of the Patch Work Screen*, appeared in the autumn of 1725.[39] The preceding decade had been disastrous for Jacobites. Starting with the reprisals following the failure of the Fifteen, these years brought one hardship after another. Imprisonments and executions, the threat of new taxes, renewed vigour in the enforcement of the penal laws, and increased surveillance made life perilous for Catholics and suspected Jacobites, while the exposure of the Atterbury plot brought new severities, including in 1723 Walpole's imposition on the Catholic community of a levy of 100,000 pounds.[40] Jacobitism was 'at a low ebb, with its morale so shaken that another spontaneous rising like the '15 was unthinkable'.[41] Even among the hard-core faithful restoration began to seem a lost cause. Barker never ceased working for the cause, however, lending it her support up to the last years of her life, as we saw earlier in her contribution

[37] Letter of 19 Mar. 1718 from London; BL Stowe MS 232, 'Jacobite Correspondence, 1717–1719'. For a transcription and translation of the letter from the original French, see Doc. Rec. 26, 37 n. 88. During this time, when mail across the Channel was closely watched, it was standard practice to open suspected letters, copy out their contents, and send them on. See G. V. Bennett, *The Tory Crisis in Church and State, 1688–1730: The Career of Francis Atterbury, Bishop of Rochester* (Oxford: Clarendon P., 1975), 211.

[38] *PWS* was advertised 13 June 1723 in the *Evening Post* (No. 2165) as 'This day . . . publish'd' and, somewhat unusually, was steadily promoted in the *EP* over the next three months, at least ten more ads appearing. *PWS* was listed in the *Monthly Catalogue* No. 4, June 1723, 2, its inset tales amusingly Curllicized as, for example, 'The Religious Adulterer', 'The Perfidious Adultress', and, my favourite, 'The Unaccountable Wife; or the Matrimonial Bawd'.

[39] *Lining* was advertised in the *Monthly Catalogue* No. 30, Oct. 1725, 111, described as 'a Collection of Novels recommending virtuous Love' for the 'farther Entertainment of the Ladies'.

[40] There were risings in 1708, 1715, and 1719. For a readable narrative overview, see Bruce Lenman, *The Jacobite Risings in Britain 1689–1746* (London: Eyre Methuen, 1980), and Frank McLynn, *The Jacobites* (London and New York: Routledge and Kegan Paul, 1985).

[41] Lenman, *Jacobite Risings*, 195.

of the 'od present' to the newly resurgent movement to canonize 'our holy King'. Perhaps she was able to keep alive her
belief in the ultimate triumph of Jacobite hopes. But the post-
Atterbury fictions suggest otherwise, or more accurately
perhaps, suggest a struggle to accommodate her faith in the
transcendent virtue of the Stuart cause to the bleak events of
recent history, to negotiate what has aptly been termed a 'crisis
over the dissonant claims of principle and practical survival'.[42]
Read through the lens of this crisis, *Patch-Work Screen* can be
seen to register a complex elegiac response to the collapse of
Jacobite political ambitions while its sequel, *Lining of the Patch
Work Screen*, can be seen to explore the dilemma of the
Jacobite subject in a time of defeat, when she or he is torn
between rival claimants to the throne and forced into positions
of ideological compromise.

This is not to say that the patchwork narratives are Jacobite
works in an overt, systematic, or even sustained way. First and
foremost they are studies of a singular woman whose life takes
shape on the boundaries of ordinary female existence, as feminist
scholars have long recognized. My claim is rather that the
courtship plot that is an important thread of Galesia's life-story
would have been politically allusive for Barker's contemporaries
in ways likely to go unnoticed today. In a ground-breaking essay
that asks whether there was a rhetoric of Jacobitism, Howard
Erskine-Hill answers affirmatively by detailing a distinctively
Jacobite use of the image of rape, used to signify William's
conquest but also various other violations of political legitimacy.[43] He does not discuss a related counter-image that reverberates through a range of somewhat later Jacobite discourses
and furnished Barker with her central political trope: marriage (or

[42] Toni Bowers, 'Jacobite Difference and the Poetry of Jane Barker', *ELH* 64
(1997), 857–69 (859). Barker's ambivalence has much in common with that of
Mary Caesar, whose unpublished autobiographical writings, begun in 1724, have
been described by Valerie Rumbold as a 'poignant attempt to integrate an increasingly negative experience of life with a faith in the ultimate triumph of Jacobite
virtue': see 'The Jacobite Vision of Mary Caesar', in Isobel Grundy and Susan
Wiseman (eds.), *Women, Writing, History 1640–1740* (Athens: U. of Georgia P.,
1992), 178–98 (178).
[43] Howard Erskine-Hill, 'Literature and the Jacobite Cause: Was there a Rhetoric
of Jacobitism?', in Eveline Cruickshanks (ed.), *Ideology and Conspiracy: Aspects of
Jacobitism,1689–1759* (Edinburgh: John Donald, 1982), 49–69.

sexual union) as an image of wished-for political legitimacy.[44] In many Jacobite contexts the marriage trope tended to be eroticized, as if to convey the immense pain of separation or the intense desire for a union endlessly deferred. Its most characteristic expression is the image of the dashing 'lost lover' pervasive in representations of James Francis Stuart from 1715.[45] Against this background Barker's use of the marriage trope in the two patchwork narratives emerges as wholly her own. In place of the erotically charged Stuart romance favoured by other Jacobite writers she uses spinsterhood and a failure-of-marriage plot to explore by way of analogy the situation of the loyal subject when the 'lost lover' is truly, perhaps irretrievably lost.

Long before she began to make political use of the figure of the spinster, Barker had been fascinated by the literary possibilities of the image of the celibate woman. In *Exilius*, the virgin-princess Galecia belongs to the tradition of female martial valour which in the second half of the seventeenth century inspired the heroic self-fashionings of aristocratic women in France and England.[46] The heroic model of the *femme forte* continued to shape the otherwise more realistically conceived Galesia of *Amours of Bosvil and Galesia*, as when Galesia at one point fancies herself the champion of her sex, 'rank'd in the Catalogue of Heroines', for 'ridding the World' of the monstrous Bosvil (*BG* 31). But by the time Barker wrote *A Patch-Work Screen for the Ladies* the heroic virgin had undergone a change of key to become the diminished figure of the spinster, slightly peculiar, out-of-step; an odd woman. Read in the context of the Stuart romance of the 'lost lover', her unmarriedness suggests by analogy a country separated from its ruler/husband; and we begin to understand why an author not notably enamoured of the possibilities of conjugal union should permit an otherwise independent-minded heroine, a character

44 In the Mag. MS poem, 'On The kings birth-day, writ at St-Germains. 1694:' (fos. 42r–v) Barker imagines England as a wayward wife who promises to renounce her sexual crimes to ensure her husband's, i.e. James's, return.

45 Monod, *Jacobitism*, 62–9. The use of love song to address the exiled Stuart monarch can be traced back to at least 1694: see Pittock, *Poetry and Jacobite Politics*, 48. For examples of the translation of political affairs into amatory terms in contemporary poetry, see Erskine-Hill, *Poetry of Opposition*, 71–4.

46 Barash, *EWP*, esp. 32–40.

more attuned to the muses than to men,[47] to rue the collapse of one marriage proposal after another.

For Galesia's uncharacteristic regrets, so at odds with the 'secret Disgust against Matrimony' (*PWS* 133) expressed elsewhere in the narrative, are meant to supply a kind of allegorical shorthand for the trials and disappointments of the Jacobites since the period of wandering and exile began in 1688. 'I could *hope* nothing, *propose* nothing, but I was cross'd or disappointed therein, e'er I could arrive at Accomplishment', Galesia muses sadly, 'I began to believe Providence had ordain'd for me a *Single Life*' (*PWS* 139). She speaks here, I suggest, less as a woman than as a study in exemplary Jacobite quietism, a follower of Fénelon perhaps, passively resigned to an acceptance of God's will. As her auditor puts it, underscoring the Fénelonian point, Galesia has been granted a 'Mind submissive and resign'd' and in spite of her losses can 'hope for more prosperous Days for the Time to come' (*PWS* 140). She is at once repining England and Jacobite perseverance in a season of little hope.

Once their Jacobite underpinnings are recognized, elements of *Patch-Work Screen* that seem incomprehensible or even inept begin to take on meaning. Take, for example, the famous failure of the Galesia plot to achieve closure. The apparent irresolution has prompted a fair amount of commentary, both admiring and smug. The 'book ends *in media res*'; the heroine 'remains in the limbo of the unconcluded *Patch-Work Screen*'; her fate 'is not resolved; one cannot make a finished screen of the ambiguous fragments'.[48] Patricia Meyer Spacks seems uncertain whether to chalk up the 'ostentatious incoherence' of the narrative method to incompetence or to an indifference to

---

[47] See, for example, the ode 'The *Necessity* of *Fate*' (*PWS* 141), to which Galesia's mother responds by saying, 143, in what reads very like a benediction, 'if there be a *fatal Necessity* that it must be so, e'en go on, and make thyself easy with thy fantastick Companions the Muses'.

[48] Patricia Meyer Spacks, *Imagining a Self: Autobiography and Novel in Eighteenth-Century England* (Cambridge and London: Harvard UP, 1976), 66; Josephine Greider, 'Introd'., *A Patch-Work Screen for the Ladies*, ed. Josephine Greider (New York and London: Garland, 1973), 12; Mary Anne Schofield, *Masking and Unmasking the Female Mind: Disguising Romances in Feminine Fiction, 1713–1799* (Newark: U. of Delaware P., and London and Toronto: Associated UPs, 1990), 75.

craft that amounts to a 'disclaimer of serious intent'.[49] It is true
Galesia's life-story does not have a happy ending or much of an
ending at all, but there is a reason for this: the Stuart story still
lacks the happy ending that will bring Galesia's to a close. Once
the absence of closure is seen to be the analogue of a much
greater failure of history then we are able to bring into view the
ending that *is* there and that criticism has thus far conspicuously
failed to engage: the lengthy 'An *Ode* In *Commemoration* of the
Nativity of *Christ*', the final lines of which pray for the conversion of the 'stubborn *Jews*', a people blind, sin-hardened, and in
thrall to 'obstinate Delusions' (*PWS* 172). The reference would
have carried a strong political charge for readers attuned to the
familiar typological equation between the Jews, unconverted
after seventeen hundred years, and the no less obstinate English
people:

> Tho' suff'ring still, they still thy Laws despise,
> Since Seventeen Cent'ries cannot make them wise:
> Since from their rooted Sin they cannot part;
> Melt (for Thou canst!) the hardest Heart,
> And open Blindest Eyes:
> Make All on Earth, as All in Heav'n, join,
> Since All in Heav'n and Earth alike are Thine.
>
> (*PWS* 173)

It is thus with a prayer for the conversion of the Jews that
Barker brings closure, of sorts, to Galesia's strangely unfinished
life-story. Such an ending, bizarre at first and ignored in all
commentary on the novel, is seen to be, typologically speaking,
wholly fitting: in Jacobite contexts the conversion of the Jews
stood for that conversion of English hearts and minds that
would usher in a Stuart restoration.[50]

The Lining of the Patch Work Screen, published when Barker
was 73 and Jacobitism an all but lost cause, is Barker's bleakest
work. If *Patch-Work Screen* focuses upon the plight of the spin-

49 Spacks, *Imagining*, 69.
50 In a discussion of her poetry John T. Shawcross, 'Jane Barker', *Seventeenth-
Century British Nondramatic Poets*, *DLB*, 3rd ser. (Detroit, Washington, DC,
London: Gale-Bruccoli Clark Layman, 1993), 131. 5, notes the reference to the
conversion of the Jews but does not remark its political significance.

ster, the loyal subject denied union with her lover/king, *Lining of the Patch Work Screen* uses a bigamy trope to express the troubles of the subject divided between *de jure* and *de facto* husbands/sovereigns and in this way to deepen her analysis of Jacobite existence in a time of defeat, compromise, and political illegitimacy. Galesia is now an old woman with no story of her own to tell; we first encounter her in the lodgings where she lives alone, deprived of even the 'Society of Friends by [her] Fire-side' (180). The narrative is an assemblage of stories of the loves, sufferings, and wanderings of survivors of the Jacobite diaspora, men and women of exemplary virtue who end up in Galesia's London lodgings where they reminisce about better days. The stories they tell, many of them set in Catholic countries, are concerned to a remarkable degree with convents, priests, nuns, conversions, and the happiness to be found in the 'Society of holy Virgins' (201); several recur to memories of St-Germain, a kind of Jacobite imaginary where 'Inferiours are humble, Superiours are affable, the Women vertuous, the Men valiant, the Matrons prudent, Daughters obedient, Fathers obliging, Sons observant, Patrons readily assisting, Supplicants gratefully accepting' (222). (In view of the neglect Barker evidently experienced at St-Germain one suspects that the idealized image of the reciprocal relationship between patrons and clients reflects at once long-standing irritation and self-preserving forgetting.) The battered but virtuous survivors—men and women of staunch old-fashioned virtue who with enormous patience suffer 'Poverty, Prosecution and Punishment of all sorts' (213)—seem themselves almost ghostly as they flicker in and out of the loosely connected tales, recalling a world that exists only in memory or imagination.

Indeed, *Lining* seems in some ways a study of what it means to live outside history. The distinction Marita Sturken draws between 'history' and 'cultural memory' in her work on national biography illuminates what is meant here by the phrase living outside history. History, in her usage, refers to 'narratives that have been sanctioned in some way, that often tell a self-conscious story of the nation', whereas cultural memory refers to stories 'told outside official historical discourse, where individual memories are shared, often with political intent, to act as counter-memories to history'.[51] By the time she began *Lining*, it seems to me, Barker had come to regard fiction-making as a vehicle for promulgating Jacobite 'counter-memories' meant to exist alongside and in opposition to official history, the latter increasingly used to prop up the values and world-view of the Whig regime. Both the Magdalen manuscript and the Galesia story told in *Patch-Work Screen* engage crucial moments in recent Stuart history, chronicling in direct fashion the fall of James and the early years of his exile (the Fidelia narrative) and the final years of the reign of Charles II (*Patch-Work Screen*), where Charles's death resonates with apocalyptic significance ('as if *Dooms-day* had discharg'd it self of a Shower of black walking Animals' (*PWS* 153)). *Patch-Work Screen* also projects, in coded and allusive ways, events of national history since the death of Anne, a recent past understood as a succession of failures to unite king and kingdom, true monarch and loyal subjects. But the intense nostalgia of *Lining*, the hagiographic treatment of wandering Jacobites, the characterization of Galesia as a winter's night spinster: all suggest a pronounced shift in purpose—a deliberate turning away from history toward the preservation (in Sturken's terms) of unsanctioned cultural memories, as in this final work Barker undertakes not to rewrite history so much as to devise a narrative framework capable of accommodating elements of Catholic and Jacobite experience omitted from or distorted in the stories Protestant Great Britain told about itself.

But if the narrative looks back nostalgically to an ideally virtuous world symbolized by St-Germain, it also engages in a tough-minded way problems of economic and social survival in the early Georgian England. Emblematic in this regard is the story of Mrs Goodwife, a supporter of James who took to small trading to support her husband and children after the family lost everything in the Irish campaign (218–21). But Barker is even more interested in issues of conflicted allegiance that exercised English Jacobites on an almost daily basis in the immediate post-Atterbury period. *Lining* includes a number of stories

---

[51] Marita Sturken, 'Memory, Reenactment, and the Image', in Mary Rhiel and David Suchoff (eds.), *The Seductions of Biography* (New York and London: Routledge, 1996), 31–41 (31).

turning on bigamy (and near-bigamy), a plot vehicle that enabled her to imagine and work through the questions of legitimacy, fidelity, and troubled conscience facing those who, in rejecting the Protestant succession, were destined to be subject to one king while loyal to another. No fewer than five inset tales use a bigamy plot, including one that offers a highly compressed retelling of Behn's 'The History of the Nun'— called by Barker 'Philinda's Story out of the Book' (214)—in which the heroine arrives at the less than satisfactory solution of killing in one night two husbands.[52] As a means of giving form to the problems associated with divided loyalty two stories seem especially important. The first, the story of 'Tangerine, the Gentleman Gypsie', is concerned with the question of how to 'come home' to the political nation after years of disaffection. The title figure, a former soldier in Charles II's army whose wife married his brother in his absence, is an ageing gypsy-outlaw tired of wandering. An updated version of the gypsies and beggars used in the seventeenth century to figure the impoverished cavalier, Barker's Gentleman Gypsy is at once a wanderer in the Jacobite diaspora and a more metaphorical exile within the British political nation.[53] A chance meeting with his newly widowed wife affords him an opportunity to bring his wanderings to an end. A storyline involving a tangle of broken promises, violated vows, vagabondage, and disguise is brought to a satisfying comedic conclusion when the Gentleman Gypsy is reunited with his wife; while a spirited girl in disguise as a gypsy, his companion in his late wanderings, is at last allowed to marry her true love, who turns out to be the Gypsy's son. Bigamy—split allegiance—is resolved into lawful marriage, and the girl's 'Extravagance in leaving her Father's House' (237) has no serious consequences.

[52] For a discussion that emphasizes the differences in the two versions, see Jacqueline Pearson, 'The History of The History of the Nun', in Heidi Hutner (ed.), Rereading Aphra Behn: History, Theory, and Criticism (Charlottesville and London: UP of Virginia, 1993), 234–52. Other bigamy tales, all from Lining, include the story of Capt. Manly (182–202); the story of Tangerine, the Gentleman Gypsie, based on the 1698 Behn story 'The Wandering Beauty' (229–37); the story of double bigamy told by Amarantha (254–60); and an episode of near-bigamy included in the seduction-and-abandonment history of Malhurissa (261–6). There is, finally, a rather bizarre retelling of the story of the Portuguese nun (223–6) which, while not a bigamy story as such, involves vow-breaking on the part of a nun, who on her deathbed reflects upon the story of her 'criminal Marriage' (225).

[53] For 17th-cent. usages, see Potter, Secret Rites, 103–4.

This story ends with a pair of marriages and a dissolving of disguise: a happy ending to years of concealment, wandering, and uncertain loyalty. A tale of Jacobite wish-fulfilment, it would seem.

A later tale, however, Amarantha's 'The *Story* of *Bellemien*', uses the bigamy trope to grimmer purpose as part of a plot which would seem to express an ambivalent accommodation to the Hanoverian succession. The story involves a virtuous and loving young couple who marry secretly and then allow themselves to be persuaded by family pressures and financial exigency to renounce 'their first conjugal Vows' and commit bigamy. The narrator makes it clear we are to see the 'unhappy couple' as basically good, well-meaning people forced by the pressure of circumstances into criminality. Like the virtuous but troubled Jacobites they represent, the now doubly married man and woman seek to make the best of it. They try to bear patiently the 'Yoke' of these 'new Espousals, which courted their acceptance' (256), but nothing but trouble ensues. The man longs to return to his 'true and lawful Wife' (257), but when he does, he brings heartbreak to his second wife and infamy to his first, who is universally condemned as a whore. There can be, Barker seems to be suggesting, no satisfactory arrangement for Jacobites under present conditions. The tale is a working out in pessimistic, almost tragic terms of the Jacobite dilemma in the early Hanoverian era.

In the only extended discussion to date of Barker as Jacobite poet, Toni Bowers calls attention to elements of 'disappointment, uncertainty, and dark regret' in the St-Germain verse that in her view sit oddly with Barker's identity as one of the most uncompromising of Jacobites.[54] Bowers probably underestimates the extent to which Barker deliberately mythologizes herself in this verse, most of it from the 1690s, but her observation that Jacobites in general were caught up in a 'crisis over the dissonant claims of principle and practical survival' (859) contains a valuable insight that seems to be borne out by study of Barker's late prose fictions. I would locate the acute phase of that crisis later than Bowers does, however. If Barker can be taken as representative, then the difficult process of learning to

---

[54] Bowers, 'Jacobite Difference', 868.

live with the ideological muddle of compromise and divided allegiance may have belonged primarily to the period from 1716, when English Jacobites, Catholics most pressingly, were compelled to come to terms with the practical failure of the cause and with the retreat of the Catholic community into quietism. It was largely for this community apart that Barker wrote her patchwork narratives. Drawing upon the materials of her own life to tell the life-story of an odd woman, she created fictions of spinsterhood and bigamy in which dissident readers could find figures not only for the failure of the Stuart romance but also for their own alienated existence in Hanoverian Britain.

Romance, Readers, Communities of the Book

Recognition that Barker's career as a novelist is tied from beginning to end to Jacobite imperatives invites us to think more closely about the role of party politics in the formation of the novel and to consider the possibility that the early novel, often regarded as the most self-consciously modern of forms, was (in some of its manifestations at least) implicated in a conservative politics. Consideration of the Jacobite dimensions of her novels throws new light on the old question of who was reading the early novel and why. For whom was Barker writing or did she think she was writing? To whom might her works be expected to appeal? Who actually read her? What cultural needs did her novels serve? In 1974 Pat Rogers remarked the 'notable lack of concrete research into the size and composition' of the audience for the emergent novel.[55] A quarter-century later, despite some important work on the sociology of the early novel, the situation has not greatly changed. The extent to which the rise of the novel is linked with the rise of the middle class and the rise of a middle-class reading public is a matter 'on which there is great interest and little definitive evidence', Michael McKeon has observed; and in spite of a host of well-aired problems with the 'triple rise' thesis, scholars continue to seek links between the emergence of the genre and the development of a bourgeois

[55] Pat Rogers, The Augustan Vision (London: Weidenfeld and Nicolson, 1974), 250.

public sphere, and, less abstractly, to posit for the early novel a spectrum of urban readers new to the pleasures of reading—the semi-literate maidservants and apprentices that feature regularly in many accounts.[56] The discovery that Barker's chief publisher, Edmund Curll, targetted her prose fictions for an elite provincial audience with Tory-Jacobite leanings complicates present understandings and suggests we may need to widen considerably our angle of vision so far as the audience for the early novel is concerned.[57] Analysis of Curll's marketing of her work also confronts us with an unappreciated side of a publisher seldom noted for his relations with Jacobites, genteel lady novelists, or a gentry clientele.

Study of Curll's advertising strategies leaves no doubt that during the opening phase of her career as a novelist she was marketed as a Jacobite writer. At a time when much printed matter was sold unbound, the title-page was the bookseller's most important promotional resource, serving many of the same purposes of display as cover and dust-jacket do today. It provided copy for newspaper notices and was often posted by way of advertisement. Curll saw to it that the title-pages of Barker's earliest novels sent clear Jacobite signals. *Bosvil and Galesia* (1713), though not strictly speaking a Jacobite work, hints at the unknown author's ideological leanings with its announcement that the tale was related 'in *St.* Germains Garden'.[58] A reader who glanced at the first paragraph would

---

[56] Michael McKeon, *The Origins of the English Novel 1600–1740* (Baltimore: Johns Hopkins UP, 1987), 51. For a good summary of the difficulties that have emerged in connection with the 'triple-rise' thesis, see J. A. Downie, 'The Making of the English Novel', *Eighteenth-Century Fiction*, 9 (1997), 249–66. For an argument for the construction at around this time of an 'indeterminate but alluring "general reader" ' of the novel, see William B. Warner, 'Formulating Fiction: Romancing the General Reader in Early Modern Britain', in Deidre Lynch and William B. Warner (eds.), *Cultural Institutions of the Novel* (Durham, NC, and London: Duke UP, 1996), 279–305.

[57] McKeon, *Origins*, 52, makes a similar point: 'on the evidence of subscription lists, at least, a very large proportion of the readership of Defoe, the *Spectator*, and other "middle class" publications belongs to the nobility and gentry'.

[58] This failed courtship tale belongs, we are told, to Galesia's 'early Years'—to the extent that the story draws upon Barker's own experience this would set it in the early 1670s—but the heroine's confusion, her inability to make sense of the changing attachments of her incomprehensible lover, may catch something of the quality that Erskine-Hill, *Poetry of Opposition*, 20, detects in the (Jacobite) dramas Dryden wrote in the decade after the Revolution, which focus 'upon people in conflict or

find in its openly Jacobite references confirmation of the hint. Not only is the 'as-told-in-a-garden' frame set beside the palace of the exiled Stuarts, but the Nine Years War (as we now call it) that furnishes its backdrop is described in terms only a Stuart adherent would use—as a conflict over 'King JAMES'S Affairs'.[59] *Exilius; or, The Banish'd Roman*, her next publication, could have proclaimed its Stuart allegiances more flagrantly only by entitling itself *The Exiled Pretender*.

Newspaper advertisements suggest also that Curll sought to draw Barker's first readers from the provincial gentry. One of his earliest attempts to promote Barker, a notice in the *Post Boy* of 23 May 1713 (No. 2814) for *Love Intrigues* (as it was then entitled), attributes the 'Novel' to 'a Lady': obviously Barker had yet to acquire a following or even a name. (The following year when Curll advertised *Exilius* in the *Post Boy* (14 Aug. 1714), the name of 'Mrs. JANE BARKER' would figure prominently.) In what amounts to a fascinating instance of early niche marketing, Curll emphasizes distinctions of class. *Love Intrigues* is said to be 'Dedicated to the Countess of Exeter' and, even more remarkably, the notice is given this heading: '*Advertisement to the Lincolnshire Gentry*'. The appeal is to the social sense of a very specifically targetted readership and by extension to a broader range of readers who either belonged themselves to the upper reaches of the provincial social scale or were pleased to identify with those who did.[60]

That the notice appeared in the *Post Boy*, a tri-weekly with strong Tory leanings and a large country readership, may suggest he was aiming for a politically disaffected readership as well. The *Post Boy*, under the editorship of Abel Roper, consti-tuted the 'staple printed diet' of Tory sympathizers during the

bewildered in situations where not only values, but even the facts, are uncertain'. *BG* incorporates poems that can be dated with probability to the 1690s. It seems likely the narrative was at least partly written at St-Germain.

[59] 'King JAMES'S Affairs having so turn'd Things in *Europe*, that the War between *France* and the Allies was almost like a Civil War: Friend against Friend, Brother against Brother; Father against Son': *Love Intrigues: Or, the History of the Amours of Bosvil and Galesia, As Related to Lucasia, in St. Germains Garden. A Novel* (London: E. Curll and C. Crownfield, 1713).

[60] Cf. McBurney's speculation, 'Edmund Curll', 387, that Curll's publication of *BG* may have been motivated by a desire to supply high-toned reading matter for his newly opened bookshop in fashionable Tunbridge Wells.

last four years of Anne's reign, according to J. A. Downie.[61] It went out with the post to the provinces, where by one estimate it would have been seen by as many as 50,000 readers, including a sizeable number of Stuart loyalists.[62] Indeed, if Paul Monod's estimates are reliable, at this time perhaps one in four members of the English landed classes would have possessed loyal sympathies.[63] Curll, always a canny interpreter of market trends, must have sensed the existence 'out there' of a considerable audience of men and women with at the very least a sentimental attachment to Jacobite principles.

This speculation finds support from the discovery that Curll marketed other Jacobite romances in the second decade of the century. In the aftermath of the Jacobite rebellion in 1715 he brought out *Irish Tales* (1716), a historical romance by Sarah Butler which a scholar of Irish literature has recently described as 'a challenging fiction of contemporary political relevance: an Irish, Roman Catholic, and Jacobite work, published in Protestant, Hanoverian England, just four months after the execution of the leading Jacobite rebels for their parts in the Rebellion of 1715'.[64] *Irish Tales* provides a superb example of

---

[61] J. A. Downie, *Robert Harley and the Press: Propaganda and Public Opinion in the Age of Swift and Defoe* (Cambridge: Cambridge UP, 1979), 162. He gives the circulation figures for the *PB* at 3,000 for each issue during the Harley years, describing it as oriented toward 'tory country gentlemen' (7); for the role of *PB* in the Tory propaganda machine, see 162–4. The other two tri-weeklies, the *Post Man* and George Ridpath's *Flying Post* were Whiggish. The other main Tory press organ at this time was the *Examiner*, edited for a period in 1711 by Mrs Manley. R. B. Walker, 'Advertising in London Newspapers, 1650–1750', *Business History*, 15 (1973), 112–30, distinguishes the Tory readership of the *PB* from that of the *Gazette*, the official government newspaper, on the basis of its advertising profile: the *Gazette* catered to 'the country gentry' while the 'less specialized' *PB* would have included readers of 'the more middling sort' as well (120). For circulation figures, see James R. Sutherland, 'The Circulation of Newspapers and Literary Periodicals, 1700–30', *Library*, 4th ser. 15 (1934), 110–24 (111).

[62] Geoffrey Holmes, *British Politics in the Age of Anne* (London: Macmillan and New York: St Martin's, 1967), 30.

[63] Monod, *Jacobitism*, 271. He arrives at these estimates by figuring that between 7 and 10 per cent of the aristocracy and gentry were Catholic and most of these loyal (on some level) to the Stuarts through the 1760s; perhaps 1 per cent were nonjurors; juring Anglicans with Stuart sympathies would have brought the number to about one in four, with great variations in different counties.

[64] Ian Campbell Ross, ' "One of the Principal Nations in Europe": The Representation of Ireland in Sarah Butler's *Irish Tales*', *Eighteenth-Century Fiction*, 7 (1994), 1–16 (4). According to McBurney, 'Edmund Curll', 398, it was advertised

Curll's use of the title-page to attract readers of Jacobite procliv-ities. This one names among its characters a 'Banish'd PRINCE', a 'Constant FAIR-ONE', a 'Depos'd USURPER', while the pages that follow are populated by figures sure to stir Jacobite minds and hearts: a lover-hero who takes matters like oaths and loyalty to fathers very seriously indeed; a bloody-minded virgin-heroine active in the Irish resistance. One of the heroine's finest moments comes when, the only woman in a band of 'counterfeit Ladies', she takes part in a cross-dressed massacre: she joins a 'Noble Train of suppos'd young Virgins'—stout young men really—who promise sex to gain entry to the usurper's court and then effi-ciently reduce the startled male courtiers to a 'purple Deluge on the Floor'.[65] This is Jacobite resistance heroics at its campiest and in some ways most characteristic, and answers to the author's stated design of showing the *'strange means by which* Ireland *was once deliver'd from the Tyranny of* Turgesius *and the* Danes, *by the Beauty of a Virgin'.*[66] For reasons that must be left to other scholars to explore, the Jacobite imagination seems to have been especially stirred by displays of female martial heroics, almost as if women were expected to enact the derring-do denied their more compromised husbands and brothers.[67]

in *The Post Man*, 30 June 1716. *Irish Tales: or, Instructive Histories for the Happy Conduct of Life*, published in London for Curll and J. Hooke in 1716, was reissued in 1718 as *Milesian Tales*. The BL catalogue attributes it to Charles Gildon, who signed the dedication. Ross, 6, who so far as I know has written the only reliable modern discussion of the novel, regards Butler as an actual person but one about whom our lack of knowledge is 'nearly total'; he speculates, 7, that she was of high social rank and Catholic, but finds no evidence she was one of the Ormonde Butlers: 'All we know for certain, on the authority of Charles Gildon in his "Epistle Dedicatory" to *Irish Tales*, is that Sarah Butler was dead by 1716'.

[65] Sarah Butler, *Irish Tales: or, Instructive Histories for the Happy Conduct of Life* (London: E. Curll and J. Hooke, 1716), 70, 66, 75.

[66] *Irish Tales*, preface, [xix]. Cross-dressing themes as well as displays of female heroics figure importantly in Jacobite resistance lore. For Colonel Parker's escape in 1694 from the Tower in women's clothes supplied by his wife, see Jane Garrett, *The Triumphs of Providence: The Assassination Plot, 1696* (Cambridge: Cambridge UP, 1980), 48–9; for Lord Nithsdale's in 1716, see William Fraser, *The Book of Carlaverock: Memoirs of the Maxwells, Earls of Nithsdale, Lords Maxwell & Herries*, 2 vols. (Edinburgh, 1873). Accounts of the episode, which stressed the inge-nuity, skill, and intrepidity of Lady Nithsdale in engineering her husband's escape from the Tower, are said to have 'created a deep sensation at the Court in London, and throughout the kingdom' (*Book*, i. 437).

[67] For an early verse rendering of this theme, see Dryden's 'The Lady's Song' (written *c.*1691, published 1704), discussed by Anne Barbeau Gardiner, 'A Jacobite

The story, which is set in Gaelic Ireland between the late ninth and early eleventh centuries, during the time of the Danish invasions, uses events from the Irish past to recall more recent events, in particular James II's Irish expedition, here given a more satisfying conclusion than the one James provided in 1690 when he fled from the Boyne. The heroic plot celebrates resistance to tyranny and loyalty to one's lawful ruler. It focuses on the actions of the valiant 'few' who offered resistance to the slavish tyranny of an unlawful monarch, the 'few' who 'knew not how to bow their Necks in subjection to any but a lawful Prince, or stoop to any thing beneath their free Liberties, and Obedience to their own Kings . . .' (3). Historical parallels and an unmistakably Jacobite idiom must have made the politics of *Irish Tales* absolutely clear. Ross has argued otherwise, however. He thinks the Jacobite and Roman Catholic thrust of the novel would have been 'almost wholly inaccessible' to Butler's contemporaries.[68] My analysis of Curll's promotional strategies would suggest the converse, that there existed at this time a sizeable number of readers who would have sought out *Irish Tales* precisely *for* its political aspect. If so, then it is significant that among the titles advertised on the final leaf, Curll should give top billing to Barker's heroic romance. The notice for *Exilius* fills up nearly the entire first page—evidence that it was the leading work of Jacobite popular fiction in Curll's list at this time.[69]

Another Curll-sponsored Jacobite romance from this same

Song by John Dryden', *Yale University Library Gazette*, 61 (1986), 49–54. Cf. the manuscript poem from the 1690s, 'The Female Heroine. Or the Loyall Fair One's Noble Resolution', which calls upon women to take up the heroism no longer practised by men: 'Come Brisk Lasses let's unite | Arm, Arm your selves, your foes to fight, | Let us Perform Heroick Deeds | And Cast off all our Female Weeds' in order to 'redeem our Mangled Laws' and place the 'Lawfull King' on the throne. The speaker rejoices that 'our Great King by female strength, | From Exile was brought home at length' (Yale, Osborn b. 111, pp. 53, 54). Another version is found in Bod., MS Firth d. 13, fo. 43.

[68] Ross, 'One of the Principle', 16.

[69] Its twenty-three lines give titles for the eight interlocking tales making up *Exilius*, supplied no doubt by Curll—titles such as '*Clelia and Marcellus*: Or, The Constant Lovers', 'The Lucky Escape: Or, The Fate of *Ismenus*', and '*Piso*: Or, The Lewd Courtier'. The one other book mentioned on the page, receiving only three lines of type, is *BG*, sporting here the title 'The *Sincere* VIRGIN: Or, The Amours of *Bosvil* and *Galesia*. A NOVEL'.

period offers additional insight into the appeal of these works in their political moment. This one, said to be 'Done from the *French* by a LADY', was first published in 1715 as the *German Atalantis* and was reissued in 1718 and again in 1721 with the even more pointed title *Hanover Tales*.[70] The action of this romance moves across a familiar Jacobite terrain—a kingdom in revolt, brave and noble men in exile, a haughty usurper, noble resistance to unlawful rule. Like all such politically encoded romances *Hanover Tales* offers imagined solutions to seemingly intractable political problems, but more directly than either *Exilius* or *Irish Tales* it seeks to promote acceptance of the change of state. Anxiety and confusion are displaced onto a fable in which contrasting feminine responses to thwarted love offer metaphors for responses to changes of state. Baritia (i.e. Britain) is the Jacobite figure. Torn between duty to her father and desire for a banished lover, refusing to marry without her father's (lawful) consent, she resolves to abandon herself to grief and sullen retirement. Happily, Baritia's father is eventually reconciled to the match and permits her to devote herself to her 'faithful, tender, and most constant Love' for her Fradonia (143). So far we have a fairly straightforward rendering of the Jacobite predicament brought to a satisfying wish-fulfilment conclusion. But the ideologically correct Jacobite response of Baritia in the novel's foreground is contrasted with that of Calista, who stands for accommodation to the Hanoverian regime. When her first beloved dies in battle she too devotes herself to grief, but when commanded to remarry by her parents she does so, albeit reluctantly, and to her surprise finds contentment in the new relationship. *Hanover Tales*, appropriately enough given its otherwise inexplicable title, is a fable of compromise and acceptance, permitting its conflicted readers

---

[70] *The German Atalantis: Being, A Secret History of Many Surprizing Intrigues, and Adventures transacted in several Foreign Courts. Written by a Lady*, no publisher named. The *Monthly Catalogue* for Feb. 1715 advertises it as published by Curll. The unsigned author's 'advertisement' (1715) calls attention to the political charge of the title while seeming to disavow political intent: 'It is hoped no Offence will be taken at the Title, since none is intended by it, and therefore 'tis best to conclude with the Royal Motto, *Evil be to him that Evil thinks*'. Although *German Atalantis* (or *Hanover Tales*) is sometimes attributed to Mary Hearne, a signed receipt in the Upcott Collection (BL Add. MS 38,728, fo. 37r) indicates its author was one Robert Busby.

the pleasures of identification with an uncompromisingly loyal Jacobite position while making available a respectable position of accommodation. Like other historical romances from 1715–20, and like the bigamy plots strongly featured in *The Lining of the Patch Work Screen*, the dual storyline offers a way, finally, of working through ambivalent feelings towards the Hanoverian succession.

We might now take up more fully the question of who read Jane Barker in this period and why by considering the nature of the Jacobite historical romance—*Exilius*, *Irish Tales*, and, in more complicated ways, *Hanover Tales*. Works such as these, coded, oblique, politically allusive, and intensely idealizing, would doubtless have supplied the 'Jacobite faithful' with the special 'pleasures of complicity and solidarity', as Valerie Rumbold has said of Mary Caesar's Jacobite writing.[71] The escapist fantasy they delivered would have appealed, it seems likely, to a broader readership as well, one consisting of over-lapping groups of political and cultural dissidents. At the core would have been a 'self-sustaining, recognisable minority who rejected the social, political and religious order installed after 1688'—the Jacobite faithful—and around it a 'shifting cloud of individuals, families and connexions', not necessarily Jacobite, drawn for various reasons into opposition to the new Whig order.[72] For readers such as these Jacobite historical romances, like their precursors the heroic romances of the seventeenth century, would have delivered alternative worlds of high princi-ple and uncompromising ideals—a retreat from the sordid real-ities of the compromised Hanoverian present—as well as the pleasures of imagined resistance.

Few accounts of the early novel take notice of historical romances or their readers since by no stretch of the critical imagination can they be assimilated to any strand of the evolu-tionary 'triple rise'. And herein, perhaps, lies part of their signif-icance to scholars today. These romances serve to remind us that an insistent focus upon the urban middle-class reader is, in the words of Paul Hunter, a 'vast simplification of the readership

---

[71] Rumbold, 'Jacobite Vision', 179.
[72] Daniel Szechi, *The Jacobites: Britain and Europe 1688–1788* (Manchester and New York: Manchester UP, 1994), 12.

spectrum'. What distinguishes novel readership in the eighteenth century, he stresses, is 'not its confinement to a particular class or group' but rather 'its social range': the appeal of the
novel 'spanned the social classes and traditional divisions of
readers'.[73] Yet even Hunter's examples tend to move us down
the social scale, to the clerks, apprentices, and domestic servants
presumed to be fairly recent recruits to the pleasures of reading.
My work on Curll's marketing of Barker's novels suggests that
we must also look up the scale, as well as out of London, if we
are to develop a full and reliable picture of the early readership
of popular fiction. The fact that Edmund Curll trafficked in
Jacobite popular fiction during the opening years of the
Georgian era is evidence of a robust demand for such wares.[74]
With an uncertain political nation working through anxieties
around the new succession, with some Jacobites and many
Tories seeking face-saving ways to compromise with the new
order, and with even Whigs unclear what to make of a German-
speaking Lutheran monarch, Curll knew there was money to be
made selling idealized nostalgic romances with a Jacobite edge.
His doubtless well-calculated appeal in 1713 to 'the
Lincolnshire Gentry' suggests as well that in his analysis the
early market for prose fiction was more elite than many
accounts would have us believe.[75]
  I would like to suggest by way of speculative conclusion that
Barker's Jacobite fictions may have circulated through and
served to promote bonding within politically estranged commu-

---

[73] J. Paul Hunter, 'The Novel and Social/Cultural History', in John Richetti (ed.),
The Cambridge Companion to the Eighteenth-Century Novel (Cambridge:
Cambridge UP, 1996), 19.

[74] Cheryl Turner, *Living by the Pen: Women Writers in the Eighteenth Century*
(London and New York: Routledge, 1992), 50; McBurney, 'Edmund Curll', 386,
writes: 'any publishing venture by Curll was a strong indication that a lucrative
market for such a product existed'.

[75] Pat Rogers, *Robinson Crusoe* (London: Allen and Unwin, 1979), 102, specu-
lated that in 1710–29 the audience for popular fiction probably overlapped 'with
the traditional literary public' more than we might have imagined. Subsequent work
on subscription publication and dedications in the first half of the century lends
support to this speculation. See W. A. Speck, 'Politicians, Peers, and Publication by
Subscription 1700–50', in Isabel Rivers (ed.), *Books and their Readers in
Eighteenth-Century England* (Leicester: Leicester UP and St Martin's P., 1982),
47–68; Pat Rogers, 'Book Dedications in Britain 1700–1799', *British Journal for
Eighteenth-Century Studies*, 16 (1993), 213–33.

nities, or what have been called 'subaltern counterpublics'.[76] If this is so, then further attention to the political orientation of early popular prose fictions might usefully complement and complicate the view of the novel as agent of *national* cultures and identities that appears to be gaining ground in recent accounts of the early novel. Deirdre Lynch and William Warner have made an intriguing case for the constitutive role of the novel in the formation of national imagined communities. Novels, they point out, are uniquely mobile. They are able to 'circulate among a diverse readership within the nation', crossing lines of gender and class and mobilizing desire by 'triggering identification with a central character and transporting readers into alternate desires'. They thus serve to promote a sense of national belonging and unity: 'When novel reading traverses the social boundaries within the nation, novels' popularity can seem an index of the nation's essential coherence'.[77] Yet in the case of Jacobite romances a different mechanism of identification seems to be at work.

The imaginative counter-worlds created in Jacobite historical romances promote identification not only with characters but also, perhaps more crucially, with other readers, making available communal recognitions serving to nourish a sense of kinship among constituents of various estranged communities—Tory, Catholic and Jacobite, male and female—and to support shared antipathies to the new order. The circulation of such romances among the disaffected may indeed have enabled the formation within the larger national community of 'subaltern counterpublics', or 'parallel discursive arenas', as Nancy Fraser puts it, in which 'members of subordinated social groups invent and circulate counterdiscourses to formulate oppositional interpretations of their identities, interests, and needs'.[78] To acquire, say, *Exilius* with a view toward reading and then passing it on to another of the tribe of the politically righteous was to position oneself alongside imagined others at the cultural periphery.

[76] The phrase is from Nancy Fraser, 'Rethinking the Public Sphere: A Contribution to the Critique of Actually Existing Democracy', in Craig Calhoun (ed.), *Habermas and the Public Sphere* (Cambridge, Mass., and London: MIT P., 1992), 109–42 (123).

[77] Lynch and Warner, 'Introduction', *Cultural Institutions of the Novel*, 4.

[78] Fraser, 'Rethinking', 123.

The popularity of Jacobite romance in its own moment suggests, we might say, the existence of a reading public that understood itself less in terms of unity and coherence than of national heterogeneity—a patchwork public, if you will.

5

A Writer for Pay

IN an oft-cited passage Galesia, asked whether she prefers Philips or Behn, replies with 'blunt Indignation' that *they ought not to be nam'd together* (*PWS* 108). This emphatic repudiation is usually read as an effort on Barker's part to dissociate herself from Aphra Behn or, more precisely, to dodge the ill-repute that pursued the scandalous Behn after her death and indeed into our own century.[1] Perhaps this is so. But to stress the distance between these two writers is to risk obscuring the extent to which Barker, by the end of her writing life, had come to embrace an authorial identity suggestive less of Orinda's genteel amateurism than of Behn's market-place professionalism. If one implication of the last chapter is that Barker's eighteenth-century prose fictions carried on her Tory predecessor's pro-Stuart agenda in a post-revolutionary Jacobite idiom, an implication of the findings presented in this one is that Barker's orientation to the market-place of print may resemble Behn's more closely than many scholars have cared to consider, as well. Barker was no denizen of Grub Street, to be sure. She did not attempt to live off the proceeds of her pen in the often hand-to-mouth fashion of Behn (or Defoe or Haywood); she did not adopt the unapologetic topicality of Tory journalist and pamphleteer Delarivier Manley or write for the stage like Mary Davys, Mary Pix, or Susannah Centlivre or issue urgent political broadsheets in the manner of Elinor James. But she did write for pay and the paying public, and in the two patchwork narratives, written when she was very elderly, Barker assessed in suggestive ways her real, if perplexed, identification with the commerce of letters.

---

[1] A good summary of the ambiguous legacy of Behn's reputation is offered by Jeslyn Medoff, 'The Daughters of Behn and the Problem of Reputation', in Isobel Grundy and Susan Wiseman (eds.), *Women, Writing, History 1640–1740* (Athens: U. of Georgia P., 1992), 33–54.

The present chapter considers Barker's prose fictions in relation to that complex of shifts we call the transition from manuscript to print, the transformation from a literary culture that
was 'aristocratic, amateur, authoritarian, court-centered' to the
'print-based, market-centered, democratic literary system' we
know today.[2] We have seen that in her early and middle years
Barker enjoyed a surprisingly varied career as a literary amateur
circulating verse within manuscript networks, including a
Cambridge coterie and courtly circles at St-Germain. But with
the unsolicited print-publication in 1713 of her manuscript
work *The Amours of Bosvil and Galesia* she was forced to
adapt, willy-nilly, to the new conditions of the market-place.[3]
Thereafter she would publish all her works save one with
Edmund Curll, the canny if famously unscrupulous print entrepreneur whom Pope was neither first nor last to propose as a
perfect symbol for the low excesses of modern literary
commerce.[4] Within a decade her reorientation to print was
complete, and the patchwork novels from the 1720s show her
cultivating a place for herself within the new community of
print, having developed for that purpose a public voice suitable
for addressing a diverse and impersonal reading public.

The discussion that follows pursues the paradox of the figure
I call *Janus* Barker, an aged woman who remained stubbornly
attached to the high ideals of the Stuart age and yet was able to
produce experimental fictions notable for the way they inscribe,
in Bakhtin's phrase, the 'tendencies of a new world still in the
making'.[5] The last chapter stressed the backward gaze, her
devotion to a conservative political credo; this one considers the

---

[2] Alvin Kernan, *Samuel Johnson and the Impact of Print* (Princeton: Princeton
UP, 1987), 4.

[3] For a useful account of the development over the 18th cent. of female literary
professionalism, see Cheryl Turner, *Living by the Pen: Women Writers in the
Eighteenth Century* (London and New York: Routledge, 1992). For a more theoretical analysis of the careers of five early female novelists, see Catherine Gallagher,
*Nobody's Story: The Vanishing Acts of Women Writers in the Marketplace,
1670–1820* (Berkeley and Los Angeles: U. of California P., 1994).

[4] For Curll's career, see Ralph Straus, *The Unspeakable Curll* (London:
Chapman and Hall, 1927); Peter Murray Hill, *Two Augustan Booksellers: John
Dunton and Edmund Curll* (U. of Kansas Library Ser. No. 3, (Lawrence: U. of
Kansas Libraries, 1958).

[5] M. M. Bakhtin, *The Dialogic Imagination: Four Essays*, ed. Michael Holquist
and trans. Caryl Emerson and Michael Holquist (Austin: U. of Texas P., 1981), 7.

distinctively modern gaze of an septuagenarian writer-for-pay whose view takes in a commercialized order of booksellers, Grub Street hacks, and women literary professionals, a novelist prepared to embrace a whole new world of 'smear'd' possibilities for writing women. Ironically, it was a world less and less open to female political interventions.

The Passage into Print

It is no easy matter to say when exactly Barker began to write for the press. *Poetical Recreations* (1688) almost certainly reached print without her consent, as we saw in Chapter 1, and such appears to have been the case with her next printed work, the courtship novella *The Amours of Bosvil and Galesia* (1713), a cautionary tale of bungled love-making. Important clues to the genesis, authorial intentions, and early textual history of this work can be found in a pair of dedications. The dedication written for the revised 1719 edition insists that the publication six years earlier of the novella (under the title *Love Intrigues*) had come as a distressing surprise.[6] 'I was extreamly confus'd', she writes to the countess of Exeter, dedicatee of both editions, 'to find my little Novel presenting itself to your Ladyship without your Leave or Knowledge' (*BG* 2).[7] She is unable to explain 'by what Concurrence of Mistakes' the dedication saw print before the countess had granted her patronage, a violation of protocol a dyed-in-the-wool conservative like Barker would have regarded as both a grave offence against hierarchy and a terrible personal embarrassment. (Other aristocratically oriented poetic amateurs of middling origins, Katherine Philips and Mrs Rowe for example, express just such dismay when they fear they might be suspected by a noble female patron of similar breaches of protocol.)[8] Barker apologizes for the 'Indecorums and

---

[6] A 'corrected' version of *BG* appeared as the last part of the two-volume *EN* (1719), along with an unrevised *Exilius*.

[7] The countess of Exeter was the former Elizabeth Brownlow of Belton, Lincolnshire, who married John Cecil, 6th earl of Exeter, in 1699 and lived at Burghley House until her death in Nov. 1723.

[8] Three letters to Charles Cotterell show Phillips anxious lest the duchess of York, whom she sought as her patron for *Pompey*, should learn of others seeing

Breaches of Respect' committed when the novel was first published, thanks the countess for this 'Opportunity to beg Pardon for the Offences committed by the other', acknowledges her patron's graciousness in extending protection to 'this large Composure' (*BG* 2), that is, the two-volume *Entertaining Novels* (1719), and concludes, in the conventionally flattering manner of dedications, with praise for the countess's 'Condescention, in raising me from my Obscurity' (*BG* 4).[9]

It may be well to reflect briefly on the significance of what must be called, for want of a better word, the sycophancy of this address. Female displays of subservience, even those directed toward a female patron, make critics uncomfortable nowadays. Most prefer to see early women writers as 'pioneers', boldly assertive adventurers in a brave new world of print. Witness the way critics turn in embarrassment from the solemnly deferential formalities of Behn's later dedications to celebrate the in-your-face impudence of her early, unpatronized 'punk prostitute' phase.[10] Such critical discomfort is understandable, perhaps,

---

copies before she did: 'I had rather it never should [be presented to the duchess], than that she should hear it is gotten into other Hands before': see Thomas, *Collected Works*, ii, letters XX, XXI, XXII. The quote is on 64. Mrs Rowe was similarly alarmed when she got wind of Edmund Curll's plans to preface an unauthorized volume of her poems with an account of her life. To the countess of Hertford she wrote: 'I am in pain till you know I am entirely ignorant of *Curl*'s romance of my life and writings': see Theophilus Rowe (ed.), *The Miscellaneous Works in Prose and Verse of Mrs. Elizabeth Rowe* (London: R. Hett and R. Dodsley, 1739), ii. 177.

    [9] In the 'third edition' of *EN* (1736) appeared a dedication to the countess of Exeter dated from Wilsthorp, 10 June 1715, which begins 'I am delighted in having Permission to lay this Work [*Exilius*] at your Ladyship's Feet . . .'. Since *Exilius* had appeared in Aug. 1714 without a dedication, Barker must have sought and received the countess's patronage sometime during the year following its publication.

    [10] The notable exception is Deborah Payne, who has closely analysed Behn's problematic position in the Restoration patronage system. In ' "And poets shall by patron-princes live": Aphra Behn and Patronage', in Mary Anne Schofield and Cecilia Macheski (eds.), *Curtain Calls: British and American Women and the Theater, 1660–1820* (Athens: Ohio UP, 1991), 114, she points out that in Behn's later, patronized plays, her dedications—to the duke of York, the earl of Arundel, the earl of Rochester—are written 'in the most humorless and sanctimonious of tones' as Behn came to assume, without irony, the voice of the patronized male playwright. Most critics prefer the mocking and outrageous Behn of Catherine Gallagher's 'Who was that Masked Woman? The Prostitute and the Playwright in the Comedies of Aphra Behn', in Regina Barreca (ed.), *Last Laughs: Perspectives on Women and Comedy* (New York: Gordon and Breach, 1988), 23–42. It has since appeared, modified, as a chapter in *Nobody's Story*. See Payne, ' "And poets" ', 116–17, for a valuable critique of Gallagher.

but a proper account of women's writing practices during this transitional period requires that we acknowledge and attempt to make sense of what Pat Rogers, aware of the inadequacy of his terminology, describes as the 'prevailing note of sycophancy' sounded in dedications at a time when authors, men and women alike, found themselves poised between older aristocratically based patronage systems and the more egalitarian possibilities of the developing world of print. 'There is no equivalent concept in the existing lexicon', he points out; ' "deference" is about the nearest, but that is largely passive, and sycophancy was an active and sometimes dynamic ingredient in social transactions'. He concludes that we 'cannot conceptualize the issues raised by the dedication until the terminology is made more precise'.[11] To recognize that Barker's novella is part of a social transaction is to see more clearly the transitional nature of writing at this time. To modern eyes *Bosvil and Galesia* looks like a market-place commodity: it was, after all, sold in London bookshops, bears Curll's name on the imprint, and includes a verse puff piece by George Sewell, hack originator of such Curll classics as *A Treatise on Flogging*.[12] But the deferential gestures of the second dedication indicate how fully Barker continued to identify with a traditional clientelistic literary economy: it is her aristocratic patron, not the bookseller or the buying public, whom she thanks for raising her from her obscurity.

Study of the unauthorized dedication, intended evidently for the eyes of the countess and her young daughter only, throws light on the earliest readership of *The Amours of Bosvil and Galesia* and perhaps on Barker's original literary purposes. The dedication begins conventionally enough:

To send abroad the Composure of leisure Hours, as at first I was very timerous, so (had not the sweet Reflections of Your Ladyship's experienc'd Goodness emboldned me to skreen this little Novel under your auspicious Protection) it had for ever lain Dormant; and which indeed,

---

[11] Pat Rogers, 'Book Dedications in Britain 1700–1799: A Preliminary Survey', *British Journal for Eighteenth-Century Studies*, 16 (1993), 213–33 (230).

[12] 'To Mrs. *Jane Barker*' is reprinted in *Posthumous Works of Dr. George Sewell* (London: Henry Curll, 1728), 47–9. Since he addresses Barker as '*Galesia*, Fair unknown', it is reasonable to conclude the lines were commissioned by Curll.

now it does humbly prostrate it self before you, can have no other
Pretensions, than to be Half an Hours Amusement to Your Ladyship.[13]

The information that the story had long 'lain Dormant' is interesting, for in combination with internal evidence it confirms the
impression that the novella had been drafted much earlier,
perhaps at St-Germain (where the framing fiction is set).
Otherwise we learn only that Barker intended the 'little Novel'
to be read by the countess and perhaps others in her circle.
More revelatory are the confessional lines that follow.
Remarkably, they express hope that the countess's daughter be
spared the troubles the author had experienced as a girl—'may
[she] never intangle her Noble Person in those Levities and
Misfortunes the ensuing Treatise describes me unhappily to
have struggled with'—and in this way disclose the autobiographical basis of the story, something Barker assuredly would
not have done had she thought the dedication destined for
public view. The 'corrected' 1719 dedication, which *was*
intended for print, is wholly devoid of self-reference, never mind
the tone of woman-to-woman intimacy so striking in the original version, and is swollen instead with praise of the countess.[14]
Comparing these dedications one gets the strong sense that in its
earlier form the story of Bosvil and Galesia was written for, and
meant to circulate within, a small, select, sympathetic, and
almost certainly feminine circle of élite readers.

Further evidence that the 1713 version of *Bosvil and Galesia*
was never intended for public consumption, at least not in the
form in which it saw print, is found in other kinds of revisions.
For one thing, Barker saw to it that the little novel be given a
more dignified title, presumably the one she originally intended.
Although it is usually known today by the 1713 title, *Love
Intrigues; or, The History of the Amours of Bosvil and Galesia*,

---

[13] Dedication, *Love Intrigues; or, The History of the Amours of Bosvil and
Galesia* (London: Curll and Crownfield, 1713), cited hereafter as *LI*.
[14] Similarly, when Barker prepared her 'Poems Refering to the times' for presentation at court she removed lines she feared savoured of self-preoccupation, including a forty-two-line passage from 'Fidelia & her friend on the Revolution' in which
a Protestant 'friend' tempts her to betray the Stuart cause with promises that she will
be hailed a 'Saviouress', a 'Heroine', and a 'phisician to the state'. She restored the
lines in the Magdalen MS copy, where the poem is entitled 'Fidelia and her friend'
(fos. 25v–27).

I have no doubt that the opening phrase, hinting at sexual misconduct in the manner of the scandal chronicle, was Curll's contribution. The term *amour*, according to the *Oxford English Dictionary*, had as its primary meaning love affair, love-making, or courtship (hence Congreve's description of *Incognita* as an 'intricate amour') and referred only secondarily to an illicit love affair, whereas the slightly off-colour *intrigue* was more likely to refer to a 'clandestine illicit intimacy' and was therefore used to flag scandal fiction—hence Manley's *Court Intrigues* (1711), and, later, Haywood's *The Secret History of the Present Intrigues of the Court of Caramania* (1727).[15] Barker must have insisted upon the less salacious title in 1719, and I think we should too; everything about the phrase *love intrigues* savours of the bookseller.

She also carefully revised the narrative proper with a view toward elevating and generalizing what must have seemed, in print, even with its already strong sense of didactic purpose, an indecorously personal account. Conceived in the tradition of advice to a young lady, *Bosvil and Galesia* warns against the perils of vanity. In Barker's hands, however, the traditional *vanitas* theme becomes less an occasion for moral persuasion than a vehicle for analysis of the psychology of vanity, especially the seemingly infinite capacity for self-deception possessed by a young woman in love. In addition to countless verbal adjustments in the interest of economy, precision, and focus, she added poems and fragments of poems and revised others,[16] incorporated bits of proverbial wisdom, and strengthened the theme of religious resignation. Where the revised version ends with an affirmation of trust in providence that rounds itself off

---

[15] Cf. Dryden's usage in *Marriage à la Mode* (1673), cited in the *OED*: 'Intrigue, Philotis! that's an old phrase; I have laid that word by: amour sounds better'. In titles *amour* was one of those coded terms, like the word *novel* itself, used to signal a small story of courtship and love in polite society, as in the 22 Nov. 1718 advertisement (one of Curll's) for Mary Hearne's *The Female Deserters*, described as 'the Amours of some Ladies of Quality of the first Rank' (*PB*, No. 4576).

[16] The revisions made to 'I wish'd my self unsprung of Human Race' (1713) on its way to becoming 'O wherefore was I born of human Race' (1719) show Barker giving more direct expression to Galesia's almost overwhelming sense of abjection. For example, a triplet that reads, '*For what is more disgraceful to a Maid | What Pangs so sharp her tortur'd Soul invade, | As this sad Curse*—Deserted and betrayed' (58) is compressed to read, '*For what is more disgraceful to a Maid, | Than to be scorn'd like me, like me betray'd*' (40)—one of many changes for the good.

on a note of pious formality, the original ending had been abrupt, spare, and uninstructive: 'Thus I have impartially pointed out to you this unhappy Scene of my Life', the narrator says, 'which the Bell now ringing to Prayers shall put a Period to' (*LI* 71). (In contrast the moralized 1719 ending reads: 'But where we take Vertue for our Guide, God and our good Angels helps us thro'; and tho' we meet with many Rubs to make us stumble or reel, yet the good Hand of Providence is ready to lend Support, that we shall not fall into Ruin or Confusion' (*BG* 46–7).) One might expect the heightened piety and didacticism of the 1719 text to make it the duller of the two, but the opposite is true. It is as if the elevated framework permitted Barker to probe more deeply Galesia's vulnerabilities and to give fuller play to the darker, less respectable elements of her personality, including her rage and her sexuality.[17] Galesia emerges from the revisions more spiteful, self-punishing, and sexually humiliated—a more complex and interesting character, in short.

All the evidence points, then, to the likelihood that an intimately self-revelatory narrative of advice had been hijacked out of its natural manuscript setting to become, in the bookseller's vulgarizing phrase, a tale of *Love Intrigues*. However, it is by no means clear how Curll might have come into possession of a copy, although a clue may be found in the second name found in the imprint: that of Cornelius Crownfield, the sober and estimable Cambridge University Printer.[18] Crownfield's involvement in the project seems more than a little odd, for he would never again involve himself with Barker or for that matter with anything as lightweight as popular prose fiction, and hereafter his dealings with Curll would be minimal. However, from at least 1702 Crownfield was established as a bookseller in his own right and from time to time published various titles of his own. In 1710–12 he did seem to be branching out a bit (publishing Tacquet, Varenius, Theophrastus, Minucius Felix, for example) and it may be, as Don McKenzie has suggested, that his

<hr/>

[17] See Jane Spencer, 'Creating the Woman Writer: The Autobiographical Works of Jane Barker', *Tulsa Studies in Woman's Literature*, 2 (1983), 171, 173; Margaret Anne Doody, 'Jane Barker', *British Novelists, 1660–1800, DLB* 39, part I (Detroit: Gale Research Co.–Bruccoli Clark, 1985), 28.

[18] For Crownfield's career prior to 1712, see D. F. McKenzie, *The Cambridge University Press 1696–1712*, 2 vols. (Cambridge UP, 1966).

association with Curll just at that time represents a short-lived interest in extending his list to include fiction, although nothing is known of his actual share in *Bosvil and Galesia*.[19]

Curll may have sought a partnership with Crownfield in order more readily to tap the local market. Cambridge was a major distribution centre only some forty miles away from Wilsthorp, where Barker was living at the time, and from Burghley House, home of the volume's dedicatee, and we know from a 1714 advertisement for *Exilius* that Curll was attentive to matters of local distribution.[20] But it seems at least as likely that it was Crownfield who initiated publication. Barker is known to have had important literary connections with Cambridge in the previous century.[21] *Poetical Recreations* got into print in part through the agency of some Cambridge scholars, one a neighbour in Lincolnshire, and a copy found its way into the Trinity College library of a fellow Lincolnshire man, Sir Isaac Newton, one of a small number of volumes of poetry to be found among his books.[22] It seems reasonable to speculate that Crownfield somehow acquired a copy of *Bosvil and Galesia* and, recognizing its publication value, contacted the London-based Curll as someone already positioned to reach the national audience for popular fiction. In any event, he would have needed a partner in London, for at this time all printed material was required by law to have the name of a London bookseller in the imprint, which meant that a provincial printer would require 'a London agent to supply not only the London trade but also the provincial booksellers who normally

---

[19] I am grateful to the late Don McKenzie for this information.

[20] *Post Man*, 14 Aug. 1714. In addition to being sold in London (by J. Roberts), Barker's 'new Entertaining Romance' was sold by Mr Palmer, a bookseller in Stamford, the market town closest to Wilsthorp. Such arrangements were in fact characteristic of print distribution systems at this time. Terry Belanger, 'Publishers and Writers in Eighteenth-Century England', in Isabel Rivers (ed.), *Books and their Readers in Eighteenth-Century England* (Leicester: Leicester UP and New York: St Martin's P., 1982), 9, observes: 'Even in 1700, provincial readers tended to acquire their books through provincial dealers, and they did so increasingly throughout the century'.

[21] These earlier connections are difficult to trace. The one Cambridge friend I have been able to follow, John Newton ('Philaster'), became the rector of King's Cliff, Northamptonshire, in 1689, dying in 1714.

[22] John Harrison, *The Library of Isaac Newton* (Cambridge: Cambridge UP, 1978), 70–1.

depended on their London agents for supplies'.[23] It seems on the whole more likely, then, that Crownfield sought out Curll than the reverse.

In any event, Crownfield would soon retire to the sober respectability of his academic publications and leave in place a long, productive, and somewhat puzzling association between Curll and Barker. Curll was known already for his aggressive marketing of salacious books,[24] and in 1713 had yet to publish a novel—*Bosvil and Galesia* would be his first—nor had he established the association with women writers that was to become a marked feature of his publishing practices. (His list would eventually include works by Delarivier Manley, Susannah Centlivre, Mary Hearne, Sarah Butler, Martha Fowke, and Elizabeth Thomas, among others.) How the famously scurrilous bookseller and a genteel Lincolnshire writer came into a professional relationship must remain a mystery, but we know that from this point on Curll, alone or in partnership, would bring out all her works save the final novel, published during a period when Curll, buffeted by legal problems, was in temporary retirement.[25]

Since no contemporary commentary on *Bosvil and Galesia* has survived, we can only guess at the reasons for its modest success—and it is worth noting that such popularity as Barker was to enjoy in her own lifetime appears to have derived from this novella along with the following year's *Exilius*. They appeared together in 1719 in the two-volume *The Entertaining Novels of Mrs. Jane Barker*, which was reissued late in 1735 and again in 1743.[26] Barker is best known today for the gender-and-

---

[23] David Foxon, *Pope and the Early Eighteenth-Century Book Trade*, rev. and ed. James McLaverty (Oxford: Clarendon P., 1991), 3–4.

[24] According to William H. McBurney, 'Edmund Curll, Mrs. Jane Barker, and the English Novel', *Philological Quarterly*, 37 (1958), 386, 'as early as 1710 Curll's shop at the Sign of the Dial and Bible was well known for its scurrilous and sensational publications' and his name 'synonymous with unethical publishing methods'.

[25] See Straus, *Unspeakable Curll*, ch. 6, for the story.

[26] The 'third edition' of *Entertaining Novels* (London: Bettesworth, Hitch, and Curll, 1736) by 'the late Mrs. Jane Barker' was advertised in the *London Magazine* monthly catalogue in Sept. 1735. It was advertised 13 May 1736 in the *London Evening Post* as part of a ten-volume collection of novels intended for the 'Entertainment of Gentlemen and Ladies'. EN was advertised 11 Sept. 1731 in the *Daily Post* in 'Four Pocket Volumes', printed for Bettesworth and Hitch, and in 1736 in the *London Evening Post* as part of a ten-vol. set. A 1743 edition came out

genre innovations of *A Patch-Work Screen for the Ladies*, a work which has been judged 'one of the most important, if ignored, works in women's literary history',[27] but neither this work nor its sequel, *The Lining of the Patch Work Screen*, appears to have made much of a ripple. Neither went into a second edition.

The story of an adolescent girl's coming to sexual consciousness, covering her fifteenth to eighteenth years, the *Amours of Bosvil and Galesia* focuses upon the trials of a heroine too easily betrayed by her own feelings. By any reckoning it is an extraordinary piece of writing. Like other works in the feminocentric amatory tradition, to which it bears an interestingly ironic relation, the narrative may be read as a complex instance of the 'heroinizing of artifice and fictional duplicity' and analysed along lines laid down by Ros Ballaster in *Seductive Forms*.[28] Yet Barker's novella possesses an immediacy and psychological realism seldom felt in the narratives of Behn, Manley, and Haywood. There is the frankness of the psychological content for a start. *Bosvil and Galesia* is a study in female sexual obsession; it deals sympathetically with the rage, shame, self-deception, jealousy, and violent fantasies of a heroine who, for all her outward prudence and self-control, suffers a range of mortifying sexual and emotional needs. Although feminine abjection had been put on display in tragic drama and Ovidian complaint, seldom was it adjusted to the ordinary gradations of daily existence within the intimate spaces of prose narrative. Episodes such as that in which Galesia watches her well-merited fury with her lover sink into depression and histrionic self-blame ('my Anger [turned] against myself, my wretched self, that woful and unworthy Thing' (*BG* 32)) or that in which she sends him horns on his wedding day, and then denies, even to

under the imprint of C. Hitch. Closer bibliographical scrutiny might reveal that they are not 'editions' but rather reissued sheets of the 1719 edition, suggesting perhaps a publisher's attempt to move slowly selling material. The relative scarcity of surviving copies, with not even more than one 'edition' in the BL, leaves this matter open to bibliographical investigation.

[27] Josephine Donovan, 'Women and the Rise of the Novel: A Feminist-Marxist Theory', *Signs*, 16 (1991), 441–62 (452).

[28] Ros Ballaster, *Seductive Forms: Women's Amatory Fiction from 1684 to 1740* (Oxford: Clarendon P., 1992), 3.

herself perhaps, 'any malicious Intent' (*BG* 44), invite us to
share in a quite ordinary, but no less devastating for that, sense
of shame. Galesia, it has rightly been observed, is an important
figure in popular fiction by women precisely because she is an
'early bearer of women's experiences'.[29] One would like to
know how she was read by her contemporaries.

That the novella probably originated within private manuscript circles may help account for one of its most interesting
features, its curiously oblique relation to the conventions of
popular amatory fiction. Much of the best work on *Bosvil and
Galesia* connects it to the courtship tale (on the one hand) or the
seduction tale (on the other). However, even discussions which
notice that much of the power of the narrative resides in the
way the action 'subverts the conventions of earlier romance by
communicating a cynical view of love and a dread of a woman's
surrender to a man's power' fail to appreciate that the story
unfolds with a strange disregard for the pull of amatory convention, either in its seventeenth-century heroic forms or the early
eighteenth-century seduction-and-betrayal incarnations discussed
by Ballaster.[30] Far from exalting transcendent love in the old
heroic fashion (as Barker had done in *Exilius*) or tracing the fall
into sexual ruin in the manner of the more recent seduction tales
of Behn and Manley (as she would do in some of the inset tales
in *A Patch-Work Screen for the Ladies*), this ironized romance
presents the portrait of a heroine who exists in a kind of sexual
limbo outside the confines of the amatory plot in any of its
expected manifestations.[31] The real story, from beginning to
end, is the inward cost of her refusal of that plot, and it is a

[29] Paula R. Backscheider and John J. Richetti, introd., *Popular Fiction by Women
1660–1730: An Anthology* (Oxford: Clarendon P., 1996), xix.

[30] Wilson, xxxviii. For *BG* in relation to romance, see Jane Spencer, *The Rise of
the Woman Novelist: From Aphra Behn to Jane Austen* (Oxford and New York:
Basil Blackwell, 1986), 64–6; and Kristina Straub, 'Frances Burney and the Rise of
the Woman Novelist', in *The Columbia History of the British Novel*, ed. John
Richetti (New York: Columbia UP, 1994), 199–219, esp. 203–5. For the development of romance more generally, see Ballaster, *Seductive Forms*, 42–66.

[31] Obviously I depart here from Spencer's reading of Galesia as romance heroine.
What I find most interesting about Galesia, in fact, is the extent to which she
remains *outside* the conventions of the romance plot within an alternative plot sceptical about the validity of those conventions. I concur entirely, however, with
Spencer, *Rise*, 65, that one of Barker's purposes was to 'make the single life a new
kind of heroine's destiny'.

story tangled in ambiguities as Galesia struggles to read several opaque texts—chief among them the motives of a perversely incomprehensible lover and her own propensity for self-deception. Barker seems to have regarded *Bosvil and Galesia* as a cautionary tale, as indeed it is, but in a deeply ironic way. For Galesia is the victim not of male sexual predators but of a too fastidious adherence to codes of female virtue. The effect of Barker's subversive narrative—and in this instance that overworked adjective seems about right—is to expose feminine modesty and prudence as forms of self-suppression as likely to breed shame and humiliation as to ensure personal happiness and a well-ordered household. I know of nothing like it in published fiction from this period.

The next year saw the publication of *Exilius; or, the Banish'd Roman*, another work conceived within the matrix of late seventeenth-century manuscript culture.[32] Barker wrote a preface in which for the first time in her writing life she appeals to an impersonal buying public ('Tho' I cannot Fee my Fancy with the Hopes of Praise or Profit from the following Book, yet I am willing to plead its Cause, and deliver it with as fair a Title as I can to my Readers Approbation . . . .' (sig. A2)). Yet a substantial portion of *Exilius* had been completed many years earlier, parts having circulated in manuscript under the title *Scipina* among her Cambridge friends. Like *Poetical Recreations* and the more recent *Bosvil and Galesia*, *Exilius* is best regarded as a manuscript work in print, the product of the interplay of different but far from distinct literary cultures. Indeed, one lesson of this transitional phase of Barker's literary career is that the two cultures, manuscript and print, often depicted as separate and even opposed, are not in practice distinguishable but coexist rather as sets of overlapping and interpenetrating expressive possibilities. Another is that, though the interconnections may have been weakening, many of the invented narratives now gathered together under the rubric 'the early novel' have important links with manuscript coterie traditions that remain virtually unexplored.

---

[32] Its coterie origins are discussed in Ch. 4 above.

The Patchwork Narratives: 'buy these Patches up quickly'

After the publication of *Exilius* in 1714 another nine years would pass before Barker would bring out a new work of prose fiction. *A Patch-Work Screen for the Ladies* (1723), written after the collapse of her Jacobite political hopes, represents a decisive change in orientation for Barker, a turning point in her relationship to the reading public. Up until this point the imaginative writings that had come out under her name had been intended to circulate in manuscript within select, familiar, and relatively closed reading communities: friendship coteries late in the Restoration period, the St-Germain exile community after the Revolution, a feminine and aristocratically centred reading circle in her local neighbourhood. Print-publication seems to have been unsought (*Poetical Recreations, Bosvil and Galesia*) or a much later choice (*Exilius*). In contrast to these earlier works, *A Patch-Work Screen for the Ladies* (1723), the first eighteenth-century work by Barker not to appear under the auspices of a titled woman,[33] was composed for a large, impersonal reading public whose members Barker could no longer rely upon to share her values, prejudices, angers, and identifications. The political poetry from the turn of the century, it will be recalled from Chapter 3, confronted us with an outspoken, self-righteous, heavy-handedly partisan poet whose call for uncompromising sectarianism was directed toward a tight band of co-religionists. So monovocal a mode of address would have to change, obviously, if Barker were to meet the requirements of market-driven literary expression. The dialogism that first revealed itself in 1718 when Barker made the Catholic Fénelon 'speak *English*, in the Dialect of the Church of *England*' emerges into broader, more hybridized, and more various expression in *A Patch-Work Screen for the Ladies*, a remarkably

---

[33] Barker's dedicatory practices were somewhat unusual, according to findings summarized by Rogers in 'Book Dedications'. He reports, 225, that woman-to-woman dedications were not common in the 18th cent., although they would become more so as the century went on. Out of a total sample of 856 attributable dedications, he locates only seven woman-to-woman dedications prior to 1750 as compared with twenty-one after mid-century. These numbers are clearly quite low, however. The topic merits further investigation.

miscellaneous work composed by a market-place author for a national public.

The innovative hybrid narrative method widely acknowledged to be a defining feature of this work has won much praise, especially from feminist critics intrigued by the suggestive interplay between gender and genre. Margaret Doody was one of the first to call approving attention to the experimental 'generic mixture'; more recently Carol Shiner Wilson has called it a 'lively hybrid genre'.[34] Elizabeth Wahl finds that the patchwork metaphor and narrative method enabled Barker to define 'the novel as a peculiarly feminine pursuit' and furnish the narrative with a 'peculiarly "feminine" form'; Josephine Donovan uses Bakhtin to discuss Barker's blurring of the 'line between literature and nonliterature', concluding that the 'critical, polyvocal, "patch-work" perspective' produces the 'feminist critical irony' employed to critique the patriarchal social and economic order.[35] What has not been remarked is that the self-conscious generic diversity of this work is to a great extent a function of Barker's new sense of herself as a market-place author and signals a new understanding of the relationship of author to reader.

Virtually every element of *Patch-Work Screen* testifies to her effort to translate the essentially private, interior, and autobiographical concerns of *Bosvil and Galesia* into a public register. Toward this end she uses a technique which might be compared to collage and assemblage—a patching together of scraps of inherited forms so as to accommodate within the confines of a single female-centred narrative kinds of experience traditionally excluded from popular fiction, resulting in a 'patchwork' of

---

[34] Doody, 'Jane Barker', 29. Wilson, xxxix. Not all critics have been so admiring. John Richetti, *Popular Fiction Before Richardson: Narrative Patterns 1700–1739* (Oxford: Clarendon P., 1969), 237, calls the framework narrative 'a very old product . . . with the new ideological wrappings of the female moral sensibility'. Patricia Meyer Spacks, *Imagining a Self: Autobiography and Novel in Eighteenth-Century England* (Cambridge and London: Harvard UP, 1976), 66, is downright harsh: the novel lacks 'any apparent focused, conscious purpose'; it is 'an almost incoherent melange of happenings related to one another only by the often peripheral involvement of the heroine'.

[35] Elizabeth Wahl, 'Jane Barker', in Paul Schlueter and June Schlueter (eds.), *An Encyclopedia of British Women Writers* (New York and London: Garland, 1988), 24. Donovan, 'Women and the Rise', 453, 462.

modes, manners, voices, and genres—including verse epistles, ballads, odes, prophecies, moral essays, even versified recipes. (A recipe for French onion soup begins, wonderfully, 'Take a large Barn-door Cock, and all his Bones break' (151).) She also seeks to redefine in public terms the narrative space in which Galesia relates her story. In *Bosvil and Galesia*, as we have seen, Barker directs much of her creative energy toward establishing a relationship of intimate sympathy with her (female) readers: the 'as-told-to' framing fiction in which Galesia is shown confiding in her friend Lucasia thematizes an essentially private relation between author/speaker and reader/listener. The beginning of *Patch-Work Screen* could scarcely be more different in intent or effect. Cast in the form of a stage coach journey and featuring a round of story-telling on the part of the five passengers, three men and two women, the frame brings to mind various predominantly male 'journey' narratives at the same time that it suggests modes of story-telling that are public, communal, and mix-gendered.

The first three tales, crime stories, are told by the men; they are followed by a grotesque tale of murder and dismemberment told by Galesia with her own brand of grisly relish (the body, chopped up and tossed into the common sewer, is recovered 'Piece-meal as it was, as also the Head' (64)); a young lady brings things to a close with a tale of illicit convent love. After this exchange of mostly gender-inflected stories, Galesia's offering being characteristically odd, the coach overturns and a mode of story-telling associated with the road is turned on its head as well. The scene of story-telling now shifts from the mixed company of the coach to the feminized space of an aristocratic country house, where Galesia is invited to tell her history to a noble lady and her 'women', that is, female attendants, and at the same time to add scraps of her own writing to an ongoing patchwork screen. Thus does Galesia resume the life-story begun in *Bosvil and Galesia*, but with a difference. It is as if Barker uses this long and complicated framing fiction, with its succession of allegorized stories, tellers, auditors, and sites, to redefine Galesia-as-storyteller along the public lines suggested by the motif of passengers in a coach and then, by means of the spill, to relocate the scene of story-telling within female space and, more particularly, at the site of the patchwork screen. The movement is broadly suggestive of its author's own journey toward an innovative narrative art that is at once hybridized, female-centred, and public.

Barker is intent also upon positioning the narrative within the here-and-now of an expanding field of 'novels', 'authentic memoirs', 'histories', and such. The crime stories told in the coach may represent a nod toward Daniel Defoe and popular criminal narrative more generally, as has been suggested;[36] the inset tales of seduction and betrayal punctuating the narrative proper may gesture toward Eliza Haywood, who, since 1719, when she published the first part of the 'bestselling' *Love in Excess*, had flooded the market with enormously popular amatory fictions. Whether or not Barker was paying ironic homage to the two writers who in 1723 might be said, with only some exaggeration, to divide the field of popular fiction between them, there can be no doubt that in this 'History *reduc'd into* Patches' (51) she sought to reach an expanding market for popular prose fiction and did so by producing a broadly inclusive fiction, responsive to a variety of contemporary influences and suitable for a pluralistic reading public, whose members, conceived now as consumers, are frankly urged to '*buy these* Patches *up quickly*' (54).[37]

Although Barker left no explicit statements on Defoe, whose sympathetic renderings of upward social mobility I expect she would have found suspect,[38] the preface to *Patch-Work Screen*

[36] Michael F. Shugrue, 'The Sincerest Form of Flattery: Imitation in the Early Eighteenth-Century Novel', *South Atlantic Quarterly*, 70 (1971), 248–55 (253) argues that the frame represents an effort to capitalize on the popularity of Defoe's criminal narratives.

[37] Since it is generally assumed and routinely asserted of virtually any moment in the 18th cent. that it 'saw a rapid expansion of the field of popular fiction', it is worth pointing out that, while in actual fact the century saw long stretches of flat and even declining production as far as new titles were concerned, 1723 was indeed a boom time for new works of popular prose fiction. For an overview of biblio-graphical studies establishing this point, see J. A. Downie, 'The Making of the English Novel', *Eighteenth-Century Fiction*, 9 (1997), 249–66. He reports, 254, that in the 1720s the number of new titles just about doubled the output of the previous decade, reaching a peak at mid-decade at around twenty new titles per annum.

[38] Although deeply interested in patterns of social mobility, she tended to focus on deserving members of the higher orders who lose caste: see, for example, in *PWS*, the nurse's story (119–22); and in *Lining*, 'The Story of Mrs. Goodwife' (218–21) and 'The History of Dorinda' (238–47).

shows that she wanted the work to be viewed in opposition to the extended prose narratives we now associate with his name. 'And why a HISTORY reduc'd into Patches?' she imagines the reader asking, 'especially since HISTORIES at Large are so Fashionable in this Age; viz. Robinson Crusoe, and Moll Flanders; Colonel Jack, and Sally Salisbury?' (51). (The final item in the series, The Authentick Memoirs of the Life Intrigues and Adventures of the Celebrated Sally Salisbury (1723), is not by Defoe, of course. I shall return to it shortly.) Given that, except for Robinson Crusoe, Defoe's authorship of these narratives was unknown at this time and that for most readers even Crusoe was a book 'without an author, a book which did not need an author',[39] it is misleading to represent Barker as asserting her place alongside the leading male novelist of her time, as is sometimes done. She seems instead to be using a code familiar to her readers to distinguish her own brand of fiction-making—fiction, it should be recalled, for 'the ladies'—from the low, gritty, popular, more or less criminal stories signified by the names of their protagonists. That same year the author of The Highland Rogue (1723) claimed to be presenting 'not the adventures of a Robinson Crusoe, a Colonel Jack, or a Moll Flanders, but the actions of the Highland Rogue, a Man that has been too notorious to pass for a mere imaginary Person' (sig. A2v). The preface to Richard Falconer laments that in the present day 'Shakespear, and Ben Johnson, must give way to Robinson Crusoe, and Colonel Jack; as well as Dryden and Otway to Moll Flanders, and Sally Salisbury'.[40] In 1725 the Dublin Journal commented that 'Your Robinson Crusoe's, Moll Flanders's, Sally Salisbury's and John Shepard's' have been 'as greedily read by People of the better sort, as the Compilers of Last Speeches and Dying Words by the Rabble',[41] which might suggest the existence of a 'better sort' of reader who found in works such as these opportunities for literary slumming. An

---

[39] Not until the 1770s and 1780s were these works clearly tied to Defoe: see P. N. Furbank and W. R. Owens, 'Defoe and Francis Noble', Eighteenth-Century Fiction, 4 (1992), 301–13 (301).

[40] William Rufus Chetwood, preface, The Voyages, Dangerous Adventures, and Imminent Escapes of Capt. Rich. Falconer (1720; London: Marshal, Chetwood, Cox, and Edlin, 1724).

[41] Qtd. in Pat Rogers, Robinson Crusoe (London: Allen and Unwin, 1979), 128–9.

anonymous 1727 novel, *The Hermit*, observes that '*Robinson Crusoe*, *Moll Flanders*, and Collonel *Jack* have had their Admirers among the lower Rank of Readers'.[42]

That Barker sought to elevate her own readership by comparison with a lower or at least more salacious rank of readers is further suggested by the allusion to the *Authentic Memoirs of Sally Salisbury* (1723), a cheerfully obscene semi-pornographic story of a woman who aspires to be '*a First-Rate Whore*' attributed to one Capt. Charles Walker. Sally Salisbury, née Pridden or Priddon, was a notorious real-life courtesan whose knife attack on John Finch kept her name much in the press in the early months of 1723. Well before the trial at the Old Bailey was over 'authentic memoirs' were hitting the bookstalls. In March the *Authentic Memoirs* was advertised in the *Monthly Catalogue*; by May a second edition had been announced, said to include a key and an account of her trial. One might have expected Barker to pass over the memoir in silent disdain or denounce it as an example of everything offensive in modern writing. (Two years later in *The Lining of the Patch Work Screen* she would condemn the 'Stories of our Times' as being 'so black' that authors 'can hardly escape being smutted, or defil'd in touching such Pitch'.)[43] Barker may never have read *Sally Salisbury*[44]—indeed, one wonders why she might want to—but she could hardly have been unaware of the notoriety surrounding the real-life woman or the popular appeal of the tabloid-style stories circulating in print. That she should name *Sally Salisbury* in her preface suggests a desire to situate *Patch-Work Screen* among the very latest offerings while distinguishing it from the more popular (coarse, obscene, smutty) ways of telling a story about contemporary life.

Undoubtedly this novel addressed to 'the Ladies' belongs to what Cheryl Turner calls an 'emerging orientation towards female readers', an orientation discernible early in the seven-

---

[42] Preface, *The Hermit: Or, the Unparalled Sufferings and Surprising Adventures of Mr. Philip Quarll, An Englishman* (London: Warner and Creake, 1727), sig. A3.

[43] She is contrasting modern stories with 'Those honourable Romances of old *Arcadia, Cleopatra, Cassandra*, &c.': see *Lining*, 252.

[44] This possibility is supported by a peculiarity of the dating. Walker's Epistle Dedicatory is dated 8 Mar. 1723, some five weeks after Barker's preface 'To the Reader'.

teenth century in an outpouring of feminine conduct guides and instructional materials devoted to women's social and familial duties, and later in works of feminist advocacy, poetry—Sarah Fyge's *The Female Advocate* (1686) and Lady Mary Chudleigh's *The Ladies Defence* (1701)—as well as educational tracts, Bathsua Makin's *An Essay to Revive the Antient Education of Gentlewomen* (1673), and Mary Astell's *A Serious Proposal to the Ladies* (1694–7) being two of the best known (Turner, *Living by the Pen*, 23). It is an item of orthodoxy in feminist and mainstream accounts alike that early novels were written for and read by a largely, if not exclusively, female audience. Turner accepts as broadly true this generalization but points out that it 'obscures interesting detail about the readership, including the possible extent of male interest in this material'. She believes that men, especially young men, probably read fiction by women but were reluctant to admit to it (*Living by the Pen*, 131). Examination of the preliminary matter in works by Behn, Manley, Haywood, as well as by less studied novelists of the 1720s such as Penelope Aubin and Mary Davys substantiates Turner's point. These writers evidently expected a mixed audience for their work. Penelope Aubin, for example, repeatedly targets the 'giddy youth' of both sexes, as she puts it in the preface to *The Strange Adventures of the Count de Vinevil and His Family* (1721), sturdily addresses another novel of the same year to '*true-born* English, *and* Antient Britons' (preface, *The Life of Madam de Beaumont*, sig. A4v), and the following year declares her quarry to be the '*ductile Souls of our Youth*' (preface, *The Noble Slaves*, xi). Mary Davys dedicated *The Reform'd Coquet* (1724) to 'the Ladies of Great Britain' and sought to impress her lessons upon the '*young unthinking Minds of some of my own Sex*' (preface, x), but reveals that the work was read first in manuscript by some young men at Cambridge.

All of which suggests we need to be more cautious in our claims about female readership than has been customary and more imaginative, perhaps, in our reading of the evidence. In the case of Jane Barker it is at least possible that references to 'the Ladies' constituted a strategy, whether Barker's or Curll's or jointly conceived we cannot know, for recruiting an elite readership. Such references may have operated, in other words, to raise a narrative such as *Patch-Work Screen* above what must have seemed a sea of trashy popular fiction and distinguish its readership from that invoked, probably by Charles Gildon, in a famous 1719 attack on *Robinson Crusoe* when an invented version of Defoe brags that the volume is bought up by any 'old Woman that can go the Price of it'.[45] Barker's titular 'ladies' may function as part of a strategy of dissociation, a vehicle for constructing class distinctions within a rapidly expanding literary field that now comprehended a much wider spectrum of readers and reading matter than would have been imaginable in the 1680s when Barker's coterie verse first saw print.

The View from the Leads

Literary history, when it mentions Barker at all, situates her within narratives of modernity, connecting her prose fictions with new ideologies of bourgeois femininity and gender separatism and stressing features that associate them with the 'emerging' or 'rising' novel or their creator with the 'emerging' or 'rising' woman novelist. She has been assigned an innovatory role in the development of the domestic novel (Richetti, Spencer); identified as a precursor of the Richardsonian novel (Doody); credited with pioneering the new genre in its 'hybrid, "unofficial", polyvocal' aspect (Donovan).[46] It is certainly true that the patchwork narratives from the 1720s register in striking ways the emergence of the new ideology of domestic womanhood—these are, after all, works that posit a social and literary space belonging specifically to the ladies, something Behn, for example, would not have dreamed of doing apart from exotic settings such as convents—but it is equally true and almost unappreciated that they resist, often with sly humour, newly fashionable notions of the private, domestic, apolitical female self. Any serious attempt to take Barker's measure as a novelist must be prepared to read her late prose fictions as refusals, as well as inscriptions, of new understandings of domestic womanhood.

---

[45] Charles Gildon, *The Life And Strange Surprizing Adventures of Mr. D—De F—, of London, Hosier* (London: J. Roberts, 1719), ix.

[46] See Richetti, *Popular Fiction*, ch. 6; Spencer, *Rise*, 62–70; Doody, 'Jane Barker', 24; Donovan, 'Women and the Rise', 443.

The point may be illustrated by a fresh look at a well-known passage from the preface of *Patch-Work Screen* concerning ladies at the tea-table. This brief fable about women, politics, and patches, although often cited, deserves full quotation:

for, whenever one sees a Set of Ladies together, their *Sentiments* are as differently mix'd as the *Patches* in their Work: To wit, *Whigs* and *Tories, High-Church* and *Low-Church, Jacobites* and *Williamites*, and many more Distinctions, which they *divide* and *sub-divide*, 'till at last they make this *Dis-union* meet in an harmonious *Tea-Table* Entertainment. This puts me in mind of what I have heard some *Philosophers* assert, about the *Clashing* of *Atoms*, which at last *united* to compose this glorious Fabrick of the UNIVERSE ('To the Reader', 52; fonts reversed).

This evocation of the rage of party resolved into feminine tea-table harmony would appear at first to offer an image of bourgeois womanhood *triumphans*, as Carol Shiner Wilson seems to suggest when she comments that women in this passage are shown to be 'more reasonable than men': they 'try to create communities that strive for harmony, taking the disparate patches of bitterly oppositional politics and religion of the day—Whigs, Tories, Jacobites, Williamites, and so forth—and sewing them together to "compose this glorious Fabrick of the UNIVERSE" '.[47] This description requires some qualification, however. Wilson does not remark that the party references in this passage point away from the present to the recent past, to political divisions that were particularly acute during the 1690s ('*Jacobites* and *Williamites*') and the years of Queen Anne's reign ('*Whigs* and *Tories, High-Church* and *Low-Church*'). The passage looks back, in other words, to more politically turbulent periods that, for better or for worse, tolerated considerably more difference than was the case in the decade following the Whig ascendance of 1714, which saw the proscription of the Tories from office and renewed suppression of both Catholics and Jacobites. This should alert us to the possibility that Barker's seemingly feminist-utopian vision of woman-sponsored social harmony contains ironies Wilson's reading does not allow for.

[47] Wilson, xl.

To bring these ironies into focus it is helpful to recall the cultural meanings associated at the time with the symbolically resonant tea-table. An important element in the discursive construction of new ideals of bourgeois womanhood, the tea-table stood throughout the century for 'a larger feminizing and civilizing force at work in British culture', as Beth Kowalski-Wallace has demonstrated.[48] Already in the century's opening decades, tea-tables evoked a 'feminized' space and were linked metonymically with the emerging cult of domesticity, which (as is well known) posited a separate and complementary feminine sphere in opposition to a masculine one that was public, commercial, and political.[49] What is remarkable about Barker's little fable is that, although the tea-table at its centre is constructed as a feminine space, it emphatically does not constitute a complementary realm. This tea-table does not, that is to say, offer a haven from or 'feminized' alternative to the public world but is rather the political sphere in microcosm, the tensions and divisions of the supposedly masculine public world replicated within a gathering of women whose political views and affiliations are 'as differently mix'd as the *Patches* in their Work'. The scene might, then, be said to represent an oblique (and jaundiced) glance at the newly fashionable definitions of femininity that drained women of their political identities while relegating them to cosy protected spaces invoked by metonymic tea-tables.

Barker's distaste for the new Domestic Woman emerges more clearly still when her tea-table scene is read against that found in one of the famous Party Rage numbers of the *Spectator*.[50] In these essays Addison promotes the new bourgeois ideal ('Female Virtues are of a Domestick turn' (i. 349)) by means of a battery

---

[48] Beth Kowalski-Wallace, 'Tea, Gender, and Domesticity in Eighteenth-Century England', *Studies in Eighteenth-Century Culture*, 23 (1994), 131–45 (133).

[49] For these changes as they are registered in literature by women, see Spencer, Todd, Ballaster, Gallagher, McDowell. For the related phenomenon of the emergence of the 'culture of sensibility' as part of what is now often described as the 'feminization' of English culture across the 18th cent., see G. J. Barker-Benfield, *The Culture of Sensibility: Sex and Society in Eighteenth-Century Britain* (Chicago and London: U. of Chicago P., 1992) and Stephen Copley, 'Commerce, Conversation and Politeness in the Early Eighteenth Century Periodical', *British Journal for Eighteenth-Century Studies*, 18 (1995), 63–77.

[50] Donald F. Bond (ed.), *The Spectator*, 5 vols. (Oxford: Clarendon P., 1965).

of urbanely misogynistic images intended to deflect tender woman away from the coarsening divisiveness of politics. In No. 57, 5 May 1711 he calls attention to the disfiguring effects of 'Party Rage' upon feminine beauty—it lends an 'ill-natured Cast to the Eye' and 'disagreeable Sourness to the Look', flushing the face 'worse than Brandy' (i. 243)—and, in a scene which Barker would surely have found deeply annoying, treats his readers to the spectacle of amazonian beauties nearly coming to blows across the tea-table. His modish recommendation elsewhere that 'furious Partizans' abandon politics so as to fulfil their rightful roles as gentle mothers and faithful wives is one that I expect Barker could have stomached only with difficulty (No. 81, 2 June 1711, i. 349). Nor would she have appreciated the way he snidely exempted 'superannuated motherly Partizans' from his strictures on the grounds that there was 'no danger either of their spoiling their Faces, or of their gaining Converts' (i. 243). In Barker's recast version of the scene the politically engaged women who assemble around the tea-table—not, *pace* Addison, a great toast or fierce Penthesilea among them—are made to figure a vision of female collectivity based on acceptance of political difference rather than its suppression or sublimation into maternal tenderness.

My contention that Barker's fictions 'for the Ladies' at once map and refuse shifts in gender ideology can be further developed with reference to a richly suggestive episode from *Patch-Work Screen*, one of the best known in Barker's fictions: Galesia's expulsion from her garret-retreat. Galesia, for those who do not know the episode, has found a place of intellectual retreat in the garret of her Westminster lodgings, a cramped but liberating room into which she withdraws as if into 'a Cave on the Top of *Parnassus*' (122). There she reads, writes, studies, reflects; sometimes she steps out onto the leads where, as Jane Eyre will do a century later, she looks out on the wider world in a gaze that links a view from the heights with female intellectual freedom. The freedom is short-lived. Galesia one day admits into her retreat a pregnant woman, seduced, abandoned, and in flight from the parish authorities, and is thereafter forbidden further use of her study, now a sexually contaminated space, lest she 'encounter more Adventures, not only like this, but perhaps more pernicious' (132). One of the remarkable features of this expulsion from Parnassus is the reimagining of Parnassus itself. A mountain has been reconceived as a womb-like female space—'a Cave', a *'Den'*, most startlingly, a 'Hole'. These yonic images underscore the strongly gendered and sexualized meaning of the events that transpire within this space, which all but demand feminist interpretation so forcibly do they suggest the cultural policing of female sexuality on the one hand and the silencing of female creativity on the other. For Spencer the scene expresses Barker's own fear that 'poetry will unleash the dangers of sexuality'. Doody discerns traces of women writers' struggles with the 'prohibitions of propriety'.[51] Straub, who has developed the fullest reading of this episode, sees a return of the sexuality the poet-heroine must hold at bay in order to fulfil her literary and intellectual ambitions, feminine sexuality amounting to a 'fall' that inevitably threatens to obstruct the heroine's desires to 'rise' as a writer'.[52] All would agree that the scene stages a conflict between a woman's sexual and intellectual needs projected against the backdrop of restrictive gender ideologies that serve to close both down.[53]

These psychosexual readings are compelling on their own terms and yield insight into the dynamics of female anxieties of authorship, but I am a bit troubled by the anachronistic conclusions to which they sometimes tend. Take, for example, that apparently Brontean view from the leads. One critic has associated Galesia's gaze out at the city with a 'release from the claustrophobia of middle-class female life'[54]—an interpretation that works better for Thornfield than for the London of Charles II (where this part of the story is set) or of the 1720s (when the novel was written). The intellectual freedom Galesia seeks consists less in longing for release than desire for connection— connection with a world of books, buildings, laws, established order, and public discourse, in Lacanian terms, the 'symbolic order'. Notice, for example, that the passage which describes the view from the leads uses wit and classical allusion to invoke

[51] Spencer, *Rise*, 67; Doody, 'Jane Barker', 30.
[52] Straub, 'Frances Burney', 205.
[53] A somewhat different reading is offered by Donovan, 'Women and the Rise', 461–2, who stresses Galesia's cultural marginality, the 'peripheral standpoint' which enables Barker to criticize patriarchal society.
[54] Straub, 'Frances Burney', 204.

a world that is urban, public, and national—a pre-eminently
Augustan world:

I us'd frequently to walk to take the Air, or rather the Smoke; for Air,
abstracted from Smoke, is not to be had within Five Miles of *London*.
Here it was that I wish'd sometimes to be of *Don Quixote's*
Sentiments, that I might take the *Tops* of *Chimneys*, for *Bodies* of
Trees; and the *rising Smoke* for *Branches*; the *Gutters of Houses*, for
Tarras-Walks; and the *Roofs* for stupendous *Rocks* and *Mountains*.
However, though I could not beguile my Fancy thus, yet here I was
alone, or, as the Philosopher says, never *less alone*. Here I entertain'd
my Thoughts, and indulg'd my solitary Fancy. Here I could behold the
Parliament-House, *Westminster-Hall*, and the *Abbey*, and admir'd the
Magnificence of their Structure, and still more, the Greatness of Mind
in those who had been their Founders . . . (124–5).

The passage develops a satiric view from above of the contemporary urban landscape, an acerbic look at the city's blackened
air, great piled-up roofs, and smoking chimneys that is mocking
at once of London and the mildly quixotic desires of the heroine, who would see trees, rocks, and mountains where only
smoky roofs are to be found. Galesia indulges her solitary fancy
all right, but she does not celebrate the richness of her imagination—on the contrary she somewhat smugly congratulates
herself upon 'not beguil[ing] my Fancy thus'—nor does she
protest against her domestically confined circumstances as more
self-consciously cramped heroines would later do. Her meditations run instead upon public and national themes. She admires
the grandeur of official Westminster architecture and contem-
plates the greatness of mind and spirit that could build
Parliament, the law courts, and the Abbey ('one Place for the
establishing good Laws; another for putting them in Practice;
the Third for the immediate Glory of God' (125)). The perspective is that of a Stuart loyalist appalled by the increasingly self-
interested modern spirit that sets itself against traditional
notions of kingship and communal good, for a little later in the
passage Galesia takes up the theme of the events contributing to
the fall of the house of Stuart: 'I was amaz'd', she tells us, 'to
think how those *Law Makers* [Parliament in the time of Charles
I] cou'd become such *Law-Confounders*'. Only a very 'wicked
Spirit', she concludes, could have 'persuaded them to bring so
barbarous an Enterprize to so sad a Conclusion' (125). In

Barker's view a woman writer is nourished by solitary retreat, to be sure, and haunted by sexual anxieties; but she is also the bearer of a consciousness that seeks to understand itself and female existence in relation to the currents of national public life. Those seeking more historically grounded models for female authorship for this period than those currently available would do well to consider taking as a starting point the episode of Galesia on the leads.

Toward this end I would like to propose a reading of this symbolically resonant episode that connects its gender-and-genre themes to Barker's own moment. This interpretation draws upon the conceptual frame developed by Paula McDowell for her work on what she calls women's 'metaphors of self', their sense of identity at this transitional moment when modes of subjectivity were undergoing crucial shifts.[55] According to McDowell, the seventeenth century saw the emergence of the beginnings of a distinctively modern understanding of the female self—the unique, solitary, autonomous, politically disempowered, and gendered self of modern liberal individualism. By the turn of the century (Mary Astell) and even earlier (Margaret Cavendish) aristocratic and genteel women writers were 'beginning to perceive the self in recognizably modern ways as gendered, autonomous, and unique' (125) and to identify themselves with gendered subject-positions. Such a mode of identification was at once enabling and limiting. The greater cultural authority granted to women writing 'as women' offered a range of new expressive possibilities but these possibilities were 'predicated on women's acceptance of new subject-positions that distanced them from immediate participation in state affairs' (292). McDowell contrasts this new mode of subjectivity with one more characteristic of middling women in the seventeenth century. These were women—a good example is the printer and polemicist Elinor James—who 'tended to envision the self in more traditional ways as social, collective, and essentially unsexed' (19). James and others of her ilk, women writers 'little hampered by crystallizing ideologies of femininity' (17–18), were able, with little ambivalence or self-doubt, to

---

[55] Paula McDowell, *The Women of Grub Street: Press, Politics, and Gender in the London Literary Marketplace 1678–1730* (Oxford: Clarendon P., 1998), esp. ch. 4.

address public matters in print. These writers constitute an important but almost unrecognized tradition of female political activism, in part because they were still able to envision themselves as 'part of an unbroken continuum with the state' (19).

Barker occupies, one might say, the space between these two models, writing in a kind of *broken* continuum with the state and producing fictions at once cutting-edge and reactionary. If anyone in this period sought to chart the emergent modern self in its sometimes baffling singularity, it was Jane Barker. The Galesia fictions are arguably the most acute studies of female subjectivity before Richardson, delineating with remarkable clarity a new kind of female self—individuated, self-conscious, disempowered, and alienated. But these fictions also react against the modernity they limn. The episode in which Galesia is banished from the garret expresses, it might be argued, distrust of the new model of Domestic Woman, of an ideal that severs what McDowell has shown to be the traditional links between women and the political realm. The sense of loss generated by Galesia's removal *as a woman* from the site of literary creativity figures the greater loss bound up in women's withdrawal more generally from older, more politically engaged modes of literary activity. Remember what Galesia is denied when she is forbidden passage onto the leads: a commanding vision from above of Parliament and Westminster Abbey, the world of law, lawmakers, national history, and public affairs. The garret episode stages psychosexual conflicts within Galesia, to be sure, but it projects larger cultural conflicts as well, and would seem indeed to figure Barker's dissatisfaction with definitions of womanhood that threatened to cut women off from participation in the national life. The banishment from the leads simultaneously registers and resists the new cult of domesticity.

More Trouble on Parnassus

When Barker wrote the patchwork narratives she was an old woman, already in her seventies, and since at least the 1680s she had been brooding on what it means to be a writing woman. Representations of the writing self abound in these final narratives, forming a thread that weaves itself through an otherwise miscellaneous assemblage of materials, taking the place, one might say, of the more straightforward autobiographical concerns of *Bosvil and Galesia*. These authorial self-representations function in various ways. They enable Barker to revisit her origins as a writing woman, reflect on shifts that had transformed the literary environment over her long writing life, express distaste for women's increasing political disenfranchisement, and in other ways bring to a kind of fruition a process of authorial self-examination discernible as early as the poems on poetry in *Poetical Recreations*. Analysis of these late self-figurations reveal new dimensions of *Janus* Barker as well. Once again, much of what is most interesting in her work arises from the way their author simultaneously inhabits two different mental worlds—or, one might say, the space between—leaving her alive to the requirements of both and at home in neither. This chapter concludes by looking at a few of the most important of these self-figurations.

The preface to *A Patch-Work Screen for the Ladies*, much of it written in the extravagantly allegorical style characteristic of much political writing at this time, is obsessed with the figure of the female poet as exile, as Virtuous Outsider. This figure, which owes something to Jacobite mythology and something to late Stuart elaborations of the image of the outcast-poet, the latter popularized by Abraham Cowley and widely appropriated by royalist women of Barker's generation, had haunted Barker's fiction-making imagination since at least *Bosvil and Galesia*.[56] The Virtuous Outsider makes a dramatic entrance in the final paragraphs of the preface, where an allegorized version of 'Jane Barker', an intellectually aspiring poet, tumbles Icarus-like into the text. The passage begins with a mischievous glance at doctrines of female intellectual inferiority. '*Forgive me, kind Reader, for carrying the Metaphor too high*'—the reference is to her earlier invocation of classical atomic theory—'*by which means I am out of my Sphere*'—woman's lower mental sphere, that is to say—'*for my high Flight in Favour of the Ladies, made a mere* Icarus *of me, melted my Wings, and tumbled me*

[56] The immense importance of Cowley to the poetic self-representations of late Stuart women writers is explored in my 'Cowley Among the Women: Literary Tradition as Zone of Contact' (forthcoming).

Headlong down, I know not where' (53). 'Jane Barker' falls to earth among a throng of joyful people '*of all Ages, Sexes, and Conditions*', but she is expelled from their company when verses are discovered in her pockets. They mark her as '*one of that Race of Mortals who live on a certain barren Mountain*'— Parnassus—"*till they are turn'd into* Camelions'—poets were proverbially said to live upon air, like chameleons—'*so* [she] *was forc'd to get away, every one hunching and pushing* [her], *with Scorn and Derision*' (53). The poet is, in short, an exile in her own land.

The scene recalls the disturbing dream-vision in *Bosvil and Galesia* in which the poet-heroine, forced to climb a mountain, is snatched away and then condemned by an 'angry Power'— a kind of demonic male muse, described also as her '*uncouth Guardian*'— to a life of '*Want, and Woe, and Banishment*' (25). In its narrative context the dream would seem to figure the woman writer's troubled relation to her sexuality;[57] at the same time it underlines and in a sense ratifies Galesia's status as outsider: hereafter she is to be cursed with Cassandra's fate, 'inspired but outcast', as Carol Barash has said.[58] When Barker recast the story for the preface of *Patch-Work Screen* she used the same elements—a female poet ascends a mountain and returns to scorn, derision, and banishment—but in keeping with the more public and political scope of the 1723 narrative, gave them wider application. Banishment is now understood in relation to the state of the nation, specifically Walpole and the politico-financial scandal of the South Sea Bubble. For it turns out that '*their* Patch-Work Scheme'—the Bubble—was soon to burst, '*was blown up about their Ears, and vanish'd into Smoke and Confusion; to the utter Ruin of many Thousands of the Unhappy Creatures therein concern'd*' (53). (Significantly, at this time Walpole was widely known as the 'Skreen-Master General' or just 'the Skreen' in reference to his role in concealing the

---

[57] See Straub, 'Frances Burney', 204. In 1719 Bosvil attempts to 'tumble' Galesia down the mountain, a revision that supports Straub's reading of the scene as an enactment of Barker's fears about sexuality seducing her away from her poetic commitments.

[58] Barash, *EWP*, 153, reports that in Stuart contexts the 'inspired but outcast Cassandra was often used as a figure for the woman writer and political actor at court'.

involvement of highly placed Whigs in the Bubble.)[59] In this strikingly topical version of the expulsion from Parnassus, poetry is counterposed not to sexual fulfilment and conventional feminine destiny, as had been the case in *Bosvil and Galesia*, but rather to the greed, frenzy, narrowly self-serving views and unlimited appetite for wealth of a social order gone mad with financial speculation and other modern get-rich schemes. (Toward the end of the narrative two South Sea Directors enter the text ready to relieve the Lady's husband of 10,000 pounds. Galesia is appalled: 'if I had never so much to spare, I wou'd not put a *Shilling* into *that* or *any other* Bubble' (152).)[60] The outcast female poet is made to stand, then, in symbolic opposition to a corrupt and mercenary Whig order, of which the South Sea Bubble is centrally emblematic. In Jacobite code the Bubble means political corruption, as Jacobite scholar Murray Pittock has observed, and such a code 'seems to have been accessible to a very wide audience'. In Barker's usage the association serves also to construct the female poet as prophetic outcast, speaking moral truths others are more likely to try to screen.[61]

The final paragraph of the preface to *Patch-Work Screen* moves outward to reflect more broadly on the strikingly modern phenomenon of female literary professionalism. Galesia, who figures the new writing woman, now walks into

[59] A paper dated March 1721 (Royal Archives, SP 46/20) transcribes a satiric mock-advertisement under the heading, 'A famous Skreen now to be sold to the best Bidder', with the comment, 'There is hardly a Child in London but now calls Walpole the Skreen, and he is strangely exposed and ridiculed every where. It happens often in England that one Witty Word or Turn has a very great effect on the greatest affaires.' I am grateful to Edward Corp for bringing this paper to my attention. For a summary of Walpole's role as 'Skreen-Master General' in the aftermath of the South Sea Bubble, see Bruce Lenman, *The Jacobite Risings in Britain 1689–1746* (London: Eyre Methuen, 1980), 196–7.

[60] She also includes 'The *Prophesy*', which warns that when 'a Noise in the South | Shall fill ev'ry one's *Mouth*' then England should 'beware of *Undoing*' (*PWS* 152).

[61] Murray G. H. Pittock, *Poetry and Jacobite Politics in Eighteenth-Century Britain and Ireland* (Cambridge: Cambridge UP, 1994), 69. He makes a similar point about Anne Finch: her 'A Song on the South Sea' criticizes 'the male mercantile world of stockbroking' from a marginalized female position (78). In *Memoirs of a Certain Island Adjacent to the Kingdom of Utopia* (1725) Eliza Haywood uses South Sea scandal to establish the moral frame of her scandal chronicle of Georgian England, linking the corruptions of love with the corruptions of greed epitomized by the Enchanted Well, i.e. the South Sea Co.

the text, stretching legs cramped with 'having been long sitting at her Work'. The word *work*, which until our own century referred in feminine contexts to *needlework*, sets up the terms of an allegory about new conceptions of women's work and, more specifically, the emergence of a generation of women (patchworkers) who have made words their work: women who produce texts, that is to say, as well as textiles. Barker draws for her patchwork analogies upon the familiar topos of the oppositionally linked needle and pen ('the needle not the pen is their only proper instrument') but gives this typically misognynistic figure a new spin.[62] If the needle and pen usually stand for contradictory or opposed forms of women's work, Barker collapses the distinction between needle/textile and pen/text in order to redefine writing as a form of women's work while at the same time suggesting changes in the female relationship to writing over the course of her life. The fine but troublesome needlework of the past, when women engaged in '*the working of* Point *and curious* Embroidery' is thus contrasted with the messy but more congenial patch-work/pen-work of the present day:

And, upon my Word, I am glad to find the Ladies of *This Age*, wiser than *Those* of the *Former*; when the working of *Point* and curious *Embroidery*, was so troublesome, that they cou'd not take *Snuff* in Repose, for fear of soiling their Work: But in *Patch-Work* there is no Harm done; a smear'd Finger does but add a *Spot* to a *Patch*, or a *Shade* to a *Light-Colour*: Besides, those curious Works were pernicious to the Eyes; *they* cou'd not see the *Danger themselves* and *their Posterity might be in*, a *Thousand Years hence, about I know not what*—(54; fonts reversed).

The work of the pen is healthier than that of the needle, less harmful to the eyes; and it permits a degree of messiness not tolerated by older literary codes which barred women from taking snuff, for example, '*for fear of soiling their Work*'.

---

[62] Her patchwork metaphors may also owe something to the analogy between modern 'Writing-Artists' and fabric manufacturers developed by Shaftesbury in his essay on 'Miscellaneous Reflections'. The 'patchwork' manner invented by modern miscellany writers uses 'cuttings and shreds of learning, with various fragments and points of wit, [which] are drawn together and tacked in any fantastic form': see John M. Robertson (ed.), *Characteristics of Men, Manners, Opinions, Times, etc.*, 2 vols. (Gloucester, Mass.: Peter Smith, 1963): ii. 159.

Among modern patchworkers a dirty finger (*'smear'd'* with ink?) contributes to the tonal complexity of the product (*'does but add a* Spot *to a* Patch, *or a* Shade *to a* Light-Colour'). Living by the pen, in other words, is a great advance upon the troublesome, pernicious, restrictive, overly fussy work associated with living by the needle. But it is not without losses. Patchwork *is* a tad coarse, especially when compared with older forms of work that are fine, exquisite, feminine, unsmudged by ink; but patchwork is vital and expressive, open to the world and more responsive to a wider range of stimuli than the *'curious Works'* which once occupied women's attention, limited their gaze, and, in several senses of the phrase, destroyed their vision. The Jane Barker who speaks in this preface is, I would suggest, a self-conscious modern, the female literary professional; and in the patchwork allegory which closes her address 'To the Reader' she honours her own position as a writer-for-pay in the now well-established culture of print.

The Galesia narrative that follows, however, includes as part of its framing fiction a nostalgic scene of idealized, patronage-based literary production that stands in counterpoise to the image of soiled but robust market-place writing developed in the preface. This scene, which evokes the considerable attractions of an older, aristocratically oriented, and more sheltered literary system, occurs when Galesia, having been dumped from the stage-coach into a river, seeks refuge at a country house, one of the main traditional sites of literary production, where she will tell her life-story to a noble Lady. After being conducted through a series of apartments decorated with rich and beautiful needlework, she is brought into a room furnished in patchwork, 'most curiously compos'd of rich Silks, and Silver and Gold Brocades'. The only piece remaining to be finished is a screen, to which Galesia is invited to contribute scraps of her own writing—poems and such, most of them written and in some cases published much earlier by Barker herself. When Galesia adds her textual patches she is, allegorically speaking, carrying forward a feminine work-in-progress that extends back through the generations while at the same time aligning her earlier work with a literary economy based upon manuscript exchange within networks of aristocratic protection. The worked furnishings, we learn, are the product of 'poor

Gentlewomen' employed by the Lady's ancestors and dependent upon them for protection from 'Distress, and evil Company' (74). Read against the image of nascent professionalism developed in the preface, this scene of protection/dependency within the confines of the aristocratic household expresses ambivalence toward earlier modes of female authorship. The loveliness and opulence of the fabrics suggest nostalgia for a mode of literary production associated with noble patronage that may in turn be linked to a fantasized desire for what Laura Rosenthal, writing on Behn, characterizes as an 'idealized, pre-print exchange that binds communities and creates noble friendships'.[63] But the passivity imposed upon the 'poor Gentlewomen'—they must await a time when 'Friends could dispose things for their better Settlement' (74)—hints at the attractions of an alternative literary economy, one in which a woman writer can seek out readers '*to buy these* Patches *up quickly*' (54). The fingers of a Jane Barker and her sister novelists may be a bit 'smear'd', especially when imagined alongside the pale hands of the Orindas and Philomelas and Ardelias (and Galesias) who preceded them, but the opportunity to write for pay enables them to enjoy an economic independence unknown to the gentlewomen and genteel amateurs of a previous era.

The ambivalence that marks Barker's perception of herself as a literary professional in the final decade of her writing life surfaces most poignantly in '*Galecia*'s Dream' from her final work, *The Lining of the Patch Work Screen*. In this strange dream-vision Galesia is taken one last time to Parnassus, to witness the annual coronation of Orinda—Katherine Philips (1632–64), the Matchless Orinda—as Queen of Female Writers. Once again she is banished from the mountain. The familiar dynamic of rejection and exile re-enacted in this episode suggests an allegory of literary rejection and even belatedness, but the dream-vision is not the purely nostalgic gesture of homage to a poetic precursor that it may seem at first to be. There is no gainsaying Barker's admiration for Orinda, whose

[63] Laura J. Rosenthal, 'Owning Oroonoko: Behn, Southerne, and the Contingencies of Property', in Mary Beth Rose (ed.), *Renaissance Drama*, NS 23 (Evanston: Northwestern UP and the Newberry Library Center for Renaissance Studies, 1992), 33.

name she invokes on more than one occasion in order to associate Galesia with the genteel amateur traditions of the previous century; but as a model for Galesia's creator, Orinda was less satisfactory. Indeed, by the 1720s the kind of pristine female authorship she epitomized, amateur, courtly, coterie-bound, and manuscript-based, had come to seem a bit anachronistic—not least to women who wrote for money, as Philips never did. More and more women writers had come to understand themselves along lines suggested by the examples of hard-working, highly marketed, and self-consciously professional practitioners, print-world writers such as Delarivier Manley, who published her last work in 1720, Eliza Haywood, the best-selling novelist who over the course of the decade churned out at least thirty-five novels, ten in 1725 alone,[64] and Mary Davys, who this same year brought out a two-volume edition of her collected *Works*, in which, without apology, she asserted her right to publish for pay.[65] Although Barker in 'Galecia's Dream' looks back to the seventeenth century for her own origins and identity as a woman writer, she measures the privileges of that genteel past against the economic requirements of the present. By ending the dream with a final expulsion from Parnassus— Galesia is given some pieces of gold and ordered to leave—she creates a memorable image of the genteel amateur's descent into the fallen world of literary commerce. The dream-vision offers, then, a fitting (and fittingly ambiguous) final retrospective on a writing life that spanned nearly half a century and took Barker from one literary economy to another.

The dream begins with an enigmatic prelude. Galesia is on a journey, walking 'somewhere'. After passing a host of fearful sights and being assailed by nightmarish visions she comes at last upon a lush, fertile valley where all is abundance and constancy: she thinks it 'a terrestrial Paradice' (274). Her happiness is interrupted by the appearance of a 'strange and hideous Giant' named Omrison, an evil sorcerer who pursues her, as he

---

[64] Turner, *Living by the Pen*, 38.
[65] '[A] *Woman left to her own Endeavours for Twenty-seven Years together, may well be allow'd to catch at any Opportunity for that Bread, which they that condemn her would very probably deny to give her*': Mary Davys, Preface, *The Works of Mrs. Davys: Consisting of Plays, Novels, Poems, and Familiar Letters*, in 2 vols. (London: H. Woodfall, 1725), i. viii.

has many others, but who fails, hampered by rotten and broken toes. She runs away down a hill and is offered refuge at the bottom by a 'good Philosopher', an astrologer at Astrea's court, who takes her to his cave where she is joined by a tutelary spirit in the form of 'a pretty young Man' (275). He in turn takes her by the hand and leads her up a hill, which he tells her is Parnassus, in order to conduct her to 'the Annual Coronation of *Orinda*', though why a coronation should be an annual event remains unclear. They arrive too late for the ceremonies, however: Orinda is already crowned. Galesia is installed in a corner where, unobserved, she can watch the celebrations. Orinda is seated on a throne; in her hand is a golden pen for a sceptre and on her head a crown of laurel; she is adored as 'Queen of Female Writers' by a band of bards that includes Abraham Cowley and Pierre Corneille, who cast themselves at her feet, praise her in verse, and exalt her wit and virtue. Weirdly enough, the adoring male poets are joined by a choir of huge, gold-winged grasshoppers, a flock of nightingales, and finally a band of fairies. Crickets and beetles provide music for dancing.[66] Galesia is eventually noticed by the Fairy Queen (not Orinda, who remains forever oblivious of her devoted daughter-poet) and hastily sent on her way, but not without a gift—or is it a rebuke?—from the Fairy Queen: a handful of gold.[67]

The presence at the coronation of a choir of grasshoppers, a detail puzzling at first, helps make intelligible features of this dream-vision that might otherwise seem merely bizarre. These singing insects, said to be 'pretty Creatures in form of Grasshoppers, with Golden Wings, but as large as new born Babes' (276) are meant to invoke a long tradition of metaphorical usages linking poets and grasshoppers. In an essay that throws much light on Barker's purposes, Don Cameron Allen points out that the grasshopper had served since antiquity as a

---

[66] The association between poets and crickets was evoked by Barker in the Magdalen poem 'Reflections on mr Cowleys words, The Muses fleece lys dry': 'Tis ominous to treat a poet ill, | As tis our merry chimny guests to kill | A poet like a cricket where he comes, | Bodes good or ill, as he findes warmth or crums' (Wilson, 330).

[67] 'And whether she [the Fairy Queen] was angry to see a Mortal in that Assembly; or that she was excited by Charity, is unknown; but she took a Handful of Gold out of her Pocket, and gave [it] to one of her Gentlemen-waiters, bidding him carry it to that Mortal, and command her away from thence': *Lining*, 277.

figure for the natural poet-singer who devotes his life to careless summery song; by the mid-seventeenth century, in royalist contexts, the grasshopper had come to represent the aristocratic poet singing out of political season.[68] (Recall, for example, Lovelace's famous 'The Grasshopper', discussed at length by Allen.) Barker would certainly have been familiar with these more recent usages and probably with the earlier ones as well, but at the front of her mind she seems to have had the emblematic grasshoppers invented by Plato for a fable about poetry in the *Phaedrus*. According to the story told by Socrates to Phaedrus, grasshoppers were once a race of song-loving men; the souls of these natural singers live on in the bodies of grasshoppers and, when they die, 'they inform the Muses in Heaven who now worships them here below' (qtd. in Allen, 85). Barker's Parnassian grasshoppers, gathered to praise Orinda, evoke then classical associations between grasshoppers, poetry, song, and literary acclaim to offer an unusual tribute to the matchless Orinda in the strange but strangely fitting Platonic heaven envisioned by Barker.

But the scene also contains ambiguities expressive of Barker's conflicted allegiance to the tradition of female genteel amateurism. What, for example, are we to make of that handful of gold with which Galesia is sent on her way? Gold could stand for whorishness or chastity, female corruption or female virtue; it could signify the degeneration of the times or the pure gleam of transcendent value. Does the gold thrust into Galesia's hands stand for literature's debasement in the money-driven market-place? The taint of writing for pay? Corruption, greed, and venality more generally? Or is it meant to suggest female moral excellence such as that evoked by Sir Thomas Overbury when he famously likened a virtuous widow to 'purest gold'? Ambiguous too is the image of Katherine Philips on her Parnassian throne, with a golden pen for her sceptre. Does she stand for a feminine literary ideal regrettably vanished from contemporary life? Or for an increasingly outdated and perhaps even faintly absurd model of female authorship? For it must now be admitted that there is something a bit silly about the

[68] Don Cameron Allen, *Image and Meaning: Metaphoric Traditions in Renaissance Poetry* (Baltimore: Johns Hopkins P.,1960), 80–92.

whole business of a Queen of Women Writers, surrounded as she is by a chorus of adoring bards, singing insects, and dancing fairies, Platonic ancestry notwithstanding. The whole episode smacks of a fay extravagance that seems even more unreal in the light of the surrounding narrative, which is preoccupied with questions of economic survival in a very contingent eighteenth-century London.

Several critics have discerned in this scene an expression of Barker's regret for her own belatedness. Noting that Galesia arrives too late to see the actual coronation and then withdraws to a corner, Jane Spencer speculates that the episode may reflect Barker's own sense 'late in her life that she has survived into a new and uncongenial age when the great tributes to the poet she admires are over, and that she herself has failed in her ambition to "reach fair ORINDA's Height" '.[69] I think this true, and the source of much of the wistfulness Spencer is right to say pervades the dream-vision. The vision may also project a market-place professional's nostalgia for a vanished world in which writing remains 'Orindan', uncontaminated by its association with commerce, and acknowledge in an oblique if rueful way that its author, for all her amateur origins and affiliations, operates herself within a world of print capitalism shaped by the likes of Edmund Curll, geared toward national readerships, and oiled by Grub Street contrivances. Banished from Parnassus with a handful of gold and unnoticed in any case by its fantastically idealized Queen, Galesia figures her creator's recognition that as a novelist for pay she no longer defines herself through the genteel literary codes with which she had identified for the better part of her writing life. For all her considerable regrets, it is with the fallen commercialized literary world that Jane Barker has cast her lot.

[69] Spencer, 'Creating', 178.

Epilogue

THE view of Barker proposed in this study has emphasized continuities linking her with her own time and place even if, ironically, these links call into question the feminist paradigms that brought her to our attention in the first place. Approaches which stress her kinship with other women writers serve well the feminist literary historical aim of reconstructing the lineages and networks of female affiliation which for their part bring significance to the study of early modern women's writings, but their effect is to distort the nature of Barker's literary achievement and, less happily still, to obscure much of what is most distinctive in her work. Barker was above all a transitional writer, and a singular one. Not only did she undertake to chronicle the interior life of a woman whose destiny was to espouse poetry and the single life—her remarkable ode 'The *Necessity* of *Fate*' depicts its female speaker as set apart from birth for the austere requirements of 'the Muses Congregation'[1]—but she occupies a singular position in literary history as well. She stands alone, without 'daughters', but in standing alone can be said to figure a space in which class and gender dynamics— indeed, the larger shape of politics and national identity—are in dramatic flux. So attuned is her imagination to the ambiguities of cultural change that she is able to embody this state of flux in especially complex ways, creating in her late work in particular fictions which suggest the possibility of emergent, dimly discerned, and only barely expressible narrative lines for women. By means of the ambiguous episode of the Unaccountable Wife from *A Patch-Work Screen for the Ladies*, a tale of female same-sex desire told before 'lesbian' had emerged as a name or a recognizable social category, I will suggest that in moments of interpretative indeterminacy such as these Barker's fictions point toward a space between cultural

---

[1] *PWS* 143. 'The *Necessity* of *Fate*' first appeared in *PR* and was slightly revised for *PWS*.

formations that constitutes an 'elsewhere', a space outside or, if that is too utopian, at the outer margins of the controlling narratives of Barker's culture, in this instance its narratives of compulsory matrimony. In thinking about the significance of this fragment from lesbian prehistory, I am reminded of what a post-colonial critic has observed of Yeats's writing, which for all its failures of representation 'constantly, if a little perplexedly, invoke[s] those moments of disintegration which open the space for another history and another sexuality'.[2]

Virgins, Old Maids, and Spinsters

Barker is one of very few English writers of her century to render sympathetically and at the centre of her narratives a woman who makes for herself a meaningful life outside marriage. She is not the only novelist to affirm the value of the single life for women, of course. Sarah Scott would do so in *Millenium Hall* (1762) as would Charlotte Brontë later and with much greater passion in *Shirley* (1849) and *Villette* (1853), and even in Barker's own time an expressed preference for the single life served as something of a convention in amatory fiction to suggest by way of shorthand the moral excellence of a heroine destined either for marriage, seduction, or rape (*Clarissa* most famously). We saw in Chapter 4 that in the patchwork narratives the heroine's election to the single life, her spinsterhood, carries Jacobite implications; it will now be seen that this theme gains additional resonance read as a response to an anti-old-maid discourse that emerged in nascent form in England in the final decades of the seventeenth century and remained in malignant play through much of the course of Barker's writing life.[3]

In a careful and well-documented treatment of the discursive construction of the old maid as a 'new caste' of women 'defined

[2] David Lloyd, *Anomalous States: Irish Writing and the Post-Colonial Moment* (Dublin: Lilliput P., 1993), 5.
[3] Amy Louise Erickson, *Women and Property in Early Modern England* (London and New York: Routledge, 1993), 47, uses a passage from Barker's 'A Virgin Life' to illustrate her claim that the 'sneering epithet "old maid" and the derogatory use of "spinster" ' came into use late in the seventeenth century.

and maligned solely on the ground of their never-marriedness',
Susan S. Lanser shows that antipathy to the never-married
woman, detectable as early as the 1670s, had attained by the
1690s a virulence that would persist over the next several
decades and would issue in attacks on old maids as, among
other things, 'nasty, rank, rammy, filthy Sluts'. (In the *Satyr
Upon Old Maids* (1713), from which Lanser quotes, unmarried
women are reviled as 'so disgusting and dangerous that they are
urged to throw themselves into the "vilest" marriages to
"*Lepers* and *Leachers*", "*Zanies*", or "*Dolts*" just to avoid
being "piss'd on with Contempt" for their singleness'.)[4] A term
of opprobrium and contempt for much of the first half of the
eighteenth century, in the second half the epithet 'old maid' lost
much of its negative potency as the figure of the spinster came
to be recuperated into a domestic economy which would eventually yield the irritating but basically innocuous figure of
Austen's Miss Bates. Lanser convincingly connects these
changes in the construction of the never-married woman to new
conceptions of national identity, which she argues were tied to
anxieties about population growth which were themselves
bound up in British commercial and financial expansionism.
Failure to reproduce was a failure to serve British imperial
ambitions. This analysis, illuminating on its own terms, affords
yet another perspective on Barker's recurrent position as, culturally speaking, odd woman out. To insist on the value of the
single life, as she was to do over and over again, was to refuse
the call for teeming wombs in the service of expansionistic
understandings of national identity; it was to express in another
idiom a chronically alienated relation to British national life.

'A Virgin Life', first published in *Poetical Recreations* (1688),
responds quite directly to the cautionary anti-old-maid
discourses which even at this relatively early date, parts of this
poem suggest, were used to frighten young women into matrimony. The poem seeks, in fact, to undo the false image of the
never-married woman then under discursive construction. In its

---

⁴ Susan S. Lanser, 'Singular Politics: The Rise of the British Nation and the
Production of the Old Maid', in Judith M. Bennett and Amy M. Froide (eds.),
Singlewomen in the European Past, 1250–1800 (Philadelphia: U. of Penn. Press,
1999). I am indebted to this article for much of the terminology employed in this
discussion.

earliest version the contentedly celibate speaker declares herself undismayed by sneering references to her identity as an 'Old Maid'. Such 'slights or scorns' are 'Goblings' used to rush young women into marriages they neither want nor need: she will remain 'Fearless of Twenty five and all its train, | Of slights or scorns, or being call'd Old Maid, | Those Goblings which so many have betray'd' (*PR* 12). It has gone unnoticed that when Barker revised the poem for the Magdalen Manuscript around the turn of the century she expanded the three lines just quoted to six, presumably in order to combat more strenuously the opprobrium attached to the 'antiquated name' that 'scorn fix'd' to what a marginal note identifies as the name 'old maid':

> Fearless of twenty-five and all its rage,
> When Time and beauty endless wars ingage,
> And Fearless of the antiquated name,
> Which oft makes happy maid turn helpless dame,
> The scorn fix'd to that name our sex betray,
> And often makes us fling our selves away.[5]

> (*KR* 360)

Interestingly, this section is revised and expanded yet again for *A Patch-Work Screen* in 1723, where in a passage reminiscent of *Rape of the Lock* (1712–17) more is made of 'polite' courtship rituals and fashionable notions of feminine beauty,[6] although anxiety to defuse the contempt directed at the old maid—'the Scorn and Lumber of Mankind'—remains.

> When once *that Clock has struck* [age twenty-five], all Hearts retire,
> Like *Elves*, from *Day-break*, or like *Beasts* from Fire,
> 'Tis Beauty's *Passing-Bell*; no more are slain;
> But dying Lovers all revive again,
> Then every Day some new Contempt we find,

---

[5] In *A Serious Proposal to the Ladies*, part I (London: R. Wilkin, 1694), 132–3, Mary Astell used similar language in an effort to rehabilitate the idea of the old maid: the unmarried woman is 'quite terrified with the dreadful Name of *Old Maid*' and 'to avoid this terrible *Mormo*, and the scoffs that are thrown on superanuated Virgins, she flies to some dishonourable Match as her last, tho' much mistaken Refuge'. *Mormo*, the editors of *KR* tell us, 362, is Greek for 'bugbear'.

[6] The conceit of the dying lover revived may deliberately echo a couplet in Canto 5: 'She smil'd to see the doughty Hero slain, | But at her Smile, the Beau reviv'd, again' (ll. 69–70): see Geoffrey Tillotson (ed.), *The Rape of the Lock and Other Poems* (London: Methuen; and New Haven: Yale UP, 1940), 201.

As if the Scorn and Lumber of Mankind.
These frightful Prospects, oft our Sex betray;
Which to avoid, some fling themselves away.

(*PWS* 139–40)

At least twice, then, Barker returned to these lines, updating them for their moment in what may have seemed a somewhat lonely struggle to reclaim for women the dignity of the single life by confronting head on constructions of the old maid as 'a despicable cultural identity'.[7]

The affirmations of celibacy and the single life central to the Galesia fictions took shape alongside, and are inevitably caught up in, the anti-old maid discourse. This is most evident in *A Patch-Work Screen for the Ladies*, where Galesia's mother serves as a comparatively mild mouthpiece for the cultural orthodoxies regarding women, marriage, and reproduction. She cautions her daughter that her 'uncouth'—odd, strange—persistence in singleness serves to 'frustrate the End of our Creation'. Galesia should seek to become 'a good Mistress of a Family', an 'obedient Wife', 'discreet Governess of [her] Children and Servants', and 'friendly Assistant to [her] Neighbours, Friends, and Acquaintance'—for this is the 'Business for which you came into the World'. Despite what Galesia calls her 'secret Disgust against Matrimony' she cannot deny her mother's words: they 'were Truths which Reason would not permit me to oppose' (*PWS* 133). Yet moments such as these, which seem almost to endorse the reproach directed toward the never-married woman, are unusual in Barker's fictions and constitute indeed a kind of palimpsestic overlay upon an older and very different understanding of Galesia's identity as virgin-heroine, an identity whose origins are elsewhere, in French traditions of the *femme forte*.

Galesia first appeared as a minor character in *Exilius*, the heroic romance begun in the 1680s, as 'Galecia', a proud and virginal Numidian warrior-princess. Her valiant entrance—she gallops into the text on horseback pursuing a panther—attests

---

[7] Lanser, 'Singular Politics', 298. Barker was not entirely alone, of course: Lanser, 298–300, discusses a similar effort on Astell's part in the 1690s and points out that as early as 1673 Richard Allestree's *Ladies Calling* 'urges singlewomen not to be "frighted" by society's "vulgar contemt" and "causeless Reproaches" ' (298).

to her literary beginnings as a *femme forte*, the warrior woman popularized in French heroic romance.[8] (We may pick up reverberations of this figure in the scene in Behn's *Oroonoko*, also written in the 1680s, in which a heroically rendered Imoinda—steady, fearless, and great with child—turns on her pusillanimous English pursuers with poisoned arrows.) Galecia's mode of virginity entails taking the man's part: 'She was a Lady of a masculine Spirit, and undervalu'd the little Delicacies of her Sex, making the Study of Philosophy, and the Laws of her Country, her chief Business' (*Exilius*, ii.32). She also manages nearly to kill her troublesome lover by running him through with a sword—something a later, more realistically conceived Galesia can only fantasize about, though fantasize she does with heroic gusto.[9] If in *Exilius* virginity is associated with appropriations of male forms of power, in *Bosvil and Galesia*, begun perhaps in the 1690s, it is associated with access to specifically female forms of power, especially those linked with poetry and healing, and it is to celebrated literary virgins that this incarnation of Galesia looks for models for her sense of identity. Two are particularly important: Clorin, faithful shepherdess of the Fletcher play by that name, virgin, healer, and recluse heroically devoted to the memory of her dead lover; and Cassandra, the slightly unhinged prophetess of classical literature destined to speak truths that go unheeded.[10] These are ambiguous identifications, to be sure, but on the whole virginity in *Bosvil and Galesia* offers a potent image of the female self and is understood to be a positive withdrawal from the world of men, marriage, and reproductive obligation—precisely the world that throughout much of *Patch-Work Screen* an ambivalent Galesia finds herself unable wholly to accept or defy.

---

[8] For the French origins, see Carolyn C. Lougee, *Le Paradis des femmes: Women, Salons and Social Stratification in Seventeenth-Century France* (Princeton: Princeton UP, 1976); Ian Maclean, *Woman Triumphant: Feminism in French Literature 1610–1652* (Oxford: Clarendon P., 1977); Joan DeJean, *Tender Geographies: Women and the Origins of the Novel in France* (New York: Columbia UP, 1991).

[9] 'I resolv'd his Death, and pleas'd myself in the Fancy of a barbarous Revenge, and delighted myself to think I saw his Blood pour out of his false Heart'; by the end of her fantasy, she imagines an annual festival being held in her honour for ridding the world of 'so formidable a Monster as Bosvil' (*BG* 31).

[10] Ultimately Cassandra is raped, of course, but it is to the earlier phase of her career as disregarded prophetess that Barker appears to refer.

The translation of the heroic virgin of the early narratives into the diminished figure of the spinster in *Patch-Work Screen* occurs alongside larger cultural transformations that issued (broadly speaking) in a literary shift from the idealized, aristocratic, and heroic modes of the seventeenth century to the everyday, domestic concerns of the next, a shift discernible in Barker's increasingly 'novelistic' engagement with the here-and-now of contemporary life in the late prose fictions. But the more realistic rendering of the spinster in the patchwork narratives (1723–6) reflects important developments in Barker's fictional aims as well, not least her deepening understanding of her purposes as chronicler of unconventional and even unaccountable modes of female existence. *Patch-Work Screen* is the culmination of a lifelong endeavour to lend respectability to what one feels must have been Barker's own lived preference for the single life and celibacy over marriage and sexual relations with men. Her strategy in *Exilius* was to write virginity in a heroic register; within the intimate confines of *Bosvil and Galesia* she developed a more realistic treatment of her virgin-heroine that turns upon a deeply sceptical and indeed subversive use of the conventional courtship plot, as was seen in Chapter 5. The next stage in her radical reconceptualizing of female existence occurs in *Patch-Work Screen* and is advanced through two linked strategies. First, she displaces onto the inset tales various bits and pieces of the courtship plot, in this way pushing to the margins the amatory concerns that occupied the foreground of *Bosvil and Galesia* and, second, in the space thus cleared in the core narrative she inserts the figure of an unmarried woman who manages to convert her earlier resolve 'to espouse a Book' (*BG* 15) into an identity as a singlewoman poet. It is crucial to Barker's purposes that the human ties binding Galesia to patriarchal structures of male domination and control should over the course of the narrative be severed. Her male relations die— first her brother, then her father—and, conveniently, so do two of her most eligible suitors (one is executed for highway robbery; another commits suicide). By the close of the narrative and with the assistance of the androcidal author, Galesia manages to slip free of the diffusive psychosexual bonds that caused her such misery in *Bosvil and Galesia* and establish an identity as a writing woman independent of patriarchal lineage bonds and Britain's reproductive imperatives. She even receives the belated blessings of her mother who, shortly before she too is brought to her deathbed, declares herself resigned to her daughter's strange but now settled preference for her 'fantastick Companions the Muses' (*PWS* 143). In the finish Galesia is not wed, raped, seduced, abandoned, or dead. She writes, and she remains single.

An Unaccountable Wife

Galesia's release from the conventions of the courtship plot and the marital economy it implies has its dark analogue in the story of the Unaccountable Wife, an inset tale about a woman who refuses marriage in a manner so radical even Galesia finds it inexplicable. Most of the other inset tales in *Patch-Work Screen* serve as reminders of the amatory plot that Galesia's life-story rewrites. Stories of seduction, betrayal, female vulnerability, and male perfidy, they may be said to represent the more familiar trajectories of the heroine's destiny, maps of the heterosexual/marital road not taken. Among them the tale of the Unaccountable Wife stands by itself. The story of a curious *ménage à trois* that turns out to be less, or more—at any rate other—than had appeared, this inset tale focuses upon the strange conduct of a well-born woman who defies the claims of husband, children, kin, community, and ultimately the persuasions of the queen, to live in poverty with a female servant whom she calls her 'only Friend'. For years, it seems, wife, servant, and husband had shared a bed and sex life; both women had had children by him. The situation is well known in the community, where gossip has it that the wife was made to acquiesce in her husband's sexual desires. The action begins when the husband, tired of this arrangement and increasingly unwilling to bear the expense of a brood of illegitimate children, decides to send servant and children back to the woman's parish. To the astonishment of everyone, the wife now proclaims her presumed sexual rival her 'only Friend' and, to greater astonishment still, follows the banished servant into the country, refusing to return even when offered a pension by the queen. For the remainder of her life, we are told, she supports the servant and her children by begging in the streets.

In rehearsing the story of a wife who deserts the matrimonial order that she herself declines to enter, Galesia in effect recasts her 'secret Disgust' into a highly visible and indeed hugely transgressive refusal. For the Unaccountable Wife chooses not only penury and social isolation but also, even more unaccountably, a lower-class woman for her partner. The wife's self-chosen exile from both the matrimonial and the sex-class systems of her time stages what we might think of as a doubly queer version of the more hesitant sexual withdrawal enacted by Galesia in the core narrative. Unanswerable questions abound. What took place in the three-way conjugal bed? Were the two women sexually intimate during the triangulated phase of their relationship? Did they *ever* become intimate? Did the servant, a muted presence in the story, return the wife's vehement if obscure passion? Was the wife what a later era would call 'lesbian'? Was the servant? Galesia, openly perplexed by the strange story she recounts, seems to regard the wife's actions as proceeding from a species of desire so bizarre as to baffle understanding. She returns again and again to her own sense of bewilderment: the wife's 'unaccountable' conduct inspires 'amazement', 'great amazement', the 'greatest amazement possible'; her actions are 'unheard-of', 'impossible', 'strange', 'extraordinary', 'incredible', 'amazing'. Nor is the Lady who listens to the story and furnishes the final summing-up any more comprehending: surely the Unaccountable Wife must have been 'under some Spell or Inchantment' to have behaved 'in so strange a manner' (*PWS* 149).

The incomprehension of narrator and auditor converges with other failures of interpretation to stage a scene of misrecognition in which readers today are able very clearly to see (though perhaps without Barker's intending or even realizing it) the way in which within heteropatriarchy, as Judith Butler puts it, the 'ambiguities and incoherences' inhering in a multiplicity of sexual practices are 'suppressed and redescribed' within the framework of a masculine/feminine binary.[11] The wife's cleaving quite unexpectedly to the servant reveals, that is to say, the wrong-headedness of the phallocen-

---

[11] Judith Butler, *Gender Trouble: Feminism and the Subversion of Identity* (New York and London: Routledge, 1990), 31.

tric logic by which various members of the community—kin, friends, neighbours, more distant gossips—make what sense they can of the odd but by no means unprecedented situation. Inevitably they read what looked like a male-dominated sexual triangle through assumptions about wifely submission to a husband's desires: 'All this'—the *ménage*, including its unusual sleeping arrangement—'her Friends knew, or at least suspected; but thought it Complaisance, not Choice in her; and that she consider'd her own Imperfections, and Deformity; and therefore, was willing to take no Notice of her Husband's Fancy in the Embraces of this Woman her Servant'.[12] *He* must have insisted upon the arrangement; *her* participation must be 'Complaisance, not Choice'. When the husband attempts to convince Galesia's mother of his wife's passionate refusal to part from the servant, he meets with incredulity: 'Can you imagine me so stupid', the mother bursts out, 'as to believe your Wife can persist in such a Contradiction of Nature? It is impossible a Wife should oppose her Husband's Desire in parting with such a Woman' (*PWS* 145). Even when the wife runs off to join the servant, an action one might have thought capable of unsettling the most entrenched of phallocentric assumptions, the community continues to believe the husband was somehow behind it all: 'there arose a Murmuring', reports the narrator, 'as if he had made his Wife away; and when he told them the manner of her Departure, they would not believe him, the thing in itself being so incredible' (*PWS* 147). When the wife remains with the servant even after her husband's death, the community's capacity for interpretation collapses altogether. Shorn of the explanatory fiction of male desire and female complaisance, the wife's behaviour—perplexing, singular, perverse as it had seemed all along—becomes 'unaccountable'.

The tale exposes both the fiction of the enchanting phallus and the inadequacy of what Joan DeJean calls a culture's 'fictions of the feminine'—its 'received ideas about female

---

[12] This reference to 'deformity' may contain a hint of the widely assumed link between same-sex desire and an enlarged clitoris: see Valerie Traub, 'The Psychomorphology of the Clitoris', *GLQ: A Journal of Lesbian and Gay Studies*, 2 (1995), 81–113.

desire, its expression, its plot, and its fate'.[13] It shows quite vividly how various 'readers' struggle to bring what they see into line with what they believe to be true about female nature and desire—even when events reveal the almost risible rift between assumption and actuality. What had been read as his desires may have been, in part at least, the wife's; and when the triangulated male–female circuit is replaced by a female–female bond (with the husband receding from view) the notion that a man is a needful presence in women's lives dissolves, leaving a discourse subversive of other cultural 'fictions of the feminine'. Just how subversive can be gauged by comparing the relationship of the two women with that typically presented in male pornographic fantasies of the period. In pornographic representations woman's desire for woman flourishes in environments from which men are largely absent—convents, girls' schools, seraglios, and the like, the assumption being that sex between women is a weak substitute for the 'real' thing. The same assumption governs the convention by which female lovemaking is presented as a prologue to 'proper' sexual congress,[14] implying once again that female homoerotic desire occurs in a space created by masculine absence and that such desire will—upon happy discovery of the penis or renewed acquaintance with it—resolve itself into a dear girlish memory. Such is the case, famously, in *Fanny Hill*: Fanny's interest in lesbian sex wilts at first sight of a penis. From such phallocentric assumptions Barker's story of an Unaccountable Wife departs fully. The husband shares a bed with the two women and, we are given to believe, has impregnated them both. It is all the more striking, then, that the phallic nexus—imagined to be primary, compelling, all-sufficing, and all-explanatory—gives way to a female–female relation. The wife's attachment to her servant, 'unaccountable' though it might be, must be read as a rejection of, not a prelude to, the 'real' thing.

---

[13] Joan DeJean, *Fictions of Sappho 1546–1937* (Chicago and London: U. of Chicago P., 1989), 22.

[14] See Janet Todd, *Women's Friendship in Literature* (New York: Columbia UP, 1980), 322; Lillian Faderman, *Surpassing the Love of Men: Romantic Friendship and Love Between Women from the Renaissance to the Present* (New York: William Morrow, 1981), 23–8.

A Matter of Class

My frankly celebratory feminist/lesbian reading depends, it must now be said, upon a suppression of a crucial element of the inset tale: the narrator's moral outrage over the wife's bewildering but clearly reprehensible behaviour. The language of her narration is charged with the kind of negative energy customarily reserved for castigations of such forms of female sexual misconduct as, for example, same-sex physical intimacies. (Fielding's *The Female Husband*, written two decades later, abounds with examples.)[15] The Unaccountable Wife is a 'Shame to Woman-kind'; she has 'offended God, disgrac'd her Family, scandaliz'd her Neighbours'; she possesses an 'Interiour thoroughly degenerated'; her behaviour is a 'Contradiction of Nature' (*PWS* 146, 145). To the modern ear a discourse shot through with references to shame, offence, disgrace, scandal, degeneration, and unnaturalness reverberates with specifically sexual disapproval. Yet when returned to the context of the story these gestures of disapprobation are seen to point toward an earlier understanding of the 'natural', and one begins to realize that the narrator's condemnation is not exactly or, to be more accurate, not exclusively a response to same-sex improprieties. What is unaccountable about the wife, what makes her at once a puzzle and a 'Shame to Woman-kind' is not just that the object of her obsessive attachment is a woman: it is that the woman is a servant.

Although the narrator clearly shares my fascination with (to use the idiom of our age) the story's protolesbian content, she reads this material through a different set of emphases. Where I see resistance to an oppressive heteropatriarchal order, she sees a dangerous threat to a social system that depends upon continued subordination of the 'lower orders'; where I see (and want to applaud) a disruptive desire that opens a space for a wider range of erotic possibilities for women, she sees (and roundly

---

[15] In Henry Fielding, *The Female Husband and Other Writings*, ed. Claude E. Jones (1746; Liverpool: Liverpool UP, 1960), 29, 30, lesbian acts are 'monstrous and unnatural'; 'brutal and shocking'; 'abominable and unnatural pollutions'. For a discussion of the Fielding pamphlet, see Terry Castle, 'Matters not fit to be mentioned: Fielding's *The Female Husband*', *ELH* 49 (1982): 602–22.

condemns) an erosion of class distinctions. In the description that follows, for example, the attention of the disgusted narrator is fixated upon the spectacle of role inversions, the mistress cleaning, washing, and scouring while the 'vile Wretch' who should be doing the work of the household dawdles about at her pleasure:

[The mistress] was extremely kind to this Woman, to a Degree unheard-of; became a perfect Slave to her, and, as if she was the Servant, instead of the Mistress, did all the Household-Work, made the Bed, clean'd the House, wash'd the Dishes; nay, farther than so, got up in the Morning, scour'd the Irons, made the Fire, &c. leaving this vile Strumpet in Bed with her Husband; for they lay all Three together every Night (*PWS* 145).

Notice that the implied sexual improprieties ('for they lay all Three together every Night') amount to little more than an afterthought. Given the way dress functions metonymically to express symbolic relations among class, power, and the social order in the period,[16] it is predictable that abhorrence of the vile servant would emerge most powerfully in the moment when, decked out in the mistress's clothes ('very good lac'd Linnen, having clean Gloves on her Hands'), she is found perched on a 'handsome Velvet Chair' while the wife washes dishes (*PWS* 145–6). The 'violent Passion' the sight provokes in Galesia's mother reflects the story's investment in the maintenance of social hierarchy. When the events that function in my reading to expose the operations of heterosexist power regimes pass through the prism of the narrator's class-based mode of viewing social relations, they are refracted into the story of an uppity servant and her socially irresponsible mistress. The wife's refusal of compulsory matrimony is thus understood primarily as a story of transgression against class hierarchies that, on one level at least, reaffirms its author's conservative commitment to the existing social order.[17]

[16] See Terry Castle, *Masquerade and Civilization: The Carnivalesque in Eighteenth-Century English Culture and Fiction* (London: Methuen, 1986), esp. 55–7.

[17] Barker's rooted conservativism on social matters, including her reluctance to challenge outright the principle of female subordination, has much in common with that of Mary Astell, who also endorsed the single life as a way of extending to women a degree of autonomy while leaving the system of male domination in place.

Yet other interpretative possibilities exist. If the drama of collective misrecognition discussed earlier suggests one of the ways redescription operated to mask lesbian existence throughout the early modern period, the narrator's struggle to make sense of the wife's bizarre attachment to a lower-class woman may suggest an effort at interpretation specific to this moment. It is by now well known that during this period there existed no positive discursive identity for the woman who prefers women, though negative categories were certainly available: sexual intimacies between women could be represented in male-oriented pornography, to take one such category, or in openly hostile attacks (upon monstrous tribades, for example, or politically scheming upper-class sapphists). Around this time, however, one begins to find intimations of other less accountable 'lesbian' preferences surfacing in such muted, refracted, oblique, ambiguous, fragmentary, and more or less uncomprehended forms as the episode of the Unaccountable Wife. Lanser, in her work on what she calls the 'sapphic picaresque', has identified a number of narratives from this period that acknowledge the possibility of strong same-sex preferences in women but 'exhibit a collective failure of accountability' around the meaning and naming of female homoerotics.[18] They include, in addition to the Barker story, writings by Defoe (1706), Manley (1709), Haywood (1722), Bianchi (1744; translated into English, probably by Cleland, in 1751), and the anonymous *Travels and Adventures of Mademoiselle de Richelieu* (1743).[19] In these works female homoerotic relations are 'puzzling, fascinating, and morally and sometimes sexually ambiguous', are tied to adventuring and mobility, 'as if no conventional domestic frame can or should contain them' (4), and together create a discursive 'space of speculation' in which no single explanation of female same-sex erotic behaviour prevails. The period during which they were

See Ruth Perry, *The Celebrated Mary Astell: An Early English Feminist* (Chicago and London: U. of Chicago P., 1986), and 'Mary Astell and the Feminist Critique of Possessive Individualism', *ECS* 23 (1990), 444–57.

[18] Susan S. Lanser, 'Sapphic Picaresque: Perspectives on Heteropatriarchy and Homoadventuring', unpub. paper.

[19] For the latter, see Carolyn Woodward, ' "My Heart So Wrapt": Lesbian Disruptions in Eighteenth-Century British Fiction', *Signs: Journal of Women in Culture and Society*, 18 (1993), 838–65.

produced represents, Lanser argues, a 'moment of resistant fluidity' in the midst of shifts in sex/gender ideologies that marked the transition from hierarchical patriarchalism (based on models of sameness) to modern heteropatriarchy (based on gender difference).[20] The sapphic picaresque 'thus operates metatextually, structuring an ideological wandering in terrain being vacated by one model of sexuality but not yet charted by another one' (7). Barker's story of an Unaccountable Wife embodies just such a suspended moment of openness and fluidity before the consolidation later in the century of the hetero-sexualized gender identities which came to underpin the modern sex/gender system.

Lanser's analysis provides a final context for thinking about what has become by now a familiar dynamic in the approach to Barker's prose fictions developed in this study. Her stories of female life enact themselves, one might now say, in the space between shifting class-and-gender paradigms. If the story of the Unaccountable Wife occupies a discursive field 'being vacated by one model of sexuality but not yet charted by another', it also brings into play two different interpretative frames, one belonging to an established social world understood primarily in terms of rank and hierarchy and the other implying a world-in-the-making in which sex/gender difference will come to predominate. From the largely gendered perspective of today, the tale's protolesbianism is the vivid figure in the carpet; but from the class-based perspective of then, the homoerotic figure dissolves into another set of patterns, one in which gender and sexuality, though far from negligible, form not figure but background. So it is with Barker's eighteenth-century prose fictions generally: they partake in various ways of this quality of fluid indeterminacy and seem, as a result, imbued with a sense of exilic loneliness, of living in another's time or place or—as might be said of the tale of the Unaccountable Wife—of inhabiting the space between.

---

[20] Lanser, 'Singular Politics', 298, defines heteropatriarchy as 'a system of male dominance that posits sexual complementarity as the basis not only of personal desire but of social order'.

Janus *Barker Revisited*

This book has taken up questions of sexuality and gender when the texts have seemed to invite them but has departed from models of difference and oppositionality when other approaches seemed more fruitful. I am certainly not suggesting that we jettison models of difference or abandon insights hard-earned by a feminism that has taught us how to read the silences and gaps of women's past through the lens of gender exclusion. But if this study teaches us anything it is that feminocentric paradigms conceal as much as they reveal and, for historically minded readers, may impose unacceptable distortions. By examining Barker's religious and political affiliations, her immersion in a mixed-gender literary manuscript culture, her continuities with so-called 'male literary traditions' as well as with other women writers, her identifications with universities, learned men, and academic medicine, and her unfolding loyalties to the modern market-place of print, we have seen some of the ways she lived and wrote as part of her own time and place. Indeed, an account of her multiple engagements with early modern culture offers, if not a rebuke, at least a challenge to treatments that assign women to a private feminine sphere and women writers to feminocentric lines of ascent—constructs which, for this period anyway, seem more and more the products of our own separatist imaginings.

A corrective to what might be called the romance of feminocentrisim, *Jane Barker, Exile* is a plea for the importance of the particular case as well. Single-figure studies have not exactly been enjoying a boom these days. Enthusiasm for the broad sweep of cultural studies has invigorated literary study in countless ways but does little to encourage investigation of individual writers, except perhaps as they offer entry into strange, opaque, or hitherto unvisited parts of a culture. Those of us committed to reconstructing women's past find ourselves faced with the paradoxical situation that we know at once a good deal more and less about early modern women writers than ever before. Thanks to the efforts of the feminist recovery project we can consult reliable versions of a myriad of texts that were virtually unknown only a decade or two ago, but our information about the authors, occasions, composition, reception, and literary contexts of these works remains in many cases nearly as meagre as ever. Feminist scholars for a while now have expressed 'concern over what many view as the drive to conceptualize women's literary history before essential archival and bibliographical studies have even been truly begun',[21] as Margaret Ezell has written, and have urged directing greater energy toward uncovering basic facts regarding the lives and writing circumstances of individual women writers. I would like to think that the findings emerging from this study of one woman's singular literary career sufficiently demonstrate the value of particulars too easily trampled in the rush for theoretical models and broad cultural generalizations.

At the beginning of this book I noted that Barker's works were largely without influence or lasting impact. I should like to end by considering briefly what it might mean that Barker had no 'daughters' or for that matter mates. In the face of the silence of her contemporaries one can do no more than speculate on why Barker failed to leave a discernible imprint on her culture, but I have come to believe that writers in the generation succeeding Barker paid her little heed for the excellent reason that they would have seen her as one of history's losers many times over: a Jacobite, a Roman Catholic, an unreconstructed spinster, an admirer of Rochester, Cowley, and the literary culture of the Restoration, a novelist who announced at the outset of her final—and evidently quickly forgotten—novel that her pen 'scrapes an old Tune, in fashion about threescore and six years ago'. What could the tart asperities of a Jane Barker have to say to women learning to wring out of feminine sensibility an up-to-date 'moral authority'? To progressive women like Sarah Scott and Sarah Fielding and the later Eliza Haywood Barker must have looked every bit the anachronism she felt herself to be. No, if we are to appreciate Barker we must seek her significance not in narratives of continuity, lineage, and influence but rather in contemplation of the strangeness of her own stranded practices.

If Barker's successors learned little from her, we can. If their

---

[21] Margaret Ezell, *Writing Women's Literary History* (Baltimore and London: Johns Hopkins UP, 1993), 168 n. 5.

mistake (as we might anachronistically dub it) was to see in her only what had passed, ours is to focus too exclusively on those elements that lend her a spurious modernity—when what is needed is a reading method which allows us to crisscross dialectally between Now and Then, to accommodate difference and continuity, to take account of the rich multiplicity of historical contexts that inform her work—cultural, literary, political, social, scientific, and biographical—as well as the ways her texts speak to readers today. What I am calling for is no more than standard protocol for study of canonical male authors of the period, of course, but is seldom sought much less achieved in treatments of women. I hope that this biography of a literary career suggests some ways we might bring to the study of early women writers a mode of attention at once more minute and more inclusive than has been the case. For such study we will need to develop knowledge and expertise, depth and discrimination, a finer sense of the complex tug-and-pull between Now and Then that constitutes any engagement with the past: we must strive to be Janus-faced in the finest sense of the term.

Bibliography

MANUSCRIPT SOURCES

Beinecke Library, Yale University
    Osborn b. 111
Bodleian Library, Oxford
    MS Eng. misc. c. 116
    MS Eng. poet. e. 87
    MS Firth d. 13
    MS Rawl. poet. 155
    Thorn-Drury d. 3 (George Thorn-Drury's interleaved annotated copy of vol. 3 of the 2nd edition of Giles Jacob's *The Poetical Register* (1723))
British Library, London
    Add. MS 10,118
    Add. MS 21,621
    Add. MS 21,896
    Add. MS 27,406
    Add. MS 38,728
    Add. MS 43,410
    Stowe MS 232
Houghton Library, Harvard University
    MS Eng 612
Lincolnshire Archives Office
    4/422
    Ch. P 1709, box 4/14 (Ness Deanery)
    'Schedules and Letters of Attorney, 1717'
    'Kesteven Quarter Sessions. Papists' Estates. Rolls. 1717'
Magdalen College Library, Oxford
    MS 343
Northamptonshire Record Office
    34 P/1
Public Records Office, Kew
    C11/237/28
    C33/327
    C33/329
    FEC 1/1200
    FEC 1/1201

Royal Archives, Windsor Castle
  SP 46/14
  SP 46/20
  SP 208/129
  SP 211/110
Wellcome Institute, London
  MS 5354

PRINTED PRIMARY SOURCES

ASTELL, MARY, *A Serious Proposal to the Ladies,* part I (London: R. Wilkin, 1694).

BARKER, JANE, *Poetical Recreations: Consisting of Original Poems, Songs, Odes, &c. With Several New Translations. In Two Parts* (London: Benjamin Crayle, 1688).

—— *Love Intrigues; or, the History of the Amours of Bosvil and Galesia, As Related to Lucasia, in St. Germains Garden. A Novel* (London: E. Curll and C. Crownfield, 1713).

—— *Exilius; or, The Banish'd Roman: A New Romance: In Two Parts, Written after the Manner of Telemachus* (London: E. Curll, 1715).

—— *The Christian Pilgrimage; or, A Companion for the Holy Season of Lent* (London: Curll and C. Rivington. 1718).

—— *The Entertaining Novels of Mrs. Jane Barker. In Two Volumes* (London: A. Bettesworth and E.. Curll, 1719).

—— *A Patch-Work Screen for the Ladies; or, Love and Virtue Recommended: In a Collection of Instructive Novels. Related After a Manner Intirely New, and Interspersed with Rural Poems,Describing the Innoocence of a Couontry-Life* (London: E. Curll and T. Payne, 1723).

—— *The Lining of the Patch Work Screen; Design'd for the Farther Entertainment of the Ladies* (London: A. Bettesworth, 1726).

—— *The Entertaining Novels of Mrs. Jane Barker, of Wilsthorp in Northamptonshire,* 3rd edn. (London: Bettesworth, Hitch, and E. Curll, 1736).

BARTHOLIN, THOMAS, *Bartholinus Anatomy; Made from the Precepts of his Father,* trans. Nicholas Culpeper and Abdiah Cole (London: John Streator, 1668).

BEHN, APHRA, *A Pindaric Poem to the Reverend Doctor Burnet, On The Honour He Did Me of Enquiring After Me and My Muse.* (1689).

[BUSBY, ROBERT], *The German Atalantis: Being, A Secret History of Many Surprizing Intrigues, and Adventures Transacted in Several*

Foreign Courts. Written by a Lady (London: Curll, 1715; reissued as *Hanover Tales*, 1718).

BUTLER, SARAH, *Irish Tales: or, Instructive Histories for the Happy Conduct of Life* (London: Curll and J. Hooke, 1716; reissued as *Milesian Tales* 1718).

CAVENDISH, MARGARET, *Poems, and Fancies: Written by the Right Honourable, the Lady Margaret Countesse of Newcastle* (London: J. Martin and J. Allestrye, 1653).

—— *CCXI. Sociable Letters, Written by the Thrice Noble, Illustrious, and Excellent Princess, the Lady Marchioness of Newcastle* (London: William Wilson, 1664).

CHETWOOD, WILLIAM RUFUS, *The Voyages, Dangerous Adventures, and Imminent Escapes of Capt. Rich. Falconer* (1720; London: Marshal, Chetwood, Cox, and Edlin, 1724).

DANGERFIELD, THOMAS, *The Case of Tho. Dangerfield: with Some Remarkable Passages that happened at the Tryals of Elizabeth Cellier the Popish Midwife, and the Earl of Castlemain* (London: for the Author, 1680).

DAVYS, MARY, *The Works of Mrs. Davys: Consisting of Plays, Novels, Poems, and Familiar Letters*. 2 vols (London: H. Woodfall, 1725).

Delightful and Ingenious Novels: Being Choice and Excellent Stories of Amours, Tragical and Comical (London: Crayle, 1685).

[EGERTON], SARAH FYGE, *Poems on Several Occasions, Together with a Pastoral*. London: J. Nutt, [1706].

GILDON, CHARLES, *The Life And Strange Surprizing Adventures of Mr. D—— De F——, of London, Hosier* (London: J. Roberts, 1719).

GOODALL, CHARLES, *The Colledge of Physicians Vindicated, And the true State of Physick in this Nation Faithfully Represented* (London: Walter Kettilby, 1676).

—— *The Royal College of Physicians of London Founded and Established by Law* (London: for Walter Kettilby, 1684).

The Hermit: Or, the Unparalled Sufferings and Surprising Adventures of Mr. Philip Quarll, An Englishman (London: Warner and Creake, 1727).

HICKES, GEORGE, trans, *Instructions for the Education of a Daughter, By the Author of Telemachus* (London: Jonah Bowyer, 1707).

KILLIGREW, ANNE, *Poems by Mrs Anne Killigrew* (London: Samuel Lowndes, 1686).

Miscellany Poems and Translations by Oxford Hands (London: Anthony Stephens, 1685).

Ovid's Epistles, Translated by Several Hands (London: Tonson, 1680).

[RAMSAY, ANDREW], *The Life of François de Salignac De la Motte*

Fénelon, Archbishop and Duke of Cambray (London: Paul Vaillant and James Woodman, 1723).

ROGERS, TIMOTHY, *The Character of a Good Woman, Both in a Single and Marry'd State* (London: John Harris, 1697).

ROWE, THEOPHILUS (ed.), *The Miscellaneous Works in Prose and Verse of Mrs. Elizabeth Rowe,* 2 vols. (London: R. Hett and R. Dodsley, 1739).

SEWELL, GEORGE, *Posthumous Works of Dr. George Sewell* (London: Henry Curll, 1728).

SINGER, ELIZABETH, *Poems on Several Occasions. Written by Philomela* (London: John Dunton, 1696).

TATE, NAHUM, *Poems Written on Several Occasions.* 2nd edn. 'enlarged' (London: B. Tooke, 1684).

PRINTED SECONDARY SOURCES

ADEN, JOHN M., *Pope's Once and Future Kings* (Knoxville: U. of Tennessee P., 1978).

ALDEN, JOHN, 'Pills and Publishing: Some Notes on the English Book Trade, 1660–1715', *Library,* 5th ser. 7 (1952), 21–37.

ALLEN, DON CAMERON, *Image and Meaning: Metaphoric Traditions in Renaissance Poetry* (Baltimore: Johns Hopkins P., 1960).

ANDREADIS, HARRIET, 'The Sapphic Platonics of Katherine Philips, 1632–1664', *Signs: Journal of Women in Culture and Society,* 15 (1989), 34–60.

ARBER, EDWARD (ed.), *British Anthologies.* 10 vols. (London: Henry Frowde, 1899–1901).

ARMSTRONG, NANCY, *Desire and Domestic Fiction: A Political History of the Novel* (New York and Oxford: Oxford UP, 1987).

AVELING, J. C. H., *The Handle and the Axe: The Catholic Recusants in England from Reformation to Emancipation* (London: Blond and Briggs, 1976).

BACKSCHEIDER, PAULA R., *Spectacular Politics: Theatrical Power and Mass Culture in Early Modern England* (Baltimore and London: Johns Hopkins UP, 1993).

—— and RICHETTI, JOHN J. (eds.), *Popular Fiction by Women 1660–1730: An Anthology* (Oxford: Clarendon P., 1996).

BAKHTIN, M. M., *The Dialogic Imagination: Four Essays,* ed. Michael Holquist and trans. Caryl Emerson and Michael Holquist (Austin: U. of Texas P., 1981).

BALLASTER, ROS, *Seductive Forms: Women's Amatory Fiction from 1684 to 1740* (Oxford: Clarendon P., 1992).

BARASH, CAROL, 'The Political Possibilities of Desire: Teaching the Erotic Poems of Behn', in Christopher Fox (ed.), *Teaching Eighteenth-Century Poetry* (New York: AMS P., 1990), 159–76.

—— *English Women's Poetry, 1649–1714: Politics, Community, and Linguistic Authority* (Oxford: Clarendon P., 1996).

BARKER-BENFIELD, G. J., *The Culture of Sensibility: Sex and Society in Eighteenth-Century Britain* (Chicago and London: U. of Chicago P., 1992).

BEAL, PETER, *Index of English Literary Manuscripts, 1450–1700*, 4 vols. (London and New York: Bowker and Mansell, 1980–93).

—— *In Praise of Scribes: Manuscripts and their Makers in Seventeenth-Century England* (Oxford: Clarendon P., 1998).

BEASLEY, JERRY C., *Novels of the 1740s* (Athens: U. of Georgia P., 1982).

—— 'Politics and Moral Idealism: The Achievement of Some Early Women Novelists', in Mary Anne Schofield and Cecilia Macheski (eds.), *Fetter'd or Free? British Women Novelists, 1670–1815* (Athens and London: Ohio UP, 1986), 216–36.

BEIER, LUCINDA, *Sufferers and Healers: The Experience of Illness in Seventeenth-Century England* (London and New York: Routledge and Kegan Paul, 1987).

BELANGER, TERRY, 'Publishers and Writers in Eighteenth-Century England', in Isabel Rivers (ed.), *Books and their Readers in Eighteenth-Century England* (Leicester: Leicester UP and New York: St Martin's P., 1982), 5–25.

BELL, MAUREEN, PARFITT, GEORGE, and SHEPHERD, SIMON, *A Biographical Dictionary of English Women Writers 1580–1720* (Boston: G. K. Hall, 1990).

BENNETT, G. V., *The Tory Crisis in Church and State, 1688–1730: The Career of Francis Atterbury, Bishop of Rochester* (Oxford: Clarendon P., 1975).

BLACKEY, ROBERT, 'A War of Words: The Significance of the Propaganda Conflict Between English Catholics and Protestants, 1715–1745', *Catholic Historical Review*, 58 (1973), 534–55.

BLOCH, MARC, *The Royal Touch: Sacred Monarchy and Scrofula in England and France*, trans. J. E. Anderson (London: Routledge and Kegan Paul, 1973).

BLOM, F., BLOM, J., KORSTEN, F., SCOTT, G., *English Catholic Books 1701–1800: A Bibliography* (Aldershot, Hampshire: Scolar P., 1996).

BODDY, MARGARET, 'The Manuscripts and Printed Editions of the Translation of Virgil Made by Richard Maitland, Fourth Earl of Lauderdale, and the Connexion with Dryden', *N&Q*, NS 12 (1965), 144–50.

BOND, DONALD F. (ed.), *The Spectator*, 5 vols. (Oxford: Clarendon P., 1965).

BOSSY, JOHN, *The English Catholic Community 1570–1850* (London: Darton, Longman, and Todd, 1975).

BOWERS, TONI O'SHAUGHNESSY, 'Sex, Lies, and Invisibility: Amatory Fiction from the Restoration to Mid-Century', in John Richetti (ed.), *The Columbia History of the British Novel* (New York: Columbia UP, 1994). 50–72.

—— 'Jacobite Difference and the Poetry of Jane Barker', *ELH* 64 (1997), 857–69.

BRACHER, FREDERICK (ed.), *Letters of Sir George Etherege* (Berkeley: U. of California P., 1974).

BROOKS, HAROLD F. (ed.), *The Poems of John Oldham* (Oxford: Clarendon P., 1987).

BROOKS-DAVIES, DOUGLAS, *Pope's Dunciad and the Queen of the Night: A Study in Emotional Jacobitism* (Manchester: Manchester U., 1985).

BRÜCKMANN, PATRICIA, 'Catholicism in England', in Robert P. Maccubbin and Martha Hamilton-Phillips (eds.), *The Age of William III and Mary II: Power, Politics, and Patronage 1688–1702* (Williamsburg, Va.: The College of William and Mary, 1989), 82–8.

BUTLER, JUDITH, *Gender Trouble: Feminism and the Subversion of Identity* (New York and London: Routledge, 1990).

Calendar of the Stuart Papers, 7 vols. (London: HMSO, 1902).

CAMERON, WILLIAM J., 'John Dryden's Jacobitism', in Harold Love (ed.), *Restoration Literature: Critical Approaches* (London: Methuen, 1972), 277–308.

CANFIELD, J. DOUGLAS, 'Royalism's Last Dramatic Stand: English Political Tragedy, 1679–89', *Studies in Philology*, 82 (1985), 234–63.

CASTLE, TERRY, 'Matters not fit to be mentioned: Fielding's *The Female Husband*', *ELH* 49 (1982): 602–22.

—— *Masquerade and Civilization: The Carnivalesque in Eighteenth-Century English Culture and Fiction* (London: Methuen, 1986).

CHARTIER, ROGER, 'Laborers and Voyagers: From the Text to the Reader', *Diacritics*, 22 (1992), 49–61.

CHILDS, JOHN, *The Army, James II, and the Glorious Revolution* (Manchester: Manchester UP, 1980).

CLARK, ALICE, *Working Life of Women in the Seventeenth Century* (1919; London and New York: Routledge, 1992).

CLARK, J. C. D., *English Society 1688–1832: Ideology, Social Structure and Political Practice During the Ancien Regime* (Cambridge: Cambridge UP, 1985).

CLIFTON, ROBIN, 'The Popular Fear of Catholics during the English Revolution', *Past and Present*, 52 (1973), 23–55.

COLE, CHRISTIAN, *Historical and Political Memoirs* (London: J. Millan, 1735).

COLE, SUSAN, 'Princess Over the Water: A Memoir of Louise Marie Stuart (1692–1712)', *Royal Stuart Papers*, 18 (Royal Stuart Society, 1981).

COLLEY, LINDA, *Britons: Forging the Nation 1707–1837* (New Haven and London: Yale UP, 1992).

COOK, HAROLD J., *The Decline of the Old Medical Regime in Stuart London* (Ithaca and London: Cornell UP, 1986).

—— 'The Rose Case Reconsidered: Physicians, Apothecaries, and the Law in Augustan England', *Journal of the History of Medicine*, 45 (1990), 527–55.

COPLEY, STEPHEN, 'Commerce, Conversation and Politeness in the Early Eighteenth Century Periodical', *British Journal for Eighteenth-Century Studies*, 18 (1995), 63–77.

CRAWFORD, PATRICIA, 'Printed Advertisements for Women Medical Practitioners in London, 1670–1710', *Society for the Social History of Medicine: Bulletin*, 35 (1984), 66–70.

CROMPTON, VIRGINIA, ' "For when the act is done and finish't cleane, | what should the poet doe, but shift the scene?": Propaganda, Professionalism and Aphra Behn, in Janet Todd, (ed.), *Aphra Behn Studies* (Cambridge: Cambridge UP, 1996), 130–53.

CRUICKSHANKS, EVELINE, and CORP, EDWARD (eds.), *The Stuart Court in Exile and the Jacobites* (London and Rio Grande: Hambledon P., 1995).

CURTIUS, ERNST ROBERT, *European Literature and the Latin Middle Ages*, trans. Willard R. Trask (1953; Princeton: Princeton UP, 1990).

DALTON, CHARLES (ed.), *English Army Lists and Commission Registers 1661–1714*, 6 vols. (London: Eyre and Spottiswoode, 1892–1904).

DAVIS, JAMES HERBERT, JR., *Fénelon* (Boston: G. K. Hall-Twayne, 1979).

DAY, CYRUS LAWRENCE, and MURRIE, ELEANORE BOSWELL *English Song-Books 1651–1702: A Bibliography with a First-Line Index of Songs* (London: Bibliographical Society at the UP, Oxford, 1940 (for 1937)).

DE BEER, E. S. (ed.), *The Correspondence of John Locke*, 8 vols. (Oxford: Clarendon P., 1976).

DEJEAN, JOAN, *Fictions of Sappho 1546–1927* (Chicago and London: U. of Chicago P., 1989).

—— *Tender Geographies: Women and the Origins of the Novel in France* (New York: Columbia UP, 1991).

DONOVAN, JOSEPHINE, 'Women and the Rise of the Novel: A Feminist-Marxist Theory', *Signs*, 16 (1991), 441–62.

DOODY, MARGARET ANNE, 'Deserts, Ruins and Troubled Waters: Female Dreams in Fiction and the Development of the Gothic Novel', *Genre*, 10 (1977), 529–72.

—— *The Daring Muse: Augustan Poetry Reconsidered* (Cambridge: Cambridge UP, 1985).

—— 'Jane Barker', *British Novelists, 1660–1800, in DLB* 39, part I (Detroit: Gale Research Co.–Bruccoli Clark, 1985), 24–30.

DOWNIE, J. A., *Robert Harley and the Press: Propaganda and Public Opinion in the Age of Swift and Defoe* (Cambridge: Cambridge UP, 1979).

—— 'The Making of the English Novel', *Eighteenth-Century Fiction*, 9 (1997), 249–66.

ECCLES, AUDREY, *Obstetrics and Gynaecology in Tudor and Stuart England* (London and Canberra: Croom Helm, 1982).

EPSTEIN, JULIA, 'Writing the Unspeakable: Fanny Burney's Mastectomy and the Fictive Body', *Representations*, 16 (Fall 1986), 131–66.

—— *The Iron Pen: Frances Burney and the Politics of Women's Writing* (Madison: U. of Wisconsin P., 1989).

ERICKSON, AMY LOUISE, *Women and Property in Early Modern England* (London and New York: Routledge, 1993).

ERSKINE-HILL, HOWARD, 'Pope: The Political Poet in His Time', *ECS* 15 (1981–2), 123–48.

—— 'Literature and the Jacobite Cause: Was there a Rhetoric of Jacobitism?', in Eveline Cruickshanks (ed.), *Ideology and Conspiracy: Aspects of Jacobitism, 1689–1759* (Edinburgh: John Donald, 1982), 49–69.

—— *Poetry of Opposition and Revolution: Dryden to Wordsworth* (Oxford: Clarendon P., 1996).

ESTCOURT, EDGAR E., and PAYNE, JOHN ORLEBAR, *The English Catholic Nonjurors of 1715: Being a Summary of the Register of their Estates* (London: Burns and Oates, [1885]).

EZELL, MARGARET J. M., *The Patriarch's Wife: Literary Evidence and the History of the Family* (Chapel Hill and London: U. of North Carolina P., 1987).

—— (ed.), *The Poems and Prose of Mary, Lady Chudleigh* (New York and Oxford: Oxford UP, 1993).

—— *Writing Women's Literary History* (Baltimore and London: Johns Hopkins UP, 1993).

FADERMAN, LILLIAN, *Surpassing the Love of Men: Romantic Friendship and Love Between Women from the Renaissance to the Present* (New York: William Morrow, 1981).

FERGUSON, MARGARET W., 'Running on with Almost Public Voice: The Case of "E.C." ', in Florence Howe (ed.), *Tradition and the Talents of Women* (Urbana and Chicago: U. of Illinois P., 1991), 37–67.

—— 'Renaissance Concepts of the "Woman Writer" ', in Helen Wilcox (ed.), *Women and Literature in Britain 1500–1700* (Cambridge: Cambridge UP, 1996), 143–68.

FERGUSON, MOIRA, *First Feminists: British Women Writers 1578–1799* (Bloomington: Indiana UP; Old Westbury, NY: The Feminist P., 1985).

FETTERLY, JUDITH, *The Resisting Reader: A Feminist Approach to American Fiction* (Bloomington: Indiana UP, 1978).

FIELDING, HENRY, *The Female Husband and Other Writings*, ed. Claude E. Jones (1746; Liverpool: Liverpool UP, 1960).

FISCHER, SANDRA K., 'Elizabeth Cary and Tyranny, Domestic and Religious', in Margaret P. Hannay (ed.), *Silent But for the Word: Tudor Women as Patrons, Translators and Writers of Religious Works* (Kent, Oh.: Kent State UP, 1985), 225–37.

FISSELL, MARY E., *Patients, Power, and the Poor in Eighteenth-Century Bristol* (Cambridge: Cambridge UP, 1991).

FITZMAURICE, JAMES, 'Jane Barker and the Tree of Knowledge, and Learning at Cambridge University', *Renaissance Forum*, 3 (1998), URL: www.hull.ac.uk/Hull/EL Web/renforum.

FLETCHER, ANTHONY, 'The Decline and Fall of the Lusty Woman', *TLS* (15 Dec. 1995), 8.

FLINT, JAMES, 'James II and the English Benedictines', *American Benedictine Review*, 39 (1988), 113–32.

FOLEY, HENRY, *Records of the English Province of the Society of Jesus*, 7 vols. (London: Burns and Oates, 1879).

FOSS, MICHAEL, *The Age of Patronage: The Arts in England 1660–1750* (Ithaca: Cornell UP, 1971).

FOXON, DAVID, *Pope and the Early Eighteenth-Century Book Trade*, rev. and ed. James McLaverty (Oxford: Clarendon P., 1991).

FRANK, ROBERT G., JR., *Harvey and the Oxford Physiologists: Scientific Ideas and Social Interaction* (Berkeley: U. of California P., 1980).

FRASER, NANCY, 'Rethinking the Public Sphere: A Contribution to the Critique of Actually Existing Democracy', in Craig Calhoun (ed.), *Habermas and the Public Sphere* (Cambridge, Mass., and London: MIT P., 1992), 109–42.

FRASER, WILLIAM, *The Book of Carlaverock: Memoirs of the Maxwells, Earls of Nithsdale, Lords Maxwell & Herries*, 2 vols. (Edinburgh, 1873).

FURBANK, P. N., and OWENS, W. R., 'Defoe and Francis Noble', *Eighteenth-Century Fiction*, 4 (1992), 301–13.

Fuss, Diana, *Identification Papers* (New York and London: Routledge, 1995).

Gable, A. T., 'The Prince and the Mirror, Louis XIV, Fénelon, Royal Narcissism and the Legacy of Machiavelli', *Seventeenth-Century French Studies*, 15 (1993), 243–68.

Gallagher, Catherine, 'Who was that Masked Woman? The Prostitute and the Playwright in the Comedies of Aphra Behn', in Regina Barreca (ed.), *Last Laughs: Perspectives on Women and Comedy* (New York: Gordon and Breach, 1988), 23–42.

—— *Nobody's Story: The Vanishing Acts of Women Writers in the Marketplace, 1670–1820* (Berkeley and Los Angeles: U. of California P., 1994).

Gardiner, Anne Barbeau, 'A Jacobite Song by John Dryden', *Yale University Library Gazette*, 61 (1986), 49–54.

—— 'Elizabeth Cellier in 1688 on Envious Doctors and Heroic Midwives Ancient and Modern', *ECL* 14 (Feb. 1990), 24–34.

Gardiner, Dorothy, *English Girlhood at School: A Study of Women's Education through Twelve Centuries* (Oxford: Oxford UP and London: Humphrey Mildord, 1929).

Garrett, Jane, *The Triumphs of Providence: The Assassination Plot, 1696* (Cambridge: Cambridge UP, 1980).

Genet-Rouffiac, Nathalie, 'Jacobites in Paris and Saint-Germain-en-Laye', in Eveline Cruickshanks and Edward Corp (eds.), *The Stuart Court in Exile and the Jacobites* (London and Rio Grande: Hambledon P., 1995), 15–38.

Gibbons, G. S., 'Mrs. Jane Barker', *N&Q*, 11th ser. 12 (30 Sept. 1922), 278–9.

Ginzburg, Carlo, *The Cheese and the Worms: The Cosmos of a Sixteenth-Century Miller*, trans. John and Anne Tedeschi (Baltimore: Johns Hopkins UP, 1980).

Greer, Germaine, 'How to Invent a Poet', *TLS* (25 June 1993), 7–8.

—— *Slip-Shod Sibyls: Recognition, Rejection and the Woman Poet* (London: Viking, 1995).

—— Hastings, Susan, Medoff, Jeslyn, and Sansone, Melinda (eds.), *Kissing the Rod: An Anthology of Seventeenth-Century Women's Verse* (New York: Farrar Straus Giroux, 1989).

Gregg, Edward, 'The Politics of Paranoia', in Eveline Cruickshanks and Jeremy Black (eds.), (Edinburgh: John Donald, 1988), 42–56.

—— 'New Light on the Authorship of the *Life of James II*', *English Historical Review*, 108 (1993), 947–65.

Greider, Josephine, Introd. *A Patch-Work Screen for the Ladies*, ed. Josephine Greider (New York and London: Garland, 1973).

GRUNDY, ISOBEL, 'Women's History? Writings by English Nuns', in Isobel Grundy and Susan Wiseman (eds.), *Women, Writing, History 1640–1740* (Athens: U. of Georgia P., 1992), 126–38.

GUNTHER, R. T., *Early Science in Oxford*, ix: De Corde *by Richard Lower, London 1669*, trans. K. J. Franklin (Oxford: for the Subscribers, 1932).

HAGEMAN, ELIZABETH H., 'Women's Poetry in Early Modern Britain', in Helen Wilcox (ed.), *Women and Literature in Britain 1500–1700* (Cambridge: Cambridge UP, 1996), 190–208.

—— and SUNUNU, ANDREA, ' "More Copies of it abroad than I could have imagin'd": Further Manuscript Texts of Katherine Philips, "the Matchless Orinda" ', *EMS* 5 (1995), 127–69.

HARRIS, TIM, 'London Crowds and the Revolution of 1688', in Eveline Cruickshanks (ed.), *By Force or By Default? The Revolution of 1688–1689* (Edinburgh: John Donald, 1989), 44–64.

—— SEAWARD, PAUL, and GOLDIE, MARK (eds.), *The Politics of Religion in Restoration England* (Oxford: Basil Blackwell, 1990).

HARRISON, JOHN, *The Library of Isaac Newton* (Cambridge: Cambridge UP, 1978).

HAYDON, COLIN, *Anti-Catholicism in Eighteenth-Century England, c.1714–80: A Political and Social Study* (Manchester and New York: Manchester UP, 1993).

HAYTON, DAVID, 'The Propaganda War', in W. A. Maguire (ed.), *Kings in Conflict: The Revolutionary War in Ireland and its Aftermath 1689–1750* (Belfast: Blackstaff P., 1990), 106–21.

HENDERSON, G. D., *Chevalier Ramsay* (London: Thomas Nelson and Sons, 1952).

HIGGINS, IAN, *Swift's Politics: A Study in Disaffection* (Cambridge: Cambridge UP, 1994).

HILBERRY, CONRAD, *The Poems of John Collop* (Madison: U. of Wisconsin P., 1962).

HILL, GEORGE BIRKBECK (ed.), *Lives of the English Poets by Samuel Johnson*, 3 vols. (New York: Octagon Books, 1967).

HILL, PETER MURRAY, *Two Augustan Booksellers: John Dunton and Edmund Curll* (U. of Kansas Library Ser. No. 3; Lawrence: U. of Kansas Libraries, 1958).

HINNANT, CHARLES H., 'Anne Finch and Jacobitism: Approaching the Wellesley College Manuscript', *Journal of Family History*, 21 (1996), 496–502.

HOBBS, MARY, *Early Seventeenth-Century Verse Miscellany Manuscripts* (Aldershot: Scolar, 1992).

HOBBY, ELAINE, *Virtue of Necessity: English Women's Writing 1649–1688* (Ann Arbor: U. of Michigan P., 1989).

HOLMES, GEOFFREY, *British Politics in the Age of Anne* (London: Macmillan and New York: St Martin's, 1967).

—— and SZECHI, DANIEL, *The Age of Oligarchy: Pre-industrial Britain, 1722–1783* (London and New York: Longman, 1993).

HUFTON, OLWEN, *The Prospect Before Her: A History of Women in Western Europe*, i: *1500–1800* (New York: Alfred A. Knopf, 1996).

HUNTER, J. PAUL, 'The Novel and Social/Cultural History', in John Richetti (ed.), *The Cambridge Companion to the Eighteenth-Century Novel* (Cambridge: Cambridge UP, 1996), 9–40

JAMESON, FREDRIC, 'Religion and Ideology', in Frances Barker *et al.* (eds.), *1642: Literature and Power in the Seventeenth Century* (Colchester: U. of Essex, 1981), 315–36.

JONES, GEORGE HILTON, *Charles Middleton: The Life and Times of a Restoration Politician* (Chicago and London: U. of Chicago P., 1967).

KERNAN, ALVIN, *Samuel Johnson and the Impact of Print* (Princeton: Princeton UP, 1987).

KERRIGAN, JOHN, *Motives of Woe: Shakespeare and 'Female Complaint': A Critical Anthology* (Oxford: Clarendon P., 1991).

KING, KATHRYN R., 'Galesia, Jane Barker, and a Coming to Authorship', in Carol J. Singley and Susan Elizabeth Sweeney (eds.), *Anxious Power: Reading, Writing and Ambivalence in Narrative by Women* (New York: State U. of New York P., 1993), 91–104.

—— 'Jane Barker, *Poetical Recreations*, and the Sociable Text', *ELH* 61 (1994), 551–70.

—— 'The Unaccountable Wife and Other Tales of Female Desire in Jane Barker's *A Patch-Work Screen for the Ladies*', *Eighteenth Century*, 35 (1994), 155–72.

—— 'Jane Barker, Mary Leapor and a Chain of Very Odd Contingencies', *English Language Notes*, 33 (1996), 14–27.

—— 'Jane Barker and her Life (1652–1732): The Documentary Record', *ECL* 21, NS 3 (1997), 16–38, with the assistance of Jeslyn Medoff.

—— *The Poems of Jane Barker: The Magdalen Manuscript* (Oxford: Magdalen College Occasional Paper 3, 1998).

KORSHIN, PAUL J., 'Types of Eighteenth-Century Literary Patronage', *ECS* 7 (1974), 453–73.

—— Afterword, *ELH* 64 (1997), 1091–1100.

KOWALSKI-WALLACE, BETH, 'Tea, Gender, and Domesticity in Eighteenth-Century England', *Studies in Eighteenth-Century Culture*, 23 (1994), 131–45.

LANSER, SUSAN S., 'Singular Politics: The Rise of the British Nation and the Production of the Old Maid', in Judith M. Bennett and Amy M.

Froide (eds.), *Singlewomen in the European Past, 1250–1800* (Philadelphia: U. of Penn. Press, 1999).
—— 'Sapphic Picaresque: Perspectives on Heteropatriarchy and Homoadventuring', unpub. paper.

LART, C. E. (ed.), *The Parochial Registers of St.Germain-en-Laye: Jacobite Extracts of Births Marriages and Deaths*, 2 vols. (London: St Catherine P., 1910–12).

LAURETIS, THERESA DE, *Technologies of Gender: Essays on Theory, Film, and Fiction* (Bloomington and Indianapolis: Indiana UP, 1987).

LENMAN, BRUCE, *The Jacobite Risings in Britain 1689–1746* (London: Eyre Methuen, 1980).

LEWALSKI, BARBARA KIEFER, *Writing Women in Jacobean England* (Cambridge and London: Harvard UP, 1993).

LILLEY, KATE, 'True State Within: Women's Elegy 1640–1700', in Isobel Grundy and Susan Wiseman (eds.), *Women, Writing, History 1640–1740* (Athens: U. of Georgia P., 1992), 72–92.

LLOYD, DAVID, *Anomalous States: Irish Writing and the Post-Colonial Moment* (Dublin: Lilliput P., 1993).

LOISEAU, JEAN, *Abraham Cowley's Reputation in England* (Paris: Henri Didier, 1931).

LORD, GEORGE DE FOREST (ed.), *Poems on Affairs of State: Augustan Satirical Verse, 1660–1714*, 7 vols. (New Haven and London: Yale UP, 1963–75).

LOUGEE, CAROLYN C., *Le Paradis des femmes: Women, Salons and Social Stratification in Seventeenth-Century France* (Princeton: Princeton UP, 1976).

LOVE, HAROLD, 'Manuscript Versus Print in the Transmission of English Literature, 1600–1700', *BSANZ Bulletin*, 9 (1983), 95–107.

—— *Scribal Publication in Seventeenth-Century England* (Oxford: Clarendon P., 1993).

LOVELL, TERRY, 'Subjective Powers? Consumption, the Reading Public, and Domestic Woman in Early Eighteenth-Century England', in Ann Bermingham and John Brewer (eds.), *The Consumption of Culture 1600–1800: Image, Object, Text* (London and New York: Routledge, 1995), 23–41.

LUNN, DAVID, *The English Benedictines, 1540–1688: From Reformation to Revolution* (London: Burns and Oates and New York: Barnes and Noble, 1980).

LYNCH, DEIRDRE, and WARNER, WILLIAM B., 'Introduction', *Cultural Institutions of the Novel* (Durham, NC, and London: Duke UP, 1996).

McBurney, William H., 'Edmund Curll, Mrs. Jane Barker, and the English Novel', *Philological Quarterly*, 37 (1958), 385–99.

MacCarthy, B. G., *The Female Pen. Women Writers: Their Contribution to the English Novel 1621–1744* (Oxford: Blackwell for Cork UP, 1946).

Macdonald, Hugh (ed.), *John Dryden: A Bibliography of Early Editions and of Drydeniana* (Oxford: Clarendon P., 1939).

McDowell, Paula, 'Consuming Women: The Life of the "Literary Lady" as Popular Culture in Eighteenth-Century England', *Genre*, 26 (1993), 219–52.

—— *The Women of Grub Street: Press, Politics, and Gender in the London Literary Marketplace 1678–1730* (Oxford: Clarendon P., 1998).

Mack, Phyllis, *Visionary Women: Ecstatic Prophecy in Seventeenth-Century England* (Berkeley: U. of California P., 1992).

McKenzie, D. F., *The Cambridge University Press 1696–1712*, 2 vols. (Cambridge UP, 1966).

McKeon, Michael, *The Origins of the English Novel 1600–1740* (Baltimore: Johns Hopkins UP, 1987).

Maclean, Ian, *Woman Triumphant: Feminism in French Literature 1610–1652* (Oxford: Clarendon P., 1977).

McLynn, Frank, *The Jacobites* (London and New York: Routledge and Kegan Paul, 1985).

Madan, Falconer (ed.), *Stuart Papers Relating Chiefly to Queen Mary of Modena and the Exiled Court of King James II*, 2 vols. (London: J. B. Nichols and Sons, 1889).

Marotti, Arthur F., *Manuscript, Print, and the English Renaissance Lyric* (Ithaca and London: Cornell UP, 1995).

Martensen, Robert L., ' "Habit of Reason": Anatomy and Anglicanism in Restoration England', *Bulletin of the History of Medicine*, 66 (Winter 1992), 511–35.

Martinolich, Jean, 'Self-Effacement in Patriarchal Education: An Analysis of Milton's Eve and the Narrative Voice in Jane Barker's "A Farewell to Poetry, With a Long Digression on Anatomy" and "An Invitation to my Learned Friends at Cambridge" ', unpublished paper.

Medoff, Jeslyn, 'Dryden, Jane Barker, and the "Fire-Works" on the Night of the Battle of Sedgemore (1685)', *N&Q*, NS 35 (June 1988), 175–6.

—— 'The Daughters of Behn and the Problem of Reputation', in Isobel Grundy and Susan Wiseman (eds.), *Women, Writing, History 1640–1740* (Athens: U. of Georgia P., 1992), 33–54.

—— ' "A temerity allmost to madness": Jane Barker as Jacobite

Poet/Historian', paper presented at Northeast American Society for Eighteenth-Century Studies, Sept. 1996.

MELVILLE, A. D., *Ovid: The Love Poems* (Oxford and New York: Oxford UP, 1990).

MERMIN, DOROTHY, 'Women Becoming Poets: Katherine Philips, Aphra Behn, Anne Finch', *ELH* 57 (1990), 335–55.

MILLER, JOHN, *Popery and Politics in England 1660–88* (Cambridge: Cambridge UP, 1973).

—— *James II: A Study in Kingship* (1978; London: Methuen, 1991).

MINER, EARL (ed.), *The Works of John Dryden*, iii: *Poems 1685–1692* (Berkeley and Los Angeles: U. of California P., 1969).

MONOD, PAUL KLÉBER, *Jacobitism and the English People, 1688–1788* (Cambridge: Cambridge UP, 1989).

—— 'Jacobitism as Court Culture and Popular Culture', paper delivered at Northeast American Society for Eighteenth-Century Studies, Sept. 1996.

MORGAN, FIDELIS, *A Woman of No Character: An Autobiography of Mrs Manley* (London and Boston: Faber and Faber, 1986).

MORILLO, JOHN, 'Seditious Anger: Achilles, James Stuart, and Jacobite Politics in Pope's *Iliad* Translation', *ECL* 19 (May 1995), 38–58.

MULVIHILL, MAUREEN E., 'A Feminist Link in the Old Boys' Network: The Cosseting of Katherine Philips', in Mary Anne Schofield and Cecelia Macheski, (eds.), *Curtain Calls: British and American Women and the Theater, 1660–1820* (Athens: Ohio UP, 1991), 71–104.

NAGY, DOREEN, *Popular Medicine in Seventeenth-Century England* (Bowling Green, Oh: Bowling Green State Univ. Popular P., 1988).

NEEDHAM, GWENDOLYN B., 'Mary de la Riviére Manley, Tory Defender,' *Huntington Library Quarterly*, 12 (1948–9), 253–88.

NICOLSON, MARJORIE HOPE, *The Breaking of the Circle: Studies in the Effect of the 'New Science' Upon Seventeenth-Century Poetry*. rev. edn. (New York: Columbia UP, 1960).

PARFITT, GEORGE, *English Poetry of the Seventeenth Century*, 2nd edn. (London and New York: Longman, 1992).

PATTERSON, ANNABEL, *Censorship and Interpretation: The Conditions of Writing and Reading in Early Modern England* (Madison: U. of Wisconsin P., 1984).

PAYNE, DEBORAH C., ' "And poets shall by patron-princes live": Aphra Behn and Patronage', in Mary Anne Schofield and Cecilia Macheski (eds.), *Curtain Calls: British and American Women and the Theater, 1660–1820* (Athens, Oh: Ohio UP, 1991), 105–19.

PEARSON, JACQUELINE, 'The History of *The History of the Nun*', in Heidi Hutner (ed.), *Rereading Aphra Behn: History, Theory, and*

Criticism (Charlottesville and London: UP of Virginia, 1993), 234–52.

PELLING, MARGARET, 'Medical Practice in Early Modern England: Trade or Profession?', in Wilfrid Prest (ed.), *The Professions in Early Modern England* (London: Croom Helm, 1987), 90–128.

—— and Webster, Charles, 'Medical Practitioners', in Charles Webster (ed.), *Health, Medicine and Mortality in the Sixteenth Century* (Cambridge: Cambridge UP, 1979), 165–235.

PERRY, RUTH, *The Celebrated Mary Astell: An Early English Feminist* (Chicago and London: U. of Chicago P., 1986).

—— 'Mary Astell and the Feminist Critique of Possessive Individualism', *ECS* 23 (1990), 444–57.

PITTOCK, MURRAY G. H., *Poetry and Jacobite Politics in Eighteenth-Century Britain and Ireland* (Cambridge: Cambridge UP, 1994).

POOVEY, MARY, *The Proper Lady and the Woman Writer: Ideology as Style in the Works of Mary Wollstonecraft, Mary Shelley and Jane Austen* (Chicago and London: U. of Chicago P., 1984).

PORTER, ROY, *Health for Sale: Quackery in England 1660–1850* (Manchester and New York: Manchester UP, 1989).

POTTER, LOIS, *Secret Rites and Secret Writing: Royalist Literature, 1641–1660* (Cambridge: Cambridge UP, 1989).

PRESCOTT, SARAH, 'Resolv'd to espouse a Book', *TLS* (9 Jan. 1998), 21.

REYNOLDS, MYRA (ed.), *The Poems of Anne Countess of Winchilsea* (Chicago: U. of Chicago P., 1903).

RICH, ADRIENNE, 'Compulsory Heterosexuality and Lesbian Existence', in *Blood, Bread, and Poetry: Selected Prose 1979–1985* (New York and London: Norton, 1986. 23–75).

RICHETTI, JOHN J., *Popular Fiction Before Richardson: Narrative Patterns 1700–1739* (Oxford: Clarendon P., 1969).

ROBERTSON, JOHN M. (ed.), *Characteristics of Men, Manners, Opinions, Times, etc*, 2 vols. (Gloucester, Mass.: Peter Smith, 1963).

ROPER, ALAN, *Dryden's Poetic Kingdoms* (New York: Barnes and Noble, 1965).

ROGERS, PAT, *The Augustan Vision* (London: Weidenfeld and Nicolson, 1974).

—— *Robinson Crusoe* (London: Allen and Unwin, 1979).

—— 'Book Dedications in Britain 1700–1799: A Preliminary Survey', *British Journal for Eighteenth-Century Studies*, 16 (1993), 213–33.

ROSENTHAL, LAURA J., 'Owning Oroonoko: Behn, Southerne, and the Contingencies of Property', in Mary Beth Rose (ed.), *Renaissance Drama*, NS 23 (Evanston: Northwestern UP and the Newberry Library Center for Renaissance Studies, 1992), 25–58.

ROSS, IAN CAMPBELL, ' "One of the Principal Nations in Europe": The

Representation of Ireland in Sarah Butler's *Irish Tales*', *Eighteenth-Century Fiction*, 7 (1994), 1–16.

RØSTVIG, MAREN-SOFIE, *The Happy Man: Studies in the Metamorphoses of a Classical Ideal*, 2nd edn. (Oslo: Norwegian Universities P., 1962).

RUMBOLD, VALERIE, 'The Jacobite vision of Mary Caesar', in Isobel Grundy and Susan Wiseman (eds.), *Women, Writing, History 1640–1740* (Athens: U. of Georgia P., 1992), 178–98.

RUSSELL, K. F., *British Anatomy 1525–1800. A Bibliography of Works published in Britain, America and on the Continent*, 2nd edn. (Winchester: St Paul's Bibliographies, 1987).

RUVIGNY AND RAINEVAL, MARQUIS OF, *The Jacobite Peerage* (Edinburgh: T. C. and E. C. Jack, 1904).

SAID, EDWARD W., 'The Mind of Winter: Reflections on Life in Exile', *Harpers*, 269 (Sept. 1984), 49–55.

SAWDAY, JONATHAN, *The Body Emblazoned: Dissection and the Human Body in Renaissance Culture* (London and New York: Routledge, 1995).

SCHOFIELD, MARY ANNE, *Masking and Unmasking the Female Mind: Disguising Romances in Feminine Fiction, 1713–1799* (Newark: U. of Delaware P., and London and Toronto: Associated UPs, 1990).

SCHWOERER, LOIS G., 'Propaganda in the Revolution of 1688–89', *American Historical Review*, 82 (1977), 843–74.

—— 'Women and the Glorious Revolution', *Albion*, 18 (1986), 195–218.

SCOTT, GEOFFREY, ' "Sacredness of Majesty": The English Benedictines and the Cult of King James II', *Royal Stuart Papers*, 23 (Huntingdon: The Royal Stuart Society, 1984).

—— *Gothic Rage Undone: English Monks in the Age of Enlightenment* (Bath: Downside Abbey, 1992).

SCOTT, JONATHAN, 'England's Troubles: Exhuming the Popish Plot', in Tim Harris, Paul Seaward, and Mark Goldie (eds), *The Politics of Religion in Restoration England* (Oxford, Basil Blackwell, 1990), 107–31.

SEIDEL, MICHAEL, 'Crusoe in Exile', *PMLA* 96 (1981), 363–74.

—— *Exile and the Narrative Imagination* (New Haven and London: Yale UP, 1986).

SHAWCROSS, JOHN T., 'Jane Barker', *Seventeenth-Century British Nondramatic Poets*, *DLB*, 3rd ser. 131 (Detroit, Washington, DC, London: Gale-Bruccoli Clark Layman, 1993), 3–6.

SHELL, ALISON, 'Popish Plots: *The Feign'd Curtizans* in Context', in Janet Todd (ed.), *Aphra Behn Studies* (Cambridge: Cambridge UP, 1996), 30–49.

SHUGRUE, MICHAEL F,. 'The Sincerest Form of Flattery: Imitation in the Early Eighteenth-Century Novel', *South Atlantic Quarterly*, 70 (1971), 248–55.

SINCLAIR, H. M., and ROBB-SMITH, A. H. T., *A Short History of Anatomical Teaching in Oxford* (Oxford: Oxford UP, 1950).

SMITH, HILDA L., *Reason's Disciples: Seventeenth-Century English Feminists* (Urbana: U. of Illinois P., 1982).

SPACKS, PATRICIA MEYER, *Imagining a Self: Autobiography and Novel in Eighteenth-Century England* (Cambridge and London: Harvard UP, 1976).

SPECK, W. A., 'Politicians, Peers, and Publication by Subscription 1700–50', in Isabel Rivers (ed.), *Books and their Readers in Eighteenth-Century England* (Leicester: Leicester UP and St Martin's P., 1982), 47–68.

SPENCER, JANE, 'Creating the Woman Writer: The Autobiographical Works of Jane Barker', *Tulsa Studies in Women's Literature*, 2 (1983), 165–81.

—— *The Rise of the Woman Novelist: From Aphra Behn to Jane Austen* (Oxford and New York: Basil Blackwell, 1986).

—— 'Women Writers and the Eighteenth-Century Novel', in John Richetti (ed.), *The Cambridge Companion to the Eighteenth-Century Novel* (Cambridge: Cambridge UP, 1996), 212–35.

STANGLMAIER, KARL, *Mrs. Jane Barker: Ein Beitrag zur Englischen Literaturgeschichte* (Berlin, 1906).

STAVES, SUSAN, *Players' Scepters: Fictions of Authority in the Restoration* (Lincoln and London: U. of Nebraska P., 1979).

STIEBEL, ARLENE, 'Subversive Sexuality: Masking the Erotic in Poems by Katherine Philips and Aphra Behn', in Claude J. Summers and Ted-Larry Pebworth (eds.), *Renaissance Discourses of Desire* (Columbia and London: U. of Missouri P., 1993), 223–36.

STRAUB, KRISTINA, 'Indecent Liberties with a Poet: Audience and the Metaphor of Rape in Killigrew's "Upon the saying that my Verses" and Pope's *Arbuthnot*', *Tulsa Studies in Women's Literature*, 6 (1987), 27–45.

—— 'Frances Burney and the Rise of the Woman Novelist', in *The Columbia History of the British Novel*, ed. John Richetti (New York: Columbia UP, 1994), 199–219.

STRAUS, RALPH, *The Unspeakable Curll: Being Some Account of Edmund Curll Bookseller* (London: Chapman and Hall, 1927).

STURKEN, MARITA, 'Memory, Reenactment, and the Image', in Mary Rhiel and David Suchoff (eds.), *The Seductions of Biography* (New York and London: Routledge, 1996), 31–41.

SUTHERLAND, JAMES R., 'The Circulation of Newspapers and Literary Periodicals, 1700–30', *Library*, 4th ser. 15 (1934), 110–24.

SZECHI, DANIEL, *The Jacobites: Britain and Europe 1688–1788* (Manchester and New York: Manchester UP, 1994).

TAYLER, HENRIETTA, *Lady Nithsdale and her Family* (London: Lindsay Drummond, [1939]).

THOMAS, PATRICK (ed.), *The Collected Works of Katherine Philips: The Matchless Orinda*, 2 vols. (Stump Cross, Essex: Stump Cross Books, 1990).

TILLOTSON, GEOFFREY (ed.), *The Rape of the Lock and Other Poems* (London: Methuen; New Haven: Yale UP, 1940).

TODD, JANET, *Women's Friendship in Literature* (New York: Columbia UP, 1980).

—— *The Sign of Angellica: Women, Writing, and Fiction 1660–1800* (London: Virago P., 1989).

—— (ed.), *The Works of Aphra Behn*, i: *Poetry* (London: William Pickering, 1992).

—— *The Secret Life of Aphra Behn* (London: Andre Deutsch, 1996).

TOMLINSON, JOHN, *Cultural Imperialism: A Critical Introduction* (London: Pinter, 1991).

TRAUB, VALERIE, 'The Psychomorphology of the Clitoris', *GLQ: A Journal of Lesbian and Gay Studies*, 2 (1995), 81–113.

TRICKETT, RACHEL, *The Honest Muse: A Study in Augustan Verse* (Oxford: Clarendon P., 1967).

TURNER, CHERYL, *Living by the Pen: Women Writers in the Eighteenth Century* (London and New York: Routledge, 1992).

VIETH, DAVID M., *Attribution in Restoration Poetry: A Study of Rochester's Poems of 1680* (New Haven and London: Yale UP, 1963).

WAHL, ELIZABETH, 'Jane Barker', in Paul Schlueter and June Schlueter (eds.), *An Encyclopedia of British Women Writers* (New York and London: Garland, 1988).

WALKER, KEITH (ed.), *The Poems of John Wilmot Earl of Rochester* (Oxford: Basil Blackwell, 1984).

WALKER, R. B., 'Advertising in London Newspapers, 1650–1750', *Business History*, 15 (1973), 112–30.

WALLER, A. R. (ed.), *The English Writings of Abraham Cowley*, 2 vols. (Cambridge: Cambridge UP, 1905–6).

WALSH, MICHELINE KERNEY, 'Toby Bourke, Ambassador of James III at the Court of Philip V, 1705–13', in Eveline Cruickshanks and Edward Corp (eds.), *The Stuart Court in Exile and the Jacobites* (London and Rio Grande: Hambledon P., 1995), 143–53.

WARNER, WILLIAM B., 'Formulating Fiction: Romancing the General

Reader in Early Modern Britain', in Deidre Lynch and William B. Warner (eds.), *Cultural Institutions of the Novel* (Durham, NC, and London: Duke UP, 1996), 279–305.

WARTER, JOHN WOOD (ed.), *Southey's Common-Place Book*, 4th ser., 4 vols. (London: Longman, Brown, Green, and Longmans, 1851).

WEBER, HAROLD M., *Paper Bullets: Print and Kingship under Charles II* (Lexington: U. of Kentucky P., 1996).

WEIL, RACHEL J., 'The Politics of Legitimacy: Women and the Warming-pan Scandal', in Lois G. Schwoerer (ed.), *The Revolution of 1688–1689: Changing Perspectives* (Cambridge: Cambridge UP, 1992), 65–82.

WELDON, BENNET, *A Chronicle of the English Benedictine Monks from the Renewing of their Congregation in the Days of Queen Mary, to the Death of King James II* [London: J. Hodaes, 1882].

WIESNER, MERRY E., *Women and Gender in Early Modern Europe* (Cambridge: Cambridge UP, 1993).

WIKBORG, ELEANOR, 'The Expression of the Forbidden in Romance Form: Genre as Possibility in Jane Barker's *Exilius*', *Genre*, 22 (1989), 3–19.

WILLEN, DIANE, 'Women and Religion in Early Modern England', in Sherrin Marshall (ed.), *Women in Reformation and Counter-Reformation Europe: Public and Private Worlds* (Bloomington and Indianapolis: Indiana UP, 1989), 140–65.

WILLIAMS, J. A., 'English Catholicism under Charles II: The Legal Position', *Recusant History*, 7 (1963), 123–43.

WILLIAMSON, MARILYN L., *Raising Their Voices: British Women Writers, 1650–1750* (Detroit: Wayne State UP, 1990).

WILSON, CAROL SHINER (ed.), *The Galesia Trilogy and Selected Manuscript Poems of Jane Barker* (New York and Oxford: Oxford UP, 1997).

WILSON, KATHLEEN, *The Sense of the People: Politics, Culture and Imperialism in England, 1715–1785* (Cambridge: Cambridge UP, 1995).

WILTSHIRE, JOHN, 'Fanny Burney's Face, Madame D'Arblay's Veil', in Marie Mulvey Roberts and Roy Porter (eds.), *Literature and Medicine during the Eighteenth Century* (London and New York: Routledge, 1993. 245–65).

WINN, JAMES, *John Dryden and his World* (New Haven and London: Yale UP, 1987), 525–31.

WITTREICH, JOSEPH, *Feminist Milton* (Ithaca and London: Cornell UP, 1987).

WOODWARD, CAROLYN, ' "My Heart So Wrapt": Lesbian Disruptions in Eighteenth-Century British Fiction', *Signs: Journal of Women in Culture and Society*, 18 (1993), 838–65.

WOUDHUYSEN, H. R., *Sir Philip Sidney and the Circulation of Manuscripts 1558–1640* (Oxford: Clarendon P., 1996).

WYMAN, A. L., 'The Surgeoness: The Female Practitioner of Surgery 1400–1800', *Medical History*, 28 (1984), 22–41.

YOUNG, SIDNEY, *Annals of the Barber Surgeons* (London: Blades, East and Blades, 1890).

ZARET, DAVID, 'Religion, Science, and Printing in the Public Spheres in Seventeenth-Century England', in Craig Calhoun (ed.), *Habermas and the Public Sphere* (Cambridge and London: MIT P., 1992), 212–35.

Index